Ordering Tang China

Ordering Tang China

CULTURAL MEMORY, EMPEROR TAIZONG, AND THE *ESSENTIALS*

Kelly Ngo

LEVER
PRESS

ASIANetwork Books

Series Editors:
Erin McCarthy (St. Lawrence University)
Lisa Trivedi (Hamilton College)

ASIANetwork Books strives to publish high-quality, original monographs, edited collections, and translations that embody a rigorous liberal arts approach to Asian Studies. A collaboration with ASIANetwork, a consortium of Asian Studies faculty at 160 colleges, the series seeks to fill a space between works that address the critical pedagogical strategies of the Asian Studies classroom and works of specialized scholarship that engage a broad readership outside higher education. Manuscripts published in the ASIANetwork Books series, no matter how narrowly focused, are expected to raise broad questions of interest for the public and demonstrate classroom utility for Asian Studies.

Titles in the Series

Vikash Yadav and Jason Kirk, *The Politics of India under Modi: An Introduction to India's Democracy, Economy, and Foreign Policy*

A complete list of titles in the series can be found at www.leverpress.org

Lever Press (leverpress.org) is a publisher of pathbreaking scholarship. Supported by a consortium of higher education institutions focused on, and renowned for, excellence in both research and teaching, our press is grounded on three essential commitments: to be a digitally native press, to be a peer-reviewed, open access press that charges no fees to either authors or their institutions, and to be a press aligned with the liberal arts ethos.

The complete manuscript of this work was subjected to a fully closed ("double-blind") review process. For more information, please see our Peer Review Commitments and Guidelines at https://www.leverpress.org/peerreview

Cover illustration: Image of the earliest extant edition of the *Essentials for Bringing about Order from Assembled Texts* (*Qunshu zhiyao* 群書治要) (*circa* 10th century) from the Tokyo National Museum.

DOI: https://doi.org/10.3998/mpub.14467609
Print ISBN: 978-1-64315-070-3
Open access ISBN: 978-1-64315-071-0

Library of Congress Control Number: 2024934988

Published in the United States of America by Lever Press, in partnership with Michigan Publishing.

To my parents and my sister

In memoriam
Venerable Master Chin Kung AM
Professor Clayton Chou

Contents

Member Institution Acknowledgments

Lever Press is a joint venture. This work was made possible by the generous support of Lever Press member libraries from the following institutions:

Amherst College
Atlanta University Center Consortium
Berea College
Bowdoin College
Carleton College
Central Washington University
Claremont Colleges
Claremont Graduate University
Claremont McKenna College
Clark Atlanta University
College of Saint Benedict & Saint John's University
The College of Wooster
Davidson College
Denison University
DePauw University
Grinnell College
Hamilton College
Hampshire College
Harvey Mudd College
Hollins University
Iowa State University
Keck Graduate Institute
Knox College
Lafayette College
Macalester College
Middlebury College
Morehouse College
Morehouse School of Medicine
Norwich University
Occidental College
Penn State University
Pitzer College
Pomona College
Randolph-Macon College

Rollins College
Santa Clara University
Scripps College
Skidmore College
Smith College
Spelman College
Susquehanna University
Swarthmore College
Trinity University
UCLA Library
Union College
University of Idaho
University of Northern Colorado
University of Puget Sound
University of Rhode Island
University of San Francisco
University of Sheffield
University of Vermont
Vassar College
Washington and Lee University
Whitman College
Whittier College
Willamette University
Williams College

Acknowledgments

I am humbly indebted to and ever grateful for
the counsel and writings of scholars past and present,
the assistance of librarians around the world,
the support of the Lever Press team, and
the unconditional love and guiding lights of my parents and my sister,
without which this work would not have been possible.

Technical Notes

The transliteration of non-English terms and the sources consulted for biographical, reign, and dynasty dates, information on texts, and the translation of official titles in this work are as follows.

Except for non-English terms that have an established or commonly used transliteration among academic sources, I adopt the Pinyin, Hepburn, Revised Romanisation, and Quốc ngữ systems for the transliteration of Chinese, Japanese, Korean, and Vietnamese terms, respectively. Quotation from writings that use alternative transliteration systems are modified accordingly for consistency. Chinese, Japanese, and Korean characters are provided for the first mention of relevant persons, texts, and places. All titles of traditional primary sources are translated into English. Unless otherwise indicated, the translations are my own. The main sources of biographical, reign and dynasty dates are:

- The China Biographical Database Project of Harvard University (https://projects.iq.harvard.edu/cbdb/home);
- Rafe de Crespigny, *A Biographical Dictionary of Later Han to the Three Kingdoms (23–220 AD)* (Leiden: Brill, 2007);
- Jiang Liangfu 姜亮夫, *Lidai mingren nianli beizhuan zongbiao* 歷代名人年里碑傳總表 (Table of birthplaces and years of life [with epitaphs and biological sources references] of eminent people of successive dynasties) (Taipei: Shangwu yinshuguan, 1970);
- Michael Loewe, *A Biographical Dictionary of the Qin, Former Han and Xin periods (221 BC – AD 24)* (Leiden: Brill, 2000);

- William H. Nienhauser Jr. and Michael E. Naparstek, eds., *Biographical Dictionary of Tang Dynasty Literati* (Bloomington: Indiana University Press, 2022);
- Seiichi Iwao, ed., *Biographical Dictionary of Japanese History* (Tokyo: Kodansha International and International Society for Educational Information, 1978);
- Sen'ichi Hisamatsu, *Biographical Dictionary of Japanese Literature* (Tokyo: Kodansha International and the International Society for Educational Information, 1976);
- Edward L. Shaughnessy, *Sources of Western Zhou History: Inscribed Bronze Vessels* (Berkeley: University of California Press, 1991);
- Endymion P. Wilkinson, *Chinese History: A New Manual* (Endymion Wilkinson, 2022);
- Victor Cunrui Xiong, *Historical Dictionary of Medieval China* (Lanham, MD: Rowman & Littlefield, 2017);
- Zheng Jinsheng, Nalini Kirk, Paul D. Buell, and Paul U. Unschuld, *Ben Cao Gang Mu Dictionary Volume 3 Persons and Literary Sources* (Oakland: University of California Press, 2018), and
- *Zuo Tradition Zuozhuan Volume 3*, trans. Stephen Durrant et al. (Seattle: University of Washington Press, 2016).

For information on texts, including their textual histories and attributions, I consulted:

- David R. Knechtges and Taiping Chang, eds., *Ancient and Early Medieval Chinese Literature: A Reference Guide – Parts One, Two, Three and Four* (Leiden: Brill, 2010–2014);
- Cynthia L. Chennault et al., eds., *Early Medieval Chinese Texts – A Bibliographical Guide* (Berkeley, CA: Institute of East Asian Studies, 2015); and
- Michael Loewe, ed., *Early Chinese Texts: A Bibliographical Guide* (Berkeley: The Society for the Study of Early China and the Institute of East Asian Studies, University of California, 1993).

Translations of official titles are from Charles O. Hucker, *A Dictionary of Official Titles in Imperial China* (Taipei: Southern Materials Center Inc., 1985) with modifications.

INTRODUCTION: THE *ESSENTIALS FOR BRINGING ABOUT ORDER FROM ASSEMBLED TEXTS* IN CONTEXT

In 626, Li Shimin 李世民 succeeded his father to become the second emperor of the Tang dynasty (618–907) at the age of 28. He became known as Emperor Taizong 太宗 (r. 626–649) of Tang China.[1] Having been preoccupied with military campaigns since his teenage years, Taizong was conscious that he lacked the formal learning traditionally thought to prepare a prince for governing an empire. However, the period of his reign, named "Constancy Revealed,"[2] became synonymous with exemplary rulership. The years of Taizong's reign came to be known among later courts as the "good government of Zhenguan,"[3] and lauded as one of the most successful rulerships in the history of imperial China. Although this early period of Tang China has been the subject of scholarly endeavors in fields such as politics, history, art, and culture, what seems to have largely eluded researchers to date is a statecraft text that was completed for Emperor Taizong shortly after he ascended the throne.[4] That text is the *Essentials for Bringing about Order from Assembled Texts* (*Qunshu zhiyao* 群書治要[5]—the "*Essentials*").[6]

The *Essentials* is one of the earliest extant anthologies in China designed for educating an emperor on cultivating ethical character and governing the state. As its title suggests, this seventh-century anthology articulates a distinctive political philosophy through its collection of readings that are excerpted from a total of 68[7] canonical, historical, and masters[8] writings, as well as their commentaries.[9] The compilation took place within a broader enterprise of consolidating the fledgling Tang empire and legitimating its succession by reinstating cultural and literary traditions. As an imperial commission that was completed not long after Taizong promulgated his political manifesto, the *Essentials* throws considerable light on the nature of his political orientation and the theoretical underpinnings of his government administration. Whereas the *Essentials of Governance from the Zhenguan Reign* (*Zhenguan zhengyao* 貞觀政要) (the "*Zhenguan Essentials*") by the Tang historian Wu Jing 吳競 (*c.* 669–749)[10] offers the earliest extant account of the practice of government by the Zhenguan court, the *Essentials for Bringing about Order from Assembled Texts* provides the political discourse that plausibly informed it—the theory to their praxis. Moreover, the formalization of political norms and values within the *Essentials*, that are seen to define the Zhenguan rulership, arguably served to distinguish Tang China from its Sui (581–618) predecessors. Insofar as the *Essentials* was used by the Zhenguan ruling elite and later courts in China and abroad, its compilation and transmission offers unique insight into the political thought of the early Tang and its contribution to a shared vision of good governance in East Asia.

Intriguingly, the *Essentials* is characterized by an in-built temporal dynamism. It was composed for the contemporary needs of Emperor Taizong, and it invokes the past by drawing upon pre-existing writings, but always with a view to the future of the Tang ruling house, and even the reuse of the text itself by posterity. In light of these characteristics, I have chosen the critical hermeneutic of cultural memory, as theorised by Jan and Aleida Assmann (collectively, "the Assmanns"),[11] to try to illuminate the circumstances, procedures, purposes, and interests pertaining to the *Essentials*' appropriation of the past. Studying the past from a memory perspective differs from the analytical categories of history and tradition:

> [Memory] differs from history in that its stated focus of interest lies not in the past as such but in its successive retrospective configuration; and it

> differs from tradition in that it is not static or conservative, but – because of its responsiveness to an ever-evolving present – dynamic and innovative.[12]

Cultural memory functions to impart collective identity and profile, to reconstruct the past within present frames of reference, to institutionalize the social heritage and the collective experience, and to build and sustain a value system.[13] The elements of cultural memory assist an understanding of this imperially commissioned corpus of knowledge, from why it was compiled, who was involved, and how it was composed and disseminated, to what it tells us about political discourse during the Zhenguan era, and its significance in China and East Asia throughout time.

I endeavor to address the following three main questions in this study:

- How and why does the *Essentials* present as a cultural memory text of the Zhenguan reign-period?
- As a cultural memory text, how does the *Essentials*' articulation of cultural knowledge offer normative guidance for, and inculcate the formative values of, the Zhenguan ruling elite?
- How do the above findings contribute to the political thought and practice of the Zhenguan era, including the import for subsequent polities within China and abroad?

In responding to these questions, I investigate the political, intellectual, and cultural circumstances that surrounded the commissioning of the *Essentials*, including the key actors involved. I examine a variety of primary and secondary sources to elucidate the political thought and practice of the Zhenguan ruler and his court, and to trace the historical transmission and reception of the *Essentials* in China, Japan, Korea, and Vietnam. The primary sources include paratexts, official records, and historical writings, and they span a timeframe from the Zhenguan reign-period through the twentieth century. Reflecting upon the cultural memory embodied in the *Essentials* and its influence on the making of cultural memory by later generations of ruling elites, I look at the broader significance of its compilation and transmission for Zhenguan political thought and practice in China and East Asia.

It is pertinent to note that the traditional historiography does not provide a comprehensive account of Emperor Taizong and his government. Instead, the extant documentation proffers a rather incomplete and skewed picture of the Zhenguan reign. The historical record is incomplete because Taizong spent most of his time among the secluded palace community, where it is likely that he received advice, discussed policy matters, and took some decisions in the absence of his officials and the court recorders.[14] The received sources present a skewed account for the following reasons. First, Chinese history is traditionally written with a moral-didactic purpose and biographical details tend to depict individuals as stereotypes of relevant roles, focusing only on those particulars that accord with an exemplary or minatory account of their persona.[15] Second, the records were written by contemporary and later officials who upheld a court-centered rulership model and were interested in idealizing Taizong's reign accordingly, not least to advance their influence over their emperor, his succession, and the palace community.[16] Third, the Zhenguan ruler constructed an exemplary reputation based on moral ideals of sagely rulership through his political and literary writings, such as self-authored edicts, poems, and rhapsodies.[17] Fourth, Taizong may have directly influenced certain contemporary records, as exemplified by his directions on the historiography of the Xuanwu Gate Incident that had secured his rise to power.[18] Indeed, Denis Twitchett writes that the Zhenguan reign "gradually acquired a popular image that bore only an indirect relationship with the actual historical events."[19] Considering the above limitations, I have cautiously included primary sources of the Zhenguan ruler's prose writing on statecraft, Wei Zheng's 魏徵 (580–643) remonstrations, and Li Jing's 李靖 (571–649) conversations with Taizong, with the majority of anecdotes concerning the Zhenguan court attested by at least two sources. Given that the *Essentials* and historiographical records were curated or produced by scholar-officials, it is not unexpected that they may share emphases on prioritizing worthy talent and heeding remonstrance. From the perspective of cultural memory and what can be known about the Zhenguan court, this study is interested in whether and to what extent the historical statecraft writings excerpted in the *Essentials* resonates with the norms and values upheld by Emperor Taizong and his court officials, how they may have wished to be seen by others, and how later generations of the ruling elite, scholars-officials, and historians chose to remember them.

The *Essentials* has been researched since the nineteenth and twentieth centuries in Japan and China, respectively. The corpus of secondary literature broadly encompasses three strands of enquiry. First, there are studies on textual collation and reconstruction, as well as historical Chinese linguistics, which concern the formal record of the text and its various editions. Extensively mined for the fragments of texts it preserves, the *Essentials* provides a reference for correcting recensions of its sources that remain extant, and for rediscovering those sources that are otherwise lost. As such, the anthology has been the subject of many textual studies concerning historical linguistics, and the collation and reconstruction of its extant and non-extant sources, respectively. For example, various editions of the *Essentials* have assisted with variant text enquiries into the recensions of *Master Guan* (*Guanzi* 管子),[20] *Master Wen* (*Wenzi* 文子),[21] and the *Mao Tradition of Commentary on the Odes*.[22] Several editions of the *Essentials* have been studied for the textual collation and reconstruction of its sources, including the *Records of the Three Kingdoms* (*Sanguo zhi* 三國志),[23] the *Art of War* (*Sunzi* 孫子),[24] *Master Yu* (*Yuzi* 鬻子),[25] the *School Sayings of Confucius* (*Kongzi jiayu* 孔子家語),[26] *Master Shi* (*Shizi* 尸子),[27] the *Spring and Autumn Annals of [the States of] Wu and Yue* (*Wu Yue chunqiu* 吳越春秋),[28] the *Records of the Historian* (*Shiji* 史記), and the *History of the Former Han Dynasty* (*Han shu* 漢書).[29]

Second, there are studies of the *Essentials* as part of the history and culture of Tang China and its international cultural dialogue. Such research sheds light on the historiography of the Zhenguan era,[30] the historical reception of the statecraft anthology in China and Japan, including its status as a "recovered text" (*yicun shu* 佚存書),[31] and how it has contributed to Japanese culture as an imperial reader and a reference text for codicology, paleography, and collation.[32] This strand of enquiry has also studied the *Essentials* as a manifestation of the political discourse associated with the state of Qi 齊 during the Spring and Autumn period (722–476 BCE),[33] as a reflection of early Tang classicist scholarship by reference to the canonical section of the "Monograph on Classics and Literature" (*jingji zhi* 經籍志) in the *History of the Sui Dynasty* (*Sui shu* 隋書),[34] and the development of the *Old Master* (*Laozi* 老子) scholarship during the Tang dynasty.[35]

Third, there are studies on the political discourse of the text and how it is read as political advice literature.[36] The political studies typically focus on the traditional paradigm of a Confucian government presented by the *Essentials*, either generally or by reference to various tropes.[37] They have also attempted to distill the editorial intent by comparing the excerpts of certain sources with their received "full-text" versions.[38]

The above scholarship is mostly written in Chinese, Japanese, or Korean. While writings in the Japanese language had little impact on Chinese-language scholarship and *vice versa*, this situation has started to change in recent years, as evidenced by the 2010 doctoral thesis by the Korean scholar Kim Kwang-Il 金光一 that was written in Chinese and includes a detailed review and analysis of the Japanese literature.[39] Kim has also written on the *Essentials* in the Korean language.[40] Although the *Essentials* is referred to in several English books and articles, their treatment of the anthology is limited to brief and descriptive remarks as they are concerned with other subjects of Tang China,[41] or the English translations of certain sources compiled within the *Essentials*.[42] Thus, Fan Wang's book chapter, "Reading for Rule: Emperor Taizong of Tang and *Qunshu zhiyao*,"[43] and my article "Cultural Memory of Early Tang China in the *Qunshu zhiyao* 群書治要 (*Essentials for Bringing about Order from Assembled Texts*),"[44] appear to be the first published works on the *Essentials* in the English language.

While the existing scholarship is long-standing and broad-ranging, the discourse generally suffers from a lack of critical and comprehensive analysis of important aspects relating to the textual history of the *Essentials*. Questions that warrant further investigation include the prolific factors that led Emperor Taizong to commission the work that became the *Essentials*, why those members of the editorial team were chosen to undertake the commission, the extent to which the *Essentials* was read by the Zhenguan ruler and his court, how the *Essentials* was transmitted to and received by later courts in imperial China and elsewhere, and how each of the historical and extant editions of the *Essentials* factored into the life of the text.

Recent decades have witnessed topical interest in the text across East Asia. First, the *Essentials* has featured in Sino-Japanese diplomacy. Two hundred years after the text was reintroduced to China from Japan, the late Chinese ambassador and vice minister of foreign affairs Fu Hao 符浩 (1916–2016) received a photographic reprint of a further edition of the *Essentials* from a member of Japan's imperial family in 1996.[45] In 2018, yet another edition of the *Essentials* (the "Eisei Bunko edition") formed part of a collection of classical Chinese texts given to the National Library of China by the former Japanese prime minister Hosokawa Morihiro 細川護熙 (1938–present) for the fortieth anniversary of the Sino-Japanese Treaty of Peace and Friendship. To facilitate public access to the donated books, which were reported to be the largest collection of Chinese texts received from Japan, the National Library of China reprinted texts from each of the four traditional bibliographical divisions of canonical, historical, masters, and literary writings, and the Eisei Bunko edition was chosen as one of the first four books to be reprinted in 2019.[46] Second, the *Essentials* has been the subject of international conferences. A public forum on the *Essentials* organized by the *Mingpao Monthly* journal and Sage Education Association in Hong Kong during April 20–23, 2013, was attended by over two thousand delegates from the government, business, and higher education sectors of mainland China, Hong Kong, Taiwan, Malaysia, and Singapore.[47] Since 2019, the Chinese University of Hong Kong and the National Cheng Kung University of Taiwan have jointly held an annual international academic symposium on the *Essentials* in Tainan, Taiwan.[48] Scholars from mainland China, Hong Kong, Japan, Korea, and Taiwan, have presented at the symposia and edited volumes of their conference papers are published each year.[49] Notwithstanding such substantial interest in the *Essentials*, there remains a dearth of European-language literature on this medieval Chinese anthology. While other political advice literature concerning the Zhenguan reign-period has been translated into non-Chinese languages, there are only limited, partial translations of the *Essentials*, and I have been unable to find a complete translation of the text in any European language.

This volume builds on the body of research in the Chinese, English, Japanese, and Korean languages that have variously studied the *Essentials* as a matter of textual enquiry, cultural history, and statecraft discourse. Of the extant editions of the *Essentials*, I focus on the edition that was first published in 1787 during the Tenmei 天明 reign-period (1781–1789) of Heavenly Emperor Kōkaku 光格天皇 (r. 1780–1817) in Japan and is commonly referred to as the "Tenmei edition." It is the second extant edition from Japan that was introduced to China after the *Essentials* had become lost on its native shores sometime around the fourteenth century,[50] and it remains one of the most widely circulated editions. The quotations from the *Essentials* in this study are sourced from a photographic reproduction of the Tenmei edition[51] that was first published in 1926 as part of the *Four Branches of Literature Collection* (*Sibu congkan* 四部叢刊).[52] In the following sections, I introduce cultural memory theory, and outline the other chapters.

0.1 CULTURAL MEMORY

The concept of "cultural memory" was introduced by Jan Assmann *circa* 1989 as a body of knowledge that enables a society of a particular time and place to construct a view or an understanding of the past and thereby define their collective identity.[53] He argues that every culture connects its individual members to the experience of a shared meaningful world through common norms and stories.[54] J. Assmann identifies the following characteristics of cultural memory: (i) "[t]he concretion of identity or the relation to the group"; (ii) the "capacity to reconstruct"; (iii) its "formation"—"[t]he objectivation or crystallization of communicated meaning and collectively shared knowledge"; (iv) its "organization"—"the institutional buttressing of communication" and "the specialization of the bearers of cultural memory"; (v) its "obligation"—"a clear system of values and differentiations in importance which structure the cultural supply of knowledge and the symbols," and (vi) three types of "reflexivity": practice-reflexivity in interpreting common practice through proverbs, maxims, and rituals; self-reflexivity in drawing on itself to explain, distinguish, reinterpret, criticize, or otherwise operate in a social context, and its reflecting the self-image of the group through a preoccupation with its own social system.[55]

Reading these characteristics together with later literature by Jan and Aleida Assmann, this study understands "cultural memory" as knowledge that is objectified and stored in symbolic forms that may be transmitted from one generation to another.[56] Such knowledge is "cultural" as it pertains to the norms, values, and concerns that define the society at a particular moment in time. The knowledge is "memory" in the sense of being information that has been re-membered from the past by assembling available data in the present. The idea is that consciousness of social belonging depends on shared language, knowledge, and memory, and the communication of such common meaning, as in the form of a shared history, gives rise to a sense of community.[57]

Cultural memory is characterised by formal, institutional communication and cultivated by specialist carriers of memory, who selectively reclaim and reconstruct knowledge of the remote or recent past from which the society derives an awareness of its unity and peculiarity. Who is responsible for inscribing the cultural memory in the *Essentials*? J. Assmann observes that the imperial culture in which the center dominates the periphery is always borne by an elite minority that symbolizes the social identity of the whole.[58] As such, Emperor Taizong and his court officials count as members of the elite responsible for the cultural memory embodied by the *Essentials* (collectively, the "Zhenguan ruling collective"). Arguably, the Zhenguan ruling collective need not be limited to the four editors of the *Essentials*—Wei Zheng, Chu Liang 褚亮 (560–647), Xiao Deyan 蕭德言 (558–654), and Yu Shinan 虞世南 (558–638).[59] By virtue of being the sovereign, Taizong represented the intellectual culture of the Tang polity and its ruling elite.[60] As the *Essentials* was compiled by court officials with his approval, it may be taken to represent the shared views of the Zhenguan court on statecraft generally. Admittedly, the court officials were but one group that sought to influence the emperor's policy decisions as Taizong "spent most of his waking hours" with the palace community, which included his immediate family, women, eunuchs, entertainers, religious figures, and technical experts.[61] Although Taizong took decisions that were not necessarily discussed with his court officials and he was advised by others, I look to the court officials as those being formally and directly charged with assisting Taizong's administration of government. It must be noted that tensions existed between the Zhenguan ruler and his official advisers. For example, there is evidence showing that Taizong was motivated to mollify opposition and rehabilitate his image as a fratricidal usurper by recruiting his most outspoken remonstrator, Wei Zheng, from rival ranks and following his counsel more in the early years of his reign than later on.[62] However, there was also a consensus between the Tang emperor and their officials that their government should be committed to enacting the ideals of the past, and their dynasty should be known as an example of ritual correctness and improvement.[63] In the context of Tang dynastic consolidation, I contend that those tensions could be taken as confirmation that certain checks and balances were working—that the ideals of Taizong's remonstrators imposed certain limitations on his unbridled personal ambitions, and that the scholar officials were, on balance, successful in building the ethical foundations of the dynasty.

Elements of cultural memory theory, such as institutional communication and reconstruction of cultural knowledge, thus facilitate investigation of how the cultural knowledge in the *Essentials* came about and the relevant factors from the contemporary context that shaped its production. For example, why was such cultural knowledge needed, how was it compiled, what purposes was it intended for, who was involved, and how it was received?

Cultural memory is strictly concerned with the remembered past and not the past *per se*.[64] The knowledge is binding through the provision of normative guidance that enables the members of a society to learn its cultural values, share common points of view, and subscribe to its collective identity. Indeed, the cultural memory contains cultural messages that are addressed to posterity and intended for continuous reuse.[65] These aspects of cultural memory theory help to probe into how the *Essentials* was read, and what it meant for its readers throughout time.

Cultural memory exists in working and reference modes, and may transition between those modes over time, or become forgotten altogether as a society prioritizes new and different information in response to the ever-evolving needs of the present and future.[66] In the working mode of cultural memory, the knowledge is being used in the contemporary context to define and support the cultural identity, normativity, and orientation of a society.[67] In the reference mode, the knowledge forms part of the cultural archive of texts, images, and rituals that are stored and potentially available for reinterpretation and reuse in a future context.[68] Cultural forgetting can be active or passive. Whereas active forgetting involves intentional acts of destroying, erasing, or censoring of the documented past, passive forgetting is implied in non-intentional loss or neglect that results in the object of cultural memory falling out of the frames of attention, assessment, and usage.[69] I argue that both the active working and archival reference modes of cultural memory are identifiable in the *Essentials*. The cultural memory exists in the reference mode while the text remains in circulation, as its knowledge is available for retrieval and reuse. Whenever the *Essentials* is being studied or consulted by the ruling class of a society, it may form part of the cultural working memory of that time.

The theoretical framework of cultural memory lends itself to this study of the *Essentials* as an analytical tool that is suited to the nature of its subject-matter. Chinese political philosophy is embedded in a textual and historical tradition from which generations of the ruling elite sought to derive their guiding norms, cultural symbols, and collective values. The notion of reclaiming, reconstructing, and re-presenting inherited cultural knowledge is consistent with the development of classicist scholarship itself. Confucius (551–479 BCE) is traditionally known for editing the *Odes*, the *Documents*, the *Rituals*, and the *Music*,[70] and generations of classicist scholars would recycle, reinterpret, rearticulate, and reauthorize the tradition for their own times.[71] Cultural memory theory thus offers a befitting methodology to engage with the repertoire of the *Essentials* that is derived from past writings for present purposes of governance. The elements of cultural memory theory pose questions of how the cultural knowledge embodied by this composite work has come about and what factors from the contemporary context shaped its production. Answering those questions yields fresh insight into how the *Essentials* manages information and formalizes new meaning that nurtures the collective identity of Zhenguan society and provides its normative orientation. Moreover, cultural memory creates a "framework for communication across the abyss of time,"[72] that facilitates a meaningful exploration of the vicissitudes of the *Essentials*' existence and its experience of "shifts of meaning,"[73] that is, how it was used and what it means for the political elites over time both in China and abroad. This study therefore draws on the theory of cultural memory to guide a critical analysis of the interplay of present and past in the formation, contents, and transmission of the *Essentials*, and its contribution to the political thought and practice of China and East Asia since the Zhenguan reign through to the present.

0.2 CHAPTER OUTLINE

This volume is divided into four chapters. Chapter 1 argues that the *Essentials* is a cultural memory text of the Zhenguan period of Tang China by examining the circumstances surrounding its compilation through the elements of institutional communication, reconstruction of cultural knowledge, and binding nature. How the cultural memory worked during and after the Zhenguan years is explored in Chapters 2 to 4. Chapter 2 analyzes how the cultural memory served to inform the political thought, profile, and practice of the Zhenguan ruling collective through the cultural symbol of the worthy official. Chapter 3 discusses how the cultural memory offered guidance to Emperor Taizong and his court and shaped their collective identity through narratives about remonstration, historical remonstrances that typically invoked the past, and shared knowledge and values. Chapter 4 follows the dissemination of the *Essentials* to explore the extent to which the Zhenguan cultural memory contributed to the political discourse of later courts of imperial China and her neighbours, Japan, Korea, and Vietnam. I conclude by drawing together the various themes and findings of the book as a whole and examining insights into the political thought and practice of the Zhenguan ruling elite from the compilation and transmission of the *Essentials*.

CHAPTER ONE

A CULTURAL MEMORY CANON OF THE ZHENGUAN ERA

In this chapter, I explore how and why the *Essentials* forms a part of the written cultural memory of the Zhenguan era. I operationalize elements of cultural memory theory to understand why the text was commissioned, who was involved, how it was received by its principal reader, how it took its shape, and how it works as a reference text. The pertinent cultural memory elements are summarized as institutional communication, reconstruction of cultural knowledge, and binding nature.

1.1 INSTITUTIONAL COMMUNICATION

Cultural memory enables a society to construct a narrative picture of the past and through this process develop an image and identity for themselves. This picture of the past involves an objectivation of shared meaning and knowledge, the communication of which is institutionally sponsored or supported, and the cultivation of which presupposes expertise on the part of its transmitters.[1] I argue that such characteristics of institutional communication are patently identifiable in the *Essentials* as a text that was compiled under imperial auspices in the early years of the Zhenguan reign-period by specialists, and then approved and disseminated by the sovereign himself.[2]

I begin by examining key factors that led to the imperial commissioning of what became the *Essentials*. Compiling such an anthology served to demonstrate the state's cultural authority and political legitimacy at a time when the new Tang empire was being consolidated by its second emperor. First, the *Essentials* underscored the cultural power of the Zhenguan rulership by its curation of the literary heritage.[3] Over 80 percent of the imperial library collection had been lost due to the misfortunes of political turbulence at the end of the Sui dynasty and a disastrous accident during transportation from its former capital of Luoyang.[4] As much as the library collection had to be rebuilt during the reigns of Gaozu 高祖 (r. 618–626) and Taizong of the Tang dynasty, its texts and records also needed to be reorganized. Such re-collecting and reordering of knowledge are seen in the assembly of selected sources that were excerpted and rearranged for the *Essentials*. Although it was merely one of many texts being produced at the time, it could be said that the *Essentials* through its distinctive configuration helped to define the literary sense of Zhenguan culture.[5]

Second, the *Essentials* commission contributed to the legitimation of the Tang ruling house and the succession of its second ruler. Compiling a new statecraft reference provided an opportunity to rearticulate the imperial vista for the new Tang era. The *Essentials* supported the Zhenguan rulership by complementing Taizong's political manifesto, informing him of the traditional discourse on Confucian governing, and signaling the civil nature of his political orientation. Presented with competing ideas of governmental administration in or around 626, Emperor Taizong chose to implement a Confucian model of government that was advocated by the Grand Master of Remonstrance and Right Assistant in the Department of State Affairs Wei Zheng over alternatives such as the legalist approach proposed by the Vice Director of the Department of State Affairs Feng Deyi 封德彝 (568–627).[6] Taizong's promulgation of the *Jin jing* 金鏡 (Golden mirror) manifesto in the second year of his reign (*c.* 628) accordingly reflected Confucian ideas of good governance. It sets out the role of an ideal sovereign and their relationships with subjects and subordinates based on historical precedents, and emphasizes the need on the part of the ruler to temper military prowess with civil virtue, to heed the counsel of advisors, to engage in self-reflection, and to exercise self-restraint.[7] It is perhaps no coincidence that Wei Zheng, who figured prominently in the Zhenguan ruler's decision to adopt a Confucian administration, also became the chief editor of the *Essentials*, a text that advocates for such government. Recruitment of Wei Zheng to high office in the Zhenguan administration from the ranks of the former crown prince Li Jiancheng 李建成 (589–626), who was Taizong's brother and rival for the throne, converted Wei Zheng, who had been a staunch opponent,[8] into a critical ally and further points to the consolidation of Tang authority.[9] It seems, however, that the newly enthroned Emperor Taizong, who had been preoccupied with military affairs since his teenage years, was relatively unversed in the scholarship traditionally thought to prepare rulers for statecraft.[10] Taizong himself is recorded to have said:

> When [We] were young and fond of archery, [We] obtained ten excellent bows, and thought none could be better. Recently [We] showed them to a bow-maker, who said; 'All are of poor quality.' When [We] asked the reason, he replied: 'The hearts of the wood are not straight, so their arteries and veins are all bad. Although the bows are strong, when you shoot the arrows they will not fly true.' We began to realize that [We] were not yet good at discriminating. We pacified the empire with bows and arrows, but [Our] understanding even of these was still insufficient. How much the less can [We] know everything concerning the affairs of the empire![11]

Having committed to pursuing a Confucian model of government but lacking in the know-how for such governance, there was a plausible need for the Zhenguan ruler to learn on the job by becoming familiar with the art of governing in the most efficient manner. Taizong himself was of the view that the historical past served as a mirror for understanding dynastic rise and fall,[12] and he expressed a clear preference for learning from the experience of former rulers to secure the longevity of the Tang ruling house.[13] Scholars have observed in Taizong "a ruler conscious of, if not obsessed by, the glories of the Han Empire, and a man who realized that one of the surest ways to validate the T'ang ... after so long a period of disunion was to replicate Han achievements."[14] That a Confucian administration was chosen by the Zhenguan ruler and foregrounded by his *Essentials*, would support Arthur F. Wright's suggestion that Taizong sought to emulate Emperor Wu of Han (r. 140–87 BCE),[15] who is known for making texts associated with Confucian scholarship part of state-sponsored learning.[16] Such interest in the educative function of historical experience is corroborated by Zhao Keyao 趙克堯 and Xu Daoxun's 許道勛 observations that the official histories completed during Taizong's reign took Emperor Wen's (r. 180–157 BCE) rulership during the Han dynasty (206 BCE–220 CE) as an instructive model, and the Qin (221–206 BCE) and Sui (581–618) regimes as cautionary warnings, and generally examined the reasons for dynastic success and failure.[17] Indeed, the Zhenguan ruler and his court were acutely aware of the Qin and Sui dynasties not having lasted beyond their respective second generations.[18] Accounts of Taizong's enquiring into the contemporary records concerning his reign[19] show a sensitivity to historical scrutiny not least in respect of its militant beginnings. The Zhenguan ruler became the crown prince in charge of all governmental and military affairs within days of murdering his two brothers in a palace coup in 626; he ascended the throne when his father abdicated two months later.[20] As the final ceremonies confirming Taizong's emperorship did not take place until late 628,[21] commissioning the *Essentials* served to display Taizong's patronage of cultural heritage and his turn from the militaristic force by which he rose to power towards civil statecraft in the orthodox Confucian tradition. The imperial order for the work that produced the *Essentials* was therefore motivated by factors ranging from the public assertion of cultural authority and demonstration of legitimate succession to the private desire to learn the political discourse for administering Confucian government and glean lessons from historical precedents. These terms of reference, whether expressly stated by Taizong or implicitly understood by his editorial team, were addressed through the form and contents of the *Essentials*, which will be discussed in Section 1.2 "Reconstruction of Cultural Knowledge."

The editors of the *Essentials* arguably qualify as "specialists" in curating its cultural memory by possessing relevant knowledge and skills, understanding the needs and aspirations of their ruler, and enjoying his trust and confidence to undertake and deliver on the commission. As the editors' work on the text was plausibly informed by the cultural milieu of classical learning and public service within their families, the following paragraphs focus on their individual backgrounds.

The editorial team was led by Wei Zheng who was then the Director of the Palace Library.[22] He was descended from a family involved in government service and historiography. The historical records show that the diplomatic efforts of Wei Zheng's great-grandfather Wei Zhao 魏釗 (dates unknown) in the service of Emperor Taiwu 太武 (r. 423–452) of the Northern Wei once saved a city from military confrontation;[23] his grandfather Wei Yan 魏彥 (d. 517) served as Secretary Aide to various nobles, edited a history of the Jin dynasty (265–420), and became a prefect for Emperor Xiaoming 孝明 (r. 516–528) of the Northern Wei,[24] and his father Wei Zhangxian 魏長賢 (d. 591) continued Wei Yan's work on the Jin dynastic history and was known for remonstrating in the Northern Qi court.[25] An avid learner since his youth, Wei Zheng was widely read in various intellectual traditions and had even trained to become a Daoist master.[26] Having served as an assistant in the Department of the Palace Library during the reign of Taizong's predecessor Emperor Gaozu, and then as Director of the Palace Library throughout the duration of the *Essentials* project,[27] Wei Zheng was plausibly familiar with all that the imperial library collection had to offer for the making of the *Essentials*. Known for offering frank and fearless advice, Wei Zheng served Taizong in offices of considerable responsibility throughout his 17 years of service.[28] His roles included: Grand Master of Remonstrance and Right Assistant in the Department of State Affairs from 626, Director of the Palace Library with the title Participant in Deliberations about Court Policy from 629, Director of the Chancellery with status concurrent with the Grand Councilor from *circa* 633, and he educated the crown prince as Grand Preceptor to the Heir Apparent from 643.[29] Wei Zheng was regarded as so vital to the Zhenguan government that his applications to retire were all declined by Taizong, and his lengthy time in office ended only on his passing at the age of 63.[30] Howard J. Wechsler notes that "Wei [Zheng], who served at [Taizong's] side for seventeen of his twenty-three years on the throne, is widely viewed as having been a prime motive force behind the success of the [Zhenguan] period."[31]

His approach to learning from the historical past must have resonated with Taizong, as Wei Zheng was entrusted with overseeing the writing of no less than five official histories between the years 635 and 642. Those works included the *History of the Liang Dynasty*, the *History of the Chen*

Dynasty (557–589) (*Chen shu* 陳書), the *History of the Northern Qi Dynasty* (550–577) (*Bei Qi shu*北齊書), the *History of the Northern Zhou Dynasty* (557–581) (*Bei Zhou shu* 北周書), and the *History of the Sui Dynasty*, being editor-in-chief for the latter work.[32] Wei Zheng also wrote interpretive pieces for the *History of the Liang Dynasty*, the *History of the Chen Dynasty*, and the *History of the Northern Qi Dynasty*, as well as the prefatory and concluding remarks that frame the chapters of the *History of the Sui Dynasty*.[33] According to Hung Kuan-Chih, Wei Zheng's input embodied the Zhenguan spirit of learning from history by connecting historical circumstances to contemporary application. In distilling the lessons to be learned, the role models to be emulated, and the principles for success or causes of failure, his historical writings provided practical inspiration with specifiable guidance.[34]

The design and crafting of the *Essentials* further benefited from the scholarly talents of the other editors: Xiao Deyan, Yu Shinan, and Chu Liang,[35] in order of age. Qualified academicians since the inception of the Zhenguan period, they numbered among the academic elite of the Institute for the Advancement of Literature. Xiao Deyan's biography in the *Old History of the Tang Dynasty* records that he was well versed in the Confucian canon and historical works, with particular mastery of the *Zuo Tradition*.[36] There was also a long tradition of public service in Xiao Deyan's family. His great-great-grandfather Xiao Sihua 蕭思話 (400–455) distinguished himself in military service under Emperor Wu 武 (r. 420–422) of the Liu Song 劉宋 regime (420–479),[37] his great-grandfather Xiao Huiqian 蕭惠蒨 (dates unknown) served as court archivist in the Southern Qi court (479–502), his grandfather Xiao Jie 蕭介 (476–548) was senior advisor to Emperor Wu 武 (r. 502–549) of the Liang dynasty,[38] and his father Xiao Yin 蕭引 (527–584) served in advisory roles for the Chen dynasty.[39] Xiao Deyan was so highly esteemed that Emperor Taizong compared him to historic Confucian exemplars. Specifically, Taizong praised Xiao Deyan for having an ethical character on par with Yanhui 颜回 (521–481 BCE) and Min Sun 閔損 (536–487 BCE), erudition that surpassed Yan Yan 言偃 (506–443 BCE) and Bu Shang 卜商 (507–400 BCE), and for being as instrumental to the revival of Confucian learning as Fu Sheng 伏生 (268–178 BCE) and Yang Zhen 楊震 (59–124).[40] Besides being the Vice Director of the Palace Library, Xiao Deyan was entrusted with educating the crown prince, and for drafting, *inter alia*, the *Records of Extended Territory* (*Kuo dizhi* 括地志), which was a comprehensive gazetteer of the empire.[41]

Both Yu Shinan and Chu Liang were known for their flair for writing and had served in former courts before assuming leading roles in the early Tang administrations.[42] Yu Shinan's grandfather Yu Jian 虞檢 (dates unknown) served as advisor for the founding emperor of the Liang dynasty, and his father Yu Li 虞荔 (503–561) was a Palace Cadet of the Heir Apparent in the Chen court.[43] Besides consulting Yu Shinan on state matters, Emperor Taizong would also study canonical and historical writings with him,[44] and once described Yu Shinan as a "walking library."[45] It seems that Taizong appreciated Yu Shinan for unreservedly offering advice and remonstration based on the examples of past rulers, and extolled his distinctions in the five areas of moral virtue, scholarship, dedication, writings, and calligraphy.[46] Indeed, the Zhenguan ruler once commented that governing the empire would not be a problem if all his ministers could be like Yu Shinan.[47] That Yu Shinan succeeded Wei Zheng as Director of the Palace Library in 633 shows that he was no less skilled than his predecessor on bibliographical and textual matters of the state.[48] The words below attributed to Emperor Taizong in the third year of the Zhenguan reign-period (629) reflects his close working relationship with Wei Zheng and Yu Shinan, and the support he received from them:

> In recent years, when We have held court to oversee affairs or taking Our leisure and enjoyment within the parks and orchards, We have always summoned Wei Zheng and Yu Shinan to attend and accompany Us. Sometimes We have planned and discussed the business of governance together, or discoursed on scriptures and canonical texts. The enlightening things We have often heard have not only brought benefit to Oneself, but one could say that this was the Way to lasting peace for the [dynasty's] state altars.[49]

Working individually or together with others, Wei Zheng and Yu Shinan were responsible for penning three of the five works of political advice literature produced during the Zhenguan years, namely, the *Concise Discourse on Emperors and Kings* (*Diwang lüe lun* 帝王略論), the *Essentials*, and the *Record of the Commendable and Contemptible Conduct of the Feudal Lords and Princes since Antiquity* (*Zi gu zhuhouwang shan'e lu* 自古諸侯王善惡錄), in order of their completion.[50] It is likely that Yu Shinan's research on past rulerships for writing the *Concise Discourse on Emperors and Kings*, which was finished in or around 627,[51] would have benefited the *Essentials* project that was completed later, in 631.

Chu Liang's great-grandfather Chu Yan 褚湮 (dates unknown) served as Palace Aide to the Censor-in-Chief in the Liang court,[52] his grandfather Chu Meng 褚蒙 (dates unknown) served as Secretary to the Heir Apparent, and his father Chu Jie 褚玠 (529–580) was Director of the Palace Library for the Southern Chen court.[53] Chu Liang had worked in the government service since the Chen and Sui dynasties. He served Emperor Taizong as an academician and senior recorder, and often advised on military campaigns.[54]

Drawing on family traditions of cultural erudition and public service, along with their scholarly background, all four editors occupied senior roles within the Zhenguan court. Serving Emperor Taizong in positions of considerable confidence and responsibility enabled their work on the *Essentials* to be informed by an intimate knowledge of their principal reader. This would include understanding his need to become familiar with the discourse on kingship and historical precedents, his preferences for making the past useful to the study and practice of government, and his mission and vision for the Zhenguan rulership. Hence, it could be said that expertise in the cultural knowledge and familiarity with Taizong qualified Wei Zheng, Xiao Deyan, Yu Shinan, and Chu Liang as specialists in mediating the relationship between the past and the Zhenguan rulership through the *Essentials*.

That the editors' completed work was met with Emperor Taizong's approval confirms the *Essentials* as an institutionally supported communication. The extant literature records that Emperor Taizong was delighted with the *Essentials* from the outset. In the same month that the *Essentials* was presented in 631, Taizong personally wrote to Wei Zheng:

> Reading what has been recorded, [We are] impressed by its comprehensiveness and conciseness. [We have] discovered matters that were hitherto unknown and unheard of. It enables us to bring about order [by] studying

> antiquity and oversee matters without doubt. Are not such accomplishments great indeed! [Wei] Zheng et al. are to be given a thousand bolts of plain silk and five hundred lengths of coloured silk. The crown prince and other princes are to be given one [copy] each.[55]

As for how the Zhenguan ruler read the *Essentials*, Fan Wang avers, based on the word attributed to his act of reading—"*lan* 覽" (to look at), that the manuscript scrolls were likely perused in silence with him appreciating their calligraphic art and textual content.[56] The positive reception of the *Essentials* by Emperor Taizong is attested by later sources, namely, the *Outstanding Models from the Storehouse of Literature* (*Cefu yuangui* 冊府元龜) encyclopedia of political essays, autobiography, memorials, and decrees, completed by Wang Qinruo 王欽若 (962–1025) and others in 1013, the *New History of the Tang Dynasty*, and the *Ocean of Jades* (*Yu hai* 玉海) encyclopedia compiled by Wang Yinglin王應麟 (1223–1296) in *circa* 1255. The *Outstanding Models from the Storehouse of Literature* includes two virtually identical entries as follows.

> Taizong expressed praise after perusing it, ordered for a copy to be circulated to each of the crown prince and other princes, and for Wei [Zheng] to be gifted two hundred bolts of silk.[57]

A version of Taizong's response found in the *New History of the Tang Dynasty* is consistent with his handwritten reply to Wei Zheng above:

> The Emperor [Taizong] was delighted by the text's comprehensiveness and conciseness. He said [addressing the editors of the *Essentials*], 'Your efforts enable us to study antiquity and oversee matters without doubt!' Especially opulent gifts were conferred.[58]

Any doubt that the "text" in this passage refers to the *Essentials* is quelled by the same quote appearing in an entry for the *Essentials* marked "*Qunshu zhiyao* of the Tang dynasty" (Tang *Qunshu zhiyao* 唐群書治要) within the *Ocean of Jades*.[59] It is likely that some references to the *Essentials* in the historical records are based on descriptions of the anthology in earlier writings rather than first-hand knowledge. However, the above passages share the same gist and present a relatively consistent narrative: that Emperor Taizong favored the comprehensive coverage and concise expression of the *Essentials*, found it to be helpful for understanding the past and for overseeing matters with confidence, generously rewarded the editors, and considered it useful enough to order for the princes to have a copy each.

The Zhenguan ruler's regard for the value of the *Essentials* may also be discerned by comparing his response to another compilation of classicist scholarship. This commission compiled standard editions of five canonical writings associated with Confucian scholarship, namely, the *Zhouyi* 周易 (Changes), the *Shangshu* 尚書 (Venerable documents), the *Mao Tradition of Commentary on the Odes*, the *Zuo Tradition*, and the *Liji* 禮記 (Records on ritual), which are collectively referred to as the "Five Classics." This work commenced in 630 and was finished to Taizong's approval as the *Standard Editions of the Five Classics* (*Wujing dingben* 五經定本) in 633. Interestingly, the section on "awards of appreciation" in the *Imperially-commissioned Categorized Writings in the Library of Deep Insight* (*Yuding yuanjian leihan* 御定淵鑑類函) compiled in 1702, cites from the *Outstanding Models from the Storehouse of Literature* that Taizong awarded "fifty bolts of silk" for the *Standard Editions of the Five Classics* and "two hundred bolts of silk" for the *Essentials*.[60] While the precise types and quantities of silk that was bestowed in respect of the *Essentials* may vary between records from different sources,[61] it seems significant that the one source records considerably more silk awarded for the *Essentials* than another compilation for statecraft education, which may well indicate a higher level of imperial approval.

Aside from Emperor Taizong's initial response to the *Essentials*, the historical record suggests that it became a reference text that he consulted. I have not found direct evidence of how the *Essentials* was read by Taizong (or read to him[62]), his princes, or the courtiers who had access to the manuscript copies. However, there is a remarkable consistency across three sources—the *Oustanding Models from the Storehouse of* Writings, the *Family Account of the Lord of Ye* (*Ye hou jiazhuan* 鄴侯家傳), and the *Memorials of Leading Officials of each Period* (*Lidai mingchen zouyi* 歷代名臣奏議)—as three officials of later Tang courts, namely, Yang Xiangru 楊相如 (*fl.* 712), Li Mi 李密 (722–789), and Li Jiang 李絳 (764–830), each commends the *Essentials* as a statecraft reference commissioned for the Zhenguan ruler.[63] Such accounts imply that the *Essentials* had been used by Taizong, and that it had proven sufficiently useful to merit presentation to the later Tang emperors. Fan Wang also observes Taizong to be an avid reader of the *Essentials*.[64] That the above sources are later or fall within the category of bureaucratic responses to the submission of a text to court, does to some extent limit how much they may reliably illuminate the Zhenguan ruler's engagement with the *Essentials*. In the absence of more specific evidence of usage, the impression of Taizong consulting the *Essentials* remains sketchy, but the possibility of the text being used by him, and his princes and courtiers, cannot be ruled out. Overall, as a work of imperial commission, compiled by officials with relevant knowledge and expertise, highly approved and likely consulted by the emperor himself, if not also, by other members of his court, the *Essentials* exhibits the characteristics of an institutionally sponsored communication that is crafted by professional historians as curators of the memory of the past. The next section will consider the editors' work in making and shaping the cultural memory in the *Essentials* as a political resource for their time.

1.2 RECONSTRUCTION OF CULTURAL KNOWLEDGE

According to Jan Assmann, the past does not just emerge of its own accord but is derived from a cultural process of construction and representation that is always guided by certain motives, aims, and expectations of the present.[65] Likewise, the historical consciousness associated with cultural memory must be "remembered" by the ruling elite retrieving, reinterpreting, and rearticulating what they regard to be worth remembering for their society.[66] Aleida Assmann writes, "[G]roups indeed define themselves by agreeing upon what they hold to be important, to which story they accord eminence, which anxieties and values they share."[67] Given that any reconstruction of the past for present purposes is infused with contemporary intentions, it is relevant to examine how and why Zhenguan cultural memory took the form of the *Essentials*. Section 1.2.1 "Textual reproduction" enquires as to how the cultural knowledge is reconstructed by the *Essentials* through the elements of selection and representation in the textual reproduction of cultural memory.[68] Sections

1.2.2 "Remembering historical practice" and 1.2.3 "Reviving classical scholarship" will engage with the "why" enquiry by focusing on the political priority attributed to historical and classical learning in early Tang China, as well as the Zhenguan ruler's inclination to learn about the traditional discourse on statecraft.

1.2.1 Textual reproduction

According to Aleida Assmann, "[Humans] do not have to start anew in every generation because they are standing on the shoulders of giants whose knowledge they can reuse and reinterpret."[69] This approximates the approach of the *Essentials*' editorial team in privileging the appropriation of existing material over original authorship. Instead of writing a new work of their own, the editors capitalized on the available know-how by repackaging and repurposing selections from extant writings to articulate the Zhenguan court's views on the business of administering an empire. I will argue below that the elements of selection and re-presentation in the making of cultural memory are manifest in the format, composition, and organization of the *Essentials*.

A selection process is implicit in the title and form of the *Essentials*. Its appellation "*Essentials ... from Assembled Texts*" and anthology format point to the text being the outcomes of various choices. Such choices include selecting which of the "assembled texts" to include from the extensive palace library,[70] what parts to excerpt from, and how much of those parts to extract for the relevant text and annotations. This style of compilation bears some resemblance to the nature of epitomes (*chao* 抄 or *shuchao* 書抄), which are texts comprised of excerpts that have been copied from one work or one type of work.[71] Excerpting a passage was one method of deriving the essence from the relevant work(s).[72] There is selection in the choice of those passages that are deemed material for copying, but the epitome may sometimes summarize or paraphrase the content of a work.[73] A compilation of excerpted materials is often denoted by the character "*yao* 要," as seen in the title of the *Essentials* and epitomes such as the *Collected Essentials of Military Principles* (*Bingfa jieyao* 兵法接要) by Sun Wu 孫武 (*fl. c.* 500 BCE) and Cao Cao 曹操 (155–220 BCE), respectively.[74] Considering that the existing statecraft references were voluminous, as exemplified by the *Imperial Conspectus* (*Huanglan* 皇覽) (approx. 680 scrolls)[75] and the *Comprehensive Digest of the Institute of the Floral Grove* (*Hualin bianlüe* 華林遍略) (approx. 600–700 scrolls),[76] it is not surprising that the inexperienced Taizong confronted a literary challenge, which gave rise to the commission's terms of reference. This is reflected in Wei Zheng's preface to the *Essentials* ("Wei Zheng's preface"), which is translated into English in Appendix 1. The relevant part is extracted below:

> [Your Majesty] finds [the writings of] the Six Classics bewildering and [the writings of] the hundred masters disparate. Exhaustive analysis of the principles and natures is fatiguing yet futile. Extensive reading without perspective broadens [one's] knowledge without grasp of the essentials. Your servants have therefore been ordered to select from divers texts, excise the irregular and irrelevant, and illuminate the instructive standards.[77]

Wei Zheng's preface makes the point that the editors of the *Essentials* were enlisted to create clarity and order for Taizong, who found the extensive literature "bewildering" and "disparate," which suggests that he barely knew where to start or how to read effectively for rulership. They do so by selecting not only the relevant texts but also excerpting their most relevant parts to provide guidance on what needs to be done in governing the empire, and the model standards and practices involved. The *Essentials* thus represents the editors' choice of what texts their emperor needed to know. In delivering the clarity and order embodied by the *Essentials*, its chief editor Wei Zheng takes care to explain its scope and dimensions:

> [This text] draws from the Six Classics to the various masters, [spans] from the [times of the] Five Sovereigns to the years of the Jin dynasty. It comprises five cases of fifty scrolls altogether. It primarily seeks [to capture] the gist of bringing about order and is thus entitled 'Essentials for Bringing about Order'.[78]

The sources are derived from canonical, historical, and masters writings. Their time frame spans from the high antiquity era of the Five Sovereigns to the Jin dynasty (265–420) of the recent past. The physical proportions of the *Essentials* come to "five cases of fifty scrolls altogether." And the title reflects the primary objective of their opus: "[to capture] the gist of bringing about order." That the relevant sources were distilled down to fifty scrolls of excerpted readings throws into relief the extent of selection involved in producing the anthology. Accordingly, McMullen describes the *Essentials* as "the seventh-century equivalent of a sizeable encyclopedia of political wisdom, intended to save the emperor reading time. It offered an efficient route to minimum learning, and that was what Taizong ... needed."[79]

Table 1.1 sets out the 68 titles from which the *Essentials* derives its contents. The sources span the first three traditional classifications of canonical, historical, and masters writings, different branches of learning (e.g., classics, history, philosophy), and different traditions of thought (Confucian, Daoist, Mohist, legalist, syncretist, logician, and strategist). As with their approach to the source titles, the editors refrained from composing their own commentary and excerpted in the form of annotations material from existing commentaries on 27 of the 68 sources.

Table 1.1. Contents of the *Essentials*[154]

Scroll (*non-extant)	**Contents**	**Author** (where specified)	**Annotated** (•)
1	*Wei Zheng xu* 魏徵序 (Wei Zheng's preface)		
	Zhouyi 周易 (Changes)		•
2	*Shangshu* 尚書 (Venerable documents)		•
3	*Maoshi* 毛詩 (Mao tradition of commentary on the *Odes*)		•

Scroll (*non-extant)	Contents	Author (where specified)	Annotated (•)
4*	*Chunqiu Zuoshi zhuan* 春秋左氏傳 (Zuo tradition of commentary on the *Spring and Autumn Annals* ("Zuo Tradition")) Part 1		•
5–6	*Zuo Tradition* Parts 2–3		
7	*Liji* 禮記 (Records on ritual)		•
8	*Zhouli* 周禮 (Rites of Zhou)		•
	Zhoushu 周書 (History of the Zhou dynasty)		•
	Chunqiu waizhuan guoyu 春秋外傳國語 (Unofficial commentary on the *Spring and Autumn Annals*—Discourses of the states ("Discourses of the States"))		•
	Hanshi waizhuan 韓詩外傳 (Exoteric commentary on the *Odes* by Han Ying)		
9	*Xiaojing* 孝經 (Classic of family reverence)		•
	Lunyu 論語 (Analects)		•

(Continued)

Table 1.1. continued.

Scroll (*non-extant)	Contents	Author (where specified)	Annotated (•)
10	*Kongzi jiayu* 孔子家語 (School sayings of Confucius[155])		•
11–12	*Shiji* 史記 (Records of the historian) Parts 1–2		•
	Wu Yue chunqiu 吳越春秋 (Spring and Autumn annals of [the states of] Wu and Yue)		
13*, 14–19, 20*	*Hanshu* 漢書 (History of the former Han dynasty) Parts 1–8		•
21–24	*Hou Hanshu* 後漢書 (History of the latter Han dynasty) Parts 1–4		
25–26	*Weizhi* 魏志 (Records of Wei) Parts 1–2		•
	Shuzhi 蜀志 (Records of Shu)		•
27–28	*Wuzhi* 吳志 (Records of Wu) Parts 1–2		•
29–30	*Jinshu* 晉書 (History of the Jin dynasty) Parts 1–2		•
31	*Liutao* 六韜 (Six quivers)		
	Yinmo 陰謀 (Secret strategies)		

Scroll (*non-extant)	Contents	Author (where specified)	Annotated (•)
	Yuzi 鬻子 (Master Yu (Yu Xiong))		
32	*Guanzi* 管子 (Master Guan)	Guan Yiwu	
33	*Yanzi* 晏子 (Master Yan)	Yan Ying	
	Sima fa 司馬法 (Methods of Sima)		•
	Sunzi bingfa 孫子兵法 (Art of war)		•
34	*Laozi* 老子 (Old master (Lao Dan))		•
	He guanzi 鶡冠子 (Pheasant Cap Master)		
	Liezi 列子 (Master Lie (Lie Yukou))		•
	Mozi 墨子 (Master Mo)	Mo Di	
35	*Wenzi* 文子 (Master Wen)		
	Zengzi 曾子 (Master Zeng)	Zeng Shen	
36	*Wuzi* 吳子 (Master Wu)	Wu Qi	
	Shangjun shu 商君書 (Book of Lord Shang)	Shang Yang	
	Shizi 尸子 (Master Shi)	Shi Jiao	
	Shenzi 申子 (Master Shen)	Buhai	

(Continued)

Table 1.1. continued.

Scroll (*non-extant)	Contents	Author (where specified)	Annotated (•)
37	*Mengzi* 孟子 (Mencius[156])		•
	Shenzi 慎子 (Master Shen (Shen Dao))		•
	Yin wenzi 尹文子 (Master Yin Wen)		
	Zhuangzi 莊子 (Master Zhuang)		•
	Wei liaozi 尉繚子 (Master Wei Liao)		
38	*Sun qingzi* 孫卿子 (Master Xun)	Xun Kuang	
39	*Lüshi chunqiu* 呂氏春秋 (Master Lü's Spring and Autumn annals)		•
40	*Hanzi* 韓子 (Master Han (Han Fei))		
	Sanlüe 三略 (Three strategies)		•
	Xinyu 新語 (New analects)		
	Jiazi 賈子 (Master Jia)	Lu Jia	
41	*Huainan zi* 淮南子 (Master Huainan)		
42	*Yantie lun* 鹽鐵論 (Discourses on iron and salt)		
	Xinxu 新序 (New order)		

Scroll (*non-extant)	**Contents**	**Author** (where specified)	**Annotated** (•)
43	*Shuoyuan* 說苑 (Garden of persuasions)	Liu Xiang	
44	*Huanzi xinlun* 桓子新論 (New discourses of Master Huan)	Huan Tan	
	Qianfu lun 潛夫論 (Discourses of a recluse)		
45	*Zhenglun* 政論 (Discourses on government)		
	Zhong Zhangzi changyan 仲長子昌言 (Admirable words of Zhong Zhangzi)		
46	*Shenjian* 申鑒 (Extended reflections)	Xun Yue	
	Zhonglun 中論 (Balanced discourses)	Xu Gan	
	Dianlun 典論 (Authoritative discourses)		
47	*Liu Yi zhenglun* 劉廙政論 (Political discourse of Liu Yi)		•
	Jiangzi wanji lun 蔣子萬機論 (Master Jiang's Discourse on myriad subtleties)	Jiang Ji	

(Continued)

Table 1.1. continued.

Scroll (*non-extant)	Contents	Author (where specified)	Annotated (•)
	Zhengyao lun 政要論 (Discourse on the essentials of governing)	Huan Fan	
48	*Tilun* 體論 (Structural discourses)	Du Shu	
	Shiwu lun 時務論 (Discourse on contemporary affairs)[157]		
	Dianyu 典語 (Normative discourses)	Lu Jing	
49	*Fuzi* 傅子 (Master Fu)	Fu Xuan	
50	*Yuanzi zhengshu* 袁子正書 (Political writings of Master Yuan)	Yuan Zhun	
	Bao puzi 抱樸子 (Master who embraces simplicity)	*Ge Hong*	

Past knowledge and learning are recast through the arrangement and style of the *Essentials*. Beyond sourcing the text and annotations, the editors re-presented their selections within the context of a new anthology. It could be said that the *Essentials* is loosely modeled on the encyclopedic anthology (*leishu* 類書) genre, which entails the compilation of materials from various sources on a particular topic or a range of topics to facilitate access to relevant information.[80] However, the *Essentials'* editors chose to pioneer a new structure to avoid the drawbacks of organizing contents by topic, such as repetition or overlap in the scope of the topics and duplication where one excerpt may be relevant across multiple topics. Wei Zheng's preface identifies the faults of existing encyclopedic compilations—that is, the *Imperial Conspectus* and the *Comprehensive Digest of the Institute of the Floral Grove* that were completed in 222 and 523, respectively:

> In the past, the *Imperial Conspectus* and the *Comprehensive Digest of the Institute of the Floral Grove* follow convention and group by subject. [Their] terms and entries reiterate each other, the introductions and conclusions are disorganized, the text and its meaning are disrupted, and the usage and study [of them] is difficult.[81]

In contrast to thematically arranged encyclopedic compendia or the typical epitome, the excerpts in the *Essentials* are selected from diverse writings, not just one text or one type of text, and they are set out in their own innovative way. First, the excerpts are divided into three bibliographical classifications following the order of the fourfold system that was formalized by Wei Zheng's Monograph on Classics and Literature in the *History of the Sui Dynasty*—that is, canonical works, historical works, masters works, and literary works.[82] Second, the excerpts and associated annotations are grouped together by reference to the title of their source. Third, the excerpts and their annotations are positioned in the order that they originally appeared within their respective sources. Wang compares the editorial approaches in the *Imperial Conspectus* and the *Essentials* as follows:

> While the compilers of *Huang lan* dismembered the original texts, drawing attention to themselves as the organising intelligence that weaved heterogenous textual fragments into a coherent moralistic narrative, *Qunshu zhiyao* foregrounded the coherence of the original works, its legitimacy derived from the authority of the classics per se.[83]

Novel meaning is made from the way that the text is manipulated by the *Essentials*.[84] The text is decontextualized by removal from its original source and appropriation within the context of a new work in various ways. The excerpts are juxtaposed with different texts from the same source and placed in relative proximity to other writings, and they are combined with different versions of, or allusions to, the same or similar ideas and narratives. The passages often become abridged by virtue of being excerpted, and some annotations involve selections from more than one commentary.[85] As for the style of written expression in the *Essentials*, the editors adopted a concise approach with the contents purporting to be self-contained extracts, gleaning the gist from each source for a complete understanding without extraneous details.[86] Indeed, Wei Zheng's preface explains that the *Essentials* breaks from the artistic expression that had characterized pre-Tang writings, by adopting a style that is functional rather than flowery and focused on conveying the essentials rather than conjuring the encyclopedic.[87]

That the *Essentials* derives new meaning from inherited writings is further evident in its presentation of a Confucian-oriented discourse and incorporation of historical material. While the *Essentials*' array of sources compiled from the pre-Tang textual tradition taps various thought traditions, as is typical of state-sponsored classical learning since the Han dynasty,[88] the corpus is more accurately characterized as "Confucian-oriented" as opposed to simply "classicist."[89] To be clear, I use the term "Confucianism" to designate the philosophical orientation associated with Confucius and his students, as well as intellectual adherents who identified themselves as followers of their teachings.[90] Although the interpretations of Confucian philosophy have been varied, Confucians generally share some basic convictions that link moral concerns with the art of governance. For example, human beings are born with the capacity to develop morally, moral development begins with reflecting on and improving one's own behavior, and people are to be regulated through the educative influence of a humane government ("*ren zheng* 仁政"), where the ruler leads by example in cultivating their moral character.[91] As Paul R. Goldin observes, "Not all Confucians agreed about what moral self-cultivation entails, or how we should go about it, but all accepted that we can and must do it, and that it is a task of utmost urgency."[92]

The Confucian orientation is exemplified by the selection of classics and masters writings within the *Essentials*. The anthology opens with passages from the Five Classics, which were considered essential to Confucian learning because some of those texts were used for instruction by Confucius and his followers, and early traditions ascribe to Confucius the tasks of compiling, editing, and composing parts of them.[93] As Michael Nylan writes, imperial patronage during the Western Han dynasty traced the teachings of the Five Classics to Confucius either directly or through the construction of scholastic lineages.[94] The excerpts from the Five Classics are followed by others from the *Rites of Zhou*, the *History of the Zhou Dynasty*, the *Discourses of the States*, and the *Exoteric Commentary on the Odes by Han Ying*, which are traditionally associated with the Five Classics. Then there are excerpts from the *Classic of Family Reverence*, the *Analects*, and the *School Sayings of Confucius*, which have been regarded as records of the teachings of Confucius himself. Moreover, 17 of the 48 masters compiled in the *Essentials* are categorized among the Confucian writings by the Monograph on Classics and Literature in the *History of the Sui Dynasty*.[95] While the term "*ru* 儒" has historically referred to those with mastery of the classical precedents from ancient texts, rites, and music, those professionally trained to serve the state, those who taught the six arts of rites, music, archery, charioteering, writing and mathematics, and to Confucius and his intellectual adherents,[96] it is the latter definition that corresponds to the category of "*ruzhe* 儒者" (the Confucian writings) in the Monograph on Classics and Literature of the *History of the Sui Dynasty* based on its description of its contents:

> Zhongni (Confucius) began transmitting [the Way of] the early ages and revising the Six Classics. His three thousand followers also received their interpretation. As for the Warring States period, the followers such as Meng Ke (Mencius), Zisi and Xun Qing (Xunzi) took Confucius as their teacher. Each had their own writings that developed the gist of his teachings.[97]

The Confucian-orientation of the *Essentials* extends to the way that the text has been excerpted from their respective sources. As Fan Wang points out, "While the excerpts are selected from a wide range of sources representing different intellectual and ideological orientations, they are shaped in ways that repeat and reinforce the same essentially Confucian messages."[98] Not only are non-Confucian sources excerpted in ways that complement Confucian beliefs or address Confucian concerns, but a considerably higher proportion is excerpted from Confucian sources compared to others:

> Of the twenty fascicles and more than 100,000 words of *Han Feizi*, only eighteen passages totalling around 2,600 words are included in the *Qunshu zhiyao*. In contrast, 124 passages totalling more than 3,800 words are excerpted from the *Analects*, a primary Confucian classic that contains fewer than 16,000 words altogether.[99]

Wang's findings are consonant with the conclusion from Chou Shaowen's dissertation that some three-fifths of the *Essentials*' contents directly relate to the Confucian tradition, based on a quantitative analysis of how much is compiled from each source and their relative proportions within each bibliographical classification.[100]

The *Essentials*' excerpts from historical writings are sourced from only eight texts but account for nearly half of its fifty scrolls. No less than twenty scrolls are devoted to content from the standard histories, including the *Records of the Historian*, the *Spring and Autumn Annals of [the states of] Wu and Yue*, the *History of the Former Han Dynasty*, the *History of the Latter Han Dynasty*, the *Records of the Three Kingdoms* (Wei, Shu and Wu), and the *History of the Jin Dynasty*, which are classified as historical works by the Monograph on Classics and Literature of the *History of the Sui Dynasty*. The footprint of historical material in the *Essentials* is extended by including materials from the *Venerable Documents*, which contains records from China's antiquity, the *Zuo Tradition*—China's earliest narrative history—and the *Discourses of the States*. Indeed, the latter two were classified among the historical writings of the Spring and Autumn period (722–476 BCE) in the Monograph of Arts and Literature in the *History of the Former Han Dynasty*,[101] with the *Discourses of the States* categorized in the historical section of the Monograph on Classics and Literature of the *History of the Sui Dynasty*.[102] Moreover, Hung argues that the *Essentials*' excerpts from the masters resemble historical writings in the way they are arranged and what they record.[103] The masters are ordered not by intellectual tradition but by the lifetimes of their attributed authors that roughly correlate with the time frames of their contents. The masters extracts thereby commence with the *Six Quivers* and the *Secret Strategies* that are traditionally attributed to the earliest author: Jiang Wang 姜望 (also known as "Jiang Shang 姜尚", *fl.* 1056 BCE).[104] The masters excerpts are often centered on the words and deeds of particular individuals, not unlike the biographical entries in traditional Chinese historiography. For example, the *Essentials*' passages from the *Six Quivers*, the *Secret Strategies*, and *Master Yan*, consist almost entirely of questions-and-answers between the relevant ruler—King Wen of Zhou 周文王 (r. 1099/56–1050 BCE), King Wu of Zhou 周武王 (r. 1049/45–1043 BCE), or Duke Jing of Qi 齊景公 (r. 547–400 BCE)—and their official advisors, Jiang Wang (who is addressed as "Tai Gong 太公"), or Yan Ying 晏嬰 (d. 500 BCE) ("Master Yan"), respectively. With minimum background detail as to where and when the dialogues took place, the excerpts focus attention on what Jiang Wang and Master Yan said by way of political advice or tactical instructions.[105] Excerpts from other sources, like the *New Order* and the *Garden of Persuasions*, mainly record historical narratives and read more like the accounts of people and events found in the historical texts than discursive masters writings.[106] It is also notable that the Han dynastic histories occupy the most number of scrolls in the *Essentials*. That twelve scrolls are devoted to excerpts from the *History of the Former Han Dynasty* and the *History of the Latter Han Dynasty* provides another indication of the extent to which the Han imperium served as a model for the Zhenguan rulership. Indeed, Wei Zheng's preface to the *Essentials* highlights that the anthology is about applying the documented past to inform contemporary rulership and learning from positive and negative exemplars among former rulers, ministers, empresses, and consorts.[107]

As signaled by the editors' choice of a new title, the distinctive political philosophy in the *Essentials*' corpus of cultural knowledge finds expression in the words of selected sources that acquire new valences and significations by being excerpted, recontextualized, and reappropriated. The cultural memory in the *Essentials* has therefore been reconstructed to reflect the editors' evaluation of the past, their historiographical approach, and their emphasis on Confucian ideas about governance. To understand why the cultural knowledge from the past was reclaimed and re-presented in this way, the next two sections identify key influences from its contemporary context, including the early Tang emperors' inclination to learn from historical experience and revival of classical scholarship, respectively.

1.2.2 Remembering historical practice

The *Essentials* was arguably shaped by the historiographical zeitgeist of its time. The contemporary utility of history was emphasized by the early Tang rulers whose reigns witnessed the compilation of official histories for nearly all the dynasties in the post-Han period, as well as the commissioning of political advice literature derived from the historical records.

On-cho Ng and Qingjia Edward Wang observe that "Unlike their predecessors who beseeched Heaven to bestow blessings on their human reigns, the Tang rulers seemed more interested in learning practical historical lessons that could help guide their rule."[108] Such interest is evidenced by the first two emperors of the Tang dynasty associating history with an eminently usable object: the mirror. Emperor Gaozu refers to the historical writings serving as a mirror and a collection of precedents in his decree ordering the compilation of the histories of the five former dynasties:

> The historiographers make record of the sovereign's words and actions so one may investigate and verify the causes of success and failure and penetrate to the essence of all change; one may thereby compile analogical models to encourage good and repress evil, one may learn much from the past and use it as a mirror for the future.[109]

As mentioned above, Taizong also considered that history afforded a mirror for understanding the rise and fall of nations. Based on taking contemporary events as reflections of patterns that have occurred in the past and the results of those patterns as indicative of outcomes in the future, the mirror metaphor meant that the historical precedent denoted a specific event that could serve as "rationale, model, or justification for a proposed future course of action."[110] Addressing the Zhenguan ruler, Wei Zheng's description of the court historians' work in his preface to the *Essentials* reflects the pragmatic approach to history as a record of past experience for informing contemporary rulership:

> The court historians of the left and right record the ruler's deeds and words to illuminate virtue, deter wrongdoing, motivate goodness, and

> punish misconduct. Thus, through their records, worthy examples leave fragrance lasting a hundred generations while unworthy examples flash warnings for a thousand years.[111]

Traditionally, history in China was written to educate about past affairs of state with explanation of political success and failure and moral evaluation based on the ethical norms and standards of canonical works.[112] But for both Emperor Gaozu and Emperor Taizong, the documented past itself also provided a resource of model precedents and practices, not least for reflecting on and learning from the accumulated collective experience.

That the early Tang emperors were keen on the contemporary utility of history is manifest in the priority attributed to writing the major histories of the preceding four centuries during their reigns. Whereas history writing had been proscribed by Emperor Wen 文 (r. 581–604) during the Sui,[113] it was promoted by Gaozu and Taizong. Shortly after founding the Tang dynasty in 622, Emperor Gaozu's court commenced compiling dynastic histories for the Northern Wei (386–534), Liang, Chen, Northern Qi, Northern Zhou, and Sui dynasties, respectively.[114] With the exception of the *History of the Northern Wei* (*Wei shu* 魏書),[115] this corpus of work was completed during Taizong's reign in 636 by a dedicated historiography office: the Institute of Historiography (*Shiguan* 史館).[116] Established in 629, the institute enabled history writing to be located at court for the first time in China's history.[117] The prominent place accorded to history writing by the Zhenguan rulership can also be seen in the Institute of Historiography being positioned near the most important governing office—initially, the Chancellery and later, the Imperial Secretariat.[118] Tatsuhiko Seo makes the point that the official historiography written from the standpoint of the Tang was indicative of which dynasties were orthodox in the period from the Jin dynasty to the Period of Disunity (220–581), and suggestive of the role of unification and continuity by the Tang.[119] Hence, the historical writings not only served to help the Tang ruling house glean lessons and avoid the mistakes of short-lived dynasties during the Period of Disunity and the Sui dynasty,[120] but also to legitimate the new Tang ruling house by conferring on it orthodox status in the line of dynastic succession.[121]

Emperor Taizong's enthusiasm for learning from past practices appears to be more than a transitory fascination. This is exemplified by his commissioning several works of political-advice literature based on historical records. In or around 627, Yu Shinan completed the *Concise Discourse on Emperors and Kings* for the Zhenguan ruler.[122] This text comprised historical narratives about rulers dating from legendary antiquity (e.g., Fuxi 伏羲 and the Yellow Emperor 黃帝) through the Sui dynasty and included commentary styled in a question-and-answer format.[123] For his sons, Taizong addressed Wei Zheng as the Director of the Chancellery in 633 as follows:

> Since antiquity, there have been very few princes able to preserve themselves and survive. This is because being born and raised amid riches and honour, they are inclined towards arrogance and idleness. Many do not understand how to draw near gentlemen and keep away from petty persons. We wish to acquaint Our sons with the former words and past deeds and We hope that they will take them as precepts and models.[124]

Accordingly, Wei Zheng composed the *Record of the Commendable and Contemptible Conduct of the Feudal Lords and Princes since Antiquity*, detailing the strengths and shortcomings of princes throughout history, which Taizong commended to his sons.[125] Emperor Taizong thus led his court officials in taking a proactive approach to learning from the documented past—examining exemplars and best practice, and reflecting on the lessons of history for moral cultivation and monarchical governance. In light of such leadership, it may be argued that the *Essentials* was just one of many texts enabling Taizong, along with his princes and court officials to tap the wealth of historical experience for securing the foundations of their newly founded dynasty.

1.2.3 Reviving classical scholarship

Why the cultural memory of the *Essentials* communicates Confucian tenets and principles is explained in part by Emperor Taizong's need for relevant discourse to support his implementation of Confucian government, as discussed in Section 1.1. The Confucian orientation of the anthology may also be rationalized by the state revival of classical scholarship advocated by the first two Tang emperors, and the interest in classical learning on the part of Taizong himself.

As part of consolidating the new dynastic government across a reunified empire, both Emperor Gaozu and Emperor Taizong showed a commitment to the development of cultural and educational institutions, with a view to strengthening Confucian scholarship. Soon after gaining control over the Sui capital in 618, Gaozu reopened three academies that taught the Five Classics as their core curriculum, namely, the Academy of State Scholars, the Imperial Academy, and the Academy of the Four Gates, and he reintroduced the civil service examination system such that examinations were taking place in Chang'an by 621.[126] The establishment of schools in all prefectures and counties throughout the empire was ordered in 624.[127] Under Taizong, the State Academy Directorate was created to oversee the schools in the capital, which were expanded to include the Academy of Calligraphy, the Academy of Law, and the Academy of Mathematics, and provided with new buildings to accommodate over two thousand students.[128] The Institute of Literary Studies, which was established by Taizong while he was a prince and later became the Institute for the Advancement of Literature, also served as a school for a smaller number of students selected from the imperial family and senior officials.[129] The civil service examinations increased in both number and frequency during the Zhenguan reign-period, and candidates would travel from the provinces to sit the examinations almost every year.[130]

Not only did the early Tang emperors promote Confucian learning by developing the educational infrastructure, but they also initiated projects underpinning a revival of the Confucian tradition in a spirit not unlike that of the Han dynasty. Emperor Gaozu in 619 ordered for the Academy of State Scholars to construct two shrines in honor of the Duke of Zhou 周公 (r. as regent 1042–1035 BCE) as the ancestral sage and Confucius as the correlate, respectively, with seasonal commemorations throughout the year, and in 625, conferred posthumous honors on Confucius' descendants.[131] Emperor Taizong reinstated the earlier tradition of commemorating Confucius as the ancestral sage with Yan Hui 顏回 (521–490 BCE) as the ancestral teacher at the Academy of State Scholars in 628; he directed each provincial school to have a shrine in honor of Confucius in 630,[132] and named 21 historical Confucian scholars to be commemorated as correlates there in 647.[133] Taizong also awarded Confucius a posthumous title and arranged for 20 families to make seasonal offerings to Confucius at a purpose-built memorial hall in Yan province in 636.[134]

By the early Tang, there were many competing editions of the classics in circulation and widely divergent interpretations in their commentaries and sub-commentaries.[135] As the texts of the Confucian canon suffered from contention over their formal record and interpretation, Emperor Taizong in 630 ordered the production of standard editions for the Five Classics, and in 638 the compilation of their orthodox commentaries and sub-commentaries.[136] The outcomes were the *Standard Editions of the Five Classics* and the *Orthodox Exegesis of the Five Classics* (*Wujing zhengyi* 五經正義), which distilled the associated scholarship and integrated diverse interpretations, thereby setting a foundation for Confucian political thought and education in the reunified empire. The *Standard Editions of the Five Classics* was disseminated throughout the empire for the benefit of those studying for the civil service examinations,[137] and the *Orthodox Exegesis of the Five Classics* became textbooks of the State Academy Directorate.[138] According to Arthur F. Wright and Twitchett, the interpretation of the Five Classics was "a way of assuring that a uniform official orthodoxy was the basis of all schooling and that this orthodoxy in turn became the basis of a common moral outlook among the elite."[139] Wei Zheng himself was praised by Taizong in 638 for editing an annotated compilation of the *Records on Ritual*, one of the Five Classics.[140] As the standardization of the Confucian canon and work on their orthodox commentaries occurred around the same time as the making of *Essentials*, it is not difficult to imagine that the latter was shaped by those contemporary projects.[141]

Emperor Taizong's personal interest in classical learning dates to his days as Li Shimin, the Prince of Qin. In or around the time that Li Shimin helped the Tang administration settle rival claims and rebellion against its sovereignty, he showed awareness that his career as a military strategist and combatant since the age of 16 had left little opportunity for formal studies.[142] Unlike the battlefield environment, the court context demanded cultural learning for statesmanship in the civil tradition and competence with the forms and conventions of court interactions. For example, Fan Wang argues that the *Essentials* introduced Taizong to a repository of ready-made quotations for polite discourse, which would help him learn to identify allusions and decipher intentions in poetic quotations, for understanding memorials and engaging in court dialogues.[143] Li Shimin received support from a community of scholarly expertise through the Institute of Literary Studies and the Institute for the Advancement of Literature, which served as his private council and secretariat at different times.[144] The Zhenguan ruler also showed admiration for and keenness to follow the exemplary personages revered by the Confucian tradition, as exemplified by King Yao (trad. r. 2357–2255 BCE), King Shun (*fl.* 2250 BCE), the Duke of Zhou and Confucius.[145] It is notable that the combined number of references to King Yao and King Shun in Taizong's *Golden Mirror* manifesto of 628 are unanimously positive and outnumber references to other individuals.[146] The *Zhenguan Essentials* records Taizong in that year, describing the ways of King Yao and King Shun and the teachings of the Duke of Zhou and Confucius being as vitally imperative as wings to a bird and water to a fish.[147] It would seem that Taizong continued to attribute importance to classical learning even towards the end of his reign, as he advised his successor in the *Model for an Emperor*:

> Those [emperors] who set in flight splendid reputations, soaring aloft with their burgeoning achievements, and shining brilliantly throughout the empire without decay, are only those who have done so on account of their learning. Such is the rationale for honoring literature ... when we reach an era when the seas and border peaks are already enjoying quiet, when the waves and dust of battle have already calmed down, we can cease the awesome exercise of the seven military virtues, and instead display the grand transformation wrought by the nine perfections [of civil government].[148]

Fresh meaning in cultural memory is thus seen to be derived from existing knowledge through the choice of texts from various sources and their reconfiguration within an anthology that is shaped by contemporary political priorities of learning from historical practice and reviving Confucian scholarship. Such selection and re-presentation involved in the *Essentials*' form, structure, and contents thus corroborate its claim as a text of Zhenguan cultural memory.

1.3 BINDING NATURE

The knowledge preserved in cultural memory is characterized by a binding nature in terms of prescribing principles or guidance to be followed (its normative function) and espousing the shared values that orient the collective identity of the society through the way they see themselves, and how they wish others to know them (its formative function).[149] Where this body of written knowledge is closed and invariable, the text becomes a canon of cultural memory that provides a secure point of reference for the normative guidance and formative values of a community.[150] Such a canon is arguably found in the *Essentials* as its form and contents remain fixed and not subject to change. How the binding nature of the cultural memory in the *Essentials* furthers understanding of the Zhenguan ruling elite and their political administration is outlined below, with fuller discussion to follow in Chapters 2 and 3.

The normative function of cultural memory alerts us to the educative nature of the *Essentials*. As a statecraft reference, it instructs an aspiring or incumbent ruler in what they should know and be, and how and why they should act. Sourcing images, concepts, principles, narratives, precedents, and commentary, from poetry and prose, the anthology purports to offer a broad base of learning to inform and support the life and work of a monarch, including a repertoire of resources to develop their cultural literacy and competence for court interactions. Designed for discerning the complexities of being a sovereign with examples of the selfless and the self-serving, and the challenges of being a government official with examples of the meritorious and the manipulative, the *Essentials* was intended to encompass a comprehensive Confucian education in emperorship.[151] To the extent that the *Essentials* was accessible to and studied by the officials and princes, those readers also stood to benefit from the text by understanding more about their ruler's role and learning how to support them.

The formative function of the cultural memory sheds light on how the cultural knowledge remembered in the *Essentials* conveys the values of the Zhenguan ruling elite and defines their collective identity and profile through what they hold to be important and how they should behave. This is because "[a]ny selective acceptance of a tradition, that is any act of reception, also entails recognition of a specific set of values."[152]

In particular, the canon of cultural memory defines the proportions of what is important by pointing to works that embody and exemplify relevant values: " ... it not only points backward to the reception of a selected work; it also looks forward to an expanding array of possible connections."[153] With the excerpts in the *Essentials* forming a recension of their respective sources, it could be said that the compilation as a whole exemplifies a reception and recognition of values to which Taizong and his court subscribed. By identifying with selected parts of certain texts in the *Essentials* for the purposes of realizing their political objectives, they positioned themselves in public discourse with the cachet of conventional wisdom.

The specifics of how the *Essentials* shaped the collective identity of the Zhenguan court by guiding their political decision-making, will be explored in the next two chapters by reference to a cultural symbol and a narrative that feature prominently within the anthology. Chapter 2 examines how the *Essentials* provides normative guidance through the cultural symbol of the worthy official and how it relates to an excellence of statesmanship that was valued by the Zhenguan ruling elite for their public profile and governmental practice. Chapter 3 considers how the *Essentials*' narratives of remonstrative advice guide Taizong and his officials to seek and offer remonstration, respectively, and demonstrates that they attributed an importance to learning from the historical past in court communications.

The theoretical framework of cultural memory undergirds an understanding of the *Essentials* that takes account of its historical, political, and cultural settings. Crafted by Zhenguan officials from existing knowledge and consulted by their ruler as principal reader, the *Essentials* constitutes an institutional communication. With the meaning of the *Essentials* being shaped by the political and cultural drivers of its time and articulated through the selection and arrangement of excerpted texts, the book is no less than a work of cultural reconstruction. And by offering normative guidance for imperial governance and providing a shared basis for communal action, the *Essentials* reinforces the Zhenguan collective identity through its compilation of selected writings. I consider how the anthology performs such cultural functions in Chapters 2 and 3.

CHAPTER TWO

A CULTURAL SYMBOL OF THE WORTHY OFFICIAL

Through the unifying vision of the editors, the *Essentials* establishes a prototype of the worthy official equipped with a cultural repertoire that is traceable across the textual tradition. Whereas Chapter 1 explored how the *Essentials* forms part of the cultural memory of the Zhenguan era, this chapter analyzes how the anthology provides normative guidance to the Zhenguan ruler and his court through the cultural symbol of the "worthy official." Using the interpretive tools of cultural memory theory, intertextuality, and profilicity, it will be argued that this educative function of the cultural memory is reflected in the political thought, profile, and practice of Emperor Taizong and his court. As a prelude to understanding the portrayal of the worthy official in the *Essentials*, the following paragraphs will briefly introduce the general meaning of the relevant Chinese term "*xian* 賢" (worthy), the preference for worthy talent in the context of government service in traditional China, and will outline the theoretical elements relevant to this analysis of the symbolic worthy official.

First, what does the term "*xian* 賢" mean in Chinese? According to the *Explanations of Simple and Compound Characters* (*Shuowen jiezi* 說文解字), which is one of the earliest surviving Chinese lexicons from the second century, the term originally meant "of many skills or talents," with its graph comprising the character for "valuable" (*bei* 貝) to signify the prized or valuable nature of competency.[1] However, this definition became obsolete as *xian* was later used to denote worthiness in character and competence.[2] Hence, the term "*xian*" is often translated in English as "worthy" and "virtuous." It is notable that when *xian* appears together or close to the character "*neng* 能," which means "capable" or a "capable person,"[3] the two characters serve to accentuate different qualities. While *xian* communicates about a person's virtue, *neng* accounts for their expertise or proficiency. This appears to be the prevailing interpretation at the time the *Essentials* was produced, as evidenced by the writings of the Tang scholar-official Kong Yingda 孔穎達 (574–648), whom Emperor Taizong commissioned to produce standardized editions of the Five Classics and their commentaries. For example, in the imperially sponsored *Orthodox Exegesis of the Five Classics*, Kong's commentary on the *Venerable Documents*, which is one of the earliest and most authoritative sources of Chinese political discourse, asserts that *xian* refers to "ethical conduct" whereas *neng* refers to "talented ability."[4] When *xian* is written on its own, it generally describes an individual of both character and competence. While the notion of "worthy" may sometimes be expressed differently among the excerpts compiled from various sources in the *Essentials*, I will use the term "worthy" to denote the dual qualification of character and competence, and address any material differences in terminology as they arise.

The historian and philosopher Ch'ien Mu 錢穆 (1895–1990) once observed, "The traditional concept in China has always been that the virtuous, or worthy, rather than an electoral majority, should represent public opinion, when it came to choosing government officials."[5] We may begin to understand the value of worthy talent and why they are preferred within the government service through the following narrative that recurs in the *Essentials*.[6] When King Zhao昭 (r. 311–279 BCE) of the state of Yan consulted Master Guo Wei 郭隈 (*c.* 351–297 BCE) about recruiting worthy officials to help seek revenge against the state of Qi, Guo suggests the historical approach of respecting those officials as teachers. Guo also cites a precedent where a ruler manages to acquire thousand-mile horses, which are fine steeds that can travel one thousand miles in a single day,[7] only after an official purchased for him the deceased remains of such a horse for five hundred gold pieces. Likening his role to that of the dead horse, Guo convinces the king to appoint him as his teacher, a move which successfully draws talent to Yan, including from the states of Wei, Qi, and Zhao, respectively.[8] The considerable price paid for the dead horse provides a memorable foil for the untold worth of the official who ingeniously resolved the horse procurement quandary. That Guo could glean lessons from the past and help the king to recruit without delay, highlights his own merits. What this anecdote portrays as invaluable is not any outstanding equine, dead or alive, but the officials—both past (unnamed) and present (Guo Wei), and particularly the abilities of the latter—to be conversant with historical practices and to make the recollected past fruitful for contemporary needs. In the same vein, the Tang dynasty scholar and official Han Yu 韓愈 (768–824) wrote in his essay entitled "Discourses on Horses," "There have always been horses that can gallop a thousand miles; but there has not always been a Bo Le 伯樂 [*fl.* fifth century BCE]."[9] By analogy to Bo Le, the horse expert who lived during the time of Lord Mu of Qin 秦穆公 (r. 659–621 BCE) and was considered rarer than the most remarkable steeds, Han Yu implies that officials able to recognize and recruit fine talent are priceless. Referring also to Yi Dun 猗頓, who lived during the Warring States period (475–221 BCE) and is known for his expertise in discerning jade, the *Essentials* provides that the art of governance relies on the wisdom of the worthy personnel, as one would depend on Bo Le and Yi Dun to examine horses and jade, respectively.[10]

Of particular relevance to this analysis of the symbolic worthy official in the *Essentials* are the following elements of cultural memory theory, intertextuality and profilicity. The theory of cultural memory alerts us to the use of symbols in constructing a social identity shared among the members of a collective by drawing on their common knowledge, memory, and language. Jan Assmann theorizes that national community is based on an imagined continuity that reaches back into the depths of time, rooted in and defined by the events and experiences of the past.[11] Membership of a collective group like the nation involves sharing and adopting its history. Given that history exceeds the boundaries of any person's lifespan, each member must learn about and identify with the group's vision of the past.[12] As the collective identity ("we") depends upon shared knowledge and memory being communicated through a common semiotic system or language, it is but an imaginary construct underpinned by factors that are "purely symbolic."[13] Investigating how cultural memory enriches understanding of ancient Rome, Diana Spencer notably provides that "Memory relies upon and is generated by the manipulation of symbols."[14] Moreover, anything can become a symbol to denote community through its structure and function.[15] It will be demonstrated that the worthy official, by virtue of what it signifies and how it is used within the *Essentials*, presents as a cultural symbol that speaks to the normative and formative functions of the cultural memory's binding nature.

The workings of intertextuality equip us to explore how a symbol derives its meaning and the parameters of its signification by tracing the patterns, layers, and dynamics in the text. The term "intertextuality" (*intertextualité*) was coined by the French philosopher and literary theorist Julia Kristeva, who advocated approaching the literary word as "an intersection of textual surfaces rather than a point (a fixed meaning), as a dialogue among several writings: that of the writer, the addressee (or the character), and the contemporary or earlier cultural context."[16] According to Jonathan Culler, intertextuality "designates everything that enables one to recognize pattern and meaning in texts" and appreciate the dimensions of signification.[17] The concept has been recognized in the reading and writing practices of pre-modern China, including their quotation, allusion, and adaptation of prior texts.[18] In the context of texts from early medieval China (220–589), Wendy Swartz explains that allusion and quotation enabled writers to amplify a text of limited words by drawing on extratextual associations and extensive systems of signification. They can enter into a dialogue with established voices by choosing interlocutor texts and positioning themselves within certain traditions.[19] Indeed, "each quotation is a new creation insofar as it rewrites that prior text, and any writing is as 'original' as its particular appropriation of available textual and cultural resources."[20] New meaning is thus realized in the choice, adaptation, contextualization, and explication of the quoted text, which makes it mean or represent something more than historical information.[21] As the *Essentials* is a text wholly composed of excerpted material, it could be said that intertextual elements are manifest in its editors' selection of source texts and their excerpts, their appropriation of those excerpts within the context of the anthology, and their inclusion of selected commentary in annotations to explain and guide its interpretation. Through intertextual links such as set phrases that occur in different texts, the *Essentials* builds a repertoire of excerpts that center on the topic of the worthy official and provides "proof" that certain meritocratic ideals are firmly embedded in the literary tradition. It could be said that the knowledge from the past, recorded in what would otherwise be disconnected sources, comes together in anthologies such as the *Essentials*. By assembling selected sources from the literary heritage and harnessing the connections between its different parts, the *Essentials* develops a political philosophy of its own.

Given that the *Essentials* was curated by an editorial team of Zhenguan officials to the approval of their ruler, its narratives naturally tell us something about the Zhenguan court itself. In this respect, the notion of profilicity helps us further understand how their collective identity is shaped by the anthology. Hans-Georg Moeller and Paul J. D'Ambrosio argue that people form an identity by curating images of themselves ("profiles") for second-order observation, whereby others can see how they wish to be seen as being seen.[22] Moeller and D'Ambrosio explain this perspective by comparing the movie experience to live theater: "The audience no longer simply sees a character but sees a character as being seen – and this invites a different form of identification. We now can identify not only with the character but at the same time also with the 'peer' who is observing him."[23] Reading the *Essentials*, rather than the full text of its sources, is akin to watching a movie. As a collection of excerpts from selected sources, the *Essentials* does not simply denote a direct engagement with those texts, but signifies further communication about those texts among the Zhenguan ruling elite: which parts of what sources are considered meaningful for and congruous with, their political objectives, and how they read those sources for governing the state. Through the compilation, the Zhenguan ruling collective presents a profile for second-order observation of how they would like to be seen, by identifying with excerpts from texts that position them in public discourse. It will be seen that such imperial representation is reinforced through confirmation by the members of the Zhenguan ruling elite as participants in the discourse.

Considering the formative influence of shared symbols on a collective's culture, self-image, and profile, the worthy official motif offers a key to unraveling the functions of cultural memory within the *Essentials*. Separate sections of this chapter will analyze how the symbolic worthy official that is adjudged more valuable than precious objects, supports the collective identity and profile of the Zhenguan ruling elite, and how the portrayal of historical exemplars provides guidance as to what statesmanship entails in the contexts of personnel recruitment and lifelong service to the state, respectively.

2.1 TREASURE TALENT

China has a long-established tradition of transmitting cultural knowledge through people. This is consistent with the fact that Chinese culture relies on human beings rather than antiquated objects or monuments to perpetuate the memory of the past. Simon Leys found that "Continuity is not ensured by the immobility of inanimate objects, it is achieved through the fluidity of successive generations."[24] For example, the tradition of formal teachings imparted from master to student is corroborated by the lineages of Confucianism and Zen Buddhism. Confucius himself had some seventy accomplished followers according to the *Records of the Historian* and *Mencius*.[25] The Chinese idiom "robe and alms-bowl handed down" conveys the knowledge transfer of art, craft, or intellectual tradition from one generation to another. This expression was derived from the handing-down of the sacred robe and alms-bowl of Bodhidharma 菩提達摩 (dates unknown) as the founding father of Zen Buddhism in China, throughout generations of succeeding patriarchs as a testament of their full qualification.[26] In the context of imperial public service and statecraft know-how, the relevant individuals were the scholar-officials. Scholars, regardless of whether they became government officials, were generally respected in the society of pre-modern China. They were ranked first among the four categories of traditional occupations, namely, scholars-officials, farmers, craftspeople, and merchants.[27] And the best scholars as adjudged in the civil service examinations, for instance, could look forward to a career in officialdom. As the popular saying goes, "Worthies are the treasures of state, Scholars are the teachers of principles."[28] The chapter entitled "On Teaching and Learning" in the *Records on Ritual*, which is one of the Five Classics, provides that rulers must not treat the officials who are responsible for teaching them as their subordinates, and accordingly, those officials need not follow the custom of facing northwards in bowing to the ruler.[29]

That worthy talent is indispensable to the political governance was not lost on the *Essentials*. Dating from the Zhou dynasty to the late Han, excerpts about public officials being valued more than precious objects were drawn from all three of its bibliographical classifications. The *Essentials*' passages offer insight into how the worthy official is portrayed and the signification attributed to them. What it means to be a worthy official for the Zhenguan ruling elite is expressed through the editors' eclectic choice of sources, the selective inclusion of their text and commentary, and their re-contextualization and re-presentation within the anthology.

First, the passages challenge the conventional idea of what is valuable or should be valued. Instead of foreign creatures, fine jades, and precious pearls, the Chinese term for "treasure," pronounced "*bao*" and written as "寶" or "珤" in the *Essentials*, becomes associated with worthy talent for the public service. Describing those officials as "*bao*" implies that they are invaluable to the state, generally rare, and potentially irreplaceable given the uniqueness of human individuals. That the exemplary service of worthy officials is preferred to exquisite objects, reflects a trend favoring the intangible over the tangible. From the first section of canonical writings, the *Essentials* establishes that worthy personnel are more valuable than exotic animals and ornamental minerals through annotated extracts. This is exemplified by the following excerpts from the *Venerable Documents* and the *Discourses of the States*, respectively:

> [Even] dogs and horses that are not native to his country he will not keep. Refrain from keeping non-native [species] as [people] are not accustomed to using them. Fine birds and strange animals he will not nourish in his state. This is because they are useless and burdensome [to the state]. When he does not look on foreign things as precious, foreigners will come to him; By not competing for foreign interests, [the state will] gain the deference of foreigners. When [what is treasured are the worthy], [his own] people near at hand will enjoy repose. Cherishing the worthy and engaging the able brings peace to those near, which in turn brings peace to those afar.30

This *Venerable Documents* passage has been chosen from its "Hounds of Lü" (*lü'ao*旅獒) chapter, where the *Essentials* adopts words attributed to the Grand Guardian Duke Shao 召公 (d. *c.*1000 BCE) advising King Wu 武 (r. 1049/45–1043 BCE) of Zhou to value and engage worthy officials rather than enjoying and cultivating foreign animals. This is because worthy talent is the only thing worth treasuring.[31] This course of action is commended by general advantages identified in the annotation of Kong Yingda. Receiving hounds from the Lü tribe becomes an occasion (for the worthy official) to remind the Zhou king to rise above the distractions of private pleasures and be mindful of serving the public interests instead. The *Essentials* omits the opening details that appear in the recension of this chapter from the Wenyuan Hall edition of the *Complete Library*: "After the conquest of Shang, the way being open to the nine tribes of the Yi and the eight of the Man, the western tribe of Lü sent as a tribute some of its hounds ... ."[32] Such elision of background information underscores the focus of the *Essentials* on providing normative guidance rather than historical completeness. The above position from the Zhou dynasty finds endorsement and elaboration in subsequent excerpts, which leaves the reader under no uncertain terms as to what should be valued and what has been valued since ancient times.

Selective inclusion of text and annotation in this *Discourses of the States* excerpt makes a persuasive case from the late Spring and Autumn period:

> Wangsun Yu (*fl.* late sixth century BCE) is on a formal visit to the state of Jin. Wangsun Yu is a high official of the state of Chu. Lord Ding of Jin (r. 511—475 BCE) held a feast in his honour. Zhao Jianzi (d. 496 BCE) asked Wang Sunyu: "Does Chu still have its white *heng* jade?" The *heng* jade is what is across the top of the girdle ornament. Wang replied, "Yes."
>
> Jianzi asked, "How long has it been a state treasure?" "Long" [in terms of] how many generations.
>
> Wang said, "It has never been a treasure. What Chu treasures are: Guan Yifu (*fl.* late fifth century BCE), This is about the worthy being treasured. who deals with the princes on model terms This is about using model terms in relations with the princes. such that Chu's ruler does not become a subject of criticism. "Criticism" means slander and ridicule. There is also the court secretary Yi Xiang (*fl.* 473 BCE), who can teach

model practices to keep the various matters of state in order "Order" means sequence. "Matters" means affairs. and constantly advises Chu's ruler of the strengths and faults such that they are mindful of the accomplishments of former sovereigns ... These are the state treasures of Chu. As for the white *heng* jade, it is a plaything of past rulers, hardly a treasure." A "plaything" being an object of amusement.33

Although jade is traditionally ascribed moral qualities of benevolence, rightness, wisdom, courage, and purity[34] and likened to the virtue of the exemplary person,[35] this passage clarifies from the outset that the state of Chu treasures not its famous *heng* jade but its worthy officials. Including annotation by Wei Zhao韋昭 (204–273), a scholar-official and historian of the Three Kingdoms period (220–280), this point is impressed upon the reader in three ways. First, "This is about the worthy being treasured" indicates that the treasures are not limited to named or specific individuals (e.g., Guan Yifu 觀射父 and Yi Xiang 倚相). Second, what Chu treasures is not theoretical virtues but the actual practice of those virtues by its officials, which is assumed to make their service valuable. The Chu high-ranking official ("high official") Wang Sunyu 王孫圉 (*fl.* late sixth century BCE) waxes lyrical about not only what the Chu officials have done, but also what they can do for Chu. It is notable that the excerpt excludes part of the annotation found in the received version of the *Discourses of the State* ("received text") from the Wenyuan Hall edition of the *Complete Library*: "not regarding treasures as treasures." As reading such annotation could raise queries as to why things termed "treasures" are not actually considered treasures, this exclusion is likely due to preventing redundancy and confusion. Also in the received text, the Chu high official Wang Sunyu goes on to enumerate six types of state treasures, including sages, jades, turtles, pearls, gold and the mountains, forests, lakes, and grasslands.[36] However, this entire final paragraph does not appear in the *Essentials*. Although Wang ultimately dismisses the *heng* jade as a plaything, in the received text he does acknowledge that jade generally counts as a treasure, as it was thought to protect grain crops and prevent drought. Exclusion of these lines from the *Essentials* passage may be to avoid detracting from the central idea of the treasures being worthy statespersons and preclude ambiguity about what should qualify as state treasures. Indeed, it is not the jade but the personnel that first comes to mind for Wang at the mention of state treasures.

Third, the annotation reinforces the idea expressed in the text that the *heng* jade is but a "plaything of past rulers," merely a dated object of personal amusement, which is hardly worth treasuring at all. Following on from the previous excerpt, the *Discourses of the States* manifests a continuity in the ruler's selfless dedication to public duty over private diversion, which will also come to distinguish the exemplary service of the worthy official.

A pattern is already discernible from these extracts of the *Venerable Documents* and the *Discourses of the States*. The *Essentials* has excerpted text where the historical protagonist explains about state treasures in conversation with another person, often in response to an enquiry about some valuable object, and frequently providing examples. This formula is reflected among the historical and masters writings within the *Essentials*. The following excerpts from the *Records of the Historian*, the *Discourses on Salt and Iron*, the *New Order*, and the *Extended Reflections*, do not contain any annotation nor do they differ materially from the received versions in the Wenyuan Hall edition of the Complete Library.[37]

This excerpt of the *Essentials* from the *Records of the Historian* records a dialogue between King Hui 惠 (r. 344–319 BCE) of Wei 魏 and King Wei 威 (r. 356–320 BCE) of Qi 齊in 333 BCE, where the latter avers that Qi's treasures are not luminous pearls but its efficacious officials:

> King [Hui] of Wei asked, "Does Your Majesty also have treasures?"
>
> King Wei [of Qi] replied, "No."
>
> King Hui said, "A state as small as mine still has ten pearls, each measuring an inch in diameter and illuminating a distance twelve chariots long. How can [Qi] a state of ten-thousand chariots be without treasure?"
>
> King Wei replied, "What we regard as treasure differs from Your Majesty. Our official Master Tan, when he defends Nancheng, the people of the state of Chu dare not to encroach, and all twelve states south of the River Si pay court. Our official Master Pan, when he defends Gaotang, the people of the state of Zhao dare not to fish from the east bank of the Yellow River. Our official Qianfu, when he defends Xuzhou, [people of the

states of Yan and Zhao offer oblations at its northern and western gates] The northern and western gates of Qi. This is about the people of Yan and Zhao offering oblations for good fortune as they fear military incursion and attack. and over seven thousand families have relocated to Xuzhou [from those states]. Our official Zhong Shou, when he safeguards against bandits and brigands, even lost property on the road will remain untouched. [Such officials] could illuminate a thousand *li* [(Chinese miles)], not just twelve chariots!"

Discomfited, King Hui left in displeasure.[38]

Aside from their lustrous forms, pearls are traditionally thought to represent the essence of water and therefore could offer protection from fire.[39] However, precious pearls do not even rate a mention when King Wei is asked about his treasures. Instead of answering the personal enquiry along the lines of pearls or other prized objects, as hinted by King Hui, King Wei wastes no words in conveying that his judgment of value differs altogether. He has chosen to value that which makes a positive and meaningful difference to his state. This passage insinuates that the state would not need pearls while there are competent officials, such as Master Tan 檀子, Master Pan 盼子, and Qianfu 黔夫, to safeguard territories against the fires of warfare (*zhanhuo* 戰火). Combined with the endorsement of King Wei, the formulaic likeness of this extract to the others signals that Master Tan, Master Pan, Qianfu, and Zhong Shou were appreciated as worthy officials, albeit not expressly specified as such in the text. Like the *Discourses of the States* passage above, this excerpt from the *Records of the Historian* squarely focuses attention on the excellent work that the named officials have contributed in service of Qi and what it means to the state.

In citing the rulership of sage kings, this passage of the *Essentials* from the *Discourses on Salt and Iron* adds the weight of historical authority and conventional wisdom to the choice of worthy officials over famous pearls and jades, or other rare and extraordinary things:

The Sui [Prince's pearl] and Master He's [jade disc] have been famous treasures for generations, but they cannot assist [a state] in crisis or prevent [its] collapse. Consequently, inspiring virtue and showcasing authority stems from the worthy officials and not the armaments, horses, [nor] the rare and extraordinary. That is why the sage rulers treasured the worthy [officials] rather than pearls and jades. In the past, Master Yan cultivated [protocol] at the banquet and quashed an [enemy] assault from a thousand miles. The incompetent [official] may have a full chest of the Sui [pearls] and He [jades], yet they would not avert [state] collapse.[40]

Although Master Yan is not expressly described as a "worthy" within this excerpt, his characterization as such may be inferred from the preceding sentence about worthy officials and the following sentence about their opposite: the incompetent official. The reader would also be able to discern that Master Yan is a worthy official through other passages in the *Essentials* (e.g., the excerpts from *Master Yan* in scroll 33). Pragmatic and public considerations underlying the preference for worthy officials are highlighted by the fact that one worthy official in the form of Master Yan could accomplish for the state what many pearls and jades cannot.

In the *Essentials*' excerpt from the *New Order* below, the worthy officials are literally placed on pedestals:[41]

Qin wanted to attack Chu and sent an envoy to Chu to inspect its treasures. On hearing about this, the Chu ruler [King Xuan (r. 369–340 BCE)] ... asked, "May the Jade Disc of He and the Pearl of the Sui Prince be displayed?" ...

Zhao Xixu advised, "This is about assessing our state's strengths and weaknesses. The treasures are in the worthy officials. Pearls and jades are [but] objects of amusement, not substantial treasure."

The ruler then entrusted Zhao Xixu to deal with this matter. Zhao erected one eastern platform, four southern platforms, and one western platform. On the arrival of the Qin delegate, Zhao said, "As the guest, please be seated on the east side." [Senior Minister Zixi, Minister of Rites Zi'ao, Lord Zigao of She, and Minister of Defense Zifan each took their position at the southern platforms, with Zhao himself at the western platform.]

Zhao said to [the Qin delegate]: "You wish to view Chu's treasures. What Chu treasures are worthy officials. Managing court officials, filling granaries, such that the people each gain what they should is Senior

> Minister Zixi here. Visiting the feudal states with jade tablets and circlets, resolving issues of hostility, developing friendly bilateral relations, such that there is no risk of warfare is Minister of Rites Zi'ao here. Safeguarding the territory and maintaining the borders without encroaching on or by neighbours is Lord Zigao of She here. Managing the regiments and battalions and organising the armaments to withstand enemy forces ... is Minister of Defense Zifan here. Contemplating the extant discourses of hegemons and gleaning lessons from the experience of order and disorder is Zhao Xixu here. Specifically for your inspection."
>
> The Qin delegate was stunned speechless. On returning to Qin, he reported to the Qin ruler, "Chu has many worthy officials, it is not the time to take advantage." And then [Qin] did not attack Chu.[42]

As a variation of the formula whereby the real state treasures are related in a dialogue between just two parties, the protagonist Zhao Xixu 昭奚恤 convinces the Chu ruler and a third party: the delegate from the state of Qin. By contributing to the bureaucratic organization, economic vitality, diplomatic relations, territorial integrity, defense readiness, and historically informed strategy, this passage portrays Chu's worthy statesmen, namely, Senior Minister Zixi 子西, Minister of Rites Zi'ao 子敖, Lord Zigao of She 葉公子高, Minister of Defense Zifan 子反, and Zhao, as the pride of their state and far more precious than jades and pearls. Indeed, their presence staves off a Qin incursion. Exclusion of information in the received version about Zhao mobilizing military officers to build the platforms and the concluding quotation from the *Odes*, keeps the attention on the officials themselves and their contribution to the normative guidance of the *Essentials*.[43]

Authored by Xun Yue 荀悅 (148–209), the Director of the Palace Library for the last Han ruler Emperor Xian 獻 (r. 189–200), this *Extended Reflections* excerpt from the *Essentials* embodies the voice of an official himself:

> Precious rarities offered from foreign territories that require extensive translation are not treasures. Good counsel offered by entrusted individuals as they prostrate [before the ruler] is the ultimate treasure.[44]

Here, the "entrusted individuals" are presumably officials whose contributions of good advice matter more than foreign gifts, and by logical inference from the preceding passages, they may be assumed to be worthy officials. Perhaps more directly than the other excerpts, the *Extended Reflections* underlines what is it about the worthy officials that makes them valuable, namely their input, guidance, and advice.

Compiled within the anthology, the above excerpts collectively convey that the importance placed on worthy officials is well-established, that such talent has been sought since the earliest times as documented in the *Venerable Documents*, and that the Zhenguan ruling collective wanted to be seen as identifying with and following this conventional wisdom. Arguably, the *Essentials* takes this matter further not least in the following two ways.

First, through the passages being located in different parts of the text, the *Essentials* offers recurring reminders to the reader that valuable items such as jades, pearls, exotic animals, and other rarities cannot compare to the worthy officials and that such talent is the only thing worth treasuring. These "truths" are shown as being recognized by rulers and officials alike, from the *dramatis personae* within the extracts to the authors of the source texts, such as Liu Xiang and Xun Yue who wrote the *New Order* and the *Extended Reflections*, respectively, and the editors of the *Essentials* themselves. The seemingly valuable are devalued in different ways: pursuing foreign assets risks conflicts of interest with other states, the *heng* jade is dismissed as just a curio, pearls can only give off visible light, and no amount of jades or pearls however famous can stave off a foreign assault. Given the shift from the superficially pleasing towards the substantively pragmatic, the reader is warned against misconceptions or distractions associated with beautiful or strange objects, using the question-and-answer format evident from three of the six excerpts. Specifically, someone enquires about treasure only to learn, in varying levels of detail, that the treasures are the worthy personnel. The preference for such talent is driven by a recognition of the strengths of available candidates as much as the need for human resources to attend to myriad matters of government. This is seen in the *Essentials*' excerpts from the *Records of the Historian*, the *Discourses of Salt and Iron*, and the *New Order*, where the service of worthy officials, individually or as a group, effectively safeguard the state territory and ward off the threat of foreign attack. In particular, the *New Order* excerpt identifies the synergy of several officials: just by excelling in their respective duties, the worthy may collectively mitigate the risk of hostilities from a state as formidable as Qin. Thus, the symbolic figure of the worthy personnel is attributed a priceless and indispensable worth.

Second, the excerpts offer insight into the diversity of roles that have been served by the worthy official, and the exemplary level of service that may be expected from them, with particular focus on the application of cultural knowledge and historical learning to statecraft. The role descriptions of the named individuals show that worthy personnel have contributed meritorious service in diverse areas ranging from foreign affairs (e.g., Guan Yifu and Zi'ao), archival records and administration (Yi Xiang) to territorial defense (e.g., Master Tan and Lord Zigao of She). Clearly, it is not the person *per se*, but their performance that bejewels the crown. The exemplary quality of their work is conveyed as much by their names being mentioned in the same breath as tangible valuables, as the complimentary remarks about their excellence in service. For example, Zhao Xixu's penetrating discernment of Qin's motives and shrewd handling of the situation exemplify how the ideal statesperson would act with percipience, wit, and unerring judgment. Zhao's presentation of each official's singular contributions to the Qin delegate develops the reader's understanding of the standards of worthy conduct that are encouraged by the *Essentials*. Perhaps King Wei is alluding to the enduring worth of the worthy official's exemplary work illuminating the standards for others by his climactic declaration: "[Such officials] could illuminate a thousand miles, not just twelve chariots!" Extrapolating from the various roles of the worthy precedents, it becomes conceivable that any member of the bureaucracy, regardless of their portfolio, position, or responsibility, can and should develop themselves to become a worthy. Moreover, given the concise nature of the *Essentials'* excerpts, it seems significant that they also include portrayals of worthy officials who glean lessons from the past for their day-to-day work. For example, Guan Yifu uses model terms in foreign relations such that the ruler enjoys an untarnished reputation, Yi Xiang keeps state affairs in order and helps the ruler learn from the experiences of former rulers by sharing model practices, and Zhao Xixu contemplates the extant discourses of hegemons and gleans lessons from political experiences of order and disorder. It must be noted that the further details provided in respect of Yi Xiang—that is, that he keeps the Chu ruler "mindful of the achievements of former sovereigns," combined with the use of word "model" to qualify Guan Yifu's diplomatic terms and Yi Xiang's practices—implies that the diplomatic terms are based on past practices rather than being Guan Yifu's own ways. Historical experience is thus highlighted as a source of benchmarks or best practices. By contributing meritorious service in their roles, including the practical application of their knowledge of historical practice to meet the needs of contemporary governance, the symbolic worthy official in the *Essentials* who may be generalized from the historical exemplars, attests to an excellence and a pattern of conduct that is valued by the Zhenguan ruler and his court.

Various ideas are reiterated—that worthy talent is priceless, that it is the only "thing" worth treasuring, and that such a person contributes exemplary work whatever their roles. Repetition through different accounts across all three bibliographical sections of the *Essentials* suggests that the worth of worthy officials was re-emphasized in the Zhenguan era, and that its ruling elite wanted to be seen as commemorating such past exemplars and encouraging existing personnel towards the same standard. This is supported by records of the political thought and decision-making attributed to Emperor Taizong and his court, which help illuminate why and how the historical worthy figures are used to symbolic effect in the *Essentials*.

First, the Zhenguan ruler himself appears acutely aware of the need to engage worthy officials to achieve lasting success. As Emperor Taizong expressed to his ministers in the second year of the Zhenguan reign-period (628), both generally and in respect of the commanders and prefects:

> The essence of governance lies [solely] in getting [the right] people. If incapable people are employed, it will be difficult to bring about ordered government.[45]
>
> We dwell deep in the palace, and Our eyes and ears do not reach far. We rely on commanders and prefects. This is in reality the group on whom order and disorder depend, so finding the right [people] is all the more essential.[46]

Over a decade later, this position purportedly remained unchanged as Taizong said to his attendant officials in the thirteenth year of the Zhenguan reign-period (639): "If We are to pacify the realm, the most important issue is employing worthy talent."[47]

Even as a prince, Emperor Taizong surrounded himself with eminent scholar-officials whom he recruited as academicians of his private council and secretariat: the Institute of Literary Studies, which later became the Institute for the Advancement of Literature. He appointed scholars to the Institute since the inception of his reign and often consulted them on ancient texts and state affairs until late in the evenings.[48]

That a talented official can be invaluable and irreplaceable reverberates in the Zhenguan ruler's remarks about Yu Shinan, one of the four editors of the *Essentials*. One time while Taizong was about to embark on an inspection tour and he was asked whether he needed his books to be brought along with the imperial carriage, he replied, "That's not necessary, Yu Shinan will be with me—he is a walking library."[49] The Zhenguan ruler's compliment captures the precious utility of being able to consult a learned official. Having this one official saves him from carting along numerous texts and having to read them himself. In mourning the passing of Yu Shinan in 638, the second Tang emperor lamented that there will never be anyone as learned as Yu Shinan among the libraries, and he no longer has anyone with whom he can discuss the books.[50]

That the exemplary service of worthy talent was highly regarded is reflected in Taizong's praise of officials from both the military and civil ranks. This is exemplified in respect of the Regional Governor Li Ji 李勣 (594–669) and Wei Zheng, respectively. Sometime during the early years of the Zhenguan reign-period, Taizong complimented Li Ji as follows:

> Taizong said to his attendant officials: "Emperor Yang of Sui did not understand how to carefully select the worthy [personnel] to guard the borders. He only knew how to build great walls far away and station soldiers across a wide area for protection against the Turks. That was how confused his sense and knowledge of things were. Now that We have deputed Li Ji to Bingzhou, We have been able to intimidate the Turks into taking flight

and achieve peace on the border. Is not this worth more than great walls stretching for thousands of miles!"[51]

Juxtaposing the stationing of a single official at Bingzhou with the great lengths employed under Emperor Yang 煬 (r. 604–618), the last ruler of the Sui dynasty to alleviate the threat of incursions by the Turks evokes the efficacy of the worthy talent. Similarly, the Zhenguan ruler extolled the reliable advice from Wei Zheng to his ministers sometime in the early years of the Zhenguan reign-period, as follows:

> At first the prefectures in Lingnan were all buzzing with talk of the rebellion of [Feng] Ang, and We certainly wanted to suppress him. Wei Zheng remonstrated with urgency, believing that We should not do it, but should merely nurture him with virtue, and that then he would surely come of his own accord without the need for a punitive expedition. We followed his plan, with the result that the area beyond Ling is at peace, and it was pacified without toil. This was better than 100,000 troops![52]

Although Wei Zheng here is not expressly described as a worthy official, it is strongly implied, not least by the praise in somewhat analogous terms: Li Ji and Wei Zheng are better than great walls extending over thousands of miles and military troops of 100,000 men, respectively. Such expressions communicate the great worth attributed to the worthy official by the Zhenguan ruler. At the same time, they underscore that what is critical is not merely manpower, but the worthy quality of those human resources.

Beyond the meritorious service of worthy officials, it is notable that Emperor Taizong personally valued their examples as "mirrors," whose guidance and advice could be used to reflect on himself and improve his faults. One long-serving official regarded as a mirror was Wei Zheng, who assisted in various capacities over 17 years (discussed in Section 1.1) and whose death was deeply mourned by the Zhenguan ruler. When Wei Zheng was absent from court on account of illness in or around 642, Taizong personally wrote to him conveying that his absence was dearly missed through an ancient saying: "Without a mirror, one is unable to see [one's] beard and brow."[53] Taizong personally composed Wei Zheng's funerary inscription and wrote the steele calligraphy.[54] After suspending court for five days to mourn Wei Zheng's passing, Taizong said to his court:

> Using bronze as a mirror, one can adjust clothes and cap. Using the past as a mirror, one can foretell rise and fall. Using a person as a mirror, one can discern strength and shortcoming. We have held on to these three mirrors to keep Ourselves from committing mistakes. Now that Wei Zheng has passed, We have lost a mirror![55]

Another entrusted advisor was Ma Zhou 馬周 (601–648), who is described by the *Zhenguan Essentials* as being skilled in debate, a capable memorialist, and having the powers of penetrating analysis. Emperor Taizong once said of Ma Zhou, "Such is Our relation with Ma Zhou that as soon as We do not see Ma Zhou for a while, We miss him."[56]

Taizong's appreciation of talent is manifest in two contemporary artworks: the *Portraits of Eighteen Academicians* in the Palace Library (date unknown),[57] and in 642, the *Portraits of Twenty-four Meritorious Officials*[58] at the Lingyan Pavilion. These life-sized portraitures were commissioned by the Zhenguan ruler to commemorate the academicians and officials whose contributions he regarded as integral to the success of his reign. Given that the standing pose was traditionally preferred for such commemorative formal paintings,[59] the lifelike representations would have resembled mirror-like images of the respective individuals. Both artworks effectively enabled Taizong to preserve those "mirrors" long after their retirement or passing for his reflection on their counsel and examples. According to Patricia Ebrey, viewers of portraits of eminent individuals admired for their cultural, political, or military accomplishments were meant to be inspired by the moral message they conveyed.[60] Insofar as the paintings were styled as character portraits—rendering moral traits of the individuals for admiration, identification, and emulation[61]—it could be said that they offered an enduring pictorial record of the inspirational statesmen and their exhortations for the Zhenguan ruler. Notably, both artworks include portraits of the *Essentials*' editors: Chu Liang and Yu Shinan in the former, and Wei Zheng and Yu Shinan in the latter. The *New History of the Tang Dynasty* records that after Wei Zheng passed away, Taizong would visit his portrait at the Lingyan Pavilion and write poetry in mourning him.[62]

To Emperor Taizong, having the input of worthy officials evidently mattered more than amassing material wealth. When the Secretarial Censor Quan Wanji 權萬紀 (d. 643) proposed in 636 to mine the extensive deposits of silver in the mountains of Xuanzhou and Raozhou for a cash windfall, Taizong responded unequivocally that what he prioritized and what the empire needed were the service of worthy officials, not more profit:

> Taizong said, "As the Son of Heaven We are exalted, and there is nothing that We lack in regard to this matter. All that We require are the acceptance of good advice and the promotion of good acts for the benefit of the common people. Moreover, even if the country were to obtain several million strings of cash, how could that compare to obtaining a single talented and virtuous person?"[63]

The notion in the *Essentials* that the worthy talent is the only thing worth treasuring is complemented in the Zhenguan ruler's comment that their advice counts as one of the few things that he (and the state) genuinely needs. That Taizong's words in the above extracts were putatively expressed in the presence of his court meant that the members of the Zhenguan ruling elite would have been aware of his views.

Based on such historical evidence about the Zhenguan rulership, it is apparent that the worthy talent mattered all the more to Emperor Taizong who harbored convictions about such officials being fundamental to imperial governance generally and indispensable to his rulership. His attitude goes some way to explaining why the *Essentials*, as a product of his commission and completed by four of his closest officials, portrays worthy talent to be worth more than anything else and their input in state affairs to be the ultimate asset. From the perspective of the Zhenguan ruling collective, the excerpts of the *Essentials* convey a clear re-emphasis in the shift from valuing objects that must be handed down as part of the material heritage, towards people. In this case, the worthy officials of the past are considered to be the real treasures, as are by implication, the worthy personnel of the present. The symbolic figure of the worthy official in the *Essentials* by its very nature necessarily relates to an excellence of statesmanship that was collectively valued by the Zhenguan ruler and his court for their public profile as well as how they performed their public service. These concerns are further examined in the next two sections.

2.2 RECOMMEND TALENT

This part considers why the worthy talent is esteemed to be invaluable in the *Essentials* by reference to their exemplary work, focusing on their role in recommending talent to and recognizing talent within the government service.

In a sermon on gratitude, Ralph W. Emerson observed that the examples of others offer sublime inspiration and transformative strength:

> [A] cause of lively gratitude is a blessing a little beyond home, the acquaintance we have, near or remote, with persons of great worth. A cultivated heart and mind, a finished character, is the most excellent gift of God, the most excellent thing out of us that we can form an idea of ... How far more exciting is this spectacle of living virtues than the dead letter which describes the same virtues. I look upon the persons of fine intellectual endowments and of magnanimous dispositions whom it is or has been my fortune to know, as my apostles and prophets. They perform to us the office of good angels; they show us to what height active virtue can be carried; the thought of them comes to us in the hour of despondency and of temptation, and holds us up from falling.[64]

The depth of personal appreciation of exemplary individuals for Christian cultivation as described by Emerson above, offers a starting point for understanding the ancient Chinese tradition of drawing upon the force and import of exemplars in personal cultivation. David N. Keightley argues that the early Chinese civilization is characterized by an inclination to trust that the past and its exemplars set a course, the following of which would yield social harmony and prosperity. He explains that in early China, "heroes were heroes precisely because they were models worthy of emulation."[65] As such personages represented reliable sources of moral guidance and commemorating their legacy would enjoin others to follow their positive example, the hero would operate as a general and symbolic lesson for others.[66] Keightley describes the stories of heroes as often pedagogical and culture-building; they were recorded and recited less for entertainment than for instruction and exhortation.[67] The Chinese hero became a hero by having emulated others, being inspired by and internalizing as their own, the examples from their past.[68] Indeed, to the early Confucians, the emulation of exemplars was the most efficient method of learning. As Donald Munro remarks, "For the Confucians, model emulation was not just one way of learning; it was by far the most efficient way, and one could inculcate any virtuous behaviour in people by presenting the right model."[69]

Such views from contemporary scholars are corroborated by the canonical writings. The *Records on Ritual*'s chapter "On Teaching and Learning," as the earliest Chinese text on pedagogy, provides: "To improve by observing each other is called learning from others."[70] According to the *Analects*, Confucius taught his students, "When you see a worthy person, think about how you can equal him."[71] (*Analects*, 4.17). Instead of achieving social order by instilling the fear of punitive sanctions for legal transgressions, Confucian thought preferred to ensure proper conduct by presenting virtuous models whose attitudes and behaviors would be emulated even in the absence of law enforcers.[72] The *Analects* records that Confucius said: "Guide them with government orders, regulate them with penalties, and the people will seek to evade the law and be without shame. Guide them with virtue, regulate them with ritual, and they will have a sense of shame and become upright."[73]

Amy Olberding's theory about exemplars in the *Analects* offers insight into analyzing the characterization of the worthy official as a positive role model in the *Essentials*. Olberding ascribes an exemplarist moral theory to the *Analects* whereby the general moral sensibility that the text proposes results from the scrutiny of exemplary figures:

> Confucius and the *Analects*' authors know, in a pre-theoretical, immediate way, whom they judge to be good people and that the various abstract moral concepts and prescriptions the text proposes are an effort to explain and characterize these people ... Its governing imperative is that we ought to seek to be like our exemplars and its generalized accounts of the virtues reflect efforts to assay, in an organized and careful fashion, what emulation of exemplars entails and requires.[74]

Olberding identifies two types of exemplars: the "total exemplar" who presents themselves as worthy of emulation in most if not all respects, and the "partial exemplar," who are exemplars for certain roles, areas of human activity, or particular virtues.[75] Arguably, a "partial exemplar" may be found in the worthy official, based on narratives within the *Essentials* identifying them as admirable statespersons. While some are lauded for exemplary service, others may suffer the injustice and ignominy of demotion, detainment, or a death sentence. As such, the cultural symbol of the worthy official personifies a behavioral norm or standard of excellence that is recognized and upheld by the editors of the *Essentials.* Like the patchwork nature of contents in the *Analects*, there is no express structure in the *Essentials* directing the reader's attention as to how the worthy official should conduct themselves. For example, there are no headings in the text indicating particular themes or topics. However, it will be seen that, as shown by Olberding for the *Analects*, locating exemplars in the *Essentials* can help to understand, *in situ*, what the worthy official would think, say, and do. Specifically, this section will consider the exemplary nature of their work in respect of facilitating the recruitment of talent for the public service.

The *Essentials* establishes a relevant feature of the worthy statesperson's contribution in this excerpt from the *School Sayings of Confucius.* The *School Sayings of Confucius* is notably considered a canonical work in the *Essentials* compared to its relegation to the masters' writings in the Qing dynasty-compiled *Complete Library of the Four Branches of Literature* (*Siku quanshu* 四庫全書). The following dialogue attributed to Confucius and his student Zi Gong 子貢 (b. 520 BCE) identifies that worthy conduct is characterized by a willingness to refer candidates of worthy talent for government service:

> Zi Gong asked Confucius, "Who are the worthy among today's ministers?" Confucius replied, "Qi has Bao Shu and Zheng has Zi Pi."
>
> Zi Gong asked, "Does not Qi have Guan Zhong and Zheng have Zi Chan?"
>
> Confucius explained, "Zi, you only know one, but not the other. Have you heard of the worthy minister as the one who exerts efforts or the one who recommends the worthy?"
>
> Zi Gong replied, "The one recommending the worthy is the worthy!"

> Confucius said, "Correct. I have heard that Bao Shu recommended Guan Zhong and Zi Pi recommended Zi Chan, but I have not heard of the latter individual [in each case] recommending anyone better than themselves."[76]

Adopting authoritative words from Confucius himself, the worthy official is depicted by the *Essentials* as someone who contributes meritorious service in two ways. They do so directly by performing such service themselves. And they also contribute indirectly by recommending worthy candidates who are able to do the same. As illustrated by the examples of Guan Zhong 管仲 (*c.* 723–645 BCE) (also known as 'Guan Yiwu 管夷吾') and Zi Chan 子產 (d. 522), this worthy qualification of their referees does not appear to be conditional on the recommended worthy making such referrals themselves.

The role of the worthy official in facilitating civil service recruitment is amplified by this passage. First, they are seen to prioritize the public interest even over their private concerns. By putting forward those they consider to be better qualified, the partial exemplars of Bao Shu 鮑叔 (also known as "Bao Shuya 鮑叔牙") (*fl.* sixth century BCE) and Zi Pi 子皮 (dates unknown) exhibit a selfless devotion to state interests, not least the staffing needs of officialdom. Indeed, this *Essentials* passage strengthens Confucius' reasoning and lends an enduring authority to the named exemplars by excluding Confucius' first sentence "I haven't met any" and the qualifier "In the past" that appears in the received version of the *School Sayings of Confucius*.[77] The positive models of Bao Shu and Zi Pi are accordingly saved from being relegated to times past so that they may continue timelessly to inspire the present for Confucius and Zi Gong, and by extension, for the readers of the *Essentials*. Hence, the willingness of Bao Shu and Zi Pi to support quality entrants to the government service denotes the selfless dedication distinguishing the work of worthy officials.

Second, the fact that the recommendations of Bao Shu and Zi Pi were accepted and implemented in the appointments of Guan Zhong and Zi Chan respectively, conveys inherent confidence in the judgments of historical worthy officials. Here, the *Essentials* arguably implies that the referrals of those worthy officials have been taken as impartial, accurate, and reliable assessments of the respective nominees. After all, the worthy official would only be inclined to provide endorsement where justified by the merits of the individual candidates.

The exemplary service of the worthy in the context of recruitment is thus defined by their capacity and willingness to refer additional worthy talent. This position is developed by the following passages from the *Essentials* that focus on the worthy official's commitment to making those referrals despite the risk or actuality of detriment to themselves. In particular, the risk of reputational damage is raised in the next excerpts from the *Zuo Tradition* and *Master Han*, respectively.

This passage from the *Zuo Tradition* features recommendations by the Jin 晉 central army commandant Qi Xi 祁奚 (dates unknown) for the staffing of various roles:

> In the third regnal year [of Lord Xiang of Lu (570 BCE)], Qi Xi requested to retire on account of old age. Age, a ground for termination of government service. The Prince of Jin asked about his successor. Successor, someone to continue the role. Qi Xi named Xie Hu, who was his enemy. The Jin ruler was about to establish Xie Hu in the position when he died. Xie Hu died. He asked again. Qi Xi replied, "Qi Wu would be acceptable." Wu is the son of Qi Xi. At that time Yangshe Zhi had just died, and the Prince of Jin asked, "Who can take his place?" He replied, "Yangshe Chi would be acceptable." Chi is Bohua, the son of Yangshe Zhi. Thus, Qi Wu was made commandant of the central army, with Yangshe Chi assisting him. Each succeeded their father.
>
> The noble man remarks that Qi Xi, in this case, showed himself capable of recommending good men. He named his enemy, but that was not ingratiation. He established his son in office, but that was not favoritism. He recommended his adjutant, but that was not about forming factions. Adjutant means "associate." ... It was quite simply because he was good that he was capable of recommending those of his kind.[78]

This extract describes the first candidate proposed to be Qi Xi's enemy, even if Qi Xi himself may not have said as much to the Jin ruler. As for the other two referrals—Qi Wu 祁午 (dates unknown) and Yangshe Chi 羊舌赤 (d. 570 BCE)—the narrative emphasizes their merits for the relevant roles by the Prince of Jin simply relying on Qi Xi's assurance that they can undertake the job, respectively. As if to dispel any suspicions of ingratiation, favoritism, and factional intrigue, the unbiased nature of Qi Xi's recommendations is then underscored by the *Essentials*' inclusion of commentary by the noble man, which may be taken as the voice of the invisible author(s) of the *Zuo Tradition*.[79] Through the noble man's words, Qi Xi is commended in the *Essentials* as a good official who is accordingly fit to recognize similar talent and willing to recommend the same. As such, he resembles the worthy official as characterized in the above extract from the *School Sayings of Confucius*. In light of the similarity of the wording used to describe Qi Xi in this excerpt and the position of a worthy official in the *Master Han* excerpt below, the analysis of Qi Xi would directly bear on the symbolic figure of the worthy official and their exemplary service. The reputational risk taken by Qi Xi for making those referrals is accentuated by the commentary. As an official about to retire, his career prospects were no longer on the line, but his reputation along with the public memory of his long service may well have been blighted. That the noble man needs to set the record straight and absolve Qi Xi of the potential charges of ingratiation, favoritism, and factionalism, insinuates that he may have faced those accusations. This message is affirmed by the way the noble man's commentary has been abridged by the *Essentials* by comparison with the received version of this *Zuo Tradition* passage.[80] Including the annotation explaining that the character for "adjutant" means "associate" in this context, draws attention to the first sentence of the noble man's commentary—Qi Xi's recommendations were untainted by personal bias. Excluding references to the *Shang Documents* and the *Odes* in the received version, and its mention of achieving "three things" with one office in the second sentence of the noble man's commentary, keeps to the point: the incumbent official is good because they are willing and able to propose disinterested nominations of those who fit the bill.

Adopting the characterization of Qi Xi from the *Zuo Tradition*, the *Essentials* draws attention to the dedication of the worthy official. Like Qi Xi, they are someone who may be distinguished by long-service in various roles, someone who is mindful of ensuring that his job continues to be duly performed after his retirement, able to offer more than one referral, and willing to make referrals regardless of the risk of damaging their own reputation. This is subtly corroborated by the events of Qi Xi's age-related retirement and his adjutant's death-in-service, which combine to illuminate the worthy official as someone who will serve for the long term and until such time that they are physically incapacitated, as in the case of old age or death, respectively.

Meritocratic appointments in the *Essentials* are emphasized through this subsequent extract from the *Zuo Tradition*, while revisiting the reputational risk involved in awarding a family member for meritorious service:

> In the twenty-eighth regnal year [of Lord Zhao of Lu (514 BCE)], Wei [Xianzi] took charge of the [Jin] administration. Wei Xianzi is also known as Wei Shu. The supervisor of the military Shi Mimu was made high officer for Wu. Jia Xin was made high officer for Qi. The supervisor of the military Du was made high officer for Pingling. Wei Wu was made high officer for Gengyang. Wu is the son of Wei Shu and his concubine. Wei [Xianzi], considering that Jia Xin and the supervisor of the military Du had exerted themselves on behalf of the royal house, In the twenty-second regnal year of Lord Zhao of Lu (520 BCE), Xin and Du led troops and received King Jing. promoted them.
>
> Wei [Xianzi] said to Cheng Zhuan, Zhuan is a high officer of Jin. "Since I have granted a district to my son, Wei Wu, will people think that I have shown favoritism?"
>
> He replied, "What are you saying? It is Wei Wu's way of comporting himself as a man that even when he is [distanced], he does not forget his ruler, "Distanced" in terms of being estranged. and when he is near at hand, he does not crowd his peers. Not crowding colleagues of the same status. In the midst of benefits he keeps his thoughts on dutifulness, Does not seek improper gains. and in straitened circumstances keeps his thoughts on purity. Without an immoderate mind. Is it not right to give him a district?
>
> In former times, when King Wu conquered the Shang, taking broad possession of all-under-heaven, fifteen of his brothers governed domains, and forty who had the Ji clan name governed domains. In all these cases kinsmen had been appointed. The right way of making appointments consists in nothing other than appointing the good, whether they are kin or not ... ."

When he heard of the appointments Wei [Xianzi] had made, Confucius considered them dutiful. He said, "Near at hand he does not fail his kin, A reference to appointing Wei Wu. while at a further remove he does not fail in his way of making appointments. Appointing based on worthiness. This can be called dutifulness." When he heard of the command to Jia Xin, he considered it loyal. Loyal for rewarding meritorious service to the royal house first. "Wei [Xianzi's] appointments are dutiful and his commands loyal. He will have a long posterity in the domain of Jin!'[81]

This passage considers the idea of impartial appointments in a new context. Instead of recommending new candidates to a superior, the "dutiful" official here personally determines the awards granted to existing officials. Given that the behavioral pattern of Wei Xianzi 魏獻子 (d. 509 BCE) is similar to Qi Xi above and the worthy official Xie Hu 解狐 (d. 570 BCE) discussed below, references to the "dutiful" official in this excerpt may plausibly be read as the worthy statesperson. Comparing the *Essentials*' excerpt to the received version of the *Zuo Tradition*,[82] it is immediately obvious that large tracts of text and annotation have been excised, with the result that attention is focused squarely on the problem of perceived favoritism purportedly shown by Wei Xianzi to his son as one of the awardees. While Wei Xianzi remains confident that he has acted fairly in the matter and that his son deserves the award, he expresses concern about those who might think otherwise, although such worries were not inhibitive. These concerns arguably foreground Wei Xianzi's dedication to Jin's interests as he proceeds to award his son, thereby putting at stake both his own reputation and the reputation of his son. This narrative is used by the *Essentials* to reinforce that there is no need to disqualify eligible family or others because the "right way of making appointments consists in nothing other than appointing the good." Like Wei Xianzi, the worthy official will not hesitate to refer talent even if they may risk suffering reputational damage themselves. In addition to reassurance provided by the Jin high official Cheng Zhuan 成鱄 (dates unknown), any remaining doubt about a conflict of interest is allayed by the approval of Wei Xianzi's conduct attributed to Confucius.

The following passage of the *Essentials* excepted from *Master Han* illustrates the referral of an enemy by a worthy official:

> Xie Hu and Xing Boliu were enemies. Zhao Jianzhu asked Xie Hu: "Who could be the Governor of Shangdang?"
>
> Xie Hu replied, "Xing Boliu could."
>
> [Zhao] Jianzhu said, "Is he not your enemy?"
>
> [Xie Hu] replied, "Your servant has heard that loyal subordinates will promote the worthy without overlooking enemies and dismiss the incompetent without favoring friends."
>
> [Zhao] Jianzhu said, "Excellent!"
>
> [Xing Boliu] was then appointed as governor. On hearing about [Xie Hu's recommendation], Xing Boliu visited Xie Hu to express appreciation. Xie Hu said, "Nominating you was public. Despising you is personal. Go away, [I] despise you as before."[83]

Applying the logic attributed to Confucius and Zi Gong and the precedent of Qi Xi recommending his enemy in the first instance, Xie Hu qualifies as a worthy official by making an unbiased referral without overlooking his foe. Through the responses of Xie Hu to enquiries from Zhao Jianzhu 趙簡主 (d. 496 BCE) and Xing Boliu 邢伯柳 (dates unknown), the text emphasizes that recommending the latter for the governorship was a matter of Xie Hu putting public considerations ahead of his private enmity. Zhao Jianzhu's words draw attention to the significance of the referral, while implying that it might prove detrimental as recommending an enemy would expose Xie Hu to accusations of ingratiation. At the same time, they ultimately affirm the rightness of Xie Hu's impartial conduct. Inclusion of the dialogue between Xie Hu and Xing Boliu makes clear that the former had no intentions of finding favor with the latter. That Xie Hu could propose someone he despised while maintaining the personal grudge, not only makes him more relatable as an exemplar but also suggests that the exemplary service of the worthy remains within the reach of the average official.

That the worthy statesperson does not shy away from the risks of putting forward eligible talent in the forms of family, friends, and foes is reiterated by this passage of the *Essentials* extracted from *Master Shi*:

> Those in the world who approach the excellent are precisely the good. (For example,) one who has lost his child, if it were possible to recover it, would not discriminate among people (to help him find it). Good people (who) approach the excellent are likewise thus. This is why Yao promoted Shun in the fields and Tang promoted Yi Yin (to chief minister) from among the cooks. In promoting from within (the court), do not avoid intimates; in promoting from outside (the court), do not avoid (even your) enemies. Good people (who) approach the excellent have no (such) discrimination, and have no (such) aversion, (but rather) only (seek) the places where the excellent are.[84]

Analogous to searching for a lost child where anyone willing and able to help would be a welcome hand, this excerpt conveys that the talent search must not discriminate beyond the selection criteria based on job requirements. To act otherwise would risk never recovering the child, nor by implication, recruiting the worthy personnel. As the wording of this principle resembles the words of the worthy official Xie Hu in the *Master Han* extract, the references to "good people" in this *Master Shi* excerpt may arguably be read as a reference to worthy officials. Hence, the passage portrays the worthy official as someone who will consider all eligible individuals known to them—their intimates and enemies, and even strangers—just as Shun and Yi Yin (*fl.* 1675 BCE) once were to King Yao and King Tang (trad. r. 1675–1646 BCE), respectively.

Reading these excerpts from the *Zuo Tradition*, *Master Han*, and *Master Shi* together, there is a notable commonality among their language in the Chinese expressions relating to the making of impartial recommendations or appointments. For example, Confucius said: "Near at hand, he does not fail his kin, while at a further remove he does not fail in the way of making appointments. Appointing based on worthiness."; Xie Hu said: "without overlooking enemies ... without favoring friends," and Master Shi said: "In promoting from within (the court), do not avoid intimates; in promoting from outside (the court), do not avoid (even your) enemies." Moreover, the Chinese graphs for "only goodness" (*wei shan* 唯善) feature in the passages from both the *Zuo Tradition* and *Master Shi*. The noble man of the *Zuo Tradition* concludes that it was because Qi Xi was himself meritorious that he could recommend those of that kind. Cheng Zhuan reassures Wei Xianzi by affirming that the right way of making appointments is purely based on merit. Master Shi avers that good people nominate others without favoritism nor aversion, looking only to their merit. Extracting similar language from the canonical and masters writings generates repetition that serves to subtly remind and reinforce across the first and last bibliographical sections of the *Essentials*: the feature of impartiality in the exemplary service of the worthy official.

Bao Shuya, who was praised by Confucius in the earlier *School Sayings of Confucius* extract, fittingly fulfills the above-discussed criteria—neither avoiding intimates nor overlooking enemies. His exemplary service in recommending Guan Zhong is noted in the following two excerpts from the *Records of the Historian* concerning the hereditary house of Qi and the memoir of Guan Zhong:

> The noble scion Jiu fled to Lu, [and] Guan Zhong and Shao Hu assisted him. Xiao Bai fled to Ju, and Bao Shu assisted him. When the person of Yonglin killed Wuzhi [the lord of Qi] and discussed the enthronement of a ruler, Gao and Guo were the first to secretly summon Xiao Bai from Ju. Lu also sent out troops to escort the noble scion Jiu. Moreover, Guan Zhong was dispatched to lead troops to block the road from Ju. [Guan Zhong] shot an arrow that struck Xiao Bai's belt buckle. When Xiao Bai ascended the throne [as Lord Huan of Qi], he wanted to kill Guan Zhong. Bao Shu said, "If my lord wishes to rule Qi, then Gao Xi and Shuya will be sufficient. But if my lord also wishes to become a hegemon to the king, then you cannot do without Guan Yiwu." Lord Huan then treated [Guan Zhong] with sumptuous ritual, and making him chancellor, entrusted his government to him. The people of Qi were all delighted, and from then on [Lord Huan] became hegemon.[85]
>
> Guan Zhong (formal name Yiwu) was a native of the Ying River region. In his youth, he often traveled with Bao Shuya. Bao Shu knew that he was worthy. Guan Zhong was poor and often took advantage of Bao Shu, but Bao Shuya always treated him well, never mentioning any of these

> [matters] ... Bao Shu then recommended Guan Zhong [to Lord Huan]. Once employed, Guan Zhong was entrusted with the administration of Qi and Lord Huan thereby achieved hegemony, assembling the feudal lords nine times and rectifying the world [order]. These were all the plans of Guan Zhong. After Bao Shu recommended Guan Zhong, he himself served in a subordinate role. His descendants for generations received official emoluments in Qi and they generally became renowned high officials. The world thought less of Guan Zhong's worthiness, but much of Bao Shuya's ability to appreciate individuals.[86]

From the above excerpts, the reader learns that Guan Zhong was working for the brother of Lord Huan 桓 (r. 685–643 BCE) of Qi 齊, who was his arch-rival for rulership. Moreover, Guan Zhong's failed attempt to assassinate Lord Huan, his subsequent imprisonment, and Lord Huan's desire to execute him are also key details selected for inclusion in the *Essentials*. In other words, that Bao Shuya recommends his ruler's former assassin and the strategist of his ruler's rival is plain to the reader. This represents a variation from Xie Hu and Qi Xi nominating their respective opponents, but the stakes are higher for Bao Shuya who would likely incur the wrath of his ruler. Just as Qi Xi and Wei Xianzi did not disqualify eligible family and associates from being considered for public office, Bao Shuya does not hesitate to recommend an old friend whom he adjudges to be worthy. Particulars of the friendship between Bao Shuya and Guan Zhong in the text may seem superfluous at first glance given that it does not relate to statecraft, and much of the original has accordingly been excluded. However, the rationale later becomes obvious. The inclusion of a one-sided relationship painting Guan Zhong almost as a foe rather than a friend ("管仲貧困，常欺鮑叔 Guan Zhong was poor and often took advantage of Bao Shu") makes Bao Shuya's actions even more admirable. Any accusation of favoritism on the part of Bao Shu is further unwarranted, as he refers Guan Zhong for a position none other than his own while harboring no reservations about having to serve in a subordinate capacity should Guan Zhong be appointed. Regardless of whether Guan Zhong is a friend or enemy, he is a worthy official in Bao Shuya's opinion. Such an opinion should be and is ultimately trusted because of the evidence given in the *Essentials* of Bao Shuya's worthy credentials. This includes praise by Confucius in the excerpt where his name is first mentioned, his bold recommendation to Lord Huan, yielding of his position and the resultant regard throughout the ages as noted in Sima Qian's commentary. Such a precedent of self-sacrifice in serving state interests is underscored by the inclusion of the *Records of the Historian*'s comment that people have always thought more of Bao Shuya's ability to recognize worthy talent than Guan Zhong's worthiness and its mention of the hereditary official emoluments for his descendants.

These excerpts in the *Essentials* illustrate that by contributing exemplary service for the recruitment of talent to the bureaucracy, the worthy official is innately qualified to identify, and will not hesitate to refer, worthy talent. Indeed, they will selflessly subordinate personal interests, including sacrificing their own position and risking reputational damage or other misfortune by exclusively committing to nominating the worthy talent in the name of serving state interests. That these ideas, conveyed by accounts from different texts, spanning a time period from 570 BCE in the Spring and Autumn period to the late second century CE in the Latter Han, and reiterated across the anthology's three bibliographical sections, suggest both exemplary service by worthy officials generally and that the referral of worthy talent mattered to the Zhenguan ruling elite and their public profile. In particular, Taizong and his court wanted to be seen as valuing and encouraging exemplary service in public service recruitment. This corresponds to historical evidence of their political thought and practice that may confirm why the historical worthy officials are used to such effect in the *Essentials.*

First, the notion of the government official setting a positive role model for others accords with Emperor Taizong's exhortations to his court and their own expectations. Indeed, the *Zhenguan Essentials* records Taizong encouraging his Chief Minister of the Court of Imperial Sacrifices Wei Ting 韋挺 (590–647) to be exemplary throughout his career:

> In the sixth year of Zhenguan (632) ... Taizong wrote [to Wei Ting] ... "Be as resolute at the end as you are at the beginning and set a model for posterity. We must make future generations look up to us, as we now look up to the ancients. Would that not be exquisite!"[87]

In the same year, Taizong said to Wei Zheng:

> Whatever action We take today will be scrutinized by the world; whatever We say will be heard by the world. If We are successful in appointing the right individuals, all good people are encouraged; if by mistake We appoint renegades, the evil jostle for position.[88]

The members of the Zhenguan court were themselves conscious of setting a positive example for posterity, as exemplified by the Attendant Censor Ma Zhou's memorial to Emperor Taizong in the eleventh year of Zhenguan (637):

> [A]t the beginning of the Daye reign (605–617), the Sui Emperor Yang also laughed over the destruction of the [Northern] Zhou and Qi Dynasties. At present we look towards Emperor Yang as the latter did towards the [Northern] Zhou and Qi. Therefore, Jing Fang [a scholar (78–37 BCE) who specialized in *The Changes*] said to the Han Emperor Yuan: "I fear that later generations will view us in the same way that we now view those in the past." These words should serve as a warning![89]

By adopting these advisory words of Jing Fang 京房 (78–37 BCE), who served Emperor Yuan 元 (r. 48–33 BCE) of the Han dynasty as a Gentleman and later Governor of Wei County, Ma Zhou shows that he was aware of the rulership of the Tang empire being studied and judged by others in time.

Second, the Zhenguan ruler entrusted the members of his court with the task of discovering talent for the imperial civil service and led by example in recruiting impartially. This is evidenced by his requests to the Vice Directors of the Department of State Affairs Fang Xuanling 房玄龄 (578–648), Du Ruhui 杜如晦 (585–630), and Feng Deyi 封德彝 (568–627):

> In the second year of Zhenguan (628), Taizong said to Fang Xuanling and Du Ruhui: "As Vice Directors of the Department of State Affairs, you should help with Our cares and burdens, and broaden Our hearing and sight in the search for the [worthy] and wise."[90]

> In the second year of Zhenguan, Taizong said to the Right Vice Director of the Department of State Affairs, Feng Deyi: "The basis of achieving order lies in obtaining (the right) individuals. For some time now, We have ordered you to nominate the [worthy], but you never have anyone to recommend. The realm is a heavy responsibility, so you should share Our concerns and troubles. If you do not speak up, on whom will We rely?"[91]

Taizong believed that worthy talent exists in every generation and was concerned that they might remain unknown to him.[92] Arranging for the Vice Directors Fang Xuanling and Du Ruhui to have time to seek out such human resources by delegating matters to the Assistant Directors of the Six Ministries, the Zhenguan ruler prioritized seeking worthy talent over the trivia of bureaucratic process and hearing petitions.[93] These excerpts from a range of historical writings collectively allude to a consciousness among the Zhenguan ruling collective of the Tang dynasty having to be consolidated at the time and scrutinized by history in due course.

It appears that Taizong himself recruited talent based on merit, overlooking matters of kinship and enmities. For example, he appointed his empress' elder brother Zhangsun Wuji 長孫無忌 (594–659) and advisors to his late brother Li Jiancheng, including Wei Zheng and Wang Gui王珪 (571–639), respectively, to high offices within the Zhenguan administration. It must be noted that Wei Zheng and Wang Gui had belonged to enemy ranks, as their former superior Li Jiancheng was then the crown prince with a claim to the throne that rivaled Taizong's own.[94] Taizong appointed his brother-in-law to be chancellor against Zhangsun Wuji's offers to resign and his empress's warning about the risk of her relatives overrunning the government and monopolising power.[95] The recruitment of Ma Zhou also exemplifies Taizong's merit-based approach. In or around 631, Taizong was so impressed after reading Ma Zhou's analysis of some twenty issues in a memorial that he summoned Ma Zhou immediately and appointed him to serve as an auxiliary in the Imperial Chancellery on the same day. Ma Zhou also went on to serve as Investigating Censor and Drafter in the Secretariat.[96] Moreover, Taizong directed his officials to recruit worthy talent to support the heir apparent and other princes.[97]

An impartial and meritocratic approach to civil service recruitment by an official is further reflected in the exemplary service of Fang Xuanling, one of Taizong's veteran assistants depicted in the Portraits of Twenty-four Meritorious Officials. According to historical records, Fang Xuanling was proactive in recruiting talent since the days he served Taizong, who was then the Prince of Qin, as the Military Secretarial Aide for the Weibei 渭北 Circuit, and he would recruit talent regardless of their lowly or humble backgrounds.[98]

The Zhenguan historical records, therefore, suggest that contributing exemplary service to the practice of government and recruiting the talent to do so were foremost in the minds of both Emperor Taizong and his court. At a time when membership of the ruling elite was determined more by noble birth and entrusted referrals than by performance in the civil service examinations, the need to ensure that deserving candidates were not overlooked arguably explains why the *Essentials* places such emphasis on worthy talent being proactively referred by worthy officials. From the perspective of the Zhenguan era, the excerpts in the *Essentials* commemorate the worthy officials of the past to support contemporary worthy officials, as they were possibly the only ones who could reliably identify worthy talent and facilitate their entry into the government service. It may be said that the treasure of the worthy official is distinguished by their being willing and able to generate more treasure in discovering and putting forward further worthy talent. The symbolic figure of the worthy statesperson thus embodies a pattern of behaviors valued by the Zhenguan ruling collective. They were valued not least for informing its recruitment of the human resources to support its work in consolidating a fledgling empire and implementing a government that might bear up to the scrutiny of history. That the Zhenguan ruling collective cultivated a profile by identifying with excerpts about worthy officials facilitating talent recruitment is corroborated by recorded interactions between Emperor Taizong and his courtiers.

2.3 PRIORITIZE SERVICE

The exemplary service of the worthy official is typically distinguished by an unswerving dedication to state interests that lasts until the end of their life. That public service entails a lifelong commitment is conveyed by words attributed to one of Confucius' foremost students, Zeng Shen 曾參 (b. 505 BCE), who is also known as Master Zeng, in this *Essentials*' excerpt from the *Analects*, "The road ends only with death—long, is it not?"[99] The Zhenguan ruler and his court were known to attribute importance to officials prioritizing state governance over personal security, based on their writings and on what has been written about them. Emperor Taizong in his *Golden Mirror* manifesto upholds several exemplars in this regard. Such exemplars include Bi Gan 比干 (dates unknown) who had "his heart torn out" for remonstrating against the licentious conduct of his nephew King Zhou 紂 (*c.* 1105–1046 BCE) of the Shang dynasty (*c.* 1600–1046 BCE), and Guan Longfeng 關龍逢 (*fl.* 1650 BCE), who was executed by King Jie 桀 (d. *c.* 1600 BCE) of the Xia dynasty (2070–1600 BCE) for pointing out that the state was doomed by the king's wasteful and murderous ways.[100] It is notable that the brief manifesto accommodates two references to Bi Gan.[101] Such historic examples of self-sacrifice are echoed in the work and words of Wei Zheng, who is known to have risked his own life by outspoken remonstrations at court that would at times be humiliating and infuriating for Emperor Taizong. Indeed, Taizong was so incensed at one point that he expressed an intention to have Wei Zheng put to death.[102] Moreover, the *Essentials*' coverage of faithful ministers who serve the nation selflessly is highlighted in its preface written by Wei Zheng.[103] While sacrificing one's life may not be necessary or appropriate given familial and political considerations,[104] it will be seen that the *Essentials* espouses this "service above self" value of the Zhenguan ruling collective through its poignant portrayals of worthy officials.

The cultural symbol of the worthy official is construed by the *Essentials* as someone whose public service is characterized by a lifetime commitment. This notion is specifically conveyed by not one but two passages in the *Essentials* that are excerpted from the *Analects*. In words attributed to Master Zeng and annotation from the commentary by the Han dynasty scholar and official Kong Anguo 孔安國 (*c.* 156–*c.* 74 BCE), the first passage foregrounds the scholar-official's enduring commitment to self-cultivation:

> Master Zeng said, "A scholar-official must be strong and resolute, for his burden is heavy and his way is long. Strong means "extensive." Resolute means "steadfast and

discerning." A strong and resolute scholar-official can assume demanding responsibilities over a distant course. He takes up benevolence as his personal burden—heavy is it not? His way ends only with death—long is it not?" Taking up benevolence as one's personal task is a heavy burden—there is nothing heavier. Stopping only once death has overtaken you is a long journey—there is nothing longer.105

Playing on the literal and metaphoric meanings of the Chinese character for "way" (*dao* 道) as both a physical path and an abstract moral practice, the lifelong journey becomes a metaphor for self-cultivation[106] that points to the ethical character of the worthy official. Not only must they possess a strength of character to cultivate benevolence, but they must also remain committed to doing so throughout their life. This commitment is reinforced by a subsequent passage from the same source using words attributed to Confucius and further commentary from Kong Anguo:

The Master said, "The determined scholar-official and the benevolent person would not seek to live at the expense of benevolence, and some have sacrificed their lives to fulfill benevolence." Not seeking to live at the expense of [their] benevolence, they would die to save [their] benevolence. Hence, the determined scholar-official and the benevolent person do not [overly] cherish their lives.107

From this extract, the reader learns that the cultivated official would even sacrifice their life to remain true to their benevolent principles and leave an unblemished record of service as a positive example for others. Such association of an official's character cultivation to their state service underscores the Confucian orientation of the *Essentials*. This is because in the context of Confucian political philosophy, government officials are obliged to serve as positive role models for the community and an individual's fitness for public office is predicated on cultivated character and competent ability.[108] In the *Essentials*, the notion of "benevolence" is defined as a kindness that extends to all people and things,[109] and the perfection of one's benevolence through cultivation entails conducting oneself in accordance with propriety.[110] The cultivated person will come to select the proper course of action as naturally as "we hate a bad smell and love what is beautiful."[111] Annotation from Kong Anguo's commentary about the exacting nature of such self-cultivation serves to enhance the admirable quality of the official's life-term dedication to their moral excellence and integrity. This notion of setting a lifelong example is echoed in the words of Emperor Taizong exhorting Wei Ting to maintain integrity—"Be as resolute at the end as you are at the beginning and set a model for posterity"—in 632 (discussed in Section 2.2), the year after the *Essentials* was completed and submitted to the throne.[112]

Though the efforts of such officials upholding moral excellence and integrity may remain unknown or unappreciated at the time, their examples are seen to live on long after their death. In the words of Wei Zheng's preface: "[Although] their lives expire within a century, their renown continues beyond the millennium." Elaborating on the principles sourced from the *Analects*, the *Essentials* offers numerous historical precedents across its three bibliographical divisions. Based on Taizong's mention of Bi Gan in his *Golden Mirror*, I explore below how the *Essentials* depicts Bi Gan as an epitome of self-sacrifice for public service by the worthy official. Portrayed as a dutiful official whose remonstration costed him his life, Bi Gan is expressly named as a worthy in the *Essentials*' annotation of the *Three Strategies*.[113] He is also variously described as "faithful"[114] and "proper,"[115] and posthumously honored by the exemplary King Wu 武 (r. 1049/45–1043 BCE) of the Zhou dynasty (1046–256 BCE).[116] His historical example is invoked by the *Essentials* in the contexts of canonical writing, historical remonstrations, textual exegesis, and political discourse. No less than eleven of its sources refer to Bi Gan either by name or the way that he died. The *Essentials* alludes to Bi Gan's tragic passing in an excerpt from each of the *Venerable Documents*[117] and *Master Huainan*,[118] about King Wu of the Zhou dynasty raising a mound over Bi Gan's grave after overthrowing the Shang dynasty. The reason for such commemoration is vividly conveyed by two extracts from the *Records of the Historian*'s basic annals of the Shang dynasty and the hereditary house of Master Wei 微 of Song (dates unknown), respectively. Excised of most historical details, the reader's attention is focused on the dutiful Bi Gan suffering evisceration when his forthright and forceful remonstration draws the ire of King Zhou, and Bi Gan is put to death by having his heart cut out for inspection.[119] Bi Gan is cited a total of six times in the memoirs of three officials recorded in the histories of the Former and Latter Han dynasties without any abridgment of those mentions by the *Essentials*.[120] He is used in the *Essentials*' annotations in the *Records of Wu* concerning chancellor Lu Kai's 陸凱 (198–269) memorial to the last ruler of the Wu dynasty (222–280) Sun Hao 孙皓 (r. 264–280),[121] and in the *Three Strategies* to gloss a phase about the worthy official dying (*xianchen bi* 賢臣斃).[122] Bi Gan also features in the arguments of political philosophy propounded by *Master Shen*,[123] the *New Discourses of Master Huan*,[124] *Master Shi*,[125] the *Discourses on the Essentials of Governing*,[126] and *Master Fu*.[127]

Recurring references to Bi Gan thus cement his place as a positive exemplar of lifelong dedication and self-sacrifice in service to the state for existing and aspiring officials during the Zhenguan reign-period. He is but one of several officials that are often referred to in the *Essentials*' portrayal of the worthy public servant whose life is ended by a ruler's violent rejection of their honest remonstration. Those officials include Guan Longfeng (mentioned above), Wu Zixu 伍子胥 (d. 484 BCE), who served King Fu Chai 夫差 (r. 495–473 BCE) of the state of Wu during the Spring and Autumn period, but is ordered to commit suicide after his warning of the threat posed by the state of Yue is rejected,[128] and Chao Cuo 晁錯 (d. 154), who became mistrusted by Emperor Jing 景 (188–141 BCE) of the Han dynasty and was executed accordingly.[129] As Yuri Pines observed, "Every dynasty has its list of martyrs; almost every reign has a much lengthier list of those who escaped execution but were incarcerated, dismissed, demoted, or otherwise humiliated or punished for their outspokenness."[130]

The cultural symbol of the worthy official through Bi Gan's portrayal also offers normative guidance for rulers. Given that King Zhou lost his life and empire when the Shang dynasty was overthrown after Bi Gan was ignored and put to death, this worthy official serves as a powerful reminder for rulers to give due consideration to remonstrative advice or to at least refrain from eliminating valuable human resources. This may be evidenced by Zou Yang 鄒陽 (dates unknown) successfully securing an imperial pardon for himself after twice referring to Bi Gan's demise in a lengthy memorial to Prince Xiao of Liang, Liu Wu 劉武 (d. 144 BCE).[131] In the following passage excerpted by the *Essentials* from *Master Shen*, the onus is placed on the ruler to make the most of the faithful ministers of their times:

> It is not only in chaotic ages or among the ministers of failed states that we find a lack of loyal ministers. It is not only in well-ordered ages or among the ministers of eminent lords that we can find complete loyalty. The loyalty of people in a well-ordered age is not particularly directed toward their ministers. Nevertheless, in both well-ordered and chaotic ages, we find loyal and moral people. Ministers who desire to be loyal exist in every generation and yet lords have never yet been able to be secure in their position. Every collapsed state has faithful ministers. Whereas worthy rulers are encountered once in a thousand years, there are faithful ministers in each generation. In times of ascendance, they meet and bring about flourishing. With a muddled ruler, they meet and simply coexist. Even if rulers encounter those with the loyalty of Bi Gan or Zixu, if they are dissolute and lost in darkness, they will be infected with self-indulgence, ruin their reputation, and be killed.[132]

Read without the annotation in its original context, the above extract notes the general ineffectiveness of loyal ministers.[133] Inclusion of the annotation by the *Essentials* effectively reframes the legalist writing of *Master Shen* in a Confucian light by emphasizing that it takes the worthy ruler to bring about prosperity by working with the likes of Bi Gan and Wu Zixu, namely, the worthy officials.

Characterizing the worthy official as one who remains committed to public service even at the cost of their own life, the cultural memory in the *Essentials* is seen to reinforce the selfless dedication to the state collectively valued by the Zhenguan ruling elite. Presenting partial exemplars in the historical officials offers normative patterns of behavior for the guidance of both sovereign and subordinate. The sovereign learns to appreciate the critical counsel of worthy talent. Their subordinates are inspired to cultivate their ethical characters and contribute exemplary service for the long-term interests of the state and posterity, just as their worthy counterparts have done in the past.

Worthy talent has always been preferred in the government service of traditional China. Long after the lifetimes of historic worthy officials, their life and work are selectively remembered and memorialized through the *Essentials*, which renews their meaning and relevance for the early

Tang period. The theoretical elements of cultural memory enable an understanding of the particular significance attributed to worthy talent within the pages of the *Essentials* and its signification for the Zhenguan rulership. Through the symbol of the worthy official, the *Essentials* is seen to reconfigure cultural knowledge about exemplary public service. Information about worthy officials is scattered among various old texts. By bringing some of their excerpts together in the one anthology, connecting different parts through similar narratives and references to terms and phrases, the *Essentials* orchestrates the impression that the worthy official has been at the core of political thinking since the earliest times and puts forth a unified vision of how they work. It has been seen that worthy officials are prized for their ability to contribute an exemplary level of service, not least in recruiting talent for the bureaucracy and prioritizing service to the state above personal interests. Such a cultural symbol served to further Taizong's understanding and appreciation of the role of his court officials, while guiding contemporary officials on how to support civil service recruitment and maintain a selfless dedication in serving the state. The symbolic worthy official thus espoused the values of engaging talent and long-term commitment. Such guidance and values meant that the cultural symbol of the worthy official bore a direct relationship to the collective identity and profile of the Zhenguan ruling elite. In particular, it could define the membership of their collective in terms of who they recruited, and it could legitimate their dynastic authority through how they identified and engaged with the past. For example, the inclusion of the *History of the Former Han Dynasty* in both the Imperial Academy's core curriculum and the *Essentials* meant that knowledge of Ban Gu 班固 (32–92) and his work was virtually *sine qua non* for office at the Tang court.[134] There appears to be considerable consistency between the ideas advocated within the *Essentials*, the public profile cultivated by the Zhenguan ruling collective, and the historical evidence of their political thought and practice.

The representation of past knowledge about worthy conduct within the *Essentials* had the potential to inform and inspire emulation by contemporary officials, such that the tradition of such public service as championed by historic worthy officials might be lived out beyond the scrolls of the text and into the future. In this sense, the worthy officials themselves identify as both the subject and transmitters of the cultural memory recorded by the *Essentials*. It is not difficult to imagine readers of the *Essentials* within the Zhenguan court finding inspiration or encouragement to serve as the worthy are depicted, and thereby become carriers of the cultural memory themselves—keeping the memory of former worthy officials alive by their own example. Hence, the bearers of this cultural memory would seem to form a dynamic group that transcends time and defies stereotypes based on any particular role or rank.

That human beings shoulder the responsibility of transmitting the intellectual capital of cultural heritage is particularly illustrated by the worthy officials using their knowledge of past practices to inform their work. Such strengths resonate with the governmental emphasis on historical learning during the Zhenguan era and the active application of historical experience and writings by both Taizong and his officials. Although much has been written in hallowed texts, the written word alone cannot achieve continuity of cultural memory. Rather, it seems that the engine of cultural transmission has been and continues to be driven by individuals proactively engaging with and learning from the documented past to provide fertile ground for developing the present practices and firm foundations for imagining the future. Therefore, the construction of the worthy cultural symbol within the *Essentials* represents a reflection on why people must not only be at the heart of government, but are also key in the formation and transmission of cultural knowledge, and why people steeped in the texts of the past are the foundation of an advanced political culture.

CHAPTER THREE

REMONSTRANCES IN THE *ESSENTIALS*

Remonstrance in the Confucian context refers to an inclusive mode of persuasion that assumes a shared commitment to a common goal by the parties involved.[1] It was one of the ways that hierarchically subordinate persons in government could serve as a check on the exercise of power by their political superiors throughout imperial China,[2] as acknowledged by the general political culture.[3] As this chapter will discuss, remonstration was both a right and an obligation for political subordinates, because such corrective intervention was considered to be in the best interests of the ruler, the court, and the state.[4] Denoted by the Chinese characters: *jian* 諫 or *zhen* 箴, a remonstrance involves oral or written communication intended to influence policy decisions from one or more officials to their state leader, taking place in court or a court-like setting.[5] Such communications generally comprise a constructive judgment, some details of the matter under deliberation, appeal to principles derived from past knowledge, practice, or experience ("inherited principles"), and their demonstrated relevance to the particular matter—that is, how the particular policy decision might best be made in light of the adduced information.[6] The appeal to history in early Chinese philosophy and rhetoric was ubiquitous.[7] Indeed, for a speaker or writer to appeal to the past in court discussion was a matter of prowess in the early Tang.[8] The inherited principles may take various forms, including: (i) direct quotation from texts;

(ii) systems of social practices; (iii) sayings; (iv) descriptions of historical events, individuals, and practices; (v) something heard or known to the official, and (vi) reference to historical remonstrations.[9] The vindicative purpose of the remonstrance speeches recorded in the *Zuo Tradition* and the *Discourses of the States* is highlighted by David Schaberg:

> Remonstrances ... are remembered for the sake of vindication: with rare exceptions, who speaks well is a good man, and the resources of narration will be exploited to show how his caution was warranted, his prediction accurate, or his complaint justified. Such consistency suggests a highly selective representation of the past, a narration in which unerring hindsight has found ways to demonstrate the virtue of men and women whose stated values are given implicit sanction by the historiographers.[10]

In a compilation of essential readings for the emperor and his rulership, the considerable space devoted to recorded remonstrances makes them a noteworthy element of the *Essentials*. Twenty-nine of its 68 sources, including excerpts from all three of its bibliographical divisions, record such communications addressed to an identifiable state leader by their official on a matter of state concern. These remonstrances commonly deploy one or more references to inherited principles for persuasive effect. Like the remonstrance speeches studied by Schaberg, the remonstrances recorded in the *Essentials* are remembered to prove a point. Cultural memory theory alerts us to their normative and formative functions in providing guidance for the Zhenguan ruling elite and reinforcing its collective identity. As the nature of remonstrance entails interventions by officials to admonish, advise, and correct political superiors on their courses of action, these narratives within the *Essentials* constitute a resource for advisable patterns of behavior to inform the practices of the Zhenguan administration, espouse its values, and shape its profile.

Separate sections of this chapter will argue that Taizong and his court officials are seen to be guided by norms and values in the *Essentials* that relate to the seeking and giving of remonstrative advice, respectively. Section 3.1 analyzes how the cultural memory educates about remonstrance being a core duty of the high official, and counsel to be sought and heeded by the ruler. Section 3.2 examines how officials are guided in terms of remonstration technique, focusing on the use of inherited principles, which suggests that the Zhenguan ruling elite identified with a rhetorical style that was inspired by historical knowledge, practice, and experience. Section 3.3 analyzes how officials are guided in terms of the content of their advice, which points to the cultural knowledge and values shared by Emperor Taizong and his court.

3.1 REMONSTRATION AS A POLITICAL IMPERATIVE

The provision of remonstration is established as a fundamental duty of the high official, counsel that is critical for the longevity of rulership, and advice to be proactively sought by the exemplary ruler. This is evident through the *Essentials*' excerpts from the *Venerable Documents*, the *Records of the Historian*, the *Zuo Tradition*, the *Analects*, the *Classic of Family Reverence*, *Master Guan*, and the *Structural Discourses*, respectively. Historical evidence about Emperor Taizong suggests that these narratives in the *Essentials* may have served their normative and formative functions in guiding him to recognize this standing obligation of his high officials, to appreciate the value of remonstration, and to understand the prudence of being guided by their advice.

The theoretical basis for remonstration being the high official's core duty is established early in the text. For example, within the *Essentials*' second scroll, the annotation to the "Hounds of Lü" chapter in the *Venerable Documents* highlights that even the sagely King Wu of the Zhou dynasty needed remonstrance, so how could less enlightened rulers do without?[11] The fifth scroll contains the following narrative excerpted from the *Zuo Tradition* and annotated by Kong Anguo's commentary. When the Jin ruler Lord Dao 悼 (r. 573–588 BCE) enquires about the Wei ruler, Lord Xian 獻 (r. 576–559, 547–544), who has been expelled by his officials in 559 BCE, the music master Kuang 曠 uses the occasion to explain the official's role vis-à-vis their ruler.

> Heaven gives birth to the people and establishes rulers to oversee them and take care of them, not letting them lose [their] livelihood. There being rulers, Heaven establishes helpers for them The helpers are the high officials. to act as their teachers and guardians, not letting them exceed [their] limits.

When there is excellence, the helpers praise them; Praise means publicizing. when there are wrongs, they rectify them; Rectify means correcting. when there are troubles, they come to their aid; Relieve their difficulties. when there are failings, they change them. Great indeed is Heaven's love for the people! Why would it let one person exert his will over the people Imposing means to behave unchecked. and indulge his excesses while abandoning the nature of Heaven and Earth? This would certainly not be allowed. The *Tradition* relates how music master Kuang is able to advise comprehensively in response to the question.12

Whereas this passage forms part of the chronological collection of historical records in the *Zuo Tradition*, it serves to highlight the inherent limits on a sovereign's power and the cosmological basis for the ministerial duty to assist their ruler in the *Essentials*. Just as a sovereign possesses a heavenly mandate to serve the people, their assistants have a corollary prerogative to help guide, instruct, and support the sovereign, as exemplified by the provision of remonstrative advice. A new level of engagement with the text is envisaged by the *Essentials* through its inclusion of annotations that gloss the characters for "helper" and "rectify" as "high official" and "correct," respectively. Hence, the ruler may, in principle, be more motivated to receive and duly consider remonstrances in knowing that their high officials have the authority to correct their misconduct, rectify issues, and even replace them in the event of gross failings and presumably, intransigent conditions. Indeed, the Tang dynasty was established by Li Yuan ultimately taking the place of his ruler Emperor Yang of the Sui dynasty in 618, who was known to be displeased by remonstrances, even punishing with death those who dared to criticize his court and policy.[13]

Towards the end of the canonical works section, the ninth scroll includes words attributed to Confucius in passages from the *Analects* and the *Classic of Family Reverence*. The *Essentials* includes the complete *Analects* passage with annotation excerpted from Kong Anguo's commentary:

Zilu asked how to serve the ruler. The Master said, "Never deceive him; oppose him openly." The approach to serving the ruler is rightness without deception and one should openly oppose and remonstrate.14

If this instruction remains unclear, the same scroll elaborates by adducing virtually all of the chapter entitled "Remonstrance and Reproof" from the *Classic of Family Reverence*. Indeed, the chapter of the *Classic of Family Reverence* is compiled in the *Essentials* except for one sentence. The seemingly repetitive wording concerning those receiving remonstration, from the level of the emperor to the scholar-official, is fully included rather than ending with the emperor alone. The *Essentials* thus indicates that remonstrance forms an integral part of the official's role at each of the various levels of administration, and remonstrance should also be heeded by superiors at all levels to prevent the collapse of their respective jurisdictions. Annotation in the *Essentials* further identifies which high officials are responsible for remonstrating with the emperor and underscores that they have no choice but to remonstrate when confronted with reprehensible conduct on the part of their principal. The *Essentials*' excerpt is quoted in full below, with annotation from the commentary by the Han dynasty scholar-official Zheng Xuan 鄭玄 (127–200):[15]

> Master Zeng said, "Parental love, reverence and respect, seeing to the well-being of one's parents, and raising one's name high for posterity—on these topics I have received your instructions. I would presume to ask whether children can be deemed filial simply by obeying every command of their father."
>
> "What on earth are you saying? What on earth are you saying?" said the Master. "Of old, an emperor had seven ministers who would remonstrate with him, so even if he had no vision of the proper way, he still did not lose the empire. The seven ministers are the Grand Preceptor, the Grand Guardian, the Grand Mentor, the Bulwark on the Left, the Supporter on the Right, the Front Assistant, and the Rear Aide, who support the emperor and safeguard [them] from jeopardy. The high nobles had five ministers who would remonstrate with them, so even if they had no vision of the proper way, they still did not lose their states. The high officials had three ministers who would remonstrate with them, so even if they had no vision of the proper way, they still did not lose their clans. If the lower officials had just one friend who would remonstrate with them, they will still able to preserve their good names; The Chinese word *'ling'* means good. As lower officials do not have ministers, they rely on the assistance

of worthy friends [(i.e., friends of good character)]. if a father has a son who will remonstrate with him, he will not behave reprehensively. Hence, remonstrance is the only response to reprehensible behavior. How could simply obeying the commands of one's father be deemed filial?" Bending [the principles] to follow the commands of one's father, doing good when they are good, and doing wrong when they are wrong, while harboring grievances, how can that be filial?16

By analogy to the remonstrance expected of the filial son in serving his father, the officials are duty-bound to remonstrate and cannot simply accord with their superior's reprehensible words or deeds. That the duty to remonstrate is unavoidable derives from the necessity of remonstrance for the proper administration of government. By shaping the sovereign's approach to working with their court, the above extracts also serve a formative function for the Zhenguan ruling elite. The Zhenguan ruler is guided to recognize the fundamental duty of his high officials to encourage, correct, and assist him in serving the state, and to expect those officials to remonstrate accordingly in their advices.

The rationale for remonstrance from the perspective of the Confucian canon is corroborated by narratives about the dire consequences of not heeding such ministerial advice. The recurring theme is that the recalcitrant ruler will inevitably cause detriment to themselves and their state when they disregard the honest counsel of their well-meaning officials. Such narratives provide empirical evidence for the words in the above extract from the *Classic of Family Reverence*. The narratives are historicized for a deterrent effect, namely, actual rulers have lost their states as well as their own lives. Presenting a persuasive case for a ruler to give due consideration to remonstrance, the *Essentials* illustrates the stakes involved through Lord Huan of Qi, who is the first hegemon in a new balance of power that emerged as the Zhou order declined during the Spring and Autumn period. The lord's success and failure are shown to hinge on whether he follows the remonstrative advice of his chancellor Guan Zhong. The *Essentials*' excerpts from the *Records of the Historian* are as follows:

Bao Shu then recommended Guan Zhong [to Lord Huan]. Once employed, Guan Zhong was entrusted with the administration of Qi and Lord Huan thereby achieved hegemony, assembling the feudal lords nine times and rectifying All under Heaven. These were all the plans of Guan Zhong.[17]

When Guan Zhong was ill, Lord Huan asked, "Of the various ministers, who could be chancellor?"

Guan Zhong replied, "No one knows his ministers better than my lord."

The lord said, "What about Yi Ya?"

[Guan Zhong] replied, "He killed his son to please my lord. This is not the nature of human emotions. He will not do."

The lord said, "What about Kai Fang?"

[Guan Zhong] replied, "He turned his back on his relatives to please my lord. This is not the nature of human emotions. It will be difficult to be close to him." Kai Fang is a scion of Wei.

The lord said, "What about Page Diao?"

[Guan Zhong] replied, "He castrated himself to please my lord. This is not the nature of human emotions. It will be difficult to be familiar with him."

Guan Zhong died, but Lord Huan did not make use of Guan Zhong's words. In the end he made close use of the three men, and it was those three men who monopolized authority. When Lord Huan expired, Yi Ya and Page Diao took advantage of the favored court officials to kill the various functionaries, The various functionaries are the high officers. The favored court officials are those of approval and authority within the court. and enthrone noble scion Wu Kui as lord. The heir Zhao fled to Song. While Lord Huan was ill, the five noble scions each formed factions in vying for power. By the time Lord Huan expired, the palace was empty, and none dared encoffin [his corpse]. Lord Huan's corpse lay on the bed for 67 days, until corpse insects emerged from the doorway.[18]

That fatal ramifications for the ruler and his state can and have transpired from the failure to heed remonstrance is conveyed by the *Essentials* in unequivocal terms. First, the contrasting levels of detail afforded to Lord Huan achieving hegemony and losing authority draws attention to Guan Zhong's remonstrance. Unlike the *Records of the Historian*, the *Essentials* does not dwell on any interactions between Lord Huan and Guan Zhong that brought about political hegemony. Its excerpts simply provide that

Guan Zhong was entrusted with the administration of Qi, and that following the advice of Guan Zhong, who is known as a worthy official,[19] did lead to such positive outcomes. Such scant treatment is corroborated by another passage in the *Essentials* excerpted from the same source:

> Bao Shu said: " If my lord wishes to rule Qi, then Gao Xi and Shuya will be sufficient. But if my lord also wishes to become a hegemon to the king, then you cannot do without Guan Yiwu." Lord Huan then treated [Guan Zhong] with sumptuous ritual, and making him chancellor, entrusted his government to him. The people of Qi were all delighted, and from then on [Lord Huan] became hegemon.[20]

In contrast, the *Essentials* elaborates on Guan Zhong's final remonstration and the consequences arising from Lord Huan's disregard of it, as exemplified by the second (longer) excerpt from the *Records of the Historian*.

Second, that remonstrance is pivotal to the ongoing success of rulership is illustrated by this historical example being recounted in two different parts of the anthology. Not only is there more detail excerpted about Lord Huan's failure to follow Guan Zhong's advice from the *Records of the Historian*, but the account is amplified in a subsequent part of the *Essentials* compiled from *Master Guan*.[21] The downfall of Lord Huan is vividly seen to stem from his failure to follow Guan Zhong's advice. The lord becomes manipulated by self-interested officials who turn against him, and the state of Qi suffers political turmoil, as various parties attack each other in vying for the throne. In the end, Lord Huan is unattended in an empty palace and expires alone. Hence, a ruler would best heed the experience of Lord Huan and be guided by the remonstrative advice of their officials.

As can be expected between two different sources that were authored at different times and for different purposes, disparities exist between the excerpts of this historical account from the *Records of the Historian* and *Master Guan* within the *Essentials*. For example, in the *Master Guan* excerpt, Guan Zhong advises Lord Huan to distance himself from four officials[22] instead of three as per the *Records of the Historian*. In *Master Guan*, the lord initially follows Guan Zhong's advice by dismissing the officials, but later succumbs to doubt and reappoints them, whereas the *Records of the Historian* makes no mention at all of Lord Huan following the remonstrance. Lord Huan expires from illness in the *Records of the Historian* and from suicide in *Master Guan*. There is also a much shorter period recorded between the death of Lord Huan and the maggots emerging from the doorway: eleven days in *Master Guan* compared to 67 in the *Records of the Historian*. Such factual inconsistencies within the anthology coupled with its omission of relevant time frames—for example, the precise date of Lord Huan's death—demonstrate that the veracity of historical events is subordinated to the illustrative power of their narrative. What the *Essentials* is concerned about here is that it is crucial for the ruler to take account of remonstration. The downfall of Lord Huan is used across its historical and masters' sections to reinforce this point, presumably for those rulers who may be less inclined to listen to remonstrance. Differences in detail do not detract from the overall message, as the Chinese cultural memory was such that anecdotes were constantly recycled for historiographical edification. Moreover, reiteration was a strategy that made the anecdote more compelling. Indeed, the *Luxuriant Gems of the Spring and Autumn*, a statecraft compendium attributed to the Han dynasty scholar-official Dong Zhongshu 董仲舒 (*c.* 195–104 BCE), records an exhortation from Confucius himself for readers not to let the repeated text go unexamined as one will discover worthy principles in those parts.[23]

Throughout the *Essentials*, a similar pattern is evident among historical rulers both before and after Lord Huan, as exemplified by King Li 厲 (d. 828 BCE) of the Western Zhou dynasty (1046–771 BCE) and King Huai 懷 (r. 328–299 BCE) of the state of Chu in the Warring States period. Excerpting from the *Records of the Historian*, the *Essentials* relates that King Li is forced into exile within three years of turning a deaf ear to well-reasoned advice from his minister Duke Shao not to repress public criticism of misgovernment.[24] As for King Huai, the *Records of the Historian* states that the Chu official Qu Yuan 屈原 (*fl.* third century BCE) tried to persuade him not to trust the state of Qin nor travel there to meet with its ruler. King Huai blatantly ignores Qu Yuan's remonstrance only to be ambushed and captured by Qin troops, and he dies in Qin without returning to Chu.[25] This cautionary tale is related with characteristic economy by the *Essentials*' extract from the *Structural Discourses* that is located in its penultimate scroll:

> King Huai of Chu rejected Qu Yuan's appraisal and adopted Jin Shang's scheme. He was captured by Qin and never returned. It cannot be said that there were no strategist scholar-officials.[26]

References to the rejection of Qu Yuan's advice, his subsequent banishment from Chu, and the fall of King Huai, who loses both his state and his life, appear in earlier parts of the *Essentials* excerpted from the *Records of the Historian*, the *History of the Former Han Dynasty*, the *Discourses on Salt and Iron*, and the *Discourses of a Recluse*.[27] Without laboring the point, these passages subtly serve to prime the reader for the above sentences in the *Structural Discourses* where the moral of the story becomes manifest. Not only does the *Structure Discourses* convey that good advice is ignored at the ruler's own peril, but its location near the end of the text may also serve to embed that cautionary truth in the reader's memory. Accounts of negative exemplars like King Li and King Huai act in concert with the remonstrances recorded in the *Essentials*. References to these famous incompetents are fittingly employed by officials on an intertextual level within the remonstrances, where uttering their name alone may suffice to sway their sovereign.[28]

The *Essentials* educates the ruling party not only to listen to remonstrance, but also to actively seek such counsel. Its excerpts emphasize that sovereigns who have done so are the positive exemplars in history. The *Essentials*' excerpts from the *Venerable Documents*' chapters "Charge to Yue" and "Charge to Jiong" highlight accomplished rulers valuing and proactively seeking remonstration from their subordinates since the dawn of Chinese history. The "Charge to Yue" states:

> Morning and evening present your instructions to aid my virtue. This means remonstrative instruction and candid words should be received to benefit oneself. Suppose me a weapon of steel; I will use you for a whetstone. Suppose me crossing a great stream; I will use you for a boat with its oars. Suppose me in a year of great drought; I will use you as a copious rain ... [Let] you and your companions all cherish the same mind to [correct] your sovereign .... Oh! Yue, that all

> within the four seas look up to my virtue is owing to you. As his legs and arms form the man, so does a good minister form the sage (king).[29]

The "Charge to Jiong" provides:

> Now I appoint you [Bo Jiong] to be High Chamberlain, to see that all the officers in your department and my personal attendants are upright and correct, that they may strive to promote the virtue of their sovereign, and together supply my deficiencies.[30]

The above passages depict the Shang ruler Wu Ding 武丁 (r. 1324–1264 BCE) and the Zhou ruler King Mu 穆 (r. 956–918 BCE) seeking counsel from their officials and instructing their respective chief ministers Fu Yue 傅說 (dates unknown) and Bo Jiong 伯冏 (dates unknown) accordingly from the outset of their appointments. Including the annotation of Kong Anguo's commentary, the *Essentials* highlights that Wu Ding asked his advisory officials to always provide remonstrative instruction and candid words, and that King Mu requested all officials to help him cultivate virtue and improve on his shortcomings, regardless of their rank and proximity of relationship. These narratives are noteworthy, considering that both rulers are known for their accomplishments. For example, Wu Ding was the longest-serving Shang ruler, achieved a revival of the dynasty, extensively expanded its territory, was honored posthumously as the "lofty ancestor,"[31] and eulogized by the Shang sacrificial ode "Black bird" in the *Odes*.[32] From the perspective of Wu Ding, he credits his achievements to the support of Fu Yue. King Mu is said to have transformed the bureaucracy from being dependent on hereditary appointments to one willing to appoint worthy candidates outside of the hereditary system,[33] established the earliest legal code, and defeated the Quanrong people in the north and west of the Zhou kingdom.[34] That successful rulers value and seek to be informed by remonstrative advice is naturally reiterated by these extracts being presented closer together in the same scroll of the *Essentials* than within their original context, based on received versions of the *Venerable Documents*.[35]

Remonstrative advice is thus foregrounded in several ways by the above excerpts of the *Essentials* dating from the Shang dynasty to the

Warring States Period. It is a core duty of high officials as advised by music master Kuang, and an obligatory response in face of the ruler's reprehensible conduct as taught by Confucius. Remonstrance is also critical advice that can determine whether a rulership continues or collapses and therefore to be duly considered by rulers, whether they are a king or a hegemon, and it has been sanctioned by rulers since ancient times. The portrayal of remonstration as such a political imperative in the *Essentials*, a text compiled by Zhenguan officials and used by their ruler, indicates that the Zhenguan ruling elite publicly upheld those patterns of behavior as role models, and wanted their practice of government to be informed by remonstrance accordingly.

Information about the early Tang emperors generally and the historical narratives about Emperor Taizong appear consistent with the notion of the sovereign seeking and taking remonstration from their subordinates. Denis Twitchett writes that the early Tang emperors supported a traditionalist model where:

> ... a strong and decisive yet humane monarch ... takes careful heed of the counsel offered him by carefully selected advisers and courtiers imbued not only with administrative experience but also with the best of traditional wisdom, morality, and canonical learning; a monarch who is responsive to advice ... .[36]

Indeed, it is this exemplary image that scholars of the eighth and ninth centuries identified with Taizong, whose reign became lauded as the "good government of the Zhenguan era."[37] Historical sources commonly portray the Zhenguan ruler as one who appreciated remonstration and exhorted his court throughout his reign to be forthcoming with their advice and forthright in doing so. Sometime in the early period of the Zhenguan era, Emperor Taizong said to his high officials:

> When someone wishes to see his own reflection, he is in need of a bright mirror. When a ruler wishes to be aware of his failings, he must rely on loyal officials. If a ruler considers himself wise, officials will not assist in setting matters straight. How could he avoid danger or disaster even if he wanted to under such circumstances![38]

The Zhenguan ruler was thus acutely aware from the outset of his reign that the absence of ministerial correction could spell trouble for his rulership. Based on the following account dated to 642, Taizong's attitude to receiving remonstrative counsel seems to have remained unchanged even during the last decade of his rulership. Taizong said to Fang Xuanling and other officials:

> To know oneself is to have clear insight but this is truly difficult. For example, scholars who compose texts and journeymen with artisan skills all think that they are superior and that no one else can match them. But if celebrated craftspersons and famous writers evaluate them critically then the awkward expressions and imperfections become evident. It follows from this that a sovereign needs [rectifying and] remonstrating officials to point out his mistakes.[39]

Use of the graph for "rectify" in the Chinese description of the remonstrating official whom their ruler needs to help correct his faults, echoes the language of the earlier excerpts of the *Essentials* from the *Venerable Documents* and the *Zuo Tradition*.

Mindful of the importance of remonstrative advice, the Zhenguan ruler appears to have taken various steps to promote such input. From the first year of his reign, Emperor Taizong enabled remonstrating officials to participate in high-level meetings on important matters of state, as exemplified by an entry that records his directives in 626:

> ... whenever the grand councilors [enter] the inner court to discuss important matters of state, remonstrators should be allowed to join them and be informed of these matters. If they [speak] on an issue, their words [have] to be accepted impartially.[40]

Time and again, Emperor Taizong is seen to instruct his officials to speak fully and frankly. For example, the Zhenguan ruler said to his high officials sometime in the early years of the Zhenguan reign-period:

> You, Gentlemen, must on all accounts speak frankly and remonstrate whenever Our administration is not bringing benefit to others.[41]

Another entry records that Taizong said to Zhangsun Wuji and others in 644:

> When We now ask questions, do not hold back. You must speak of Our failings in turn.[42]

To his court, the Zhenguan ruler upheld relevant role models from the early and recent past. In an address to the Censor-in-Chief Wei Ting, the Vice Director of the Secretariat Du Zhenglun 杜正倫 (d. 658), the Vice Director of the Palace Library Yu Shinan, and the Editorial Director Yao Silian 姚思廉 (557–637) during 632, Taizong referred to the ministers Guan Longfeng of the Xia dynasty and Prince Bi Gan of the Shang dynasty as loyal remonstrators who were sentenced to death for frank criticisms.[43] In an account dated 642, Taizong recounts the practice of the late Wei Zheng, who was disposed to remonstrate on all issues—never withholding honest feedback, like the clear mirror that reflects both positive and negative:

> "We often recall how Wei Zheng remonstrated on any problem that came up. In many cases he focused on Our failings as clearly as a reflection in a bright mirror will show up every good and bad point." [Taizong] then raised his cup to [Fang] Xuanling and the others to encourage them.[44]

Taizong is thus seen to remind his officials that remonstrative advice has been fearlessly proffered before, and by their former colleague Wei Zheng in the recent past no less, so there is no reason for them not to serve in the same way. He also reassured his officials that they would not incur his wrath for being forthright or opposing his ideas.[45] Reasoning that an individual who single-handedly deals with all the multitude of state matters daily may be prone to error no matter how careful they are, Taizong emphasized to his long-serving Vice Director of the Department of State Affairs Fang Xuanling and other officials that remonstrating personnel are needed to alert himself to his own mistakes.[46] To motivate his officials to remonstrate, the Zhenguan ruler pointed out to his court that their interests were aligned with his own, and that officials share in their ruler's fate for better or worse—just as the demise of Sui Emperor Yang also spelt the end for his ministers.[47] Moreover, Emperor Taizong instructed the crown prince to accept remonstration. According to a record dated 644, Taizong would say to the crown prince:

> Though this tree may be crooked, if one can get hold of a plumbline, then it may be straightened. Even if a sovereign is without the Way, if he accepts remonstration, then he may be a sage. This is something that Fu Yue [the wise advisor to the Shang King Wu Ding (r. thirteenth to twelfth centuries BCE)] said, and you should use it to examine your own conduct.[48]

That Taizong commends Fu Yue's words to the crown prince in the above passage, suggests that the Zhenguan ruler was familiar with Fu Yue's service to Wu Ding, as documented by the *Venerable Documents* and excerpted by the *Essentials*.

The historical evidence about Emperor Taizong suggests that the cultural memory in the *Essentials* may have served their normative and formative functions in guiding him to appreciate the value of remonstration, to recognize the standing obligation of his high officials to contribute such input, and to understand the prudence of being guided by their advice. Taizong often did not enjoy receiving remonstrances, nor did he always accept and follow those that he received. However, the overall historiographical representation of the Zhenguan reign arguably demonstrates that the cultural knowledge within the *Essentials* did register in the minds of Taizong and his court. Through the remonstrances of various Zhenguan officials discussed in Section 3.2, the Zhenguan ruling elite are seen to share and subscribe to the anthology's emphasis on remonstrative advice, even if their actions do not follow the relevant exhortations and admonitions. At the very least, the historical narratives support the profile of the Zhenguan ruler cultivated in the *Essentials*' extracts, as one who liked to be seen as being receptive to remonstration.

3.2 STRATEGIES USED IN REMONSTRANCE

One distinctive characteristic among the remonstrances anthologized in the *Essentials* (the "*Essentials* remonstrances") is their frequent appeals to inherited principles. Within the context of those historical remonstrations, the inherited principles form part of the remembered past for the contemporary purposes of the remembering remonstrator. Formal records of those remonstrations add to the textual tradition over time. By excerpting from those textual records, it could be said that the inherited principles that were remembered in the past, are recollected once more, albeit reclaimed with the contextual baggage of the historical remonstration that referred to it, and reconstructed for the Zhenguan cultural memory. As such, the *Essentials* remonstrances establish that the Zhenguan ruling elite themselves valued learning from historical knowledge and identified with a rhetorical style that is inspired by the same. In this way, the remonstrances commend past knowledge and experiences as sources of meaningful, relevant, and useful references for problems of policy and governance. For officials, the historical remonstrations illustrate how the persuasiveness of political rhetoric may be enhanced through the use of such knowledge and experience. Historical evidence of and about the remonstrances of Zhenguan officials (the "Zhenguan remonstrances") confirms a commitment by the Zhenguan courtiers to using inherited principles in advices to the throne. They typically follow the patterns observable in the historical remonstrances recorded in the *Essentials* (the "*Essentials* remonstrances"). For example, over one-third of the *Zhenguan Essentials* records remonstrances by Zhenguan officials, and some 80 percent of those entries contain at least one form of inherited principles.[49] As the *Essentials* remonstrances are derived from sources of diverse writing styles, I focus on what they have in common, namely, each is a recorded version of a historical written or spoken remonstrance addressed to an identifiable state leader by their subordinate on one or more matters of state concern. The following analysis proceeds by reference to the inherited principles manifest in the *Essentials* remonstrances and juxtaposes Zhenguan remonstrances to illuminate their import. While the *Essentials* and the Zhenguan remonstrances often deploy more than one type of inherited principle, I will focus in turn on an example of each inherited principle.

3.2.1 Quotations from texts

Quotation from existing texts is a common form of invoking the authority of the past in political persuasion and occurs more frequently among the remonstrances in the *Essentials*' canonical and historical excerpts than the rest of the text. With other information in the excerpt often being abridged but rarely the quotation itself, the *Essentials* foregrounds the quote as the crucial element of the remonstration. The quote within the quote is seen to be the crux of the argument. Drawing attention to the power of direct quotation thus provides an important instruction for remonstrators—the argument requires a quote.

The popular sources for such quotes are texts from the core curriculum for prospective officials in the academies at the capital. The most cited sources in the *Essentials* remonstrances are the *Odes* and the *Venerable Documents*. Other sources quoted include the *Changes*, the *Analects*, the *Art of War*, the *Old Master*, *Master Shen*, *Master Han*, and *Master Zou* (*Zou zi* 鄒子).[50] Schaberg similarly notes that the *Odes* and the *Venerable Documents* were the most invoked texts among the remonstrance speeches in the *Zuo Tradition* and the *Discourses of the States*. Common inclusion of such quotes from the Five Classics expectedly reflects the Confucian scholarship that was promoted by the Zhenguan government. However, the *Essentials* remonstrances also cite texts other than the Five Classics. Interestingly, those quotes are sometimes truncated, as exemplified by citations of *Master Han*.[51]

In this passage of the *Essentials* excerpted from the *Zuo Tradition*, a reference to the *Zhou Documents* forms the sole basis for Qu Wuchen's 屈巫臣 (dates unknown) protest against the wanton intentions of his ruler King Zhuang 莊 (r. 613–592) of Chu in 589 BCE:

> King Zhuang wishes to take Xia Ji into his harem. Qu Wuchen, Lord of Shen, said, "This will not do. You, my lord, summon the princes to chastise the guilty, but now you are taking her into your harem because you covet her beauty. To covet beauty is licentiousness, and licentiousness is a great transgression." The *Zhou Documents* says, "Illuminate virtue, be wary of transgression." "If you rouse the princes only to become guilty of great transgression, you are not being wary. My lord should consider this well!" The king thus desisted.[52]

Read as a standalone excerpt, this *Essentials* remonstrance plausibly guides rulers and officials to remain principled in diplomatic interactions, and to make timely interventions to prevent the public interest from being endangered by the ruler's personal impulses. However, there is more to its normative function in the context of the collection of remonstrances compiled by the *Essentials*. Notwithstanding that the proposed licentiousness is condemned ("a great transgression") by the official's subjective judgment, the general warning in the cited text ("be wary of transgression") is applied as a catch-all prescription. The quotation is strategically positioned between Qu Wuchen's frank criticism and concluding exhortation, which no doubt lends credence to both elements of his advice. What is striking is that the king does not even try to challenge his official's assertion by questioning, for example, "How does licentiousness count as a transgression?" As such, the authority of the textual quotation is seen to be credibly relevant beyond any doubt or question in the minds of both parties. That this timely remonstration effectively induces the king to abandon his desired course underscores the power of invoking hallowed texts of the past. While recensions of the *Zuo Tradition* include a further sentence where Qu Wuchen paraphrases the *Zhou Documents* to mention that the long-lasting Zhou dynasty was founded by King Wen illuminating virtue and being wary of transgressions,[53] the absence of this sentence from the *Essentials* suggests that a quotation from the textual heritage can be sufficiently persuasive without any need to specify examples of compliance. Additionally, such abridgment signals a shift in the historical consciousness. Within the second-order compilation of the *Essentials*, it matters more to convey the appeal to canonical texts as part of the prowess of court persuasion than the comprehensive detail of Qu Wuchen's communication.

The practice of citing textual authority in remonstration by Zhenguan officials is exemplified by Wang Gui as Vice Director of the Chancellery. According to the following account, Wang Gui quotes from *Master Guan* to help Emperor Taizong identify an issue and correct himself:

> Early in the Zhenguan reign, Emperor Taizong and Vice Director of the Chancellery Wang Gui were having a conversation at a banquet with a palace lady at their side. She had originally been a concubine of the prince of Lujiang, [Li] Yuan (587–627). After Yuan had been defeated, she was taken over by the palace. Taizong pointed her out and said to Gui: "The

prince of Lujiang was depraved. He killed her husband and took her into his house. With that degree of cruelty he could only perish."

Gui left his seat and said, "Your Majesty, do You consider her capture by the prince of Lujiang right or wrong?"

Taizong replied, "How dare someone kill another man and capture his wife! Why then are you asking Us whether this was right or wrong?"

Gui replied, "I learned the following from [*Master Guan*]: When [Lord] Huan of Qi (r. 685–643 BCE) went to the state of Guo he asked the elders of that state: 'Why was Guo annihilated?' The elders said, 'Because its ruler approved of the good and hated the evil.' [Lord] Huan said, 'If things were as you say, then he was a wise sovereign. Why did he end up annihilated?' The elders replied, 'It was not like that. The sovereign of Guo approved of the good but he could not employ them. He hated evil people but he could not get rid of them. That is why he perished.' Now this woman is still in attendance on You. I think that in Your heart You believe that what the prince did was right. If Your Majesty does not think it wrong, then we have a case of being aware of evil but failing to get rid of it."

Taizong was very pleased. He praised these as excellent words and hastily ordered that the palace lady be returned to her family.[54]

Rather than confronting Emperor Taizong about taking the former concubine of the Prince of Lujiang and potentially risking his sovereign's wrath and indignation, Wang Gui tactfully persuades by sharing seemingly innocuous information—what he has learned from *Master Guan*. What is then presented, mirrors the situation of Taizong taking the concubine of the late prince. After the Zhenguan ruler has been briefed about the inherited principle, Wang Gui astutely segues into the matter at hand: "Now this woman is still in attendance on You." Such appeal to inherited principle enables the punchline to be delivered vicariously through the voice of the Guo elders: personal perishing and state collapse stem from the ruler's failure to do what is right and desist from what is wrong, and therefore approval of the righteous and disapproval of the wrongful requires actual implementation. The broad nature of the principles quoted from the historical texts in both the *Essentials* and Zhenguan remonstrances suggests that they are more readily applicable to other situations. Hence, such memorable quotes commend themselves to contemporary officials as remonstrance material for future reference.

3.2.2 Systems of social practices

Systems of social practices, such as ritual propriety[55] and the administration of former kings, are less frequently referred to than other types of inherited principles among the *Essentials* remonstrances. By appealing to such established systems, the remonstrance appropriates enduring practices and makes them apposite to the present situation. In the following remonstrance excerpted from the *Zuo Tradition*, Rushu Qi 汝叔齊 (dates unknown) invokes ritual propriety to provide an established baseline for judging the rulership of Lord Zhao 昭 (541–510 BCE), the Prince of Lu 魯 in 537 BCE:

> In the fifth year [of the reign of Lord Zhao of Lu], [the] lord went to Jin, he made no mistakes in ritual performance, Ritual propriety of visiting states. All the way from the ceremony recognizing his exertions in the outskirts of the city through to the presentation of gifts. The outbound involved the ceremony recognizing exertions in the city outskirts. The return involved the presentation of gifts. The Prince of Jin said to Rushu Qi, "Is the Prince of Lu not excellent in his performance of ritual?" He replied, "In what way does the Prince of Lu comprehend ritual?" The lord said, "What do you mean? A man who in no way violated ritual, all the way from the ceremony to the presentation of gifts! In what way does he not comprehend it?" He replied, "These are ceremonies. They cannot be called ritual. Ritual is that by which one keeps the domain, implements administrative commands, and does not lose his subjects. At present the issuing of administrative commands is in the hands of the great houses. In the hands of the high officials. And he cannot retrieve them. He has Zijia [Ji] but is incapable of employing him. Ji, great-great grandson of Lord Zhuang. He has violated his covenant with a great domain and bullied a small domain. A reference to the attack on Ju and annexation of its Yun territory. He takes advantage of others' difficulties A reference to the annexation of Zeng during upheaval in Ju in former years. But knows nothing of his own private affairs. Lacking awareness of one's own private challenges. The lord's holdings have been divided in four parts, and the people get their sustenance elsewhere. Elsewhere refers to the three [Huan] lineages. Nobody's thoughts are on the lord, yet he makes no plans

for a good end. No one helps to plan for the lord's conclusion. He acts as ruler of the domain, and the difficulties will affect him personally, yet he takes no thought of his situation. In these things are the very roots and branches of ritual, yet he busies himself with the petty details of ceremonial practice. This refers to prioritizing ceremonial practice. Is it not far off the mark to say that he is excellent in his performance of ritual?"

> The noble man said that in this instance Rushu Qi comprehended ritual. The Prince of Jin's rulership also suffered shortcomings at the time. Rushu Qi uses this to remonstrate indirectly.56

By being critical of the Prince of Lu, Rushu Qi presents him as a mirror for his ruler—the Prince of Jin to realize his mistaken appraisal while dispelling the misconceptions that might cause him to commit the same or similar mistakes. Rushu Qi appears to be criticizing the Prince of Lu but is indirectly remonstrating with the Prince of Qi, as confirmed by the annotation at the end of the excerpt. The remonstration specifically points to the notion of ritual propriety, which is a fundamental concept in Confucian political philosophy. The *Essentials*' excerpts from the *Analects* leave the reader with no doubt that Confucius himself felt that such system of ritual propriety underpins government. For example:

> The Master said, "Can you govern the state with ritual and a deferential approach? Then you will have [no difficulty]. "Then you will have" means it will not be difficult. If you cannot govern the state with ritual and a deferential approach, then what use is ritual alone?" "What use is ritual" means ritual cannot be used.57

Indeed, Confucius also highlights the common misunderstanding between the ceremonies and the substance of ritual: "Ritual! Ritual! They say. But is it just a matter of jades and silks? This is about ritual not being just a matter of admiring such jades and silks, as their value lies in their bringing stability to those above and order to the people."58 (*Analects*, 17.11). Interpreted according to the accompanying annotation in the *Essentials*, Confucius' remarks are echoed in Rushu Qi's argument about the purpose of ritual propriety. In other words, ritual cannot be equated with ceremonies. The futility of ritual ceremony in the absence of the ruler's cultivation of character is also the reason underlying Master

Yan's advice to the Qi ruler that the proper response to a comet sighting is not ritual or sacrificial intercession, but improving on the ruler's moral failures, as recorded in the *Essentials*.[59] Moreover, if the semblance in his argument is insufficient to allude to the *Analects*, the questions about the Prince of Lu comprehending ritual propriety echo similar queries about whether Confucius, Lord Zhao, and Guan Zhong "knows ritual" in the *Analects*.[60] This excerpt's inclusion of the noble man's commentary underscores that Rushu Qi was correct in his interpretation of the ritual system, and that he was right to remonstrate with his ruler about it. As such, established systems of social order present a form of the past that is persuasive, if not also authoritative, in the context of remonstrances of the Spring and Autumn period and among the contemporary readers of the *Essentials*.

Ritual protocol is referred to in this remonstrance by Wei Zheng in response to Emperor Taizong's order that the gifts for Princess Changle's 常樂 (621–643) marriage be double those applicable to the rank of Senior Princess, during the sixth year of the Zhenguan reign-period (632):

> Formerly, Emperor Ming of the Han Dynasty (r. 57–75) wished to enfieff his son. The emperor said, "How can Our son be treated the same as the sons of the previous emperor? He can be enfieffed at half the level of the prince of Chu [Liu Ying (d. 71)] and the prince of Huaiyang [Liu Bing (d. 87)]. Earlier histories praised this observation. The sisters of the Son of Heaven become senior princesses, and the daughters of the Son of Heaven become princesses. With the designation 'senior,' they are very much more honored than the princesses. Although there can be differences in feeling, there cannot be differences in righteousness. I fear that the logic of Your Majesty ordering the ritual for the princess to exceed that for the senior princess cannot be defended. I would ask Your Majesty to reconsider."
>
> Taizong praised the excellence of this comment.[61]

By opening with the positive example of Emperor Ming 明 (r. 57–75) of the Han dynasty and historical approval for the way he enfeoffed his son, Wei Zheng offers a reasonable justification for his criticism—it would be improper for Princess Changle as a princess to have more gifts than Emperor Taizong's sisters who are senior princesses. Aside from Emperor Ming's example serving as a mirror for Taizong's self-reflection, Wei Zheng arguably appeals to the Zhenguan ruler to live up to past compliance with ritual propriety. The reference to the historical approbation of the Han emperor subtly implies that like Emperor Ming, Taizong would himself be leaving an example for better or worse, that will be scrutinized by posterity in the fullness of time. That Wei Zheng's comments are approved by Taizong suggests that the Zhenguan ruler was amenable to such use of inherited principles in remonstration, if not also to compliance with the ritual rules for gifts to princesses.

3.2.3 Historical remonstrations

Inherited principles may also be derived from the citation of historical remonstrations, particularly those of exemplary officials who effectively persuaded their respective principals. Crafting an argument to include a historical remonstration extends the parameters of intertextuality beyond merely a direct quotation from a text to potentially the entire argument of the former official. A textual quotation or saying may provide theoretical justification, and past events may evince good or poor practice. The intertextual remonstration however works on several levels, tapping into the specific characters of the former ruler and official, their circumstances, the logic of the claims, and the eventual outcome of the remonstration.

This strategy is exemplified by the following memorial addressed to Emperor Ming 明 (r. 226–239) of the Wei dynasty by his Palace Attendant Gaotang Long 高堂隆 (d. 237). It is excerpted by the *Essentials* from the *Records of Wei* and the relevant part is set out below:

> In the past, Emperor Wen of Han was known to be a worthy ruler, his frugality brought benefit for and nourishment to the people. Yet, Jia Yi corrected him and regarded the empire as being hung upside down, with one matter that made him weep bitterly, two matters that made him shed tears, and three matters that made him sigh deeply ...

> The memorial was presented. The emperor reviewed it and said to the Secretariat Supervisor and the Secretariat Director, "Reading this memorial of [Gaotang] Long makes me afraid indeed."[62]

Here Gaotang Long refers to the advice of Jia Yi 賈誼 (200–168 BCE). That the reign of Emperor Wen 文 (r. 180–157 BCE) of the Han dynasty, which is known to be relatively ordered, still attracted such words of protest from Jia Yi enhances the reasonableness of Gaotang Long's vehement criticism about issues of his time. As this remonstration within the *Essentials* is an abridgment of the longer received version, its inclusion of the appeal to historical remonstration stands out as a critical component. The words of Jia Yi are also alluded to in a later *Essentials* remonstrance by the Western Jin general Duan Zhuo 段灼 (*fl.* late 200) excerpted from the *History of the Jin Dynasty*.[63]

Jia Yi's statement is found in a remonstration by Wei Zheng while serving as the Director of the Chancellery in the eighth year of the Zhenguan reign-period (634). The remonstration concerned an outspoken letter from the Vice Magistrate of Shan County Huangfu Decan 皇甫德參:

> In the past a letter from Jia Yi (200–168 BCE) to Han Emperor Wen (r. 180–157 BCE) included the following: "There was one [matter] that [makes] me weep bitterly and six things that [make] me sigh deeply. Ever since Antiquity letters have been submitted to the throne, most of them frank and to the point. If they were not frank and to the point they would fail to engage the ruler's mind. Frankness may look like mockery or slander. Only Your Majesty can tell whether these words were admissible or not."
>
> Taizong said, "No one but you, sir, would be able to say such things." He ordered that Decan be given twenty lengths of silk.[64]

The biography of Jia Yi in the *History of the Han Dynasty* records that Jia Yi described three types of matters in an opening statement to a lengthy remonstration: "There is one matter that makes me weep bitterly, two matters that make me shed tears, and six matters that make me sigh deeply."[65] That Jia Yi's opening statement has been commonly referred to suggests that they achieved an almost proverbial status for rhetorical usage. Inconsistencies in the ways that Gaotang Long and Wei Zheng refer to Jia Yi's words do not seem to detract from their potency, but point to the fact that illustrative power is prioritized over historicity.[66] That Jia Yi's statement is referred to in dissimilar ways and for different purposes thus speaks to the versatile use of inherited principles in political rhetoric.

A historical remonstrance may be referred to in fuller detail as demonstrated by Empress Wende 文德 (r. 626–636) in her response to Emperor Taizong blaming the death of a favored horse on an attendant responsible for feeding it:

> In the past Duke Jing of Qi (r. 547–400 BCE) wanted to execute a man over the death of a horse. Yanzi [Yan Ying, a senior stateman who had long served the Qi court (d. 500 BCE)] asked to list out his offences: "Your first crime is that the horse in your care died. Your second crime is that you are causing our sovereign to execute a man for the death of a horse. When the common people learn of this, they will surely resent our sovereign. Your third crime is that when the other lords hear of this, they will no longer take our state seriously." Duke Jing then forgave his offense. "Your Majesty has come across this case in his reading, how could You forget about it!"
>
> Taizong then changed his mind. He also said to Fang Xuanling: "The empress enlightens Us on many things; this is of very great benefit."[67]

Recounting Master Yan's remonstrative advice to Duke Jing in comparable circumstances presents a mirror for the Zhenguan ruler to reflect on his own conduct. It enables the empress to voice her own protestation through the words of Master Yan, with the benefit of his established authority as a worthy official. Invoking the past in this way also tactfully avoids confrontation as the empress is simply reminding Emperor Taizong of what he has already read about and ought to remember.

3.2.4 Sayings and something heard

The remonstrances in the *Essentials* also serve to demonstrate rhetorical strategies that may be relatively less effective. Two such strategies are invoking cultural knowledge through sayings and by mention of something "the official has heard of or known about." Due to the informal nature of sayings, references to those of obscure origins (e.g., "there's a saying ... ") may at times resemble something that the official has heard or knows, albeit presented in a seemingly more objective light. Use of sayings or adages in remonstration is recorded in approx. 27 *Essentials* remonstrances, with a positive outcome on just three occasions when it is used as the sole strategy.[68] 'I have heard ... ' is recorded in approx. 137 *Essentials* remonstrances, but successful only eight times when used alone.[69] That these techniques are commonly employed in conjunction with other strategies is likely due to their being less persuasive on their own.

From the perspective of the auditor, prefacing remonstrances with an adage or "I have heard ... " appears to enhance its reliability by shifting what could be downplayed as subjective conjecture into a seemingly detached realm of proven knowledge, practice, and experience. Aleida Assmann notes that it can be "notoriously difficult" to distinguish what one has experienced oneself from what one has been told, or what one has seen or read about.[70] By simply relating something that one has heard or knows about, the origins of what is related are undeniably vague. However, the lack of specificity may serve to enhance the versatility of the information for the remonstrator, without demanding the precision involved in recalling a prescribed passage of text or particulars of a past personage, event, or practice. Non-disclosure of the specifics of sources may also enable the contemporary official to avoid arousing potential prejudices of their ruler while making the information more relatable.

That the norms preserved in the sayings are known and accepted by the parties with little question signals the binding force of such elements of the past. This is exemplified by the following passage of the *Essentials* that has been excerpted from the *Analects*:

> Lord Ding asked, "Is there one word that can bring prosperity to the domain?"
>
> Confucius replied, "Words alone cannot do that. But there's a saying that might come close. The main point is that one word cannot make a domain prosper. "Close" means approximate. There is an approximate saying that may bring prosperity to the domain. People have a saying, 'To be a ruler is difficult; to be a minister is not easy.' If the ruler understands that it is not easy to be a ruler, this would come close, would it not, to 'one word that can bring prosperity to the domain'?" Matters cannot be realized through one word but understanding this principle, one may come close to doing so.

"And is there one word that can bring ruin to the domain?" asked the lord.

Confucius replied, "Words alone cannot do that. But there's a saying that might come close. People have a saying, 'I have no delight in being a ruler. My sole delight is making certain that no one contradicts my words.' This is about not delighting in being a ruler, and only taking delight in one's words encountering no contradiction. If he is a good ruler and no one contradicts him, that would be good, would it not? But if he is not good and no one contradicts him, this would come close to being 'one word that can bring ruin to the domain,' would it not?" If what the ruler says is good, it would be good that there is no one to contradict him. If what is said is not good, and no one dares to contradict him, then this would come close to being one word that ruins the domain.71

In the parallel pattern of question and answer, Confucius informs Lord Ding 定 (r. 509–495) of Lu each time that "there's a saying ... " instead of adopting what seems to be general knowledge as his own. In this way, the narrative subtly attributes to the remonstrative advice an independence in being sourced from the common knowledge of the educated elite, a relevance in being specifically chosen in answer to the lord's enquiry, and an objectivity in not being a mere matter of personal opinion. The fact that it is Confucius, the consummate sage, remonstrating in such a manner is more pronounced in the context of the *Essentials* compared to the *Analects*, which is filled with teachings, views, and utterances attributed to Confucius. Hence, a commendable practice for contemporary remonstrators may be implicit from the use of sayings attributed to Confucius in the *Essentials*.

Other references to sayings in the *Essentials*' remonstrations are slightly more specific as to their provenance. Advising the Prince of Jin on the issue of robbers, Master Wen 文 (dates unknown) refers to a proverb from the Zhou dynasty: "Scrutiny which reveals the fish in a pool is unlucky. The wisdom which guesses secrets is fatal."[72] Master Yan refers to a proverb from the Xia dynasty: "If my lord does not go on a journey, how can I be warm? If my lord does not go on an inspection, how can I get the help I need? Journeys and inspections form the backbone of the feudal lords' administration."[73] According to the Grand Counselor of the Palace Jia Yi's remonstration to Emperor Wen of the Han dynasty, the ancients said: "If a man does not till his fields, the empire will suffer hunger; and if a woman does not weave, the empire will suffer cold."[74] More than one adage was used by the Jin Minister Bo Zong 伯宗 (d. 576) in urging the Prince of Jin not to assist the state of Song when it was besieged by Chu in 594 BCE: "Even if the whip is long, it does not reach the horse's belly"[75] and "High and low are all in the mind."[76] Reference to the "ancients" or "proverbs" generally, or a saying from China's early history, for example, the Three Dynasties period (2070–256 BCE), attributes an objective and conventional quality to the material adduced by the advisory official in support of their arguments.

The Zhenguan remonstrations also exhibit the practice of referring to sayings, as evidenced by this memorial submitted by Ma Zhou in the eleventh year of the Zhenguan reign-period (637). The memorial is underpinned by two aphorisms along with the past experiences of individuals and dynasties:

> Since the Han and the Jin Dynasties, the princes have all been given titles and posts inappropriately, and their roles have not been determined in advance, bringing about their destruction. The rulers have known this well, but have been drowned in their private loves for particular princes. And so, though carriages in front have been overturned, those that follow after have not chosen different tracks. At present, in the cases of those beloved princes who receive favor that is overly generous, my unwise concern is not only that they may rely on [this] favor to behave arrogantly. Formerly Emperor Wu of the Wei Dynasty (r. 216–220) designated the [prince of] Chensi [Cao Zhi (192–232)] as crown prince, and when Emperor Wen [Cao Pi (r. 220–226)] succeeded, he was guarded in closed premises, in ways similar to a prison in a gaol. Because Emperor Wu had granted [the prince of Chensi] excessive favor, the succeeding emperor naturally lived in fear of him. This was how it was that Emperor Wu showed irregular love for the prince of Chensi, and happened to cause him suffering. Moreover, why should imperial sons be worried that they are not wealthy and noble? They are given the incomes from their large nominal fiefs, the number of the households of these fiefs are not few. They have fine clothes and excellent food. What more do they need? Yet year on year they are given fine gifts by special dispensation, without recorded precedent. The common saying has it: "The poor will never have to learn thrift; the rich will never have to learn extravagance"; a saying that is naturally so.

> Now Your Majesty has founded the dynasty through great sageliness. Why settle just the present generation of princes? [You] should give orders for permanent laws and ensure that these are followed for ten thousand ages.
>
> When the above memorial was presented, Taizong greatly admired it, and gave [Ma Zhou] 100 lengths of silk.[77]

Advocating for the Zhenguan ruler to implement proper regulations and secure compliance for the state's long-term interests, Ma Zhou refers to the failure of rulers since the Han and Jin dynasties to treat their princes properly. That successive generations have suffered from the same mistakes is emphasized by his allusion to the saying: "Follow the tracks of an overturned cart." Further to the generalizations, Ma Zhou recalls the negative precedent set by Emperor Wu 武 (r. 216–220) of Wei in favoring one prince over his actual successor. That spoiling the princes leads to their developing poor character and habits is underlined by a second saying (" ... the rich will never have to learn extravagance"). Such recount of historical issues saves Ma Zhou from criticizing Taizong directly and he can simply praise his ruler ("Your Majesty has founded the dynasty through great sageliness"), while encouraging ("Why settle ... ") and exhorting him ("You should ... "). Hence historical precedents and aphorisms are seen to convey the risks to the state posed by the ruler's self-indulgence while lending specificity and credibility to the overall argument.

The authority of inherited principles are also invoked by the mention of something the official has "heard of or known about," as illustrated by this passage of the *Essentials* excerpted from the *Records of the Historian*:

> When Emperor Taiwu was enthroned, Yizhi became prime minister. Yizhi is the son of Yi Yin. In Bo there was a portent and two kinds of mulberry trees grew together in the courtyard [of the palace]. Within one night they grew as large as a man could reach around with both arms. The portent means an abnormality. Two trees growing together represents a punishment for disrespectfulness. Emperor Taiwu was alarmed and questioned Yizhi. Yizhi said: "I have heard that a portent cannot overpower virtue. Does Your Majesty's government have some deficiencies? May Your Majesty cultivate virtue." After Taiwu followed his advice, the

> portentous mulberry trees withered and Yin [i.e., the Shang dynasty] again became prosperous. For this reason, [Taiwu] was called Central Ancestor.[78]

What Yizhi 伊陟 (dates unknown) has heard about, though it may not directly relate to mulberry trees, becomes the springboard for his remonstrance to Emperor Taiwu 太戊 (r. 1637–1563 BCE) of the Shang dynasty. It is assumed by both parties that what has become known to Yizhi is accurate, that the portent relates to shortcomings in the emperor's governance and may be resolved by the emperor cultivating virtue to improve his rulership. Verbalizing whatever has been heard in this way enables an individual's memories to become shared within a common discourse and part of an intersubjective symbolic system. That the advisory official has thought to share what they have heard in answer to the emperor's query makes their advice appear more relevant to resolving the issue at hand and thereby worthy of consideration. Moreover, the "I have heard ... " format without attribution of the quote to a specific source seems to provide an additional discursive space where the remonstrator can adduce arguments that are not yet sanctioned by history or form part of an authoritative text corpus. As such, "I have heard ... " connects the argument to contemporaneous oral discourse and potentially contributes a contemporary perspective on a controversial topic.

Like the historical remonstration of Yi Zhi, Wei Zheng appeals to inherited principle by reference to something he has heard in this remonstration dated to the fourteenth year of the Zhenguan reign-period (642):

> I have heard that to triumph by combat is easy, but to preserve victory is difficult. Your Majesty must be very mindful and think carefully [about this], and do not fail to think of potential danger while [living] in peace. Your achievement is evident, and virtuous teachings have again become widespread. Constantly govern on this basis, and there will be no way to overthrow the ancestral altars.[79]

Wei Zheng opens his remonstrance with what he has heard, which resembles a brief allusion to *Master Wu*.[80] The opening statement—"to triumph is easy, but to preserve victory is difficult"—forms the basis for Wei Zheng's advice to Taizong to secure the Tang empire by remaining mindful of potential dangers during times of relative peace. Although *Master Wu* is not referred to expressly, the inherited principle nevertheless appeals to the cultural literacy of the Zhenguan ruler. Through the sharing of something heard or known, both Yi Zhi and Wei Zheng are seen to attempt the establishment of common ground or a shared perspective with their respective rulers.

The remonstrance narratives within the *Essentials* provide normative guidance in various ways. Trusted by political superiors and subordinates alike in the *Essentials* remonstrances, inherited principles provide established patterns and benchmarks based on past writings, informal knowledge and sayings, and historical remonstrations. The *Essentials* guides the official to help their ruler realize mistakes and misjudgment through inherited principles that can draw on historical rulers in comparable situations (e.g., the Guo ruler who couldn't engage the good personnel), defuse what might be emotionally charged situations (e.g., when Lord Jing wanted to execute the horse attendant), and are generally applicable (e.g., "Illuminate virtue and be wary of transgressions"). Quoting well-known sayings and authoritative writings provides support for the persuader's assertions and exhortations while enhancing the efficacy of the remonstrance by establishing shared understanding between parties. Leveraging the voices of historical remonstrators, including knowledgable and established authorities (e.g., Master Yan), the advisory official can humbly minimize their own fallibility and alleviate some of the awkwardness of calling out their principal's misconduct in the course of providing counsel (e.g., breaching ritual protocol in respect of Princess Changle's pending nuptials).

3.3 CONTENT OF THE REMONSTRANCES

This section analyzes how the *Essentials* guides the substance of remonstrances by the Zhenguan court. As a circumscribed corpus of works, the *Essentials* forms a cultural knowledge base shared among Emperor Taizong and his officials. Appealing to values and material that are understood and accepted by the ruler may naturally bolster the effectiveness of remonstrance. The rhetoric of remonstration covered so far in this chapter may be complemented by analyzing the language, evidence, and ideas in the content of the advice. Below I explore the textual sources and particular political themes that demonstrate how the *Essentials* may have provided such guidance.

Although the *Essentials* is known to be often consulted by Taizong for statecraft purposes and shared with his sons, there is no extant record of the specific extent to which it was used by the Zhenguan ruler, his princes, or his officials. Such dearth of historical data may stem from the various users of the *Essentials* preferring to reference its sources rather than the anthology for clarity in their remonstrance or other communications. Simply citing the *Essentials* may beg the question of which part of the anthology their reference derives from. Indeed, direct referencing of the source texts is facilitated by the *Essentials*' contents being arranged by their respective origins. In the absence of detailed information about the usage of the *Essentials* by the Zhenguan ruling elite, I argue that such information may be gleaned to some extent from documents such as the *Model for an Emperor* and recorded remonstrances.

It is important to first explore which texts the Zhenguan ruler was familiar with and inclined to use in his writings about statecraft. Of the multitude of his poetic and prose compositions in the *Collected Writings of Emperor Taizong of the Tang Dynasty*, I focus on the *Model for an Emperor* as Emperor Taizong's personal guide to his heir-apparent on governing the state. Written well after the completion of the *Essentials* and intended to convey his definitive thoughts on emperorship with over two decades of experience on the throne, the *Model for an Emperor* affords a unique evidentiary vantage point. In presenting the finished work to his successor, Taizong is recorded to have said:

> This work provides within it [what is necessary] to cultivate yourself and to govern the state. If I should die one of these days soon, there will be nothing more to be said.[81]

Intertextual references in the language and vocabulary items employed by the *Model for an Emperor* offer insight into the political writings that Taizong was conversant with. These would have been the texts that he thought pertinent for his successor to know and learn from. Insofar as the texts referred to by the *Model for an Emperor* correlate with the contents of the *Essentials*, it may provide some clues as to the extent to which Emperor Taizong was amenable to the use of the *Essentials*.

A textual analysis of the edition of the *Model of the Emperor* recorded in the *Wenyuan Hall edition of the Complete Library*[82] against the contents of the Tenmei edition of the *Essentials*[83] reveals several key findings. First, a total of 94 texts are cited in the *Model for an Emperor* of which 60 number among the *Essentials*' 68 sources.[84] This amounts to two-thirds of the *Model for an Emperor*'s textual sources being the same.[85] Although citations of the Five Classics may be conventional in political literature, there is a distinctive breadth of sources beyond those canonical works that corresponds closely to that of the *Essentials*. That sources compiled within a statecraft reference that Taizong consulted are referred to by a subsequent writing attributed to him on that subject may be unsurprising. However, the presence of the citations within the *Essentials*' contents and the frequency with which they occur indicate that the correspondence may be more than mere coincidence. Indeed, 71 percent of the references in the *Model for an Emperor* are found in the excerpts of the *Essentials*, with some 36 percent of those references corresponding to two or more excerpts of the *Essentials*. In other words, the *Essentials* credibly accounts for most of the intertextual references in the *Model for an Emperor*. Even if those references might generally form part of the political discourse at the time, it is noteworthy that they are anthologized by the *Essentials*.

The opening sentence of the *Model for an Emperor* quotes directly from the *Changes*, which is excerpted by the *Essentials* in its canonical section. The same quote is later repeated both in whole and in part within the *Essentials*' historical and masters' sections, respectively, as shown in Table 3.1. It could be said that the opening sentence of the *Model for an Emperor* sets the tone for the entire piece as intertextual references abound through its vocabulary, phrases, and sentences.

Table 3.1. The opening sentence of the *Model for an Emperor* in the *Essentials*

Model for an Emperor	***Essentials* (scroll no. source and excerpt)**	
We have heard that "the great virtue [of Heaven and Earth] is to bestow life, while the supreme treasure for the holy sage is to occupy the [imperial] position."[120]	1 *Changes*	The great virtue of Heaven and Earth is to give life. The great treasure of the sage is to occupy the [highest] position.[121]
	14 *History of the Former Han Dynasty*	Therefore, the *Changes* provides that the great virtue of Heaven and Earth is "to give life," and the great treasure of the sage is "to occupy the [highest] position."[122]
	48 *Normative Discourses*	The *Changes* states, "The great treasure of the sage is 'to occupy the [highest] position'."[123]

The *Model for an Emperor*'s indirect references may correspond to several sources of the *Essentials* based on apparent consistency in the use of language, reasoning, and the overall meaning of its excerpts. This is evidenced by the following sentence from Section 3 of the *Model for an Emperor* entitled "Seeking Worthies," as shown in Table 3.2. The logic of the sentence—that engaging the appropriate personnel naturally enables the state to be in order—follows the causality made explicit by the text and annotation of the *Essentials*' excerpts from all three of its bibliographical sections. The Chinese characters for "gaining personnel" (*deren* 得人) are found in every one of those excerpts. As I have argued in Chapter 2, officials of character and competence were valued by the Zhenguan court and is a key cultural symbol of the *Essentials*.

Table 3.2. Seeking worthy talent in the *Model for an Emperor* and the *Essentials*

Model for an Emperor	*Essentials* (scroll no. source and excerpt)	
If in the employment [of officials] the emperor obtains the appropriate men, then the empire will rule itself.[124]	2 *Venerable Documents*	Order and disorder depend on the various officers. Order arises when the appropriate personnel are appointed to office, and disorder arises when [such] personnel are lost.[125]
	10 *School Sayings of Confucius*	Therefore, the conduct of government lies in gaining personnel.[126]
	30 *History of the Jin Dynasty (Part 1)*	When the division of duties is fully clear and those in office are [appropriate] personnel, [the ruler] realizes order without acting contrary to the natural flow.[127]
	32 *Master Guan*	Never has there been heard of an ancient sage ruler who enjoyed illustrious fame and widespread praise, and whose rich achievements and great works were celebrated by the entire realm and not forgotten by later generations that this was not due to his having [won the hearts of] men.[128]
	40 *Three Strategies*	Governing the state and giving security to one's family [is a question of] gaining the people. "People" refers to worthy persons. With Yi Yin in attendance, King Tang was ascendant. When Ning Qi arrived, the state of Qi prospered.[129]

The editors of the *Essentials* evidently chose not to exclude such repetition in the anthology. As such, the reiteration probably served to remind and reinforce salient ideas, keeping them front of mind for their principal reader: Emperor Taizong. If the Zhenguan ruler knew little of the classical learning for statecraft when he ascended the throne, it is most plausible that the texts excerpted in the *Essentials*, including their commentary in the annotations, were those he was relatively more familiar with by the end of his reign and attributed importance to in advising his heir-apparent.

Another finding is that most of the references in the *Model for an Emperor* relate to the historical writings as excerpted by the *Essentials*. They include the *Venerable Documents*, the *Records of the Three Kingdoms* (counting the *Records of Wei*, the *Records of Shu*, and the *Records of Wu* together), and the standard histories of the former and latter Han dynasties. Such appeal to historical texts and the people and events they record, is in line with the historiographical zeitgeist of the Zhenguan period, as discussed in Section 1.2.2.

It must be noted that these findings may not be universally applicable across other editions of the *Model for an Emperor* or the *Essentials*. Comparing other editions of either document may yield different results due to the disparities in wording. For example, Twitchett's translation of the *Model for an Emperor* notes the variations in wording that arise from copying errors, the use of variant text, as well as different orderings of the same characters, in the different editions that he consulted.[86] Moreover, use of the Heian edition of the *Essentials* would be less productive as only 13 of its 50 scrolls remain extant and there is less material for comparison than other editions. That the findings are not more broadly applicable does not however detract from their import for this study.

The strength of the above findings is further attenuated by the fact that several texts may be alluded to by many of the intertextual references. This makes it difficult to pinpoint with complete certainty the source(s) that Emperor Taizong may have had in mind. I have tried to mitigate this problem by distinguishing between those references that simply cite books that are found in the *Essentials* and those that appear to correspond to those texts as they have been excerpted and annotated by the *Essentials*. The reliability of trying to trace the intertextual references to the level of the specific source or excerpt is admittedly tenuous at best. Notwithstanding such empirical limitations, the overall trend by which the *Model for an Emperor* refers to the sources as they appear in the *Essentials* provides evidence of certain texts that Emperor Taizong considered relevant and useful to cite in writings on matters of state.

Taizong's study of the *Essentials* manifests in the composition and instructions of the *Models for an Emperor*. His political views on several subjects, including the priority accorded to agricultural work and classical scholarship, are also reflected in and arguably shaped by the *Essentials*. The values espoused by the anthology resonate in the content of the remonstrances submitted by the Zhenguan courtiers. While the *Essentials* is not topically arranged, its selective inclusion of excerpts and annotations provide textual interpretations that bring to light the values of the Zhenguan ruling elite. On the topic of warfare, the six military treatises found in the masters' section of the *Essentials* form a circumscribed body of texts for exploration. The military works include the *Six Quivers*, the *Art of War*, the *Methods of Sima*, the *Secret Strategies*, the *Three Strategies*, and *Master Wu* (collectively, the "military texts"). The normative guidance from the *Essentials*' military writings is seen to be strikingly consistent with the nature of Zhenguan remonstrances and Taizong's own words. I begin by discussing several key themes in the *Essentials*' military texts, which arguably provide guidance for related remonstrances during the Zhenguan years.

The prevention of warfare is unequivocally identified as the best military strategy through the *Essentials*' selections from the military texts and the historical remonstrances. First, their tactical and combative elements are all but absent. Indeed, there is no mention of battle in the *Essentials*' extracts from the *Secret Strategies* in scroll 31.[87] Significant portions of the military texts are wholly excluded from the *Essentials*, including much of the minutiae of martial strategy formulation and implementation. For example, the *Essentials* omits six chapters from the *Art of War*, including those entitled "Waging War" (*zuozhan* 作戰),

"Manoeuvring Armies" (*junzheng* 軍爭), and the "Nine Terrains" (*jiudi* 九地), and two chapters from each of the *Methods of Sima* ("Defining Rank" (*ding jue* 定爵) and "Strictness in Rank" (*yanwei* 嚴位)) and *Master Wu* ("Estimating the Enemy" (*liaodi* 料敵) and "Sudden Emergency" (*yingbian* 應變)).[88]

Second, military intervention is actively discouraged. The opening passage from the *Art of War* attributes the ultimate excellence to subduing the enemy without any fighting at all, and the details of besieging walled cities are redacted. The relevant parts of the excerpt are as follows:

> Master Sun said, " ... winning every battle is not the highest attainment. The highest attainment is to subdue the enemy without fighting. The enemy voluntarily surrenders without fighting. .... So it is that the one who handles troops well is he who causes other people's troops to surrender, but without fighting. He captures a stronghold, but without attacking it, and he takes other countries, but without a long campaign. He will always keep his resources intact while contending for the Empire, and his soldiers' weapons will not be damaged. Thus, his [triumph] will be complete."[89]

The ideal of conquering without armed confrontation is conveyed through the main text—"The highest attainment is to subdue the enemy without fighting"—and its annotation about the voluntary surrender by the opponent. Teaching that strongholds, countries, and even the empire can be won over without expending military efforts or resources, the *Essentials* unmistakably disincentivizes military recourse while detailing the potentials of conflict-free strategies.

Third, the *Essentials* substantiates its non-martial principles by reference to conventional authority and practice of the sages. Excerpts from the *Methods of Sima* associate the absence of war and strife with the best rulership since ancient times: "the good governance of [rulers with] sagely virtue."[90] Similarly, "The [sagely] king does not take any pleasure in using the army" is extracted from the *Three Strategies*.[91] Military engagement is de-emphasized, as state security is attributed to domestic factors. The *Six Quivers* records that national stability and imperial government are brought about by the ruler's perfection of moral cultivation.[92] Accordingly, the visionary Jiang Shang advises King Wen of Zhou to win over the empire by cultivating his virtue, heeding the advice of worthy officials, and extending benevolence to the people.[93] In this dialogue excerpted from *Master Wu*, the question about martial formations and strategies is answered in distinctly non-martial terms with reference to matters beyond the battlefield:

> Marquis Wu inquired, "I would like to hear about the Way [Dao] for making battle formations invariably stable, defenses inevitably solid, and victory in battle certain."
>
> Wu Qi replied, "If you are able to have the worthy hold high positions and the unworthy occupy low positions, then your battle formations will already be stable. If the people are settled in their farming and homes and [are] attached to their local authorities, then your defenses will already be solid. When the hundred surnames all acclaim my lord and condemn neighboring states, then in battle you will already be victorious."[94]

The same themes are detectable in the remonstrances of Emperor Taizong's high officials and Taizong's own words, which not only include references found in the *Essentials* but also mirror its interpretation of the military texts. Around the inception of the Zhenguan reign-period, Wei Zheng remonstrated several times against responding to the suspected rebellion by Feng Ang 馮盎 (d. 646) and Tan Dian 談殿 (dates unknown) with a punitive expedition. His advice to instead nurture the suspected rebels with virtue[95] is in essence the strategy to "subdue the enemy without fighting" from the *Art of War*. Taizong ultimately followed the advice and praised the efficacy of the non-martial approach as being "better than 100,000 troops!"[96] Wei Zheng's remonstrances corresponding to the values espoused by the *Essentials* is unsurprising, given his role as its editor-in-chief. However, similar lines of argument concerning warfare are shown by other high officials.

The Right Vice Director of the Department of State Affairs and Army Commander-in-Chief Li Jing once advised Taizong that military strategy begins with the use of benevolence and rightness before clever tactics and deception.[97] In Li's remonstrance, one hears the echoes of the *Methods of Sima*'s opening line found in the *Essentials*, that commends an orthodoxy of governing by rightness with benevolence as the foundation, and harks back to the virtue of sage rulers.[98] Moreover, the Minister of Works and Chief Compiler of the Dynastic History Fang Xuanling consistently tried to dissuade Taizong against the use of military options. Quoting King Zhuang of Chu who is recorded in the *Essentials*' excerpts from the *Zuo Tradition*,[99] Fang repeatedly reminds Taizong that "true" martiality is the cessation of military operations, as exemplified by his remonstrances on the issue of punitive expeditions against Goguryeo in 643 and 648.[100] Fang also uses the phrase "The military is a baleful instrument and war is dangerous," in remonstrances dated 642 and 648,[101] which is found, either in whole or in part, in the *Essentials*' excerpts from the *Three Strategies*,[102] as well as the *History of the Han Dynasty*,[103] the *Old Master*,[104] *Master Wei Liao*,[105] and the *Discourses on the Essentials of Governing*.[106] This was a view that was shared by Li Jing, who once advised that "The military should be used as a last resort."[107] During the fourth year of his reign, Taizong was also recorded to have said, "The military is a baleful instrument, it should only be used as a last resort."[108] Despite Taizong's martial background, his active role in taking over the Sui empire through victorious military campaigns, and the militarist policies in the latter years of his reign, he adopts a relatively conservative approach to the use of warfare in his *Model for an Emperor* that is consistent with the *Essentials*. Indeed, the section entitled "Reviewing Preparations for War" begins with none other than "The military is a baleful instrument of the state."[109]

Another poignant example of the collective values found in the *Essentials* and used for Zhenguan remonstrance is that of Fang Xuanling's petition written from his deathbed in 648, which exhorts Taizong to heed the preconditions for military sanction. Fang includes the following quotes from the *Changes* and the *Old Master* (in Table 3.3), both of which can be found in the *Essentials*' extracts from those sources, with allusions to both in its excerpts from the *Records of Wei*.

Table 3.3. Fang Xuanling's quotes and the *Essentials*

Fang Xuanling's quotes	*Essentials* (scroll no. source and excerpt)	
The *Changes* ["Hexagram 1, *Qian*"] says: "[Arrogance is] knowing how to advance, but not knowing how to retreat, knowing preservation, but not knowing destruction, knowing gain but not knowing loss ... Knowing how to advance, retreat, preserve, and destroy, but not losing one's uprightness, this then is sage person!"[130]	1 *Changes*	"[Arrogance is] knowing how to advance, but not knowing how to retreat, knowing preservation, but not knowing destruction, knowing gain but not knowing loss ... Knowing how to advance, retreat, preserve, and destroy, but not losing one's uprightness, this then is sage person!"[131]
The *Old Master* states "He who knows sufficiency is not disgraced; he who knows when to stop is not in danger."[132]	34 *Old Master*	He who knows sufficiency is not disgraced; One who knows sufficiency will renounce greed, eradicate desires, and not disgrace themselves. He who knows when to stop is not in danger.[133]
	26 *Records of Wei*	Worry about those knowing how to advance, but not knowing how to retreat, and knowing craving, but not knowing contentment, as they will suffer difficulty and disgrace, and bear regret and shame. As the saying goes, "Not knowing contentment leads to loss of what is craved. Hence, the satisfaction of knowing contentment, is lasting contentment."[134]

Aware of the angry Taizong seeking to launch another punitive expedition against Goguryeo, Fang exhorts his ruler to reconsider the military intervention, as it would only be justified on grounds of their non-fulfillment of vassal obligations, foreign incursion, or long-term disturbance, rather than emotional impulses and expansionist ambitions.[110] By alluding to the following passages from the *Methods of Sima*, the *Art of War*, and the *Three Strategies* as excerpted by the *Essentials*, his remonstrance plausibly reflects an internalization of the shared cultural knowledge and values:

> In contending for rightness and not for gain, they showed their rightness.[111] (*Essentials*' excerpt from the *Methods of Sima*)
>
> If there is no danger do not fight. The military is used as a last resort. A lord should not raise an army on account of resentment, and a general should not fight out of anger.[112] (*Essentials*' excerpt from the *Art of War*)
>
> One who concentrates on broadening his territory will waste his energies; Concentrating on broadening territory rather than practicing virtuous government is the way of desolation. but one who concentrates on broadening his virtue will be strong. Concentrating on prioritizing thrift and moderation while broadening one's moral education is the way of strength.[113] (*Essentials*' excerpt from the *Three Strategies*)

Fang Xuanling is not alone in subscribing to the ideas espoused in the above excerpts. The excerpt from the *Art of War* is similarly evoked by Chu Suiliang as Grand Master of Remonstrance in relation to mobilizing troops for a punitive expedition against Mangniji of Goguryeo in 644. Chu specifically cautions Emperor Taizong about the risks inherent in acting on personal displeasure, which effectively dissuades Taizong from the campaign. The relevant advice from Chu is as follows:

> But if by chance You are not successful, You will fail to display Your might to the distant regions, and You will inevitably become even angrier, and once more mobilize troops. If it comes to this, it will be difficult to predict security and danger.[114]

Arguably, the above excerpts from the *Changes*, the *Old Master*, and the *Three Strategies* underlie the remonstrances of Chu Suiliang as Vice Director of the Chancellery and Wei Zheng when they each try to persuade Taizong against taking over the newly pacified state of Qočo in 640.[115] Read together, the excerpts caution against the perilous pursuit of territorial aggrandizement and the consequences of not being content. Though their advices were presented at different times, it is as if they speak in unison. They question their ruler's expansionist policy of turning the territory into prefectures and counties due to the ongoing military intervention involved. Both highlight the considerable costs in both human and material resources. Chu Suiliang's remonstrance additionally points to the danger to the state, as preoccupation with the territory of the former Qočo leaves the state exposed to military threats in other areas.[116] The correctness of Chu Suiliang and Wei Zheng's counsel is later acknowledged by Emperor Taizong, who ultimately regrets his failure to heed them.[117] Moreover, Chu's quote from the Appended Explanations of the *Changes*, "In safety, do not forget danger. In times of order, do not forget disorder," recurs among the *Essentials*' excerpts from the *Changes* and other sources as shown in Table 3.4. An undercurrent of such prudent preparedness is seen in Wei Zheng's preface to the *Essentials*, which praises the caution of former rulers: "there are none who have not been [as cautious] as if driving a horse with moldering reins," and Emperor Taizong himself: "there is peace and happiness throughout the empire. Yet Your Majesty remains humble and not complacent."[118]

The absence of detailed records about the *Essentials*' historical usage by the Zhenguan ruling collective may be alleviated by indirect evidence in the way that Emperor Taizong and his officials communicate and substantiate their arguments in the *Model for an Emperor* and the Zhenguan remonstrances, respectively. The cultural memory within the *Essentials* accounts for most sources cited by Taizong's *Model for an Emperor*, whether as direct quotes or indirect references, such as allusions. This would suggest that the Zhenguan ruler was familiar with the contents of the *Essentials* and considered its eclectic selection of sources pertinent for political purposes, and sufficiently useful to commend to his successor by referring to those sources with such frequency. The normative guidance

Table 3.4. Chu Suiliang's quote from the *Changes* and the *Essentials*

Chu Suiliang's quote	*Essentials* (scroll no. source and excerpt)	
The *Changes* states, "In safety, do not forget danger. In times of order, do not forget disorder."[135]	1 *Changes*	The Master said, "He who keeps danger in mind is he who will rest safe in his seat; he who keeps ruin in mind is he who will preserve his interests secure; he who sets the danger of disorder before him is he who will maintain the state of order. Therefore, **the superior man, when resting in safety, does not forget that danger may come;** when in a state of security, he does not forget the possibility of ruin; **and when all is in a state of order, he does not forget that disorder may come.** Thus, his person is kept safe, and his states and all their clans can be preserved."[136]
	8 *Discourses of the States*	Preparedness involves providing for inadequacies. "Preparedness" means national preparedness. "Providing for inadequacies" means preparing in advance for the unexpected, not forgetting danger in times of safety.137
	14 *History of the Former Han Dynasty*	[Liu Xiang] presented a memorial that remonstrated as follows: "Your servant has heard that the *Changes* states, 'When resting in safety, do not forget that danger may arise, when in a state of security, do not forget the possibility of ruin. That is how to maintain personal safety and thereby preserve the nation and family.' "[138]
	39 *Spring and Autumn Annals of Master Lü*	Accordingly, when a worthy ruler is at peace, he contemplates danger; At peace but not forgetting danger. when he is successful, he contemplates failure; Illustrious but not forgetting lowliness. and when he has obtained something, he contemplates losing it. Loss means deprivation. One must be mindful because where there is gain, there must be loss.139

found in, and formative values espoused by, the *Essentials*' excerpts from the military texts are reflected in the remonstrances on punitive expeditions and border control from Zhenguan officials and Taizong's own words. The language used, the evidence adduced, and the conventional ideas evoked unequivocally identify the sources compiled within the *Essentials*' as a central resource for political rhetoric. There is therefore much indirect though not inconsiderable evidence of the *Essentials* being commonly used as a repertory of cultural knowledge and values for statecraft by the Zhenguan ruling collective.

Much of the *Essentials*' contents relate to the need for remonstration and records historical remonstrances. Such cultural memory reflects how the Zhenguan ruling elite construed the past and their relationship to cultural knowledge and narratives, as much as how they wanted to be seen doing so. Institutionally commissioned, compiled, and commended, the anthology represents a formal consensus between the Zhenguan ruler and his court on what they prioritized in terms of shared stories and values. They are seen to identify with textual excerpts that position them in public discourse as a group that collectively values remonstrance and the advisory role of officials for good governance, as well as the use of inherited principles in political argumentation.

Reading the *Essentials*, the ruler may develop a better appreciation for remonstration and the advisory duty of their high officials as political imperatives to enduring rulership. The portrayal of Emperor Taizong within the historical sources accords with the *Essentials*. Not only is the Zhenguan ruler aware of the importance of remonstrance but he is known to have taken various measures to encourage such inputs from his court throughout his reign. That the *Essentials* remonstrances typically appeal to inherited principles suggests that Taizong and his court valued learning from the historical past and subscribed to the authority of precedents in political rhetoric. Indeed, the Zhenguan remonstrances dating from the outset of Emperor Taizong's reign to its final decade, commonly refer to inherited principles in the same forms that are apparent in the *Essentials*, and often with the approval of the Zhenguan ruler.[119] That the cultural memory in the *Essentials* encompasses cultural values and knowledge shared by the Zhenguan ruling elite is further manifested in the words of Taizong and his courtiers. The congruence of language, views, and citation of sources between the *Essentials*, Taizong's *Model for an Emperor*, and the Zhenguan remonstrances relating to military interventions, arguably points to the contents of the *Essentials* being a political canon of writings that was familiar to and utilized by the Zhenguan administration. This corroborates their profile as a ruling elite that drew on the wealth of cultural knowledge and experience as an essential resource for statesmanship, and the practice of remonstration with reference to inherited wisdom as a way of applying the remembered past to contemporary governance.

CHAPTER FOUR

DISSEMINATION OF THE *ESSENTIALS* IN CHINA AND ABROAD

Cultural memory may be objectified in a text for a time, but it is also an ongoing process, whereby each generation of a society may choose from the archive of cultural knowledge for its collective self-image and normative orientation. Their respective choices as to what is germane and meaningful, how much to innovate and reconfigure, is illustrated by the textual history of the *Essentials*. From the Zhenguan reign-period of the Tang dynasty through to the twenty-first century, the *Essentials* has been attributed different meanings and applied to various uses. Factors such as the evolution of language, attrition of time, and the advancement of printing gave rise to different versions of the *Essentials*, including editions containing variant text and supplementary annotations. The anthology even became lost on its native shores and had to be reintroduced from abroad. This chapter explores the dissemination of the *Essentials* and its shifts of meaning throughout its transmission history in China, Japan, Korea, and Vietnam, by reference to cultural remembering and forgetting.

The dynamics of cultural memory entail processes of remembering and forgetting. Aleida Assmann identifies active and passive dimensions to each of those processes. Active cultural remembering, known as the "cultural working memory," stores and reproduces cultural knowledge for repeated performance, sustained affirmation, and continued individual and public attention.[1] In this active mode of cultural memory, the knowledge is being used in the contemporary context to define and support the cultural identity, normativity, and orientation of a society.[2] Passive cultural remembering, termed the "cultural reference memory," preserves cultural knowledge that has been withdrawn from general attention and functions like an archive "located on the border between forgetting and remembering," by storing for a time information no longer of immediate use.[3] While such stored knowledge is available, it remains inert and uninterpreted until it is reclaimed by others with their (new) frames of reference.[4] Analogous to the ancient Greek statue that has "lived through five meanings" by being copied in a Roman workshop, excavated in Rome during the seventeenth century, displayed today in a museum and made accessible to school pupils, Martin Bommas points out that ancient objects and texts generally experience a shift of meaning at least once in their lifetime.[5] It thus seems inevitable that a cultural text may acquire different or multiple meanings over time should it be remembered and reused for the cultural identity of subsequent societies. The perpetuation of cultural memory entails the storage, retrieval, and communication of the meaning that provides the basis for a group's connective structure.[6] Such transmission of meaning depends on textual continuity, preservation, and reembodiment by institutions.[7] Not only must the text remain in circulation, but they must be kept readable as language use and historical reality evolve over time.[8]

The risk of being forgotten confronts any object of cultural memory. Barbie Zelitzer observes that "Forgetting reflects a choice to put aside, for whatever reason, what no longer matters."[9] The process of forgetting has been likened to the decay of an imprint involving implicit natural and gradual erosion.[10] Cultural forgetting is considered normal:

> As in the head of the individual, also in the communication of society much must be continuously forgotten to make place for new information, new challenges, and new ideas to face the present and future.[11]

Using cultural memory to examine Pausanias' writings about the cult worship of Egyptian gods in ancient Greece, Bommas wrote:

> If not stored properly or refreshed by appropriate media [memories] will not survive the struggle of events applying for a constant place in any society's daily reality.[12]

Similar to cultural remembering, the process of forgetting is also divided into active and passive forms. Whereas active forgetting is characterized by intentional acts of erasing or censoring the documented past, passive forgetting is implied by non-intentional loss or neglect such that the object of cultural memory becomes no longer known, valued, or used.[13] Passive forgetting has been described by Anna Lucille Boozer as "perhaps the most self-evident type of forgetting among societies."[14]

These cultural memory processes thus assist an enquiry into the preservation, circulation, accessibility, and readability of the *Essentials*, and the continuity of its meaning over time. Separate sections of this chapter will look at how the *Essentials*, as a cultural memory text of the Zhenguan reign-period, fared in the reconstruction of cultural knowledge for collective identity by subsequent ruling elites in China, and how it was transmitted to and received in pre-modern East Asia.[15]

4.1 THE *ESSENTIALS* IN CHINA

By ordering copies of the *Essentials* to be made for the princes, Emperor Taizong expressed his intention for the text to be studied and used beyond the immediate period of his reign. The *Essentials* remained extant in China until sometime during the fourteenth century. First, in respect of the remainder of the Tang period, the *Essentials* appears to have lingered in the cultural reference memory, if not also at times, in the cultural working memory. There are extant records of the statecraft reference being known to and consulted by certain Tang emperors, and being read among the officialdom. Its circulation beyond the palace library would suggest that the anthology had developed a broader readership and was applied to new uses. However, the scant historical material for this period militates against drawing firmer conclusions. For example, Denis Twitchett notes that except for one draft national history, the official archives of the Institute of Historiography for the preceding reigns of the Tang dynasty, including court diaries, veritable records, and national histories, were destroyed by fire during An Lushan's 安祿山 (d. 757) occupation of the capital Chang'an in 756.[16] Writing about court politics of the late Tang period, Michael T. Dalby also commented that "the quantity and quality of ninth-century data represent a severe constraint."[17] Second, it will be seen from the extant literature that the *Essentials* was withdrawn from the cultural working memory and became passively forgotten after the Tang dynasty. Third, the *Essentials* was restored to the cultural memory in China following the reintroduction of an extant edition from Japan in 1796.

The death of Taizong and the attendant end of his reign meant the loss of the *Essentials*' immediate addressees. Disconnected from the Zhenguan institutions that had authorized its creation, valued its contents, and determined its meaning, as discussed in Chapters 1, 2, and 3, it was perhaps inevitable that the anthology would be approached differently during later periods of Tang China. Only three Tang emperors after the Zhenguan period are recorded as having knowledge of the *Essentials*, with Emperor Xuanzong 玄宗 (r. 713–756) being the earliest of the three. This would indicate that in the period between the reigns of Emperor Taizong and his great-grandson Emperor Xuanzong, the *Essentials* was likely shelved away in the archive of cultural reference memory where it was retrievable but not actively used by those Tang rulers. Nevertheless, the *Essentials* must have continued to remain accessible to and read by the officials, because emperors Xuanzong, Dezong 德宗 (r. 779–805), and Xianzong 憲宗 (r. 805–820), each became aware of the *Essentials* through their respective courtiers.

Based on the evidence of active engagement with the anthology by Emperor Xuanzong and his court, it could be said that the *Essentials* was first restored to the working mode of cultural memory during the reign of Xuanzong. Sometime during 712/713, the commandant Yang Xiangru 楊相如 (*fl.* 712) submitted a memorial to Emperor Xuanzong that contrasted the downfall of the second Sui emperor with the success of the second Tang emperor. It specifically recommended that Xuanzong study the *Essentials* to understand the principles of governing and to learn from the fine words and deeds of sagely sovereigns and faithful subordinates:

> Yang Xiangru, as Commandant of Jingyang in Changzhou, submitted a memorial about advantages during the Xiantian reign-period [712–713]: "In the past, Taizong ordered Wei Zheng to compose the *Qunshu liyao* in fifty [scrolls] that generally discourse about the merits and faults [in governing]. Your servant sincerely invites Your Majesty, to review this text at every opportunity during your daily leisure. Although it is concise and incomprehensive, it suffices to view the straightforward words of faithful officials and to know the essentials of state governance." Emperor [Xuanzong] read and approved of it.[18]

That Yang Xiangru in Changzhou 常州 was familiar with the *Essentials* suggests that it was known and studied among officials, including those at the prefecture-level of local administration. Given that the *Essentials* had begun life by being compiled for the sovereign and shared with his princes within the palace, the above record would also indicate that copies of the *Essentials*, either in whole or in part, were accessible even to those officials working in the provinces by the eighth century. Xuanzong was further encouraged to learn from the good government of the Zhenguan era by Wu Jing, who compiled the *Zhenguan Essentials* and presented it to the throne in *circa* 729. The *Zhenguan Essentials* comprises statements from Emperor Taizong, dialogues between him and his courtiers, and narrative sections, that were reconstructed from court records based on topics designed to showcase elements of their administrative culture that Wu considered to be instructional. That the contemporary scholar-officials were familiar with the *Essentials* is evidenced in the *Records of the Writings of the Hall of Scholarly Worthies* (*Jixian zhuji* 集賢注記), by the Tang high official Wei Shu 韋述 (d. 757). Although that text is no longer extant, the relevant part has survived by being excerpted in Wang Yinglin's *Ocean of Jades* encyclopedia as follows:

> During the tenth month of the thirteenth year of the Tianbao reign-period [754], there was an imperial commission for members of the

Academy to copy the *Qunshu zhengyao* and to extract its excerpts from the *Daode jing* [also known as the "*Old Master*"]. First, the Academy presented the *Qunshu liyao* composed by Wei [Zheng, who is posthumously titled] "Wen Zheng."[19] On reading it, the Emperor [(Xuanzong)] expressed his approval and ordered the making of over ten copies for the crown prince and others.[20]

Besides improving the availability of the *Essentials* by increasing the number of its copies, Emperor Xuanzong's instructions reveal intentions for further study and usage of the *Essentials*. His order for the *Essentials* to be copied and given to the crown prince indicates a high level of personal approval and recommendation of the text for the education and training of his successor. This direction echoes the order of Taizong, who also had copies of the *Essentials* made for his sons. Extraction of the *Old Master* excerpts in the *Essentials* implies that those parts had collectively acquired an independent value and utility.

The *Essentials* was presented to Emperor Dezong by the official Li Mi 李密 (722–789) in or around 780. The incident is recorded by the *Ocean of Jades*' excerpt from the *Family Accounts of Prince Ye* (*Ye hou jiazhuan* 鄴侯家傳) as follows:

Emperor [Dezong] said, "We would like to know about the essentials of the traditional governing principles, but the historical writings are extensive, and ultimately difficult to thoroughly research. Which books shall We read?"

In reply: "In the past, Wei Zheng summarized the teachings and principles from divers texts for Emperor Taizong in a compilation of fifty scrolls that was entitled *Qunshu liyao*.' There is currently a copy in the Hall of Scholarly Worthies. Also, Suzong's chancellor Pei Zunqing wrote about the accomplished and failed administrations of emperors and kings from high antiquity to the Zhenguan reign-period in sixty scrolls that were entitled, '*Wangzheng ji*' ... As the texts are available, may Your servant present them for Your perusal?"

The Emperor said, "That would be most excellent and they should be submitted at once." The texts were then presented.[21]

It would appear from the above interaction that Li Mi presented the *Essentials* to Emperor Dezong for learning traditional governing principles. Although we lack further details as to whether Dezong read the *Essentials*, and what he thought about it, the anthology was at least known to him and his court officials. Given that Li Mi served the courts of four consecutive Tang emperors—Xuanzong, Suzong 肅宗 (r. 756–762), Daizong 代宗 (r. 762–779), and Dezong—his familiarity with the contents and location of the *Essentials* would suggest that the text continued to be accessible for and studied by officials during Li Mi's long period of government service.

The *Essentials* was commended to Emperor Xianzong in a memorial by the Hanlin Academician Li Jiang sometime in the early ninth century as follows:

> In the past, Taizong also instructed Wei Zheng et al. to comprehensively select the deeds from each era and compile the *Qunshu zhengyao*. [Taizong] kept the text beside his seat and he would constantly study and reflect on it ... Your servants have carefully transcribed all fifty articles of the wise, the foolish, the successes, and the failures, onto two scrolls. Hereby presented is the *Qunshu zhengyao*, a text that was read by Taizong himself and its contents are comprehensive. Your servants humbly hope that the administration of governance improves with each day to become an everlasting dynasty and effect effortless transformations.[22]

It is notable that Li Jiang emphasizes the extent to which Taizong used the *Essentials*—he is said to have kept the text by his side for constant study and reflection. Throughout his career, Li Jiang served the emperors Dezong, Shunzong 順宗 (r. 805), Xianzong, Muzong 穆宗 (r. 820–824), Jingzong 敬宗 (r. 824–827), and Wenzong 文宗 (r. 827–840) of the Tang dynasty. As such, his knowledge of and regard for the *Essentials* provides evidence that the anthology was well-known and valued among officials through to the late Tang period.

The recentralizing efforts of Dezong and Xianzong during the late Tang were presumably informed by the *Essentials* that was recommended by their respective officials, as well as Wu Jing's *Zhenguan Essentials*.[23] According to the *Old History of the Tang Dynasty*, Emperor Xianzong admired both Taizong and Xuanzong, and was an avid reader of their administrations, having studied the court records of the good governance of their Zhenguan and Kaiyuan 開元 (713–741) periods from the outset of his reign.[24] In the second year of his reign, Xianzong humbly recognized his inferiority to Taizong and Xuanzong in governmental affairs and reminded his court officials of the need for their criticism.[25] That Xianzong enjoyed discussing court matters with his officials, encouraged them to remonstrate, and expressed displeasure when they did not join in debates,[26] resonates with the transmitted narratives about the Zhenguan ruler being receptive to remonstrance. Indeed, Xianzong is known for presiding over "the nearest re-creation of the Zhenguan court" in the late Tang dynasty.[27] Clearly, the cultural memory of the *Essentials* being the cultural knowledge that the Zhenguan ruler and his court deemed salient to statecraft is distinct from their exemplary practice of government. Nonetheless, the fact that both emperors Dezong and Xianzong knew about the *Essentials* and had the political will to follow Taizong's example makes it eminently probable that the *Essentials* was used by them and thereby reinstated to the active working memory during their respective reigns.

The *Essentials* appears to have been transmitted beyond the imperial library in the capital during the Tang dynasty. An incomplete copy of the *Essentials*' annotated excerpts from the *Zuo Tradition* dating to the reign of Emperor Gaozong was discovered among the Dunhuang manuscripts in 1921 by Marc Aurel Stein (1862–1943).[28] Identified as "S.133," it contains 127 lines of text about events from the fourth, ninth, eleventh, fourteenth, twenty-first, twenty-third, and twenty-fifth years of the reign of Lord Xiang 襄 of Lu and is currently kept at the British Library.[29] Scholars including Wang Zhongmin 王重民 and Chen Tiefan 陳鐵凡 surmise that S.133 was likely copied from the *Essentials* for private schooling purposes.[30] Based on its variant text, the S.133 manuscript is thought to date to, or be produced from a source that dates to, the early Tang period before the reign of Empress Wu Zhao 武曌 (also known as Wu Zetian 武則天) (r. 690–705).[31] The existence of S.133 indicates that this part of the *Essentials* had circulated more broadly than the central court in the reign-period immediately following Zhenguan and had acquired a separate utility from the text as a whole. Additionally, that the Commandant of Jingyang in Changzhou Yang Xiangru recommended the *Essentials* to Xuanzong is further evidence of the *Essentials* being read outside of the capital.

No one seems to know precisely how or why the *Essentials* became non-extant around the fourteenth century. However, its physical disappearance is approximately traceable among available records, and the notion of cultural forgetting assists an understanding of how the text was circulated and classified after the Tang dynasty. The *Essentials* is attested in bibliographic sources dating from the ninth century to the nineteenth century, as set out in Table 4.1. Such traces of the *Essentials* reveal four points of note.

Table 4.1. References to the *Essentials* in the extant literature

Date of completion	Author(s) or compiler(s)	Title
c. 820	Liu Su 劉肅 (fl. 806–820)	*New Anecdotes from the Tang Dynasty* (*Tang xinyu* 唐新語)[232]
c. 850	Jiang Jie 蔣偕 (*fl.* 800–899)	*Collected Essays of Li Xiangguo* (*Li Xiangguo lunshiji* 李相國論事集)[233]
945	Liu Xu 劉昫 (888–946) et al.	*Old History of the Tang Dynasty*[234]
961	Wang Pu 王溥 (922–982)	*Essential Records of the Tang Dynasty*[235]
1013	Wang Qinruo 王欽若 (962–1025) et al.	*Outstanding Models from the Storehouse of Literature* (*Cefu yuangui* 冊府元龜)[236]
1060	Ouyang Xiu 歐陽修 (1007–1072) et al.	*New History of the Tang Dynasty*[237]
1149	Zheng Qiao 鄭樵 (1108–1166)	*Universal Treatise* (*Tong zhi* 通志)[238]
c. 1198	Zhang Ruyu 章如愚 (*fl.* c. 1198)	*Critical Compilation of Divers Books* (*Qunshu kaosuo* 群書考索)[239]
c. 1255	Wang Yinglin 王應麟 (1223–1296)	*Ocean of Jades* (*Yu hai* 玉海)[240]

(Continued)

Table 4.1. continued.

Date of completion	Author(s) or compiler(s)	Title
1345	Tuoketuo 托克托 (1313–1355) et al.	*History of the Song Dynasty* (*Song shi* 宋史)[241]
1416	Huang Huai 黃淮 (1367–1449) et al.	*Memorials of Leading Officials of Each Period* (*Lidai mingchen zouyi* 歷代名臣奏議)[242]
c. 1574	Ke Weiqi 柯維騏 (1497–1574)	*Revised History of the Song Dynasty* (*Song shi xinbian* 宋史新編)[243]
1590	Jiao Hong 焦竑 (1541–1620)	*Monograph on National History, Classics, and Literature* (*Guo shi jing ji zhi* 國史經籍志)[244]
1702	Zhang Ying 張英 (1638–1708) and Wang Shizhen 王士禎 (1634–1711)	*Imperially-commissioned Categorized Writings in the Library of Deep Insight* (*Yuding yuanjian leihan* 御定淵鑒類函)[245]
1728	Chen Menglei 陳夢雷 (1669–1732) et al.	*Comprehensive Corpus of Illustrations and Books from Past to Present* (*Gujin tushu jicheng* 古今圖書集成)[246]
c. 1736	Qi Zengjun 嵇曾筠 (*fl.* 1706) et al.	*Zhejiang Gazetteer* (*Zhejiang tong zhi* 浙江通志)[247]
c. 1807	Ruan Yuan 阮元 (1764–1849)	*Bibliographical abstracts for the collection of books not included in the Four Branches [of Literature]* (*Siku weishou shumu tiyao* 四庫未收書目提要)[248]
1814	Dong Gao 董誥 (1740–1818) et al.	*Imperially-authorized Complete Anthology of Tang Dynasty Prose* (*Qinding quan Tang wen* 欽定全唐文)[249]

First, the *Essentials* formed a part of the palace library collection until the fourteenth century. The relevant monographs of the *Old History of the Tang Dynasty*,[32] the *New History of the Tang Dynasty*,[33] and the *History of the Song Dynasty*,[34] include entries about the *Essentials* and its complete or incomplete status. Such records cannot tell us whether the text was accessed or read, nor offer specifics as to how it was used. However, the bibliographical records would suggest that the *Essentials* remained extant in its entirety until sometime around the early eleventh century, as there is no record of it in the *Catalogue of the Institute for Venerating Culture* (*Chongwen zongmu* 崇文總目), which was the catalogue of the Song dynasty imperial library compiled by Wang Yaochen 王堯臣 (1001–1056) in 1042.[35]

Second, the *Essentials* remained in circulation outside of the imperial library after the Tang dynasty. After the palace library collection was obliterated by the Jingkang Incident (1125–1127) that ended the Northern Song dynasty, the founder of the Southern Song dynasty—Emperor Gaozong 高宗 (r. 1127–1129)—in 1142 ordered for the palace library to be replenished with texts procured by reference to the Tang histories and the latest library catalogue—that is, the *Catalogue of the Institute for Venerating Culture*.[36] The palace library collection was then catalogued anew in 1178 by the *Catalogue of the Imperial Library of the Southern Song* (*Zhongxing guange shumu*中興館閣書目).[37] Whereas the *Essentials* had been absent from the earlier *Catalogue of the Institute for Venerating Culture*, the record of an incomplete copy of the *Essentials* appears in the later *Catalogue of the Imperial Library of the Southern Song*. Such a reappearance implies that the incomplete *Essentials* was derived from a source outside of the palace library, which further supports the broader circulation of the *Essentials*. That only ten scrolls were recoverable suggests that the *Essentials* was by then no longer wholly extant. While the *Catalogue of the Imperial Library of the Southern Song* has not survived, its record concerning the *Essentials* is excerpted by the *Ocean of Jades* encyclopedia as follows:

> Ten scrolls. The Palace Library records an original [of the *Essentials*] by a Tang calligrapher that dates to the seventh year of the Qiandao reign-period (1171), a manuscript copy of which is stored. The scrolls number from eleven to twenty. The rest have not survived.[38]

The ten scrolls specified by the *Catalogue of the Imperial Library of the Southern Song* is consistent with the record in the Monograph on Arts and Letters of the *History of the Song Dynasty* that only ten scrolls of the *Essentials* remained in the Palace Library in 1345.[39] Hence, it appears that the anthology initially became incomplete and then lost altogether in China sometime after the late Yuan dynasty (1271–1368).

Third, the *Essentials* was classified differently at different times. It was assigned to various bibliographical categories as follows:

- the syncretists (*zajia lei* 雜家類) by the Tang histories that date from the ninth to the tenth centuries;
- the masters (*zhuzi lei* 諸子類) by the *Universal Treatise*[40] and the *Critical Compilation of Divers Books*[41] in the twelfth century;
- the encyclopedic anthologies (*leishu lei* 類書類) by the *Ocean of Jades*,[42] the *History of the Song Dynasty*,[43] and the *Revised History of the Song Dynasty*[44] that date from the thirteenth to the sixteenth centuries;
- the masters by the *Monograph on National History, Classics and Literature*[45] and the *Zhejiang Gazetteer*[46] that date from the late sixteenth to the eighteenth centuries, and
- the syncretists by the *Bibliographical abstracts for the collection of books not included in the Four Branches* [*of Literature*] in the early nineteenth century.[47]

Such variation in classification implies that the nature of the anthology was regarded differently by authors or compilers over time. The category of syncretist writings recognizes that the political discourse of the *Essentials* is compiled from sources of various intellectual and ideological orientations. The category of masters reflects the *Essentials*' distinctive Confucian outlook, and perhaps its inclusion of the masters writings from the pre-Qin period. Interestingly, the encyclopedic anthologies' classification of the *Essentials* may be read in different ways. The Chinese term "*leishu* 類書" literally means "category books" and such encyclopedic anthologies are typically characterized by bringing together a body of knowledge that is classified by category and composed of extracts from preexisting texts.[48] On this reading, the *leishu* classification would seem to be a misnomer for the *Essentials*. The *Essentials* does not resemble such a *leishu* because its contents are arranged by source rather than by subject. Nor can the *Essentials* be used as such a *leishu* repository of quotable material, in light of its text having been excerpted to convey Confucian-oriented ideas of statecraft and thus no longer directly representative of their respective sources. With the *Essentials* being neither organized nor usable as a *leishu* as described above, that designation would indicate that the *Essentials*' unique design and intended usage was not fully appreciated in the period from the thirteenth to the sixteen centuries. The overall variability in the categorizing of the *Essentials* would seem to be a symptom of its wavering status within the cultural memory, passively fading away around the fourteenth century when it became completely non-extant. Such cultural forgetting of the *Essentials* was no doubt accelerated by its gradual physical absence. On the other hand, the divergences between bibliographical lists of *leishu* and the differences in the content of those works make the "encyclopedic anthologies" classification relatively loose.[49] Hence, one might read the *Essentials* in the *leishu* category as a sign of the flexibility of that classification, with its meaning evolving to accommodate anthologies of less typical configurations.[50]

Finally, although the *Essentials* became culturally forgotten and non-extant, Wei Zheng's preface survived in the archive of cultural reference memory. Copies of Wei Zheng's preface to the *Essentials* are found in both the *Outstanding Models from the Storehouse of Literature*[51] and the *Imperially-authorized Complete Anthology of Tang Dynasty Prose*.[52] This meant that while the actual contents of the *Essentials* became lost, some memory of their historical existence was preserved through its contemporary paratext.

The likelihood of some references to the *Essentials* in the above literature being based on descriptions in earlier writings about the anthology rather than a first-hand experience of the text itself cannot be ruled out. It is also possible that further references to the *Essentials* and its usage are untraceable because the sources of its excerpts are cited instead of the anthology.

The *Essentials* was exposed to the risk of physical loss and damage due to its limited readership and circulation. Commissioned by Emperor Taizong primarily for his reference, with copies additionally ordered for his princes, there was a finite number of copies of the *Essentials* from the outset. Its location in the palace library meant that access was, in principle, restricted to the ruler and his officials.[53] Unlike other compilations like the *Standard Editions of the Five Classics* that formed part of the formal curriculum for aspiring officials, the *Essentials* was not intended for general circulation among the wider community. With the historical records only showing that Emperors Taizong and Xuanzong ordered copies for their princes,[54] and the S.133 Dunhuang manuscript of the *Essentials*' excerpts from the *Zuo Tradition* being an isolated discovery to date, the readership of the *Essentials* seems largely confined to the higher echelons of power during Tang China. Besides the above-mentioned emperors, courtiers, and princes, the anthology was presumably known to those officials charged with educating the princes during the reigns of Taizong and Xuanzong, as well as those working in the Department of the Palace Library while the *Essentials* formed part of its collection. The fact that a relatively narrow group of people were aware of the *Essentials*, combined with the few manuscript copies of it in existence, meant that the text was more at risk of being culturally forgotten and lost over time. Besides the incremental loss and damage that might be caused by general wear and tear, mould, mice, and insects, the palace library collections were decimated by the turmoil of political violence during the An Lushan Rebellion (755–763), the Huang Chao Rebellion (874–884), and the upheavals at the end of the Tang dynasty and during the Five Dynasties period (907–960), as well as devastating fires in the years 1015, 1228, and 1231. The absence of historical records showing intentional acts of destruction or suppression directed towards the *Essentials* negates the likelihood of the text being actively forgotten. However, the anthology would have been passively forgotten where its copies suffered damage, either in whole or in part, due to the impact of natural and human-made disasters on the imperial library collection.

As a text of China's manuscript age, the *Essentials* would only survive physical destruction if later generations had reason to copy and transmit it.[55] As there was an overall decline in the authority of the central government after the Zhenguan years, the Zhenguan model was largely ignored, and there was arguably insufficient political will to preserve its *Essentials*. For example, before the An Lushan rebellion, the central court was more often than not overshadowed by the influence of imperial relatives, the use of private secretariats, and the roles of specialist commissioners and eunuch assistants, as exemplified by the rulerships of Wu Zhao[56] and Xuanzong.[57] By the end of the An Lushan rebellion, Tang imperial authority had become decentralized, with the empire reduced to a patchwork of virtually autonomous provinces.[58] The government became dominated by eunuchs and dependent on provincial governors,[59] with the power struggles among them ultimately precipitating the demise of the Tang ruling house in 907.[60] These conditions of later Tang courts arguably militated against the ideal court dynamics discoursed by the *Essentials* and manifested to a degree during the Zhenguan period. Liao Yifang observes that the Tang emperors after Dezong and Xianzong stopped trying to follow the exemplary rulers of antiquity, and felt that the Zhenguan exemplar was beyond their ability.[61] Such historical backdrop goes some way to explaining why the *Essentials* was relegated to political obscurity, with its existence being mostly culturally forgotten for the rest of the Tang dynasty.

In light of the limited readership, circulation and preservation of the *Essentials* in China, the absence of sufficient copies to secure its continuous local transmission may, on balance, be more likely due to later generations of ruling elite not knowing, rather than not wishing to know, about the text. This finding may be corroborated by the sustained and widespread interest in the Zhenguan practice of government within China, as well as Japan, Korea, and Vietnam (collectively, "East Asia"). The transmission of the *Essentials* reached Japan, Korea, and Vietnam, as discussed in Section 4.2, and nearly all imperial courts in China and East Asia studied the *Zhenguan Essentials*,[62] as discussed in the Conclusion.

After several centuries of absence in China, the *Essentials* was restored for a time to the cultural working memory by the reintroduction of various editions from Japan during the reigns of Emperor Jiaqing 嘉慶 (r. 1796–1820), Emperor Daoguang 道光 (r. 1820–1850), and Emperor Guangxu 光緒 (r. 1871–1908) of the Qing dynasty. The *Essentials* came to form part of Jiaqing's reading collection shortly after its reintroduction and also the curriculum of formal learning for officialdom by the end of the nineteenth century. At the same time, the anthology was also restored to the cultural reference memory and experienced various shifts of meaning.

On learning that the *Essentials* was no longer extant on its native shores, Tokugawa Munechika 徳川宗睦 (1733–1800), who ruled the Owari domain in Japan, wished to share an extant edition with the imperial library and academies in China, and hopefully discover further editions outside of Japan.[63] Munechika arranged for Kondō Morishige to send the Kansei edition to China and three copies were dispatched via the Nagasaki customs office in 1796.[64] A further 18 copies of the *Essentials* were imported from Japan between the years 1817 to 1825 according to historical records in the *Various Accounts of Events related to the Arrival of Chinese Junks at Port* (*Tōsen shinkō narabi ni zatsuji no bu* 唐船進港并ニ雜事之部) from the *Sequel on the History of Nagasaki* (*Nagasakishi zokuhen* 長崎志續編).[65] Those copies are thought to be the Tenmei edition based on their publication in the year of 1787.[66]

A Kansei edition was included in the *Exclusive Collection of Wanwei* (*Wanwei biecang* 宛委別藏), a collection of rare books compiled by Ruan Yuan to supplement the *Complete Library of the Four Branches of Literature*. The bibliographical abstract for the *Essentials* prepared by Ruan Yuan points to two applications of the anthology. First, the *Essentials* presents the essentials for bringing about order in plain language with comprehensive coverage and relevant exhortations and admonitions. The compilation's original function as a statecraft reference was thus recognized upon its reappearance in Qing China. Second, the *Essentials* could be put to use in collating and reconstructing the works out of which it was originally compiled. This stems from the fact that by the time of the Qing dynasty, some of the anthology's sources either differed in form or had become non-extant altogether. The relevant passage from Ruan Yuan's bibliographical abstract is as follows:

> Considering the contents [of the *Essentials*] today, it is principally concerned with the essentials for bringing about order, which are expressed in an unadorned style. It is a compilation of everything related to the art of governance, including advice and admonitions. [The excerpts] of its various composite titles are from reliable early Tang editions that differ considerably from recent publications. For example, the *History of the Jin Dynasty* (in two scrolls) is [derived from] one of the eighteen editions that preceded the current *History of the Jin Dynasty*. Also, much of the *New Discourses* by Huan Tan, the *Essay on Government* by Cui Shi, the *Admirable*

> *Words of Zhong Zhangzi* by Zhong Zhangtong, the *Political Writings* by Yuan Zhun, the *Discourse on Myriad Subtleties* by Jiang Ji, and the *Discourse on the Essentials of Governing* by Huan Fan have become non-extant in recent times. As truly ancient texts in the early Tang, [the *Essentials*] may be used to recover their rough outline.[67]

Presented to Emperor Jiaqing sometime during the years 1807 to 1811,[68] the *Exclusive Collection of Wanwei* was stored in the Hall of the Cultivating Heart (*yangxin dian* 養心殿) which served as the emperor's residence and the center of governmental administration and cultural activities.[69] During the 1920s, the *Exclusive Collection of Wanwei* was discovered to be located directly behind the dragon throne in the Hall of the Cultivating Heart.[70] A record of the imperial reception of the *Exclusive Collection of Wanwei* is found in the *Notes From an Immortal's Boat* (*Yingzhou bitan* 瀛舟筆談), an assemblage of Ruan Yuan's personal and professional papers collected by his cousin and long-term staff member Ruan Heng 阮亨 (1783–1856):[71]

> Winter of 1807: Attended the imperial court in an audience with the emperor, who has browsed the [rare books] presented; received the favour of perusal and much reward.[72]

Ruan Yuan's bibliographical abstract, the location of the *Exclusive Collection of Wanwei* and the contemporaneous record by Ruan Yuan's staff, when read together are indicative of two matters. First, the collection of rare and recovered writings was, in all likelihood, positively received and actually consulted by Emperor Jiaqing. Second, the *Essentials* was plausibly read by the emperor as a valuable statecraft text rather than simply another rare book. Moreover, during the reign of Emperor Guangxu 光緒 (posthumously titled Dezong 德宗), the *Essentials* formed part of the first question of the palace examination in 1884. The *Veritable Records of Emperor Dezong (posthumously titled "Jing") of the Qing Dynasty* (*Qing Dezong shilu* 清德宗皇帝實錄) provides:

> 1884: The imperial examination for all 319 candidates including Liu Pei in the Hall of Preserving Harmony. The imperial announcement [is as follows]: … You scholars who come from the fields, study ancient teachings,

> and are deeply concerned about the present times. Here, you are to submit your essays before the main hall and respectfully listen to Our words. In the education of correct development for emperors and kings, the investigation [of things] and extension [of knowledge] comes first. As for the *Model for an Emperor*, the *Essentials for Bringing about Order from Assembled Texts*, the *Imperial Learning*, can you relate their essential meanings? Who composed the *Essentials of Governance from the Zhenguan Reign* and the *Imperial Readings of the Taiping Era*? As for the *Further Record of Remonstrations by Wei Zheng*, has it benefited the government? Besides, what are the strengths and shortcomings of [Lord Fan Wenzheng's] *Memorials on Government*, the *Collection of Exhaustive Speeches*, the *Memorials of Leading Officials of Each Period*? Learning from the ancients is the root of practising governance. Teaching about the military is the method of preparedness. Establishing strategic passes is the cornerstone of founding the country. Casting currency is the essence of managing resources. You scholars [must] articulate responses accordingly. Neither mix nor merge. We will personally review.[73]

Restored to the palace library collection not long after being rediscovered in the Qing dynasty meant that the *Essentials* would have been known and accessible to its rulers and their respective courts. The anthology was evidently valued as an imperial reader, as it was referred to alongside other examinable statecraft literature in the highest civil service examination. Moreover, the *Essentials* was conceivably circulated among the wider community in sufficient quantities to be studied by examination candidates as part of their formal training and preparation for undertaking the imperial examinations. Such importance attributed to the *Essentials* signals that the anthology was reused to some extent in defining the cultural identity of Qing China following its reintroduction. Hence, it could be said that the *Essentials* was restored to the active dimension of cultural memory for a time during the Qing dynasty.

The *Essentials*' utility for purposes of textual collation and reconstruction was recognised in Ruan Yuan's bibliographical abstract. But it had already been put to such use in the twenty-first collection of the *Collectanea of the Studio of Knowing One's Deficiencies* (*Zhi buzu zhai congshu* 知不足齋叢書) compiled by the Qing bibliophile Bao Tingbo 鮑廷博 (1728–1814) in 1801. That collection contained *Zheng Xuan's Commentary on the Classic of Family Reverence* (*Xiaojing Zheng zhu* 孝經鄭注), a text that had been non-extant but was reconstructed from its excerpts in the *Essentials* by the Japanese scholar Okada Noboyuki 岡田挺之 (dates unknown).[74] As *Zheng's Commentary* had long been non-extant in China, some scholars harbored doubts as to the authenticity of Okada's edition. However, such doubts were quelled by the philologist Qian Tong 錢侗 (b. 1778), who was familiar with a Tenmei edition of the *Essentials*, and his preface to the reprint of *Zheng's Commentary* was included in the *Collectanea of the Studio of Knowing One's Deficiencies*.[75] The *Essentials*' excerpts from its sources and their annotations provide a resource for the reconstruction of other pre-Tang writings. The sources that have become non-extant include: the *History of the Jin Dynasty* (*Jin shu* 晉書) by Zang Rongxu 臧榮緒 (415–488); *Master Shi* (*Shi zi* 尸子) by Shi Jiao 尸佼 (*c.* 330 BCE); *Master Shen* (*Shen zi* 申子) by Shen Buhai 申不害 (d. *c.* 337 BCE); the *New Discourses of Master Huan* (*Huan zi Xinlun* 桓子新論) by Huan Tan 桓譚 (*c.* 43 BCE–28 CE); *Cui Shi's Essay on Government* (*Cui Shi Zhenglun* 崔寔政論) by Cui Shi 崔寔 (*c.* 110–170); the *Admirable Words of Zhong Zhangzi* (*Zhong Zhangzi Chang yan* 昌言) by Zhong Zhangtong 仲長統 (b. *c.* 180); the *Authoritative Discourses* (*Dian lun* 典論) by Cao Pi 曹丕 (187–226); the *Political Discourse of Liu Yi* (*Liu Yi Zheng lun* 劉廙政論) by Liu Yi 劉廙 (c. 181–221); the *Balanced Discourses* (*Zhong lun* 中論) by Xu Gan 徐幹 (171–*c.* 218); *Master Jiang's Discourse on Myriad Subtleties* (*Jiang zi Wanji lun* 蔣子萬機論) by Jiang Ji 蔣濟 (d. 249); the *Discourses on the Essentials of Governing* (*Zhengyao lun* 政要論) by Huan Fan 桓範 (d. 249); the *Structural Discourses* (*Ti lun* 體論) by Du Shu 杜恕 (198–252); the *Discourses on Contemporary Affairs* (*Shiwu lun* 時務論) by Yang Wei 楊偉 (d. 52); the *Normative Discourses* (*Dian yu* 典語) by Lu Jing 陸景 (249–280); *Master Fu* (Fu zi 傅子) by Fu Xuan 傅玄 (217–278), and the *Political Writings of Master Yuan* (*Yuan zi zheng shu* 袁子正書) by Yuan Zhun 袁準 (*fl.* 250–265). Indeed, the Qing bibliographer Sun Xingyan 孫星衍 (1753–1818) was one of the first to use the *Essentials* to reconstruct lost texts. The following colophon to Sun's reconstructed *Master Shi*, published in 1806, confirms that the reconstruction was based on a copy of the *Essentials* obtained from the Japanese customs office:[76]

> The *Shizi* was published in 1799. After its printing, [it] went to the family home of Director [Sun] Fengyi. After several years, Metropolitan exam

> graduate Mr. Zhuang Shuzu inherited Hui Dong's reconstructed text. About the same time, Minister of Revenue Xu Zongyan obtained Wei Zheng's *Qunshu zhiyao* from within the Japanese customs office. Because [it] recorded the 'Exhortation to Learn' [chapter] and others [from the *Shizi*] in thirteen chapters, [he] sent [it] to me, and when I had read the ancient text [I saw it] also had several old chapter [titles] that had been lost. Relying on [my] subordinate, Classicist Hong Yixuan, [I had it] re-edited in two sections and once again published [it] in Jinan, still using the previous preface and appending this summary at the end of the [preface] section. Recorded on the twenty-ninth day of the fifth month of 1806 by [Sun] Xingyan.[77]

How the *Essentials* was used for textual collation in the works of late Qing scholars is set out in Wang Weijia's master's thesis.[78] Kim's doctoral dissertation details the non-extant commentaries and sub-commentaries excerpted in the *Essentials*' annotations.[79] That the *Essentials* was reproduced in further collective works from the nineteenth century through to the twenty-first century reflects the sustained scholarly interest and usage of the anthology, not least for collating editions and reconstructing non-extant works. Reprints of the *Essentials* are found in the *Library Series of the Hall of Canton Elegance* (*Yueya tang congshu* 粤雅堂叢書) in its third reprint dated 1857,[80] the *Four Branches of Literature Collection* dated 1919,[81] and the *Corpus of Works from Collectanea* (*Congshu jicheng* 叢書集成) in its first edition dated 1937.[82] The *Essentials* has also been reproduced within new and reprinted collectanea, as exemplified by the reprints of the *Exclusive Collection from Wanwei* in 1988,[83] the *Four Branches of Literature Collection* in 1989,[84] and the *Continuation of the Complete Library of the Four Branches of Literature* (*Xuxiu Siku quanshu* 續修四庫全書) in 2002.[85]

The publication of numerous editions with vernacular translation and punctuation in recent years suggests that the readership and study of the anthology have extended to non-specialists. Those editions include the *Classical-vernacular Essentials for Bringing about Order from Assembled Texts* (*Wenbai duizhao Qunshu zhiyao* 文白對照群書治要),[86] the *Annotated Translation of the Essentials for Bringing about Order from Assembled Texts* (*Qunshu zhiyao yizhu* 群書治要譯註),[87] and the *Essential Record of the Essentials for Bringing about Order from Assembled Texts* (*Qunshu zhiyao jinghua lu* 群書治要精華錄).[88] Contemporary scholars have composed supplements in place of the three non-extant scrolls, namely, scrolls 3, 14, and 21, as published in the *Revised Edition of the Essentials for Bringing about Order from Assembled Texts* (*Qunshu zhiyao jiaoding ben* 群書治要校訂本) dated 2015,[89] and published a sequel to the *Essentials* entitled, the *Continuation of the Essentials for Bringing about Order from Assembled Texts* (*Qunshu zhiyao xubian* 群書治要續編) in 2021.[90] Following the structure and style of its predecessor, the *Continuation of the Essentials* comprises eight volumes that are internally divided into 50 scrolls of excerpts selected from 66 texts. Its sources date from the Northern and Southern dynasties to Qing China, including standard histories and masters writings found in the *Complete Library of the Four Branches of Literature* and the *Continuation of the Complete Library of the Four Branches of Literature*, and are accompanied by annotations and vernacular Chinese translation. A shift of meaning has therefore been experienced by the *Essentials* becoming an academic reference for textual and other studies.

The last decade alone has witnessed the appropriation of a vernacularized *Essentials* for popular culture. Its Chinese editions have been reconfigured in various ways and translated into several international languages to enhance accessibility for non-specialist readers in the form of self-help literature. Since 2012, the *Qunshu zhiyao 360* series have presented the anthology in a digestible "quote for the day" fashion, with each volume containing 360 selected passages that have been abridged, translated, and topically arranged. The topics include "The Way of a Leader," "The Art of a Minister," and "Esteeming Virtues." Appendix 3 contains bibliographical details of the various editions of the *Qunshu zhiyao 360* series. That the *Qunshu zhiyao 360* series is available in Arabic, Chinese, English, French, German, Japanese, Russian, Spanish, and Vietnamese languages may serve as an indicator of contemporary interest and readership. In 2020, the content of the first three volumes of the *Qunshu zhiyao 360* in Chinese was republished as a single book with a new title to emphasize the applicability of its contents to modern society: *Wisdom of the Qunshu zhiyao for [Self] Cultivation, [Family] Harmony, [State] Governance, and [Global] Peace* (*Qunshu zhiyao zhong xiu qi zhi ping de zhihui* 群書治要中修齊治平的智慧).[91] This edition aims to improve readability by organizing the information under categories appealing to contemporary readers who may not necessarily be politicians. Those categories include parenting, harmony among spouses, and health and well-being. There are also Chinese books that aim to glean lessons from the *Essentials* for the leadership and management of modern organizations and enterprise, as exemplified by the *Reflections on the Essentials for Bringing about Order from Assembled Texts* (*Qunshu zhiyao* xinde 群書治要心得) by Xiao Xiangjian 蕭祥劍.[92] A digest of practical learnings interpreted by reference to 17 topics, Xiao's book has been translated into Korean.[93] A selection of the historical anecdotes featured in the *Essentials* was published as a standalone book: *Ancient Mirror for Modern Reflection* (*Gujing jinjian* 古鏡今鑒) in 2013, with vernacular Chinese translation and thematic chapters.[94] It could be said that these publications reflect a growing interest in learning about the *Essentials* among readers who need not be familiar with the classical Chinese language, or with the various sources by which the anthology was originally arranged.[95] Such appropriation of the *Essentials* constitutes a shift of meaning as the medieval statecraft reference has become a modern self-help guide for leadership, management, and personal development.

These modern adaptations of the *Essentials* illustrate the dynamic nature of memory and how those who remember, in whatever time or place, interact with the formative past precisely from their own situatedness in the present. The mnemonic practices involve a process of negotiation between continuity and durability, and change and malleability. While the Zhenguan cultural memory becomes relatively durable by being housed in the text of various editions,[96] the material of those houses is itself exposed to some risk of loss and damage, albeit much less than in the manuscript age, as books nowadays may be reproduced from scanned copies. There is continuity in the sense that the various vernacular translations and self-help versions of the *Essentials* are produced from its extant editions and based on the same cultural narratives, symbols, and concepts. So, how has the cultural memory enshrined in the text changed? The modern adaptations vary markedly in terms of their contents. The *Essentials* has been abridged for accessibility and supplemented with annotations, punctuation, and vernacular translation for intelligibility. It has been both extended in the form of a sequel and reduced to just its anecdotes or a selected 360 passages per volume. While some renditions cater to the needs of time-poor modern readers who may lack proficiency in classical Chinese and its typical distillation of dense cultural and intertextual references, other changes in the *Essentials* are symptomatic of its memory being actively shaped by popular culture.[97] The fact that the *Essentials*' contents are variously reconstituted to align with present realities may reflect the mosaic-like character of memory, where parts of the inherited past are often being pieced together to produce new mnemonic frameworks.[98] And how has the cultural memory in the *Essentials* been malleable? According to David Lowenthal, the remembered past is malleable and flexible as those who remember will reshape it according to contemporary needs.[99] The malleability of the *Essentials* is manifest in both its material form and format. Whereas Emperor Taizong was probably presented with scrolls of manuscript on paper,[100] the *Essentials* is now available printed in electronic, paperback, hardback, or threadbound editions, with its physical dimensions ranging from A4 and A5, to full-screen, bookmark, and pocket size. Indeed, some English volumes of the *Qunshu zhiyao 360* series have been reproduced as pocketbooks, as well as sets of 360 bookmarks.[101] The format of the *Essentials* has diversified to include punctuation, translation, vernacular annotation, and topical arrangement. Reading between the lines of such modern editions, the editorial choices inherent in their production are ubiquitous—from which topics to arrange the contents by and how to punctuate the sentences, to what details may be excluded from the abridgment. Such choices inevitably modify the inherited knowledge to a certain degree, but they are necessitated at least in part, because the cultural universe of the remembering present is constantly evolving.[102] As Barry Swartz writes:

> The present is constituted by the past, but the past's retention as well as its reconstruction, must be anchored in the present. As each generation modifies the beliefs presented by previous generations, an assemblage of old beliefs coexists with the new, including old beliefs about the past itself.[103]

The vernacular translations and self-help renditions of the *Essentials* thus indicate new perceptions of and engagements with the cultural memory inscribed in the statecraft guide to imperial discourse from the Zhenguan years of Tang China.

A further shift of meaning can be seen in the masters excerpts of the *Essentials* being circulated as a separate text. Two examples are found in the *Essentials for Bringing about Order from the Various Masters* (*Zhuzi zhiyao* 諸子治要) and the *Epitome of Masters from the Essentials for Bringing about Order from Assembled Texts* (*Qunshu zhiyao zichao* 羣書治要子鈔). For example, China's late ambassador and Vice Minister of Foreign Affairs Fu Hao recalled having studied the former at the village school in his youth during the late 1920s.[104] The oldest edition of the *Essentials for Bringing about Order from the Various Masters* that I have located is a first edition published in 1962 and appears to include the entire masters section of the *Essentials*.[105] The *Epitome of Masters from the Essentials for Bringing about Order* is an abridgment of certain parts of the masters section in the *Essentials*, starting from *Master Guan* and concluding with *Master Han*. The only edition that I have found of that text is from the *Collectanea from the Studio of Seeking Truth* (*Qiushi zhai congshu* 求實齋叢書), which dates to the reign of Emperor Guangxu and is reprinted in the *Continuation of the Corpus of Works from Collectanea* published in 1989.[106] The existence of those two editions suggests that those parts of the *Essentials* had acquired an independent value for schooling purposes following its reintroduction to Chinese society.

Since the latter half of the twentieth century, further editions of the *Essentials* transmitted from Japan, reprints of the *Essentials* within the above and later collectanea, and the local production of vernacular translations point to the *Essentials* acquiring different meanings within the cultural reference memory. There have been other editions of the *Essentials* transmitted to China from Japan since the Qing era. Two hundred years after the reintroduction of the *Essentials*, Fu Hao received a photographic reprint of the Tenmei edition from a member of the Japanese royal household in 1996.[107] This edition was subsequently collated, annotated, punctuated, and published with vernacular Chinese translation as the *Philological Translation of the Essentials for Bringing About Order from Assembled Texts* (*Qunshu zhiyao kaoyi* 群書治要考譯).[108] It seems significant that the *Philological Translation of the Essentials* includes the Chinese calligraphy writing "Ancient mirror for modern reflection" (*Gu jing jin jian* 古鏡今鑒) by Xi Zhongxun 習仲勛 (1913–2002) dated February 25, 2015. With Xi being part of China's political elite and the late father of its current president Xi Jingping 習近平 (1953–present), his calligraphy signals an official approval as well as a personal commendation of the *Essentials*. More recently in 2018, a Kansei edition printed on 25 scrolls (the "Eisei Bunko edition") formed part of the collection of ancient Chinese texts gifted to the National Library of China by the Chief Director of the Eisei Bunko Museum and former Japanese Prime Minister Hosokawa Morihiro in commemoration of the fortieth anniversary of the Sino-Japanese Treaty of Peace and Friendship. The National Library of China reprinted the Eisei Bunko edition to facilitate public access to the donated texts.[109] In the Chinese-Japanese bilingual preface to the Eisei Bunko edition reprint, the *Essentials* is identified by China's National Center for Preservation of Ancient Books as a testament to the long-standing cultural dialogue between the two countries.[110] That the *Essentials* was transmitted throughout the East Asian community, and particularly with it being read, studied, taught, and researched for so long in Japan (discussed in Section 4.2), the anthology may be regarded as a symbol of a bygone era of cultural congruity within East Asia, and the international dialogue and exchange it afforded. Reception of the Tenmei edition and the Eisei Bunko edition suggests a consciousness among contemporary state leaders in China and Japan of this common cultural heritage, as well as some long-standing political ideas and values encapsulated within the *Essentials*.

4.2 THE *ESSENTIALS* IN EAST ASIA

Beyond China, historical sources show that the *Essentials* was introduced to the courts of pre-modern East Asia. However, it is difficult to ascertain precisely when and how the anthology reached those East Asian polities. Notwithstanding those empirical limitations, this section surveys how the *Essentials* became exportable through an expanded public sphere arising from cultural congruities among the East Asian nations and their disposition towards learning from the administration of Tang China, before examining what can be known of the *Essentials*' textual history in Japan, Korea, and Vietnam.

The term "public sphere" (*Öffentlichkeit*) was coined by the German philosopher Jürgen Habermas to describe a discursive space that emerged among the bourgeois in eighteenth-century Europe.[111] Before the existence of this public sphere, there was only "representative publicness" in terms of public displays of representation by feudal authorities such as the aristocracy and the Church.[112] The public sphere served as an inclusive forum for ongoing dialogue and critical reflection on state matters among educated individuals outside of the contemporary political order.[113] Such individuals would gather as a public and participate in the discussions irrespective (theoretically) of their status and privilege.[114] Fueled by information from newspapers and political journals, the published word along with coffee houses, salons, and literary societies became the loci of political discourse in England, France, and Germany.[115] Hence, discussion and debate of political concerns were no longer confined to the conventional corridors of power but took place in a broader communicative environment premised on a putative general interest. By developing a critically debating public, such public spheres became a check on state authorities. However, the public sphere that emerged in Tang China differed somewhat in character and effect. The foreign scholars and envoys visiting Chang'an sought primarily to observe and learn from the governmental culture for the interests of their native regimes. Nevertheless, such foreign interest and scrutiny plausibly spurred the Chinese courts to formalize administrative knowledge for sharing with neighbors.

Books like the *Essentials* were exportable to pre-modern Japan, Korea, and Vietnam because those East Asian societies shared the same written language and institutional culture.[116] Such cultural commonality proved remarkably constant despite variability in their political status at various times.[117] In the formative period of East Asia—that is, from the third century BCE to the tenth century CE—China was admired for being the most populous, territorially extensive, economically developed, and culturally sophisticated country within the region.[118] The Chinese script and the written language of classical Chinese (also known as "literary Chinese" and "Sinitic") was adopted for administration, diplomacy, and literary activities by the emerging states of Japan, Korea, and Vietnam, as they had yet to develop their own writing systems.[119] The earliest records of those East Asian societies were written in classical Chinese and they adapted the Chinese characters to express their native vernacular languages.[120] The written *lingua franca* of classical Chinese enabled people throughout East Asia to read and understand the same text, even if they pronounced the words differently.[121] The Chinese graphs not only provided a universal vocabulary, but also facilitated the sharing of common views and values throughout the East Asian community.[122] Indeed, Peter F. Kornicki writes that by the eighth century at the latest, the Chinese script and the practice of classical Chinese writing had created in East Asia "a semblance of linguistic uniformity, or at least communicability, for domestic, diplomatic, and intellectual purposes."[123]

The development of political institutions in Japan, Korea, and Vietnam was extensively shaped by the knowledge and practices of China's ruling elite, particularly during the seventh and eighth centuries.[124] Like Greco-Roman antiquity in northern Europe, Chinese culture was considered "classic" in the sense of being timeless and placeless to the learned elites across East Asia. As the imported culture was less Chinese culture than elite culture, it was adopted by others as easily as did the Tang Chinese.[125] The elite culture was based on a shared literature written in classical Chinese,[126] with the texts having been transmitted to the three kingdoms of Korea (Paekche, Silla, and Koguryô) before the third century, to Vietnam since the late third century, and to Japan thereafter.[127] Books were the principal medium of cultural transmission from China to its neighboring societies in East Asia.[128] Far from being foisted on those neighbours, the Chinese texts were keenly sought after and regularly conveyed by their diplomats, visiting scholars, and monastics, as well as other travelers.[129] The pre-modern states of Japan, Korea, and Vietnam organized themselves along the lines of Chinese precedents, from the centralized bureaucracy, official titles, legal codes, revenue collection, and military conscription, to the imperial calendar and standards for weights and measures.[130] They followed the Chinese paradigm by establishing classical-style academies and the examination system to train and qualify candidates for public service.[131] Such was the interest in Chinese culture and institutions that there was a large and long-standing foreign presence in the Chinese cities during the Tang dynasty, particularly in Chang'an.[132] The foreigners included merchants and monastics who were drawn to China as the largest regional exporter and the center of the Mayahana

Buddhist world, respectively, as well as envoys and students who would come into contact with the Chinese court and its institutions, and procure Chinese texts.[133] The ruling families of Japan, Korea, and Vietnam sent their sons to study in the imperial academy or work in the imperial bodyguard.[134] While some foreign students would participate in the civil service examinations and serve in the Chinese court, most would return home with first-hand experiences to inform the development of their native institutions.[135] Hence, the policies and practices of the Tang imperial court were not the exclusive concern of local scholars and officials. Rather, the commonalities of classical Chinese language and political vocabulary, combined with close and ongoing cultural dialogue with the Chinese court extended the public sphere to include other East Asian polities and their representatives, who often spent long periods at Chang'an, observing and learning the art of governance.[136] Such conditions arguably paved the way for those foreigners to know about and be interested in the *Essentials*—an anthology about Confucian-oriented statecraft from the early Tang that is written in classical Chinese. From the perspective of China's neighbors, their political elites would draw on an international repertoire of cultural knowledge to inform and supplement their respective experiences by consulting the texts and models of China's Central Plains. Those resources were certainly shared during the Tang dynasty when the Chinese empire was at its most open and cosmopolitan.[137]

From the perspective of cultural memory theory, subscribing to the same corpus of cultural learning for statecraft involved the political elite in China, Japan, Korea, and Vietnam, in a common process of remembering and retrieving cultural knowledge. Understanding the classical Chinese language and culture was just as much a learning process for students in Tang China as elsewhere. Aspiring Chinese officials whose mother tongue was one of the Middle Chinese dialects would have found the classical Chinese no more familiar than a foreign language. Adoption of the unfamiliar, abstracting from their own immediate cultural context, and reusing the classical way of bringing about order by the ruling elite in China and East Asia, thus resonates with the process of reclaiming tradition in cultural memory.

Historical data indicates that the *Essentials* did reach the foreign courts of pre-modern Japan, Korea, and Vietnam. Based on the limited availability of extant records, the questions of how the *Essentials* as a Chinese text was transmitted abroad, when the transmission likely took place, and how it was received are answered below with cautious approximation.

The *Essentials* is identifiable as a part of Japan's cultural reference memory for over a millennium and the local working memory for some eight hundred years. Actively studied and interpreted by generations of the political, intellectual, and cultural elite, the anthology enjoyed a level of readership, engagement, and circulation over an extensive period that seems unrivaled among the East Asian community. The *Essentials* also experienced shifts of meaning throughout its historical reception in Japan.

Although precisely when and how the *Essentials* reached Japan remain unclear, scholars assume that the text was brought to Japan by Japanese ambassadors or scholars returning from Tang China.[138] Japan sent a total of 16 embassies to China during the Tang dynasty.[139] Based on historical records of those diplomatic missions, Kim Kwang-Il infers that the Japanese most likely came to know about the existence of the *Essentials* when Emperor Xuanzong granted an official delegation from Japan full access to the Chinese imperial library collection in 752.[140] The delegation was guided by the Director of the Palace Library Abe no Nakamaro (known in Chinese as "Chao Heng 朝衡," *c.* 698–c.770), who was a Japanese expatriate[141] and probably familiar with the books of interest to the Japanese party, including those that had yet to reach Japan. Members of the official mission included the Deputy Ambassador Kibi no Makibi 吉備真備 (693–775), who was familiar with and interested in Chinese writings, as he introduced numerous Chinese manuscripts to Japan and instructed the future Empress Kōken (r. 749–758, 764–770) on Chinese texts.[142] This time frame falls within the Nara period (710–794), when Japanese adoption of the laws, codes, land policies, and bureaucratic forms of Tang China reached its height and other aspects of Chinese civilization were actively introduced.[143] The *Essentials* is listed as existing in 50 scrolls in the *Catalogue of Extant Books in Japan* (*Nihon koku genzai shomokuroku* 日本國見在書目錄), that was compiled in 891 and remains the earliest extant bibliography of Chinese texts in Japan.[144]

From the early Heian (794–1185) period to the late Kamakura (1185–1333) years, the *Essentials* featured in the active dimension of Japan's cultural memory as it was read, discussed, taught, researched, and disseminated among the ruling family, court scholars, other officials, and the nobility. The Heian period is characterized as a period of remarkable cultural development centered on the imperial court with extensive emulation of Tang China by the Japanese ruling elite.[145] Kim notes that the *Essentials* was one of three titles through which the Japanese emperors learned about the principles and methods of Chinese government.[146] There was also a tradition of court lectures on those texts where the emperor would be assisted in their study by one specialist in each of the canonical, historical, and masters branches of literature.[147] No less than four emperors are recorded as having studied the *Essentials* in the standard Japanese histories. The imported manuscript would have been copied for such usage by the Japanese imperial court.

The earliest reference to the *Essentials* ("*Gunsho chiyō*" in Japanese) is found in the *Continuation of the Later Records of Japan* (*Shoku Nihon kōki* 續日本後記), which is one of the six officially sponsored histories of early Japanese history dated *circa* 850 and provides a detailed account of Emperor Ninmyō's reign (r. 833–850). On the twenty-sixth day of the sixth month of the fifth year (838) of Ninmyō's Jōwa reign-period (834–848):

> The Heavenly Emperor in the Seiryōden [(the emperor's private residence)] instructed six [tutors] to lecture on the first scroll of *Gunsho chiyō* as it contained the text of the Five Classics.[148]

Emperor Ninmyō is further described as being no stranger to the masters writings that were excerpted in the *Essentials*:

> Among the hundred masters, whether in the teachings of [the *Old Master* and *Master Zhuang*] or the writings of the *Gunsho chiyō*, there are none that He was not thoroughly conversant with.[149]

For Emperor Ninmyō and his officials to know of and have access to the *Essentials*, and for the latter to present on it, the text would have already reached Japan before the fifth year of the Jōwa reign-period.[150] Emperor

Ninmyō's grandson, Emperor Seiwa (r. 858–876) is known for admiring Emperor Taizong and adopting his Zhenguan reign name ("Jōgan" in Japanese) throughout his 18-year reign.[151] The *Veritable Record of Three Generations of Emperors of Japan* (*Nihon sandai jitsuroku* 日本三代實錄) offers two relevant entries regarding Emperor Seiwa. On the twenty-eighth day of the fourth intercalary month of the sixteenth year of his reign (874):

> In recent years, the Heavenly Emperor read the *Gunsho chiyō*. Today, he read the entire text.[152]

During the twenty-fifth day of the fourth month of the seventeenth year of Emperor Seiwa's reign (875):

> First, the Heavenly Emperor read the *Gunsho chiyō*. [His advisors] proceeded to collate and explain, with the joint Chief and Assistant Minister of the Ministry of Ceremony Sugawara no Koreyoshi [(812–880)] lecturing on the text of its chronicles, biographies, and masters, the Deputy Minister of Justice Sugano no Sukeyo [(802–880)] lecturing on the text of the Five Classics, and [Ainari Yoshibuchi (dates unknown) and the Right Division Master of the Capital and Tajima, assisted with the reading and the reading assembly, respectively].[153]

The entries about emperors Ninmyō and Seiwa indicate that the court officials themselves had studied the *Essentials* for some time and developed a certain level of expertise in the text to be able to present formal lectures and assist court readings of the anthology. Further insight into the study of the *Essentials* during the reigns of emperors Ninmyō and Seiwa is found in two prefaces to the Tenmei edition. The prefatory note dated 1785 by the Owari State Academy principal Hosoi Tokumin 細井德民 (1728–1801) highlights that the *Essentials* was often the subject of court lectures during the Jōwa and Jōgan reign-periods.[154] Moreover, the golden ages of social stability and prosperity enjoyed during the Jōwa and Jōgan eras are attributed to the teaching and learning of the *Essentials* by the Grand Master for Closing Court 朝散大夫 and Chancellor of the State Academy Directorate 國子祭酒 Hayashi Nobutaka 林信敬 (1767–1792)

in his preface dated 1787.[155] The local usage of the *Essentials* by the ruling elite in Heian Japan thus appears to have had a positive impact on local society, as recognized by later eminent Japanese officials.

Not surprisingly, the *Essentials* continued to be formally studied as exemplified by the imperial courts of Emperor Uda (r. 887–897) and Emperor Daigo (r. 898–930). The biography of Sugawara no Michizane 管原道真 (845–903), who was the third son of Sugawara no Koreyoshi 菅原是善 mentioned above, and a state university professor of literature and history, records that Michizane was commissioned to assist the imperial court with reading the *Essentials* in the fourth year of Emperor Uda's reign (892).[156] On retiring from the throne, Emperor Uda advised his eldest son and successor Atsuhito, who became Emperor Daigo, of the need to study the *Essentials* without delay. He stated:

> Although the Son of Heaven has yet to master the canonical works, the historical works, and the works of the hundred masters, does he have any regrets? Just read and study the *Gunsho chiyō* as soon as possible, do not approach it as miscellaneous writings to while away the time![157]

Emperor Uda's assertion that it would suffice for a ruler to receive his scholarly training from the *Essentials* is discussed in the *Chronicle of the Direct Descent of Gods and Sovereigns* (*Jinnō shōtōki* 神皇正統記). The *Chronicle* is a politico-historical treatise on Japan's history of imperial succession by Kitabatake Chikafusa 北畠親房 (1293–1354), who was an advisor to several Japanese emperors during the fourteenth century.[158] The primary status accorded to the *Essentials* is underscored by Chikafusa, who interprets Uda's statement to mean that there is "probably no need" for an emperor to learn any classics, histories, or masters works outside of the anthology.[159] Shortly thereafter, Emperor Daigo followed his father's advice and led his own court in continuing the tradition of studying the *Essentials* in Heian Japan:

> The Heavenly Emperor Daigo on the twenty-eighth day of the second month of the first year of his Shōtai reign-period (898), started to read the *Gunsho chiyō* in the Seiryōden. He was fourteen years old. His reading was attended by the Assistant Minister of the Ministry of Ceremony Ki

> no Haseo [(845– 912)] and the *dainaiki* (senior private secretary) Ono no Yoshiki [(d. 902)].[160]
>
> In the second month of the first year of Heavenly Emperor Daigo's Shōtai reign-period (898), the Assistant Minister of the Ministry of Ceremonial Ki no Haseo attended the Seiryōden and instructed the Heavenly Emperor on the *Gunsho chiyō*. The *dainaiki* (senior private secretary) Ono no Yoshiki ... and the court nobles [(holders of the highest three court ranks)] also prepared for the court lecture.[161]

Moreover, one of Emperor Daigo's sons—Minamoto no Takaakira 源高明 (914–983)—wrote about the *Essentials* in his *Chronicles of the Western Palace* (*Saikyūki* 西宮記), which was a guide to ritual ceremony and court protocol in 969:[162]

> Those who serve in public office may be furnished books [including, on the matter of governing principles]: the *Gunsho chiyō* (fifty scrolls) and the *Jōgan seiyō* (ten scrolls). The above Tang texts offer comprehensive coverage of all matters between the sovereign and their subordinates.[163]

Such historical records would suggest that the *Essentials* was regarded as a key source of governmental learning that was standard reading for prospective and contemporary officials in Japan. By the tenth century, its readership was no longer limited to the ruling family, the imperial court, and academicians, but had rather extended throughout the nobility and officialdom. That the *Essentials* was also copied in circulation is exemplified by the existence of a Heian edition, which remains the earliest extant manuscript produced in the tenth century from an early Tang edition of the *Essentials* and punctuated around the thirteenth century.[164]

Following the Heian era, the *Essentials* continued to be valued and reused by the shogunate ruling class and educated elite for the cultural memory of Kamakura Japan. From the eleventh to the thirteenth centuries, the *Essentials* was one of the Chinese texts studied by the leading members of the Heian imperial court, the Kamakura shogunate, and the nobility.[165] For example, the military leader Hōjō Sanetoki 北條實時 (1225–1276), who served in various important roles within the Kamakura shogunate and amassed a large collection of books that served as the state library for the Kamakura period,[166] is known to have studied the *Essentials*, and arranged for it to be copied, collated, and punctuated.[167] The production of the Kamakura edition that was overseen by Hōjō Sanetoki demonstrates that the *Essentials* remained a subject of formal interest and study during the Kamakura period.[168] Based on its variant text, the Kamakura edition is thought to be copied from a version of the *Essentials* dating to the latter half of the seventh century.[169] The Kamakura edition contains manuscript notations dating from 1253 to 1308 by the academician Kiyohara Noritaka 清原教隆 (1199–1265), Hōjō Akitoki 北條顯時 (1248–1301), and Hōjō Sadaaki 北條貞顯 (1278–1333), who were the teacher, son, and grandson of Hōjō Sanetoki, respectively.[170] The notations indicate that various parts date to different times. Whereas the canonical and masters sections were completed by the military commander Gotō Motomasa 後藤基政 (1214–1267) in 1253, much of the historical section had to be recopied during 1274 to 1276 and 1306 to 1308 to replace various damaged or missing scrolls.[171] Such recopying was made possible by the availability of copies of the original Kamakura edition produced by Miyoshi Yasushi 三善康有 (1228–1290) and Kiyohara Noritaka, respectively.[172] The notations also refer to the existence of other manuscript editions of the *Essentials* belonging to the book collections of the imperial family and academicians, and show that different parts of the Kamakura edition were collated, punctuated, and taught at various times.[173] For example, such activities took place in respect of the canonical section during 1253 to 1257, the historical section from 1250 to 1260, and the masters section during 1259 to 1260. The extent of the work in producing, preserving, punctuating, collating, and teaching the Kamakura edition during the thirteenth and fourteenth centuries, and the prominent standing of the actors involved, amply corroborate the central importance attributed to the *Essentials* in Japanese political thought by contemporary shogunate and scholars, as well as the imperial family and nobility.

The *Essentials* experienced a shift in meaning during the sixteenth and seventeenth centuries. Valued for its fine calligraphy and material, the Heian edition was divided into sections and gifted by the Kujō family to the emperor, fellow nobles, and friends. For example, the manuscript notations on the Heian edition indicate that the court nobles Kujō Kanetaka 九條兼孝 (1553–1636) and Kujō Michifusa 九條道房 (1609–1647)

gave part of scroll 37 to the Confucian scholar, Buddhist monk, and writer Omura Yūko 大村由己 (d. 1596) on an unknown date, and presented ten other sections to the Heavenly Emperor Go-Mizunoo 後水尾天皇 (r. 1611–1629) in 1625, respectively.[174] The *Essentials* thus acquired a new cultural significance. In addition to being a statecraft reference text for formal study, it also served as a piece of art for calligraphy, collection, and appreciation among the social elite.

Although there is little other evidence concerning the *Essentials* in the cultural working memory during the years between the Kamakura and Edo shogunates, the survival of the Kamakura edition ensured the continuity of the *Essentials* within the local cultural reference memory. Until the discovery of the Heian edition in 1945, the *Essentials* was thought to be solely survived by the Kamakura edition, of which 47 of its 50 scrolls remained extant by the Edo period (1600–1868).[175] That other manuscript copies of the *Essentials* did not survive is indicative of the passive dimension of cultural forgetting during the intervening years of shogunate rule that were characterized by a weakened central government.[176] Notwithstanding its three missing scrolls, the Kamakura edition remains the extant edition that is most complete and derived from a source closest in time to the edition of the *Essentials* that was originally presented to Emperor Taizong. The Kamakura edition is kept in the Archives and Mausolea Department of the Imperial Household Agency in Japan.[177]

The production of five new editions of the *Essentials* under the auspices of the Tokugawa shogunate suggests that the anthology remained at the forefront of political thought throughout the Edo period, known as the last period of traditional government in Japan. The first Tokugawa shogun Tokugawa Ieyasu (1542–1616) was instrumental in the making of the first two of those editions. Ahead of implementing new regulations that stipulated the *Essentials* as compulsory study for the court and aristocracy (including the emperors), he ordered for the production of two manuscript copies of the *Essentials* based on the Kamakura edition in 1610.[178] Completed within the same year and during Japan's Keichō era (1596–1615), the manuscripts were known as the "Keichō edition" and are found in the Cabinet Library of the National Archives of Japan.[179] The Keichō edition would serve as the base for the Genna edition that was commissioned by Ieyasu to include supplements in place of the three missing scrolls prepared by the leading Confucian advisor to the Tokugawa shogunate Hayashi Razan 林羅山 (1583–1657).[180] Completed without those supplements in 1616, the Genna edition became one of the earliest official texts to be printed with copper-block movable type made in Japan.[181] Kornicki argues that printing the *Essentials* was one way of ensuring that those texts Ieyasu considered fundamental for governance were readily available in uniform, authentic editions.[182] As Ieyasu passed away before the Genna edition was completed, it was not circulated but divided among the collateral Tokugawa houses of Owari and Kii, with the latter also receiving the movable type.[183] The Edo academician Hori Kyoan 堀正意 (1585–1643) punctuated the Genna edition and added a postscript to it during 1641 and 1642.[184] The earliest extant edition of the *Essentials* printed by copper movable type was given to the Jingū Library in 1690 by Tokugawa Mitusada 德川光貞, a Kii descendant of Ieyasu.[185] Mitusada's son, who became the eighth shogun Tokugawa Yoshimune 德川吉宗 (r. 1716–1745), obtained two further copies of the *Essentials* from the Kii clan in 1740.[186] The Owari clan oversaw the making of the two most circulated editions of the *Essentials*, namely the Tenmei edition of 1787 and the Kansei edition of 1791. Intended to correct errors in the Genna edition, the Tenmei edition was the outcome of ten years of collation through the joint efforts of Tokugawa Haruyoshi 德川治林 (1753–1773), Tokugawa Haruoki 德川治興 (1756–1776), Tokugawa Haruyuki 德川治行 (1760–1793), and leading scholar-officials, including those named in the preface by Hosoi Tokumin.[187] In 1799, the Owari clan arranged for the Tenmei edition to be collated and reprinted with punctuation, thereby resulting in the Kansei edition.[188] In 1843, Tokugawa Harutomi 德川治寶 (1771–1853) and Tokugawa Nariyuki 德川齊順 (r. 1824–1846) arranged for a reprint of the *Essentials* that was collated based on the Genna edition and completed in 1846 during Japan's Kōka era (1844–1848) (the "Kōka edition").[189] As the forms of the classical Chinese characters and their grammatical expression evolve over time, the extensive collation and punctuation that took place during the Kamakura and Tokugawa shogunates may be seen as efforts to maintain the readability of the *Essentials* for study by the contemporary ruling and educated elites.

Following the Edo era, modern Japan has seen the production of one further edition of the *Essentials*, the discovery of an extant edition, and the proliferation of academic scholarship on the anthology. Using the Kamakura edition as the base, the Archives Department of the Imperial Household Agency in Japan produced a typed version of the *Essentials* in 1941 during the Shōwa era (1926–1989), which is known as the "Shōwa edition."[190] It is notable that in a preface to the Shōwa edition, the Archives Department provides an overview of the textual history of the *Essentials*, credits the success of the Tang dynasty to the *Essentials*, and emphasizes that the text was highly valued for statecraft purposes by generations of rulers in Japan.[191] After World War II, the Heian edition was discovered among the remains of the home of the noble Kujō 九條 family in 1945. Comprising just 13 of the original 50 scrolls, the Heian edition has since been purchased and preserved as a national treasure at the Tokyo National Museum.[192] Following a process of repair and restoration, seven of the Heian edition's 13 scrolls are now accessible online, namely scrolls 22, 26, 31, 33, 35, 36, and 37.[193] Arguably, the Shōwa edition's preface and the work on the Heian edition signals a further shift of meaning for the *Essentials*. Not simply a book on statecraft or an *objet d'art*, the *Essentials* has become an item of national cultural heritage. It is a text that deserves institutional preservation and requires further explanation to be fully appreciated in the contemporary context akin to a museum object that is maintained and displayed with explanatory information cards. The *Essentials* also became a subject of academic scholarship in Japan. Research on the *Essentials* commenced in the early nineteenth century with Kondō Morishige 近藤守重 (1771–1829), an official working in the shogunate library Momijiyama Bunko, who had access to various editions of the *Essentials* that were not generally accessible at the time. Kondō wrote numerous papers about the *Essentials*, including on the production, printing, and circulation of many editions, and the process by which the Kansei edition was reintroduced to Qing China.[194] He is also recorded to have arranged for scholars trained in the classical Chinese tradition to collate the Kansei edition using the Kamakura edition in 1818.[195] The extensive corpus of research published on the *Essentials* since Kondō—from the late Edo period through to the Shōwa period—is set out in Ozaki Yasushi's 尾崎康 seminal paper "*Gunsho chiyō* to sono genson hon 群書治要とその現存本" (The *Qunshu zhiyao* and its extant editions).[196] Relevant scholars include Mori Tatsuyuki 森立之

(1807–1885),[197] Shimada Kan 島田翰 (1879–1915),[198] Uematsu Yasushi 植松安 (1885–1945),[199] Ishihama Juntarō 石濱純太郎 (1888–1968),[200] and Takagi Bun 高木文 (dates unknown).[201] The *Essentials* has remained a subject of scholarly attention in recent decades, as exemplified by the numerous studies concerning the Kamakura edition's annotation and punctuation by Sasaki Isamu 佐佐木勇,[202] Morioka Nobuyuki 森岡信幸,[203] and Mizukami Masaharu 水上雅晴.[204]

That the *Essentials* was taught to and studied by generations of Japanese emperors, shoguns, and their respective courts, offers an independent testament to the text's enduring canonical status in the local cultural memory. From imperial court lectures to the production and circulation of various editions, the historical transmission of the *Essentials* in Japan suggests that it was probably one of the few normative and formative texts that have been "actively circulated and communicated in ever-new presentations."[205] The normative aspect of the anthology is unequivocally conveyed by the bilingual preface to the reprint of the *Essentials* commemorating the fortieth anniversary of the Sino-Japanese Treaty of Peace and Friendship in 2018. Written by the National Center for Preservation of Ancient Books of the National Library of China, the preface states that generations of Japanese imperial courts regarded the *Essentials* as their model standard.[206] The formative aspect is seen in the generations of ruling elite adopting as part of their collective identity those ideas and values deemed essential for good government according to the *Essentials*. The Japanese reception of the *Essentials* thus offers a glimpse of the workings of the cultural memory in storing and reproducing the cultural capital of a society that is continually recycled and reaffirmed.

That the *Essentials* was reintroduced to China through the transmission of the Kansei edition in 1796 points to the regenerative potential of cultural memory. The East Asian cultural sphere with its common language, shared texts, and political vocabulary, facilitated a common reservoir for future functional memories among its members. As part of the cultural memory of Tang China, the *Essentials* became known and transmitted to Japan by the expanded public sphere at the time. And as part of the cultural working memory of Japan, the *Essentials* was able to be restored to the working and reference modes of the cultural memory in China.

The *Essentials* has long been a repository of governmental learning in Japan. It became standard reading with a formal program of study established for centuries of Japanese rulers, and the Kamakura and Tokugawa shogunates sponsored the production and circulation of both manuscript and print editions. Hence, although there is limited primary evidence of the readership and circulation in Japan, the findings are relatively consistent and compelling in that the *Essentials* formed a part of Japan's cultural memory for over one thousand years since its transmission during the Nara period. Given such historical engagement with the text among the ruling and educated elite, it is not surprising that Japan is home to the earliest extant editions of the *Essentials* and the earliest academic research relating to them.

Compared to the history of the *Essentials* in Japan, there is far less information available concerning its transmission and reception in Korea and Vietnam. Notwithstanding the paucity of information, Peter F. Kornicki points to the overwhelming probability of a Chinese text that is available in Japan, having already reached the Korean peninsula and the northern part of what is now Vietnam:[207]

> ... it is difficult to suppose that significantly more texts reached distant Japan than other states that could be reached overland from China. The evidence that survives for early Japan therefore, can not only be taken as valid for Japan but also as an indication of the texts that must have reached Korea and Vietnam but have not survived in any form.[208]

Liu Yujun 劉玉珺 also writes that the scale and quantity of the Chinese books transmitted to Vietnam far exceed those that were available in Japan and Korea, though few records of that have survived.[209] This would suggest that a text such as the *Essentials* may have reached Korea and Vietnam sometime before 838, the date of its first mention in the Japanese historical records.

Regarding the Korean reception of the *Essentials*, the text is referred to in a dialogue between a Korean official mission and their Japanese counterparts in 1748. In the course of a discussion about scholarly matters, Fujiwara Akitō 藤原明遠 (1697–1761) enquired:

> There has been a vast number of texts since the Han and Tang dynasties. Of those that are no longer extant in China, many have survived in our country [Japan]. For example, the *Commentary on the Classic of Family Reverence* [(*Kōkyō den*)] by Kong Anguo, the *Commentary on the Analects* [(*Rongo so*)] by Huang Kan of the Liang dynasty, the *Essentials for Bringing about Order from Assembled Texts* [(*Gunsho chiyō*)] by Wei Zheng [et al.] of the Tang dynasty, the *Classified Collection [of Quotations from Works] by Imperial Court [Scholars]* [(*Kocho ruien*)] by Jiang Shaoyu of the Song dynasty, which are by no means isolated cases. May I respectfully enquire whether those texts are also in circulation in your country [Korea]?[210]

In reply, the Korean official Cho Myŏngch'ae 曹命采 (1700–1763) said, "[We have] seen and heard of those texts, and have them all."[211] This indicates that the *Essentials* had been introduced to the Korean court sometime before 1748 and was familiar to its delegation, if not also among the local officialdom more generally. Although there is no record of the *Essentials* in sources on old Chinese texts extant in Korea, such as the *Supplemented Edition of the Reference Compilation of Documents [on Korea]* (*Jeungbo munheon bigo*)[212] in the early 1900s, and the *Complete List of Chinese Texts in Korea* (*Han'guk sojang Chungguk hanjŏk ch'ongmok*),[213] there are Korean records of other texts relating to the Zhenguan reign-period, such as the *Zhenguan Essentials* dating to as early as 950.[214] As such, there seems no reason for the Korean court not to be interested in the *Essentials* or to possess a copy of it, particularly considering the long history of Chinese writings being transmitted to the Korean peninsula. The texts were either gifted from the Chinese court to Korean ambassadorial delegations, or independently procured by official delegates, merchants, or scholars visiting China from Korea.[215] Regarding themselves as "Little China" (*Sojunghwa*小中華), the three kingdoms of Korea had the most Chinese texts (outside of China) among the East Asian cultural sphere in the period before the seventh century.[216] Almost all periodic tributary delegations from Korea requested books from the Chinese imperial court.[217] Given that the *Essentials* had been primarily kept in the

Chinese palace library, the anthology was presumably shared, either voluntarily by the Chinese court, or provided on request by an official mission from Korea. Currently, the earliest copy of the *Essentials* in Korea is a xylographic manuscript of the Tenmei edition dated 1787, which is kept at the Central Research Institute for Korean Studies.[218]

In Vietnam, the earliest extant record of the *Essentials* appears in the book catalogue of the Nguyễn court library *Thư mục nội các* 內閣書目, which was compiled on royal commission by an unnamed official in 1908.[219] Categorizing the texts into the five divisions of state and dynastic works, canonical works, historical works, masters works, and literary works, the catalogue provides for each work its title, the number of its scrolls, and the quantity of stored copies. The *Essentials* is listed among the masters writings, with the local palace library holding one copy comprising 25 scrolls.[220] This would indicate that at least one copy of the *Essentials* had been transmitted to the Vietnamese imperial court sometime before 1908. It is difficult to estimate with further precision when the anthology might have reached pre-modern Vietnam because few texts survived the extensive damage to its palace library collections during the wartime years from 1256 to 1288, 1371, the early 1400s, and 1516.[221] Preservation and management of texts in the court library collections had long been neglected.[222] As such, the catalogues of old books in Vietnam contain mostly those extant during the late Lê (1533–1789) and Nguyễn (1802–1945) dynasties.[223] Indeed, it would appear that most Chinese books reached Vietnam before 1820 based on the publication dates of the texts recorded in the *Handbook of the Academy of Classical Studies* (*Sổ tay Học viện Cổ đại* 古學書院手冊), which dates to Vietnam's French colonial period and is derived from records of the court library.[224] Liu Yujun points to many Chinese texts being introduced to Vietnam through the banishment and demotion of scholar-officials to the Annan prefectures of Huan, Ai, and Feng, which collectively received some 10 percent of the total number of banished persons (including demoted officials) during the Tang dynasty.[225] It is eminently possible that the *Essentials* became known to the local government of Ai Prefecture, then part of the distant Tang dynasty protectorate of Annan that later became Vietnam, when Chu Liang's son Chu Suiliang, who had served as chancellor during the reigns of Taizong and Gaozong, was demoted there along with his sons

Chu Yanfu 褚彥甫 and Chu Yanchong 褚彥沖 in 658.[226] Chu Suiliang was appointed prefect of Ai Prefecture and passed away there at the age of 63.[227] However, it is unknown whether Chu Suiliang or his sons brought a copy of the *Essentials* to Ai Prefecture. Given that the local presence of the *Zhenguan Essentials* is reported in the *Records of Comprehensive Enquiries about Foreign Territories* (*Shuyu zhouzi lu* 殊域周咨錄), the Ming dynasty (1368–1644) ethnological reference completed in 1574 by the diplomatic official Yan Congjian 嚴從簡 (*fl.* 1560),[228] and the 1908 book catalogue of the Nguyễn court library,[229] it is likely that the Vietnamese court would also have been interested in the *Essentials* as another Tang dynasty work related to the Zhenguan court.

As the *Essentials* comprises 50 scrolls in total, the 25 scrolls recorded in the Nguyễn court library catalogue would imply that its copy was either incomplete or an edition that had been reproduced on 25 scrolls. Three of the extant editions of the *Essentials* have been printed on 25 scrolls, namely, the Tenmei edition of 1787, the Kansei edition of 1791, and the Kōka edition of 1846.[230] With the two former editions being the most widely circulated of the extant editions and completed within the pre-1820 time frame when most Chinese texts were introduced to Vietnam, either of the Tenmei or Kansei editions (or their reprints) may be, on balance, the *Essentials* listed in the Nguyễn court library catalogue.

Most Chinese texts were brought into pre-modern Vietnam by its official missions. The books would be either gifted by the Chinese court or purchased by the visiting officials under orders of the Vietnamese court, generally as part of a tributary visit, or on request of their personal associates.[231] As the *Essentials* was kept in the palace library, the *Essentials* was more likely to be given by the Chinese imperial court, either before it became non-extant in China around the fourteenth century, or after 1796 when it was reintroduced to China through the Kansei edition.

The *Essentials* was therefore exported to pre-modern Japan, Korea, and Vietnam as they could read and understand classical Chinese literature, studied Chinese culture and institutions, and were interested in adapting the governmental model of Tang China. While the historical sources indicate that the text became part of the cultural memory in Japan, there is insufficient information to know about its reception on the Korean peninsula and what is now Vietnam.

The cultural knowledge encapsulated by the *Essentials* was remembered by the Zhenguan ruling collective for their practice of government. The anthology continued to be read by later officials who served the courts of emperors Xuanzong to Wenzong of the Tang dynasty and valued the cultural resource of the *Essentials* enough to recommend it to their respective rulers. This enabled the anthology to remain within the cultural reference memory during Tang China, even if it was not always part of the cultural working memory at the time. After becoming culturally forgotten and then lost some time in the fourteenth century, the *Essentials* appeared to be seamlessly restored to the cultural memory following its reintroduction during Qing China. Through its presence in the emperor's private library and on the palace examination papers, the *Essentials* resumed its role as a statecraft reference for the curriculum of certain generations of the Qing ruling elite. Substantial evidence of the *Essentials* shaping the cultural memory of Japanese society for a much longer period compared to China furthers our understanding of the conditions conducive to continuity of cultural memory within a society and regeneration of cultural memory within a region. Despite limited information on its transmission in Vietnam and Korea, the records of the *Essentials* in those countries affirm the importance of the cultural knowledge and influence of cultural memory within the East Asian cultural sphere. Notwithstanding its loss of function and dropping out of circulation after Tang China, the *Essentials* experienced shifts of meaning as it served as a reference for textual collation and reconstruction, academic research, and international diplomacy. Separate copies were made of its excerpts from the *Old Master*, the *Zuo Tradition*, and the masters writings, for schooling and other purposes. Moreover, the Heian edition turned into gifts of calligraphy during the sixteenth and seventeenth centuries, and later became preserved with national treasure status since the twentieth century. What the cultural memory in the *Essentials* means for the Zhenguan political thought and practice is explored in detail in the conclusion.

CONCLUSION

What can the *Essentials* and its transmission tell us about the basis, conduct, or impact of rulership during the Zhenguan era of Tang China? Analyzing the anthology through the lens of cultural memory theory affords fresh insights into the administrative culture of the Zhenguan ruling elite and their influence on later rulers in China and abroad.

The compilation and transmission of the *Essentials* support two important conclusions about political thought and practice during the Zhenguan era. First, the political thought was derived from conventional wisdom yet directed by contemporary concerns. Second, the Zhenguan political practice became exemplary and exportable through the formalization and dissemination of its political advice literature. These conclusions are addressed in turn below.

The first conclusion is underscored by the *Essentials* re-presenting cultural memory in the format of an anthology. The concept of an anthology serves dual functions of managing textual information and conveying an argument about the larger corpus of the literary tradition through the way that its contents have been chosen and compiled from the vast universe of available documents.[1] The former function corresponds to the conventional wisdom in terms of the wealth of pre-Tang literature that was available during the Zhenguan reign-period. The latter function speaks to the contemporary concerns of the Zhenguan ruler and his officials. Building on the findings related to the reconstruction of cultural knowledge within the *Essentials*, it will be seen that both anthological functions are evident in its configuration.

Anthologies often arise from a practical need to manage an abundance of textual information.[2] This is corroborated by the imperial commission for what would become the *Essentials*, being born of the need to take stock of literary heritage, and make what was considered by the editors to be relevant from the extensive collection of the imperial library accessible for the inexperienced Emperor Taizong to study effectively and efficiently. Not only did the statecraft knowledge have to be useful but it also had to be organized and presented in a way that facilitated that use. The *Essentials* was intended to convey the gist and exemplary standards[3] for the Confucian government that Taizong had committed to in his *Golden Mirror* manifesto, and for securing the foundations of the fledgling dynasty. The excerpts in the *Essentials* assisted learning by reducing the material into smaller segments that were specifically applicable and presumably easier to recall. That its text was not authored afresh but excerpted from existing literature, and classified according to source rather than theme, also enabled the *Essentials* to serve as a ready repertory of quotations and allusions for court communications. This is corroborated by Fan Wang's comments below, based a study of the *Essentials*' inclusion of the *Mao Tradition of Commentary on the Odes* and the *Exoteric Commentary on the Odes by Han Ying*:

> By instructing Emperor Taizong in the reading of the [*Classic of Odes*], the compilers of *Qunshu zhiyao* introduced him to a repository of ready-made quotations, a collective medium through which the educated elites conducted nuanced political conversations. And the ability to identify allusions to the [*Classic of Odes*], to decipher intentions embodied in poetic quotations, would enable Taizong to engage intelligently in courtly dialogues and to comprehend courtly memorials.[4]

Hence, while the *Essentials* derived its classifications and source materials from the existing literature, it appropriated and assembled the information in a new formulation.

The argument conveyed by an anthology is twofold: that its selections are important, and that this importance is uniquely derived from the assemblage of those selections that it comprises.[5] While the *Essentials* constitutes a collection of sources, the editors' choice of an original title accentuates their compendium being a source in itself. Additionally, the word "essentials" in its appellation commends its selected contents as centrally important and requisite readings. The collective coherence of the *Essentials* puts forward an argument about what matters in the cultural tradition, as dictated by the editors, given the needs and objectives of their principal reader. As Christopher M. B. Nugent writes, "Any effort to gather and categorize information will inevitably reflect the ambitions and concerns of the powers that sponsor and authorize it."[6] As discussed above, the *Essentials* articulates its ideology by decontextualizing its sources, compiling their excerpts, and reorganizing them to articulate the concepts and convictions about the Confucian model of bringing about order, as envisaged by the Zhenguan ruler and his officials. While its excerpts are no longer necessarily representative of their sources, they mediate the reader's experience of the literary inheritance concerning emperorship through the *Essentials*' own comprehensive and structured arrangement of knowledge. As an imperial commission designed to inform Taizong on rulership, the *Essentials* thus demonstrates that the political philosophy of the Zhenguan era was rooted in past knowledge, while remaining true to present needs and objectives, not least through its anthological functions of managing information and communicating about the wider corpus of texts.

Overall, it appears that the *Essentials* became a political canon that was, to some extent, familiar to and utilized by the Zhenguan ruler and his court. Historical sources contemporary to Emperor Taizong's lifetime indicate that he approved and reviewed the anthology, and had copies made for his princes. While there appears to be no detailed evidence of how the *Essentials* was read by Taizong, his princes, or the courtiers who had access to the manuscript copies, no less than three officials of later Tang courts each commend the *Essentials* as a statecraft anthology for the Zhenguan ruler. Such accounts indicate that the *Essentials* had been useful enough to present to emperors Xuanzong, Dezong, and Xianzong of the Tang dynasty, respectively. It has been seen that the *Essentials*' emphasis on the worthy official, whose public service is characterized by lifelong commitment and exemplary efforts for recruiting talent, reverberates with historical records of the attitudes and conduct attributed to the Zhenguan ruler and his officials. They are also seen to be guided by the behavioral norms and values in the *Essentials* that relate to seeking and giving remonstrative advice. The Zhenguan remonstrances even follow the strategies of invoking inherited principles, as exhibited by the remonstrances excerpted by the *Essentials*. That the *Essentials* can account for most intertextual references in the *Model for an Emperor*, and the political views advocated by Taizong and his courtiers on military intervention, may be indicative of the extent of their awareness and usage of the anthology.

Considering such limited information about the usage of the *Essentials*, this study does not claim that it equally underpinned all decisions and aspects of governance by Emperor Taizong and his officials. Rather, the discoverable correspondence between the normative guidance and cultural values in this imperially commissioned text and what can be known about the Zhenguan ruling collective points to the *Essentials* furnishing a *locus classicus* of theoretical discourse and an integral part of the political ideology of the Zhenguan ruling elite. As such, one cannot exclude the potentiality of the *Essentials* contributing to the name of Taizong's reign-period—that is, "Zhenguan"—becoming synonymous with good government in history, and to the establishment of an enduring tradition of a unified empire administered by the civil service of a central authority. As Charles P. Fitzgerald explains in his biography of the Zhenguan ruler (referred to as "Li Shih-Min"):

> Before his time unity in China had been the exception, the achievement of a few strong dynasties: feudalism and partition had been the rule. But from the seventh century onwards China has far more often, and for far longer, been united than divided. Partitions have been the consequence of partial foreign conquest, or a temporary interlude between strong dynasties. Always the T'ang tradition re-asserted itself. That tradition, of a unified empire, administered by a civil service taking its orders from one supreme central authority, was the life's work of Li Shih-Min, and it has maintained and spread in the Far East the Chinese culture, one of the great civilising forces in the world's history.[7]

The textual history of the *Essentials* reflects the exemplary and exportable nature of Zhenguan political practice. Like other political advice literature concerning the Zhenguan administration, the *Essentials* enabled Taizong's reign to be known and studied by later generations of ruling elites in China and Japan for the cultural memory of their respective societies.[8] Insofar as it is a canon of the cultural memory of Zhenguan society, the *Essentials* offers a distinctive perspective. Its influence on the cultural memory-making of later courts, as evidenced by the survival of various ideas and values advocated by the *Essentials*, bears witness to the enduring memory of the Zhenguan governmental exemplar in political history.

The Zhenguan ruler did not claim to be a perfect ruler and his reign lasted only 23 years. In the *Model for an Emperor*, Taizong sets out the shortcomings of his rulership and expressly discourages his heir-apparent from taking the Zhenguan reign as a positive role model. In its preface, Taizong wrote, "Select the wise kings to serve as your teachers: do not take me as the 'mirror of the past' for your own conduct."[9] Yet the legacy of his government sufficed to become a positive exemplar that left an indelible impact on the political culture in China and Japan. The reign of Emperor Taizong witnessed a prolific production of texts that reflect contemporary institutional thought and precedents.[10] The texts range from the histories for all preceding dynasties since the Han,[11] the first Tang ritual code,[12] the first revision of the Tang legal code,[13] standard editions of the Five Classics and their commentaries,[14] anthologies for literary composition as exemplified by the influential *Excerpts from Books in the Northern Hall*,[15] to a series of political advice literature for Taizong and his princes: the *Concise Discourse on Emperors and Kings*, the *Golden Mirror*, the *Essentials*, the *Record of the Commendable and Contemptible Conduct of the Feudal Lords and Princes since Antiquity*, and the *Model for an Emperor*. I argue that the Zhenguan series of political advice literature, along with Wu Jing's *Zhenguan Essentials*[16] (collectively, the "Zhenguan political literature"), were integral to the Zhenguan governmental practice attaining exemplary recognition and international renown. The Zhenguan political literature not only enabled Taizong and his court to cement basic ideas and values in the contemporary political discourse but also to transmit those ideas and values further in time and space, as other ruling elites could know and learn about its practice of government. This is because the knowledge that has been written down and stored can overcome the limitations of direct communication and thereby transmit cultural experiences to people who do not share any spatial or temporal connection.[17] Unlike other primary sources for the Zhenguan period, the Zhenguan political literature foregrounds the ideology of Emperor Taizong and his court in various ways. From the concerns that motivated their production, the individuals involved, through to their format, and contents, those texts present the ideas and values of Zhenguan rulership, what it considered to be good governance, and what it wanted to be known for. An example of the latter is found in the *Golden Mirror*, where Chen writes that Taizong summons the image of how he wishes his audience to think of him: as one burdened by the cares of the empire, rather than exultant with the power at his command.[18] Arguably, the *Essentials* epitomizes those functions as the governmental practices, which the Zhenguan reign became known for, do correspond to those promoted by the anthology. For example, worthy talent and critical advice are underscored as imperatives for effective government in the *Essentials*. With the anthology being compiled by Taizong's trusted courtiers, read by him, and accessible to his court, it is probably no coincidence that the Zhenguan court is remembered by history for its inclination towards identifying and promoting talent for officialdom and its receptiveness towards remonstrance.[19] Taizong is celebrated as a sovereign who surrounded himself with talented civil and military officials and made a point of seeking their opinions and heeding their advice.[20] His approach fostered a solidarity among the Zhenguan officials that supported them to "brave the dragon's scales"[21] in challenging their ruler's decisions within an atmosphere of open and frank discussion.[22] The cultural memory encapsulated by the *Essentials* for the collective identity of Zhenguan society appealed to later courts, who became interested in its government as a model exemplar, and would identify or refer to the *Essentials* as its political canon. This is exemplified by records of the *Essentials* being recommended to the Tang emperors Xuanzong, Dezong, and Xianzong by their respective officials, and forming part of the imperial reading collection and the palace examination during the reigns of the Qing emperors Jiaqing and Guangxu, respectively. The anthology has also figured as a key text of governmental learning for imperial courts and shogunates in Japan from the ninth century to the eighteenth century. Hence, the Zhenguan rulership was known to others in China and elsewhere through political advice texts such as the *Essentials*.

Among the corpus of Zhenguan political literature, the *Essentials* presents a unique perspective on the Zhenguan court by articulating the cultural memory of its time. Concerned with knowledge about the remembered past that provides a collective self-image and normative orientation, the temporal horizon of cultural memory may extend even to mythical primordial time.[23] As such, the *Essentials* embeds the political vision of the Zhenguan ruling collective within a long-term historical framework that reaches back to the legendary rulers of remote antiquity, as exemplified by its excerpts from the *Venerable Documents*. This distinctive characteristic of the *Essentials* is illuminated by a comparison with the *Model for an Emperor* and the *Zhenguan Essentials*. Written as a summary of Emperor Taizong's views on rulership to guide his successor's conduct, the *Model for an Emperor* documents the Zhenguan ruler's personal memory. His model of emperorship draws heavily on the existing knowledge in terms of intertextual references to canonical principles, historical precedents, masters philosophy, and literary writings. However, the *Model for an Emperor* is not a compilation of excerpts, but an original piece of writing, the contents of which are thematically arranged by Taizong in twelve paired chapters and narrated in his voice. As Taizong wrote in the prefatory section of the *Model for an Emperor*:

> As a means to open up [for you] the mirror of former events, [We] have broadly culled the historical record and assembled together its most essential words, to act as a clear personal admonition for your conduct.[24]

The *Model for an Emperor* is delimited by what the Zhenguan ruler identifies to be relevant for his successor based on his own learning and experience. Comprising what he remembers as the incumbent, for the benefit of the incomer, the personal political testament is thus concerned with Zhenguan ideals of governance at the level of individual memory. The *Zhenguan Essentials* captures the memory of the Zhenguan rulership from a different vantage point altogether. It was not written contemporaneously by a member of the Zhenguan court, but by the later Tang official and historian Wu Jing and presented to the throne *circa* 729, some eighty years after Emperor Taizong's life and reign. As such, it conceives of the Zhenguan government as a part of recent history, thus engaging with the social level of memory, which is termed "communicative memory."[25] It also exemplifies the legitimizing and delegitimizing functions of political memory by elaborating historical knowledge and offering a counter-memory to challenge the *status quo*, respectively.[26] Having lived through what has been described as "four violently unstable courts in which the Zhenguan ideals receded dramatically into the farthest shadows of political life," Wu lobbied for reform based on the Zhenguan model during the reign of Emperor Xuanzong.[27] Twitchett notes that the desire for a restoration of the Tang and moral regeneration of its policies constantly featured in contemporary memorials and motivated his historical compilation endorsing the Zhenguan reign.[28] The *Essentials* had already been recommended to Xuanzong by the time Wu presented his opus. Nevertheless, Wu must have thought that an account of the workings of the Zhenguan court would speak louder than the words of an anthology it purported to follow. His *Zhenguan Essentials* thus attempts to delegitimize what Chen has termed the "poisoned atmosphere of the post-Empress Wu court,"[29] while imploring Emperor Xuanzong to legitimize his rulership by learning from his great-grandfather. Like the *Essentials*, both the *Model for an Emperor* and the *Zhenguan Essentials* also emphasize recruiting worthy talent and accepting remonstration. Approximately one-sixth of the *Model for an Emperor* and one-fifth of the *Zhenguan Essentials* are devoted to those concerns, respectively.[30] However, the three texts each cover those themes from a different perspective of memory. The cultural memory within the *Essentials* links the collective identity of the Zhenguan society with the remote past and the history of rulership, arguably paving the way for Taizong and his court to follow in the footsteps of positive exemplars of former times, and become exemplary themselves. The individual memory communicated by the *Model for an Emperor* infuses Taizong's advice for the future reign of his heir-apparent with the knowledge and experience of the recent past, in hopes that the next rulership will be as good as, if not better, than his own. And the communicative memory about the Zhenguan administration itself recorded by the *Zhenguan Essentials* uses the recent past to advocate for institutional reform in the present. Hence, unlike the personal memory of the Zhenguan ruler or a historical account of his Zhenguan reign, the *Essentials* provides a direct window into the political discourse that plausibly informed the Zhenguan ruling collective, including what and how Taizong read on rulership. To the extent that the anthology was consulted by the Zhenguan ruling collective, the *Essentials* may save some of the guesswork and extrapolation *ex post facto* of the principles and precedents underlying some of their attitudes and decision-making from records concerning their practice of government. Understandably, there is often a natural discrepancy between the Zhenguan ruler and his court knowing what should be done from their *Essentials* and choosing to do so, or following through on those choices. For example, Wei Zheng was highly critical of Taizong's shortcomings during the latter years of his reign, especially his failure to maintain some of the positive practices that had characterized the earlier period of the Zhenguan era.[31] Nevertheless, those discrepancies do not appear to diminish the overall exemplary nature of the rulership, nor do they detract from the *Essentials*' role as the sourcebook for governance that has been positively exemplary and exportable.

Although the *Essentials* became non-extant on its native shores sometime during the fourteenth century, many of the political ideas and values it prescribes can be seen to shape the cultural memory of subsequent courts. This stemmed from an enduring interest in the Zhenguan governmental exemplar and widespread transmission of the *Zhenguan Essentials*. I contend that the influence of the *Essentials* on later processes of cultural memory-making may be inferred from the space occupied by the *Zhenguan Essentials* in political discourse. As the cultural memory of a society need not depend on the existence of a particular canon, it may well endure, in part or in whole, through other textual carriers:

> The crucial point is that society's acceptance of norms and values does not depend on a "sacralized," written, or in any other form symbolically coded canon. The genesis and validity of values and their translation into effective practical norms is instead based on the processes of negotiation and agreement that are part of common experience ... In general, it is sufficient if the members of a group or society can explain why they keep to their effectively operating self-images ... .[32]

This would suggest that the textual discontinuity of the *Essentials* need not equate to the loss of its ideas and ideals of good government. Indeed, later courts in China and Japan continued to remember and draw inspiration from the model exemplar of Zhenguan rulership that was likely engendered by the *Essentials* in the first place. This phenomenon is manifest in the relatively continuous and extensive transmission of the *Zhenguan Essentials*. A comprehensive overview of its dissemination by De Weerdt and McMullen provides that the text was used by emperors Daizong, Xianzong, Wenzong, Xuanzong 宣宗 (r. 846–859) of the Tang dynasty, and virtually all the courts of the Song, Liao (916–1125), Western Xia (1038–1227), Jin (1115–1234), Yuan, Ming, and Qing dynasties of imperial China.[33] The *Zhenguan Essentials* has been consulted by the ruling elites beyond China—from about the ninth century in Japan, the mid-tenth century on the Korean peninsula, and from the sixteenth century in Vietnam, with continuing interest across East Asia through to the present day.[34] Admittedly, the *Zhenguan Essentials* presents a somewhat idealized account of the Zhenguan political practice, as it was intended for the edification of Emperor Xuanzong of the Tang dynasty in hopes of political reform along the lines of the Zhenguan model. However, its portrayal of the Zhenguan court and their practice of government exhibits much of the political norms and values that are prescribed by the *Essentials*. Insofar as the *Zhenguan Essentials* corresponds to the ideas and values of the Zhenguan cultural memory in the *Essentials*, the textual continuity and widespread dissemination of the former may signify that some of the Zhenguan cultural memory could be transmitted independently of their original carrier—that is, the *Essentials*. The same may be said about the *Golden Mirror* and the *Model for an Emperor*, the complete or partial translations of which became accessible to European readers from 1735,[35] and Taizong was cited in French, German, English, Italian, and Dutch books and periodicals as a universal model of good governance from the mid- to late eighteenth century.[36]

The textual history of the *Zhenguan Essentials* offers two points of note. First, generations of the ruling elite in China remained interested in studying the "good government of the Zhenguan reign" during the time that the *Essentials* was lost. This would presumably include learning from the political ideas and values of the Zhenguan rulership that were originally informed by the *Essentials*. Considering that the reception of the *Essentials* in Japan roughly parallels that of the *Zhenguan Essentials*, it seems likely that the *Essentials* may have continued to be transmitted in China had it been able to remain extant. Hence, the disappearance of the *Essentials* in China may be attributed to the passive forgetting of cultural memory in failing to preserve the finite manuscript copies that were still in existence during the Song dynasty before they became irrevocably lost.

Second, both the *Essentials* and the *Zhenguan Essentials* were studied by the polities of East Asia. With the former articulating the theoretical discourse to which the Zhenguan ruling collective subscribed, and the latter relating their practice of government, the two texts provide complementary perspectives of theory and praxis, and it is not surprising that they were often read together in the formal learning required of government officials. Minamoto no Takaakira's ceremony and protocol guide dating to tenth-century Japan even claims that everything that an official needs to know about "the matters between the sovereign and their subordinates" is covered by those two texts. Both books were also referred to in the 1884 palace examination paper during Qing China. It may be said that the existence of the *Essentials* as the statecraft sourcebook for the Zhenguan court lends credibility to their depiction in the *Zhenguan Essentials* in the sense that the exemplary governance was the fruit of following a political canon rather than a matter of serendipitous coincidence. The relatively uninterrupted transmission of the *Essentials* in Japan, combined with that of the *Zhenguan Essentials* in East Asia, attest to the enduring influence on the cultural memory of those political norms and values espoused by the *Essentials* and attributed to the Zhenguan ruling collective by the *Zhenguan Essentials*. Therefore, through books like the *Essentials*, the Zhenguan political practice formalized certain pillars of political culture that remained at the heart of political discourse and defined fundamental principles of political thought for centuries across East Asia.

The *Essentials* is a medieval Chinese compendium that has defied typical definitions and established classifications. As a source of inherited knowledge, the *Essentials* records neither the personal experiences of an individual emperor nor a systematic exposition of the workings of a government. As a compilation of excerpted material, the *Essentials* does not present as the typical epitome nor encyclopedic anthology. As a text of theoretical discourse, the *Essentials* is not a disquisition on political philosophy or concerns in the style of a masters writing. Even among the mirrors relating to the Zhenguan reign-period, the *Essentials* seems particularly unique in its structure and composition. Instead of a manifesto communication like the *Golden Mirror*, a historical survey of rulers and princes like the *Concise Discourse on Emperors and Kings* and the *Record of the Commendable and Contemptible Conduct of the Feudal Lords and Princes since Antiquity*, a program of recommended practices like the *Model for an Emperor*, or an idealized reconstruction of court speeches and dialogues like the *Zhenguan Essentials*, the *Essentials* purports to articulate the theoretical discourse to underpin the Zhenguan rulership and its successors. For all its peculiarities perhaps, the *Essentials* has been relatively obscure among European-language scholarship in the areas of politics, history, and culture. Building on the existing corpus of research on the *Essentials* that has been largely written in the Chinese, Korean, and Japanese languages, this volume hopes to bridge the gap in the English-language scholarship by analyzing the *Essentials* using the theory of cultural memory. The various elements of cultural memory, as theorized by the Assmanns, have enabled a systematic and critical investigation into the production, contents, and transmission of the *Essentials*. The findings show that the political thought and practice of the Zhenguan era tapped hallowed texts of the past and was tempered with present concerns. The excerpts selected for inclusion in the anthology reconfigured a cultural symbol and espoused values, as exemplified by the worthy official and remonstrative advices, to provide normative guidance for the Zhenguan ruling elite and reinforce their collective identity. Insofar as it formalizes the theoretical discourse underlying Emperor Taizong's administration, the *Essentials* and its relatively uninterrupted transmission in Japan is seen to be integral to the perpetuation of the political norms and values of the Zhenguan ruling collective and the dissemination of their model practice of government to courts through time and space.

APPENDIX ONE

WEI ZHENG'S PREFACE

羣書治要序[1]

Preface to the *Qunshu zhiyao*

秘書監巨鹿男臣魏徵等奉敕撰

Compiled on imperial commission by the Director of the Palace Library and Baron of Ju Lu Your servant Wei Zheng et al.

竊惟載籍之興，其來尚矣。左史右史，記事記言，皆所以昭德塞違，勸善懲惡。故作而可紀，薰風揚乎百代；動而不法，炯戒垂乎千祀。是以歷觀前聖，撫運膺期，莫不懍乎御朽，自強不息，乾乾夕惕；義在茲乎？

In my humble opinion, the ascendance of historical writings is long-established. The court historians of the left and right record the ruler's deeds and words to illuminate virtue, deter wrongdoing, motivate goodness, and punish misconduct. Thus through their records, worthy examples may leave fragrance lasting a hundred generations while unworthy examples flash warnings for a thousand years. For this reason, if one observes the former sages who embraced the heavenly mandate as their destiny—there are none who have not been [as cautious] as if driving a horse with moldering reins, improving themselves tirelessly and ever vigilant day and night. Is that not the case?

近古皇王，時有撰述，並皆包括天地，牢籠群有。競採浮豔之詞，爭馳迂誕之說；騁末學之博聞，飾雕蟲之小伎。流宕忘反，殊塗同致：雖辯周萬物，愈失司契之源；術總百端，乖得一之旨。

In ancient and recent times, emperors and princes often have their own written works. They generally encompass the celestial and earthly, including all and sundry. They compete in the use of flowery language and dissemination of preposterous notions to flaunt their conversancy with trivial scholarship and embellish their limited skill. Indulging in the wanton rambling, various paths reach the same end. Though the discourse encompasses a thousand matters, it departs from the fundamentals of writing mastery. Though the craft covers a hundred aspects, it deviates from the objective of achieving unity.

皇上以天縱之多才，運生知之叡思，性與道合，動妙幾神。玄德潛通，化前王之所未化；損己利物，行列聖之所不能行。翰海龍庭之野，並為郡國；扶桑若木之域，咸襲纓冕。天地成平，外內禔福。猶且為而不恃，雖休勿休；俯協堯舜，式遵稽古。不察貌乎止水，將取鑒乎哲人。

With Your Majesty's many natural talents and innate wisdom, [Your] character corresponds to the Way and [Your] conduct approximates the divine. Your profound virtue and intellect have inspired civilization that is unprecedented among former sovereigns. By sacrificing Yourself for others, You have effected what exemplary sages could not. The ethnic tribes of the far north have joined our territory, the peoples of the east and west adopt our headdress, and there is peace and happiness throughout the empire. Yet Your Majesty remains humble and not complacent. When praised, You are not proud, but emulate King Yao and King Shun and follow the teachings of old. You scrutinize yourself not by [the surface of] still waters, but by [reflecting on] the examples of wise individuals.

以為六籍紛綸，百家踳駮。窮理盡性，則勞而少功；周覽汎觀，則博而寡要。故爰命臣等，採摭群書，翦截淫放，光昭訓典。

[Your Majesty] finds [the writings of] the Six Classics bewildering and [the writings of] the hundred masters disparate. Exhaustive analysis of the principles and natures is fatiguing yet futile. Extensive reading without perspective broadens [one's] knowledge without grasp of the essentials. Your servants have therefore been ordered to select from divers texts, excise the irregular and irrelevant, and illuminate the instructive standards.

聖思所存，務乎政術；綴敘大略，咸發神衷。雅致鈎深，規摹宏遠；網羅治體，事非一目。

As Your Majesty is concerned about the work of statecraft and long-term strategy, the essentials are chosen from a broad range [of texts] with comprehensive coverage of the governing structure that is not limited to any one subject.

若乃欽明之后，屈己以救時；無道之君，樂身以亡國。或臨難而知懼、在危而獲安；或得志而驕居、業成以致敗者：莫不備其得失，以著為君之難。

While enlightened monarchs redeem the times by their self-sacrifice, unscrupulous rulers jeopardize the nation by their self-indulgence. Some because of caution in times of hardship achieve security in crisis. Some become complacent under favorable conditions causing success to be short-lived. No merit or fault goes unrecorded in writing about the challenges of being a ruler.

其委質策名，立功樹惠；貞心直道，忘軀殉國；身殞百年之中，聲馳千載之外。或大奸巨猾，轉日迴天；社鼠城狐，反白仰黑，忠良由其放逐，邦國因以危亡者：咸亦述其終始，以顯為臣不易。

The faithful [ministers] contribute meritorious service, are dedicated and principled, and serve the nation selflessly. [Although] their lives expire within a century, their renown continues beyond the millennium. The wicked [ministers] are powerfully manipulative and as ineradicable as the mice living in temples and the foxes dwelling in city walls. Shunning the white and admiring the black, they imperil the state and empire by banishing the faithful and good. Such details are also fully recorded to illuminate the difficulties of serving as a minister.

其立德立言，作訓垂範；為綱為紀，經天緯地。金聲玉振，騰實飛英；雅論徽猷，嘉言美事，可以弘獎名教，崇太平之基者：固亦片善不遺，將以丕顯皇極。

They establish lasting virtue and words, leave instructions and norms, as the guide and order for the warp and weft of heaven and earth. Their cherished voices, soaring excellences, fine discourses, admirable designs, estimable speeches, and good deeds, can promote the celebrated teachings and strengthen the foundations of global peace. Thus, even the smallest goodness has not been overlooked in illuminating imperial perfection.

至於母儀嬪則，懿后良妃，參徽猷於十亂，著深誡於辭輦。或傾城哲婦，亡國艷妻，候晨雞以先鳴，待舉烽而後笑者：時有所存，以備勸戒。

As for exemplary mothers and wives in the empresses and consorts, who contributed designs among the ten advisors and who wrote stern caution on declining [to share the emperor's] carriage. Additionally, calculating wives, femme fatales, like hens that supplant the rooster in heralding the dawn and Bao Si who only laughed after the beacons were lit. They existed at times and are recorded for encouragement and admonishment.

爰自六經，訖乎諸子；上始五帝，下盡晉年。凡為五表，合五十卷。本求治要，故以治要為名。

[This text] draws from the Six Classics to the various masters, [spans] from the [times of the] Five Sovereigns to the years of the Jin dynasty. It comprises five cases of fifty scrolls altogether. It primarily seeks [to capture] the gist of bringing about order and is thus entitled the "Essentials for Bringing about Order."

但《皇覽》、《遍略》，隨方類聚，名目互顯，首尾淆亂；文義斷絕，尋究為難。今之所撰，異乎先作；總立新名，各全舊體，欲令見本知末，原始要終；並棄彼春華，採茲秋實；一書之內，牙角無遺；一事之中，羽毛咸盡。用之當今，足以鑒覽前古；傳之來葉，可以貽厥孫謀。

In the past, the *Imperial Conspectus* and the *Comprehensive Digest of the Institute of the Floral Grove* follow convention and group by subject. [Their] terms and entries reiterate each other, the introductions and conclusions are disorganized, the text and its meaning are disrupted, and the usage and study [of them] are difficult. What has been compiled here differs from former works. The *Essentials for Bringing about Order* compiles the essential readings from divers texts under a new title while preserving their names and structures to facilitate a complete understanding without extraneous details. This is akin to abandoning the flowers of Spring for the fruits of Autumn. Each extract is materially complete, and each matter is related in full. Used in the present, [the *Essentials*] suffices for reflection on and learning from the ancient past. Handed on to the future, [the *Essentials*] may provide a reference for descendants.

引而申之，觸類而長，蓋亦言之者無罪，聞之者足以自戒。庶弘茲九德，簡而易從；觀彼百王，不疾而速。崇巍巍之盛業，開蕩蕩之王道。可久可大之功，並天地之貞觀；日用日新之德，將金鏡以長懸。其目錄次第編之如左。

Reflecting on its contents may provide inspiration for related affairs. It is indeed a matter of heeding the words and not blaming the sources. The *Essentials* will hopefully promote the nine virtues by making them concise and practicable, [facilitate] learning from a hundred kings with efficiency, [enable one] to revere majestic merits and establish the imperial Way. Such accomplishments will be extensive and enduring and match the constancy revealed of heaven and earth. The constant virtue of daily practice and self-improvement enables the golden mirror to illuminate for all time. The contents [of the *Essentials*] are listed in the order on the left.

APPENDIX TWO

HAYASHI NOBUTAKA'S PREFACE TO THE *COLLATED GUNSHO CHIYŌ*

校正《羣書治要》序[1]

Preface to the *Collated Gunsho chiyō*

古昔聖主賢臣，所以孜孜講求，莫非平治天下之道，皆以救弊于一時，成法于萬世，外此豈有可觀者哉？但世遷事變，時換勢殊，不得不因物立則，視宜創制。是以論說之言日浩，撰著之文月繁；簡樸常寡，浮誕漸勝；其綱之不能知，而況舉其目乎？此書之作，蓋其以此也。先明道之所以立，而後知政之所行；先尋教之所以設，而後得學之所歸。自典誥深奧，訖史子辯博，諸系乎政術，存乎勸戒者，舉而不遺。罷朝而不厭其淆亂，閉室而不煩其尋究，誠亦次經之書也。

What the sage rulers and worthy officials of the past strived towards was none other than the Way of bringing about peace and order for all under heaven. All efforts were to resolve the issues of the times and set an example for all time. What else is worth considering? However, as generations pass, matters vary, times change, conditions differ, and it becomes necessary to establish material norms and develop appropriate institutions. Hence, oral discourses expand by the day, and written texts multiply by the month. The clear and concise are generally few and increasingly outnumbered by the frivolous and baseless. If the structure remains obscure, how can one make out the details? This was how the compilation of this text came about. First understand how the Way is established, and then know the practice of government. First ponder why the education is initiated, and then attain the objective of learning. From the deeply profound canonical writings and pronouncements to the extensive disquisitions of the histories and masters, they each comprehensively cover the art of governance, and offer encouragement and admonishment. Retiring from court, one would not resent its disorderly confusion. Secluded at home, one would not be bothered by its endless tedium. This is truly a text that comes only second to the classics.

我朝承和、貞觀之間，致重雍襲熙之盛者，未必不因講究此書之力。則凡君民、臣君者非所可忽也。尾公有見於斯，使世子命臣僚校正而上之木，又使余信敬序之。惟信敬弱而不敏，如宜固辭者而不敢者，抑亦有故也。《羣書治要》五十卷，五十卷內闕三卷。神祖遷駿府得此書，惜其不全，命我遠祖羅山補之，三卷內一卷今不傳。今尾公此舉，上之欲君民者執以致日新之美，下之欲臣君者奉以贊金鏡之明，為天下國家奠昇平之愈久，遠心曠度，有不可勝言者也。信敬預事，亦知遠祖所望，信敬是所以奉命不敢辭也。

The flourishing of harmony and prosperity in the period between our Jōwa and Jōgan eras may not be unrelated to the efforts in teaching and learning this text. Hence, those ruling the people and those serving the ruler cannot afford to overlook it. Tokugawa Munechika [(1733–1800)] being aware of this, arranged for his sons to have officials collate the text and prepare woodblocks (for printing), and for myself, Nobutaka, to write the preface. I, Nobutaka, am feeble and incompetent, that I should have firmly declined but did not dare to, was not without reason. The fifty scrolls of the *Essentials for Bringing about Order from Assembled Texts* is missing three scrolls. After moving to the Sunpu domain, Tokugawa Ieyasu [(1542–1616)] received this text. Concerned about its incompleteness, he asked my ancestor Hayashi Razan [(1583–1657)] to supplement it. Of the three missing scrolls, only one is nonextant. Now Tokugawa Munechika's undertaking hopes that leaders will achieve the excellence of daily improvement by upholding the text, and subordinates will assist the wisdom of golden mirrors by following the text, such that all domains and families under heaven may enjoy longer periods of peace and prosperity. Such vision and magnanimity are beyond words. I, Nobutaka, am aware of this matter and the wishes of my ancestor [Hayashi Razan]. I, Nobutaka, therefore followed the order and dared not to refuse.

天明七年丁未四月
Fourth month of the seventh year of the Tenmei era (1787)
朝散大夫國子祭酒林信敬謹序
Preface by Hayashi Nobutaka Grand Master for Closing Court and
Chancellor of the State Academy Directorate

APPENDIX THREE

EDITIONS OF THE *QUNSHU ZHIYAO* 360 SERIES

ARABIC

مبادئ الحكم في الصين القديمة 360. Trans. Hussein Ismail and Farida Wang Fu 王複. Beijing: Huawen chubanshe, 2016.

CHINESE

1. Chung Hua Cultural Education Centre(M)Bhd 馬來西亞中華文化教育中心. *Qunshu zhiyao 360* 群書治要三六〇 vol. 1. Taipei: World Book Co., 2012.
2. Chung Hua Cultural Education Centre(M)Bhd 馬來西亞中華文化教育中心. *Qunshu zhiyao 360* 群書治要三六〇 vol. 2. Taipei: World Book Co., 2014.
3. Chung Hua Cultural Education Centre(M)Bhd 馬來西亞中華文化教育中心. *Qunshu zhiyao 360* 群書治要三六〇 vol. 3. Taipei: World Book Co., 2015.
4. Caituan faren Tainan shi guoxue shuyuan wenhua jijinhui 財團法人台南市國學書院傳統文化基金會. *Qunshu zhiyao 360* 群書治要三六〇 vol. 4. Taipei: World Book Co., 2017.

ENGLISH

1. Chung Hua Cultural Education Centre(M)Bhd 馬來西亞中華文化教育中心. *The Governing Principles of Ancient China*. Taipei: World Book Co., 2012.
2. Chung Hua Cultural Education Centre(M)Bhd 馬來西亞中華文化教育中心. *The Governing Principles of Ancient China* vol. 2. Taipei: World Book Co., 2014.
3. Chung Hua Cultural Education Centre(M)Bhd 馬來西亞中華文化教育中心. *The Governing Principles of Ancient China* vol. 3. Taipei: World Book Co., 2017.
4. *Qunshu zhiyao san liu ling ying yi ben di yi ce* 群書治要三六〇英譯本第一冊 (English translation of the *Qunshu zhiyao 360*, vol. 1). Trans. Zhong Aide, Lai Xiuhui, and Zhong Guofeng. Taipei: Juliang International, 2013.
5. *Qunshu zhiyao san liu ling ying yi ben di er ce* 群書治要三六〇英譯本第二冊 (English translation of the *Qunshu zhiyao 360*, vol. 2). Trans. Zhong Aide, Lai Xiuhui, and Zhong Guofeng. Taipei: Juliang International, 2014.
6. *Qunshu zhiyao san liu ling ying yi ben di san ce* 群書治要三六〇英譯本第三冊 (English translation of the *Qunshu zhiyao 360*, vol. 3). Trans. Zhong Aide, Lai Xiuhui, and Zhong Guofeng. Taipei: Juliang International, 2014.
7. *Qunshu zhiyao san liu ling ying yi ben di si ce* 群書治要三六〇英譯本第四冊 (English translation of the *Qunshu zhiyao 360*, vol. 4). Trans. Zhong Aide, Lai Xiuhui, and Zhong Guofeng. Taipei: Juliang International, 2014.
8. *Qunshu zhiyao san liu ling ying yi ben di si ce* 群書治要三六〇英譯本第五冊 (English translation of the *Qunshu zhiyao 360*, vol. 5). Trans. Zhong Aide, Lai Xiuhui, and Zhong Guofeng. Taipei: Juliang International, 2014.

FRENCH

1. *Les principes de gouvernance de la Chine ancienne.* Trans. M. Massoulier. Taipei: World Book Co., 2015.

2. *Les principes de gouvernance de la Chine ancienne Tome 2*. Trans. M. Massoulier. Paris: Editions You Feng Libraire & Editeur, 2017.

GERMAN

Grundsätze des Regierens in alten Schriften 群書治要: Band 1. Trans. Anna Xiulan Zeeck. Oldenburg: Desina Verlag, 2018.

JAPANESE

1. Seiyuu Association. 群書治要360第一冊. Taichung: Seiyuu Association, 2015.
2. Seiyuu Association. 群書治要360第二冊. Taichung: Seiyuu Association, 2015.
3. Seiyuu Association. 群書治要360第三冊. Taichung: Seiyuu Association, 2016.
4. Seiyuu Association. 群書治要360第四冊. Taichung: Seiyuu Association, 2019.

RUSSIAN

Принципы государственного управления в древнем Китае: Первый том. Trans. Цзинь Цзяньхун. Hong Kong: Hong Kong Buddhist Education Foundation Ltd., 2017.

SPANISH

Los principios rectores de la antigua china. Trans. Sofia Lin. Taipei: World Book Co., 2015.

VIETNAMESE

QUẦN THƯ TRỊ YẾU 360. Trans. Nguyễn Thị Thúy Hà and Cư Sĩ Vọng Tây. Hong Kong: Hong Kong Buddhist Education Foundation, 2017.

Notes

INTRODUCTION

1. Emperor Taizong of the Tang dynasty will hereafter be variously referred to as "Emperor Taizong," "Taizong," the "Zhenguan ruler," or the "second Tang emperor."
2. Translation is based on Hilde De Weerdt and David McMullen, "Introduction: *The Essentials of Governance from the Reign of Constancy Revealed* in Context" in *The Essentials of Governance* by Wu Jing, eds. Hilde De Weerdt et al. (Cambridge: Cambridge University Press, 2020), xv.
3. It is unclear when the expression "good government of Zhenguan" was first used. A relatively early instance appears in a discussion regarding Emperor Taizong between Emperor Lizong 理宗 (r. 1224–1264) of the Song dynasty (960–1279) and the minister You Si 游似 (d. 1252). Tuoketuo 托克托 et al., *Song shi* 宋史 (History of the Song dynasty) in *Wenyuange Siku quanshu* 文淵閣四庫全書, vol. 287 (Taipei: Taiwan Shangwu yinshuguan, 2013), 684.
4. Wang Pu 王溥, *Tang huiyao* 唐會要 (Essential records of the Tang dynasty) in *Wenyuange Siku quanshu* 文淵閣四庫全書, vol. 606 (Taipei: Taiwan Shangwu yinshuguan, 2013), 481.
5. As the contents of the *Essentials* relate to the cultivation of ethical character on the part of the ruler, as well as their administration of state governance, the Chinese graph "*zhi*" in its title may be translated as "bringing about order," instead of "governance," to encompass a broader notion of enriching the lives of individuals and the state. I am greatly indebted to Professor Hilde De Weerdt for the English translation of *Qunshu zhiyao* as "Essentials

for Bringing about Order from Assembled Texts" and her kind advice on preparing my research for publication.

6. The *Essentials* is also referred to as '*Qunshu zhengyao* 群書政要' (Essentials for governance from assembled texts) and '*Qunshu liyao* 群書理要' (Essentials for regulation from assembled texts) in the *Tang huiyao* 唐會要 (Essential records of the Tang dynasty) and the *Jiu Tang shu* 舊唐書 (Old history of the Tang dynasty), respectively. The Chinese character *zhi* 治 in each case was substituted by *zheng* 政 (governance) and *li* 理 (regulation) to avoid the taboo of using the name of the third ruler of the Tang dynasty—Li Zhi 李治 (628–683), who is posthumously honoured as "Emperor Gaozong" 高宗' (r. 649–683). Sharing the same rhyme in Middle Chinese, the characters *zhi* and *li* could be used interchangeably. *Tang huiyao*, 606.481; Liu Xu 劉昫 et al., *Jiu Tang shu* 舊唐書 (Old history of the Tang dynasty) in *Wenyuange Siku quanshu* 文淵閣四庫全書, vol. 269 (Taipei: Taiwan Shangwu yinshuguan, 2013), 343; Poon Ming Kay 潘銘基, "Ri cang Ping'an shidai Jiutiaojia ben *Qunshu zhiyao* yanjiu 日藏平安時代九条家本群書治要研究" (A Study of the *Qunshu zhiyao* from Japan's Heian Period), *Journal of Chinese Studies* 67 (2018): 2–3. Chen Pengnian 陳彭年 et al., *Xinjiao Songben Guangyun* 新校宋本廣韻 (New collated Song edition of the *Guangyun* [rime dictionary]), eds. Li Tianfu 李添富 et al. (Taipei: Hongye wenhua, 2001), 62, 252.
7. The 68 sources may be counted as 66 when three of the sources—the *Records of Wei* (*Wei zhi* 魏志), the *Records of Shu* (*Shu zhi* 蜀志), and the *Records of Wu* (*Wu zhi* 吳志)—are collectively referred to as "Records of the Three Kingdoms" (*Sanguo zhi* 三國志). The 66 sources may be shown as "sixty-five" because the title of the *Discourse on Contemporary Affairs* (*Shiwu lun* 時務論) was absent from the edition produced during Genna Japan (1615–1624), but its excerpts are located after the *Structural Discourses* (*Ti lun* 體論) passages.
8. The term "masters" refers to a corpus of literature traditionally attributed to master figures from the pre-Qin period (before 221 BCE), which by the early Tang dynasty also included strategist writings: Wiebke Denecke, *The Dynamics of Masters Literature: Early Chinese Thought from Confucius to Han Feizi* (Cambridge, MA: Harvard University Asia Center, 2010), 3; Endymion Porter Wilkinson, *Chinese History: A New Manual*, sixth ed. (Cambridge, MA: Endymion Wilkinson c/o Harvard University Asia Center, 2022), 1852.
9. Twenty-seven of those sources compiled in the *Essentials* have annotations excerpted from their commentaries.
10. Wu Jing 吳兢, *Zhenguan zhengyao* 貞觀政要 (Essentials of governance from the Zhenguan reign) in *Wenyuange Siku quanshu* 文淵閣四庫全書, vol. 407 (Taipei: Taiwan Shangwu yinshuguan, 2013), 337–554.

11. Jan Assmann, "Kollektives Gedächtnis und kulturelle Identität," in *Kultur und Gedächtnis*, eds. Jan Assmann and Tonio Hölscher (Frankfurt: Suhrkamp, 1988), 9–19; Jan Assmann and John Czaplicka, "Collective Memory and Cultural Identity," *New German Critique*, vol. 65 (1995): 125–133.
12. Martin Kern, "Cultural Memory and the Epic in Early Chinese Literature: The Case of Qu Yuan 屈原 and the *Lisao* 離騷," *Journal of Chinese Literature and Culture* 9, no. 1 (2022): 135.
13. Lynn A. Struve, "Introduction to the Symposium: Memory and Chinese Text," *Chinese Literature: Essays, Articles, Reviews (CLEAR)* 27 (2005): 4.
14. David McMullen, "The Big Cats Will Play: Tang Taizong and His Advisors," *Journal of Chinese Studies* 57 (2013): 300–301, 304–307, 337.
15. Arthur F. Wright, "T'ang T'ai-Tsung: The Man and the Persona," in *Essays on T'ang Society*, eds. John Curtis Perry and Bardwell L. Smith (Leiden: Brill, 1976), 22.
16. McMullen, "The Big Cats Will Play: Tang Taizong and His Advisors": 301–304, 311, 340.
17. Jack W. Chen, *The Poetics of Sovereignty: On Emperor Taizong of the Tang Dynasty* (Cambridge, MA: Harvard University Asia Center for the Harvard-Yenching Institute, 2010), 2, 4, 13, 81–105, 153–160, 190–209, 228–237, 241–246, 296–310, 330–333, 343–376.
18. Chen, *The Poetics of Sovereignty: On Emperor Taizong of the Tang Dynasty*, 26–30; Howard J. Wechsler, *Mirror to the Son of Heaven: Wei Cheng at the Court of T'ang T'ai-Tsung* (New Haven, CT: Yale University Press, 1974), 22–26; Howard J. Wechsler, "T'ai-tsung (reign 626–49) the consolidator," in *The Cambridge History of China Volume 3: Sui and T'ang China, 589–906, Part I*, ed. Denis Twitchett (Cambridge: Cambridge University Press, 2008), 189.
19. Denis Twitchett, "How to Be an Emperor: T'ang T'ai-tsung's Vision of His Role," *Asia Major* 9, no. 1/2 (1996): 4.
20. Gong Yueguo 鞏曰國 and Zhang Yanli 張豔麗, "*Qunshu zhiyao* suo jian *Guanzi* yiwen kao 群書治要所見管子異文考" (A study of the variant text in the *Qunshu zhiyao*'s excerpts from *Master Guan*), *Guanzi xuekan* 管子學刊 (Journal of Master Guan) 3 (2015): 12–16, 34.
21. Poon Ming Kay 潘銘基, "*Qunshu zhiyao* suo zai *Wenzi* yiwen yanjiu 群書治要所載文子異文研究" (A study of the variant text in the *Qunshu zhiyao*'s excerpts from *Master Wen*), *Xingda zhongwen xuebao* 興大中文學報 (Journal of the Chinese Department of the National Chung Hsing University) 44 (2018): 1–27.
22. Ren Yu 任煜, "Ri cang Liancang chaoben *Qunshu zhiyao Shi* tanlun 日藏鐮倉抄本群書治要詩探論" (An essay on the *Qunshu zhiyao*'s excerpts from

the *Odes* in the Japanese Kamakura manuscript), *Dangan* 檔案 (Archives) 1 (2020): 33–40.

23. Lam Yatyan 林溢欣, "Cong Riben cang juanzi ben *Qunshu zhiyao* kan *Sanguo zhi* jiaokan ji qi banben wenti 從日本藏卷子本群書治要看三國志校勘及其版本問題" (A matter of textual collation and editions of the *Records of the Three Kingdoms* based on the Kamakura edition of the *Qunshu zhiyao*), *Journal of Chinese Studies* 53 (2011): 193–215.
24. Lam Yatyan 林溢欣, "Cong *Qunshu zhiyao* kan Tang chu *Sunzi* banben xitong 從群書治要看唐初孫子版本系統" (A study of the early Tang editions of the *Art of War* based on the *Qunshu zhiyao*), *Guji zhengli yanjiu jikan* 古籍整理研究季刊 (Journal of ancient book collation studies) 3 (2011): 62–68.
25. Liu Peide 劉佩德, "*Qunshu zhiyao Shuofu* suoshou *Yuzi* hejiao 群書治要說郛所收鬻子合校" (Collating *Master Yu* as received in the *Qunshu zhiyao* and the *Shuofu*), *Guan zi xuekan* 管子學刊 (Journal of Master Guan) 14 (2014): 88–90.
26. Wang Wenhui 王文暉, "Cong guxieben *Qunshu zhiyao* kan tongxingben *Kongzi jiayu* cunzai de wenti 從古寫本群書治要看通行本孔子家語存在的問題" (A study of the received *School Sayings of Confucius* based on an early manuscript edition of the *Qunshu zhiyao*), *Zhongguo dianji yu wenhua* 中國典籍與文化 (Chinese texts and culture) 4 (2018): 113–119.
27. Cai Meng 蔡蒙, "*Qunshu zhiyao* suo yin *Shizi* jiaokan yanjiu 群書治要所引尸子校勘研究" (A collative study of *Master Shi* in the *Qunshu zhiyao*), *Wenzi ziliao* 文字資料 (Textual material) 35 (2018): 84–85, 110.
28. Lam Yatyan 林溢欣, "*Qunshu zhiyao* yin *Wu Yue chunqiu* tanwei 群書治要引吳越春秋探微" (Exploring the *Qunshu zhiyao*'s excerpts from the *Spring and Autumn Annals of [the states of] Wu and Yue*), *Guji zhengli yanjiu jikan* 古籍整理研究季刊 (Journal of ancient book collation studies) 1 (2019): 19–23.
29. Hou Jianming 侯健明, "Jinzeben *Qunshu zhiyao* dui *Shiji Hanshu* jiaozheng shisan ze 金澤本群書治要對史記漢書校正十三則" (Thirteen collative corrections to the *Records of the Historian* and the *History of the Former Han Dynasty* from the Kamakura edition of the *Qunshu zhiyao*), *Guji zhengli yanjiu jikan* 古籍整理研究季刊 (Journal of ancient book collation studies) 4 (2020): 50–54.
30. Hung Kuan-Chih 洪觀智, *Qunshu zhiyao shibu yanjiu: cong Zhenguan shixue de zhiyong jingshen tanqi* 羣書治要史部研究 從貞觀史學的致用精神談起 (The pragmatism of historiography in the Zhenguan period: A study of the *Qunshu zhiyao*'s historical excerpts) (Taipei: Huamulan wenhua chubanshe, 2016).

31. Kim Kwang-Il 金光一, "*Qunshu zhiyao* huichuan kao 群書治要回傳考" (A study of the *Qunshu zhiyao*'s re-introduction), *Lilunjie* 理論界 (Theory horizon) 9 (2011): 125–127.
32. Kim Kwang-Il 金光一, "*Qunshu zhiyao* yanjiu 群書治要研究" (A study of the *Qunshu zhiyao*), Doctoral thesis, Fudan University, 2010, 21, 99–100.
33. Song Yushun 宋玉順, "*Qunshu zhiyao* fanying de Qi wenhua zhiguo linian ji qi yingxiang 群書治要反映的齊文化治國理念及其影響" (Qi political culture and its influence in the *Qunshu zhiyao*), *Guanzi xuekan* 管子學刊 (Journal of Master Guan) 2 (2018): 76–81.
34. Poon Ming Kay 潘銘基, "Lun *Qunshu zhiyao* jingbu suojian Tang chu jingxue fengshang 論群書治要經部所見唐初經學風尚" (An essay on early Tang classical scholarship as seen in the canonical section of the *Qunshu zhiyao*), *Shumu jikan* 書目季刊 (Bibliography quarterly) 53, no. 3 (2019): 1–27.
35. Huang Lipin 黃麗頻, "Lun *Qunshu zhiyao* dui *Laozi* de qujing yu shijian 論群書治要對老子的取徑與實踐" (An essay on the teachings and practice of the *Old Master* in the *Qunshu zhiyao*), *Dong Hwa Journal of Chinese Studies* 31 (2020): 1–31.
36. Fan Wang, "Reading for Rule: Emperor Taizong of Tang and *Qunshu zhiyao*" in *The Edinburgh History of Reading: Early Readers*, ed. Mary Hammond (Edinburgh: Edinburgh University Press, 2020).
37. See, for example, Liu Guangpu 劉廣普 and Kang Weipo 康維波, "*Qunshu zhiyao* de nongye sixiang yanjiu 群書治要的農業思想研究" (A study of the *Qunshu zhiyao*'s discourse on agriculture), *Theoretic Observation* 理論觀察 12 (2014): 87–90, and Liu Yuli 劉余莉 and Zhang Chao 張超, "Cong *Qunshu zhiyao* zhidao sixiang lun Rujia shengxian zhengzhi tixi 從群書治要治道思想論儒家聖賢政治體系" (An essay on the Confucian system of governance by sages based on the political discourse of the *Qunshu zhiyao*), *Confucius Studies* 孔子研究 4 (2021): 33–41, 156–158.
38. Liu Haitian 劉海天 and Li Ping 李萍, "*Qunshu zhiyao* bianzuan yuanze tanshu: guanyu 'Zhenguan zhi zhi' zhengzhi lunli sixiang zhi tedian 群書治要編纂原則探述 關於貞觀之治政治倫理思想之特點" (An analysis of the compilation principles of the *Qunshu zhiyao*: the characteristics of the politico-ethical philosophy of the 'good government of the Zhenguan era'), *Modern Philosophy* 現代哲學 2 (2019): 149–154.
39. Kim, "*Qunshu zhiyao* yanjiu 群書治要研究."
40. See, for example, Kim Kwang-Il 金光一, "*Gunseochiyo* ui ilbon jeonrae 群書治要의 일본 전래" (The transmission of the *Qunshu zhiyao* in Japan), *Junggugeomunhak* 중국어문학 (Chinese literature) 2008, no. 52: 47–70, and Kim Kwang-Il 金光一, "*Jeong-gwanjichi* uiilonseo *Gunseochiyo* 貞觀之治의 이

론서群書治要" (*Qunshu zhiyao*: the theory book of the "good government of the Zhenguan era"), *Dongyoung munhwa* 東亞文化 (East Asian culture) 2011, no. 49: 123–127.

41. The text is mentioned as one of Wei Zheng's weighty responsibilities and an expression of his philosophical eclecticism in Howard J. Wechsler's *Mirror to the Son of Heaven: Wei Cheng at the Court of T'ang T'ai-Tsung*; Wei Zheng's preface to the *Essentials* is cited as a warning to Emperor Taizong against indulging in *belles lettres* anthologies in David McMullen's *State and Scholars in T'ang China*, and articles by Denis Twitchett and McMullen provide that the *Essentials* was "very frequently referred to" in Japan as an authoritative source on politics and the sovereign's role, and "the seventh-century equivalent of a sizeable encyclopedia of political wisdom" that provided an "efficient route to minimum learning" for Taizong, respectively: Wechsler, *Mirror to the Son of Heaven: Wei Cheng at the Court of T'ang T'ai-Tsung*, 113, 168–169; David McMullen, *State and Scholars in T'ang China* (Cambridge: Cambridge University Press, 1988), 214; Twitchett, "How to Be an Emperor: T'ang T'ai-tsung's Vision of His Role": 45–46; McMullen, "The Big Cats Will Play: Tang Taizong and His Advisors": 312.
42. See, for example, Carine Defoort's *The Pheasant Cap Master: A Rhetorical Reading*, Paul Fisher's *Shizi: China's First Syncretist*, and Eirik Lang Harris' *The Shenzi Fragments: A Philosophical Analysis and Translation*. *The Pheasant Cap Master (He guan zi): A Rhetorical Reading*, trans. Carine Defoort (New York: State University of New York Press, 1997), 78–84; *Shizi: China's First Syncretist*, trans. Paul Fischer (New York: Columbia University Press, 2012), 18, 48–52, 178, 189, and 191; *The Shenzi Fragments: A Philosophical Analysis and Translation*, trans. Eirik Lang Harris (New York: Columbia University Press, 2016), 3.
43. Fan Wang studies how the *Essentials* educates an emperor in the art of governance by prescribing what and how they should read, by reference to the excerpts from the *Mao Tradition of Commentary on the Odes* (*Maoshi*毛詩) and the *Exoteric Commentary on the Odes by Han Ying* (*Hanshi waizhuan* 韓詩外傳): Wang, "Reading for Rule: Emperor Taizong of Tang and *Qunshu zhiyao*," 38–45.
44. Kelly Ngo, "Cultural Memory of Early Tang China in the *Qunshu zhiyao* 群書治要 (Essentials for bringing about order from assembled texts)," *Journal of the European Association for Chinese Studies* 4 (2023): 199–222.
45. Zhou Li 周勵, "Qiangu qishu *Qunshu zhiyao* niepan chongsheng 千古奇書群書治要涅槃重生" (An ancient and extraordinary text—the revival of the *Qunshu zhiyao*), *China Western Development* 西部大開發, 2012, no. 7: 106–108.
46. National Centre for Preservation of Ancient Books, "Yongqing wenku sizhong chuban shuoming 永青文庫四種出版說明" (Note on the publication

of the four types from the Eisei Bunko Collection), in *Qunshu zhiyao* 群書治要 (Essentials for bringing about order from assembled texts), vol. 1, (Beijing: National Library of China Press, 2019), 1–2.

47. The conference was reported in the local news, for example, the *Ta Kong Pao* 大公報 newspaper. *Ta Kong Pao* 大公報, "*Qunshu zhiyao* luntan yi gu jian jin 群書治要論壇以古鑒今" (Seminars on the *Essentials for Bringing about Order from Assembled Texts* – Using the past to reflect on the present), accessed February 17, 2022 http://paper.takungpao.com/html/2013-04/27/content_37_6.htm.
48. The conferences took place during June 3–4, 2019, September 11–12, 2020, November 24–25, 2021, September 23–24, 2022, and October 13–14, 2023, with a further conference scheduled for November 22–23, 2024.
49. See, for example, National Cheng Kung University of Taiwan, "Di yi jie *Qunshu zhiyao guoji xueshu yantao hui huiyi lunwen ji* 第一屆群書治要國際學術研討會會議論文集" (Collected papers of the first international academic symposium on the *Qunshu zhiyao*), accessed June 14, 2019 www.chinese.ncku.edu.tw/p/406-1142-194026,r1185.php?Lang=zh-tw; Lin Chao-Cheng 林朝成 and Zhang Jui-Lin 張瑞麟, eds., *Di yi jie Qunshu zhiyao guoji xueshu yantao hui lunwen ji* 第一屆群書治要學術研討會論文集 (Collected papers of the first international academic symposium on the *Qunshu zhiyao*) (Taipei: Wanjuanlou, 2020); National Cheng Kung University of Taiwan, "Di er jie *Qunshu zhiyao* guoji xueshu yantao hui 第二屆群書治要國際學術研討會" (The second international academic symposium on the *Qunshu zhiyao*), accessed September 26, 2022, https://chinese.ncku.edu.tw/p/404-1142-210922.php?Lang=zh-tw; Huang Sheng-Sung 黃聖松, ed., *Di er jie Qunshu zhiyao guoji xueshu yantao hui lunwen ji* 第二屆群書治要國際學術研討會論文集 (Collected papers of the second international academic symposium on the *Qunshu zhiyao*) (Taipei: Wanjuanlou, 2021); National Cheng Kung University of Taiwan, "Disanjie *Qunshu zhiyao* xueshu yantaohui 第三屆群書治要學術研討會" (The third academic symposium on the *Qunshu zhiyao*), accessed September 26, 2022 https://chinese.ncku.edu.tw/p/404-1142-228167.php?Lang=zh-tw.
50. Yan Shaodang 嚴紹璗, *Riben cang Hanji zhenben zhuizong jishi Yan Shaodang haiwai fangshu zhi* 日本藏漢籍珍本追蹤紀實 嚴紹璗海外訪書志 (Record of investigation on rare Chinese texts in Japan: Monograph on foreign textual enquiries by Yan Shaodang) (Shanghai: Shanghai guji chubanshe, 2005), 177–178.
51. *Qunshu zhiyao* 群書治要 (Essentials for bringing about order from assembled texts) (Taipei: World Book Co., 2013).

52. *Qunshu zhiyao* 群書治要 (Essentials for bringing about order from assembled texts) in *Sibu congkan* 四部叢刊 (Four branches of literature collection), ed. Wang Yunwu 王雲五, vols. 76–78 (Shanghai: Shanghai shudian, 1989), is a reprint of its 1926 edition.
53. Assmann, "Kollektives Gedächtnis und kulturelle Identität," 15; Assmann, "Collective Memory and Cultural Identity," 132.
54. Dietrich Harth, "The Invention of Cultural Memory" in *Cultural Memory Studies: An International and Interdisciplinary Handbook*, eds. Astrid Erll and Ansgar Nünning (Berlin: Walter de Gruyter, 2008), 86.
55. Assmann, "Kollektives Gedächtnis und kulturelle Identität," 13–15; Assmann, "Collective Memory and Cultural Identity," 130–132.
56. Jan Assmann, "Communicative and Cultural Memory," in *Cultural Memory Studies: An International and Interdisciplinary Handbook*, eds. Astrid Erll and Ansgar Nünning (Berlin: Walter de Gruyter, 2008), 110–111.
57. Harth, "The Invention of Cultural Memory," 86; Jan Assmann, *Cultural Memory and Early Civilisation: Writing, Remembrance and Political Imagination* (New York: Cambridge University Press, 2011), 113–114, 119–120.
58. Assmann, *Cultural Memory and Early Civilization: Writing, Remembrance, and Political Imagination*, 130.
59. The editors of the *Essentials* will be collectively referred to as the "editors" or the "editorial team."
60. Twitchett, "How to Be an Emperor: T'ang T'ai-tsung's Vision of His Role," 1.
61. McMullen, "The Big Cats Will Play: Tang Taizong and His Advisors," 300.
62. *Zhenguan zhengyao* 407.350–354; Wang Qinruo 王欽若 and Yang Yi 楊億 et al., *Cefu yuangui* 冊府元龜 (Outstanding models from the storehouse of literature) in *Wenyuange Siku quanshu* 文淵閣四庫全書, vol. 903 (Taipei: Taiwan Shangwu yinshuguan, 2013), 832, 907.599–605; *Jiu Tang shu* 269.668–669; Li Fang 李昉 et al., *Wenyuan yinghua* 文苑英華 (Finest flowers in the garden of literature) in *Wenyuange Siku quanshu* 文淵閣四庫全書, vol. 1339 (Taipei: Taiwan Shangwu yinshuguan, 2013), 572–573.
63. Howard L. Goodman, *Ts'ao P'i Transcendent: The Political Culture of Dynasty-founding in China at the end of the Han* (Seattle, WA: Scripta Serica, 1998), 18. David McMullen has demonstrated the integration of ritual scholarship into the Tang bureaucracy that speaks to this commitment, especially on the part of scholars: David McMullen, "Bureaucrats and Cosmology: The Ritual Code of T'ang China," in *Critical Readings on Tang China*, ed. Paul W. Kroll, vol. 1 (Leiden: Brill, 2018), 295–345.
64. Assmann, "Communicative and Cultural Memory," 113.

65. Aleida Assmann, "Canon and Archive," in *Cultural Memory Studies: An International and Interdisciplinary Handbook*, eds. Astrid Erll and Ansgar Nünning (Berlin: Walter de Gruyter, 2008), 99.
66. Assmann, "Communicative and Cultural Memory," 117; Assmann, "Canon and Archive," 97.
67. Assmann, "Canon and Archive," 100–102, 106.
68. Assmann, "Canon and Archive," 101–103.
69. Assmann, "Canon and Archive," 98.
70. Sima Qian 司馬遷, *Shiji* 史記 (Records of the historian), in *Wenyuange Siku quanshu* 文淵閣四庫全書, vol. 244 (Taipei: Taiwan Shangwu yinshuguan, 2013), 237, 246–247.
71. William Theodore de Bary, "Epilogue: Why Confucius Now?" in *Confucianism for a Modern World*, eds. Daniel A. Bell and Hahm Chaibong (Cambridge: Cambridge University Press, 2003), 363–364; Roger T. Ames, "Travelling Together with *Gravitas*: The Intergenerational Transmission of Confucian Culture," in *Confucian Role Ethics: A Moral Vision for the 21st Century?*, eds. Henry Rosemont Jr. and Roger T. Ames (Gottingen: Vandenhoeck & Ruprecht, 2016), 157, 167.
72. Assmann, "Canon and Archive," 97.
73. Martin Bommas asserts that "all ancient objects and texts [experience] a shift of meaning at least once in their lifetime": Martin Bommas, "Pausanias' Egypt," in *Cultural Memory and Identity in Ancient Societies*, ed. Martin Bommas (London: Continuum Publishing Group, 2011), 92.

CHAPTER ONE

1. Assmann, "Kollektives Gedächtnis und kulturelle Identität," 13–14; Assmann, "Collective Memory and Cultural Identity": 130–131.
2. Emperor Taizong contributed to the *History of the Jin Dynasty* (*Jinshu* 晉書), that was compiled by Fang Xuanling 房玄齡 et al., various written pieces including summations of Emperor Xuan 宣 (179–251) and Emperor Wu 武 (r. 266–290) of the Jin dynasty, as well as essays on the poet Lu Ji 陸機 (261–303), the calligrapher Wang Xizhi 王羲之 (303–361), and the practice of calligraphy. However, it is unknown whether Taizong played any role in the execution of the work that culminated in the *Essentials*, for example, reviewing drafts.
3. Chinese imperial commissions of encyclopedic anthologies (*leishu* 類書) were considered to be state projects to organize the cultural and literary

inheritance. Itō Mieko 伊藤美重子, "Ruisho ni tsuite 類書について" (On the *leishu*), *Bulletin of the Sinological Society Ochanomizu University* 24 (2005): 11.

4. Wechsler, "T'ai-tsung (reign 626–49) the consolidator," 216–217.
5. Whereas other political advice texts produced for Taizong and his princes presented accounts of historical past rulers and princes (e.g., the *Diwang lüe lun* 帝王略論 (*Concise discourse on emperors and kings*) and the *Zi gu zhuhouwang shan'e lu* 自古諸侯王善惡錄 (*Record of the commendable and contemptible conduct of the feudal lords and princes since antiquity*), the *Essentials* offers broader coverage of statecraft concerns, practices, and exemplars (*Qunshu zhiyao*, 1.22–24 (Wei Zheng's preface)). Writing about the general concept of anthology, Seth Lerer considers that "The mark of any culture's literary sense of self lies in the way in which it makes anthologies." Seth Lerer, "Medieval English Literature and the Idea of the Anthology," *Publications of the Modern Language Association* 118, no. 5 (2003): 1263.
6. Xie Baocheng 謝保成, ed., *Zhenguan zhengyao jijiao* (Collected annotations of the *Essentials of Governance from the Zhenguan Reign*) (Beijing: Zhonghua shuju, 2003), 36–37, 290; *Jiu Tang shu*, 269:672; Ouyang Xiu 歐陽修 and Song Qi 宋祁, *Xin Tang shu* 新唐書 (New history of the Tang dynasty) in *Wenyuange Siku quanshu* (Wenyuange edition of the Complete Library of the Four Branches of Literature) 文淵閣四庫全書, vol. 274 (Taipei: Taiwan Shangwu yinshuguan, 2013), 244; Sima Guang 司馬光, *Zizhi tongjian* 資治通鑑 (Comprehensive mirror in aid of governance) in *Wenyuange Siku quanshu* (Wenyuange edition of the Complete Library of the Four Branches of Literature) 文淵閣四庫全書, vol. 308 (Taipei: Taiwan Shangwu yinshuguan, 2013), 321; Wang Fangqing 王方慶, *Wei Zheng gong jianlu* 魏鄭公諫錄 (Record of the remonstrations of Lord Wei Zheng) in *Wenyuange Siku quanshu* (Wenyuange edition of the Complete Library of the Four Branches of Literature) 文淵閣四庫全書, vol. 446 (Taipei: Taiwan Shangwu yinshuguan, 2013), 180–181, 199; *Tang huiyao* 607:423; *Cefu yuangui* 904.399.
7. *Cefu yuangui*, 902.638; *Wenyuan yinghua*, 1336.367–370; Twitchett, "How to Be an Emperor: T'ang T'ai-tsung's Vision of His Role": 18–33; Wu Yun 吳云 and Ji Yu 冀宇, eds., *Tang Taizong quanji jiaozhu* 唐太宗全集校注 (Collation and annotation of the complete works of Emperor Taizong of the Tang dynasty) (Tianjin: Tianjin guji chubanshe, 2004), 125–136.
8. *Zhenguan zhengyao*, 407.370.
9. That Taizong was motivated to mollify opposing parties in consolidating the new Tang dynasty finds support in the fact that Wei Zheng's advice was accepted more in the early period of the Zhenguan reign than the later years, as complained about in Wei Zheng's remonstrations dated to 637 and

641: *Zhenguan zhengyao* 407.350–354; *Cefu yuangui* 903.832, 907.599–605; *Jiu Tang shu* 269.668–669; *Wenyuan yinghua* 1339.572–573.

10. As Li Shimin began his military career from the age of 15 and spent more than twelve years in the army where he long occupied the highest post, Charles P. Fitzgerald notes that he was accustomed to commanding armies and ordering military officers but lacked experience in statecraft: Charles P. Fitzgerald, *Son of Heaven: A Biography of Li Shih-Min, founder of the T'ang Dynasty* (Cambridge: Cambridge University Press, 1933), 125–126.
11. *Zizhi tongjian*, 308:293. Translated by Wechsler, "T'ai-tsung (reign 626–49) the consolidator," 190.
12. *Jiu Tang shu*, 269:675.
13. *Xin Tang shu*, 276:11; *Tang huiyao*, 606:481; Liu Su 劉肅, *Tang xinyu* 唐新語 (New anecdotes from the Tang dynasty) in *Wenyuange Siku quanshu* (Wenyuange edition of the Complete Library of the Four Branches of Literature) 文淵閣四庫全書, vol. 1035 (Taipei: Taiwan Shangwu yinshuguan, 2013), 363.
14. Richard W. L. Guisso, *Wu Tse-T'ien and the Politics of Legitimation in T'ang China* (Bellingham: Western Washington Press, 1978), 109.
15. Arthur F. Wright, "T'ang T'ai-Tsung and Buddhism" in *Perspectives on the T'ang*, eds. Arthur F. Wright and Denis Twitchett (New Haven, CT: Yale University Press, 1973), 250–251.
16. It is not possible to know the total content excerpted by the *Essentials* on the Han emperors from the *Hanshu* 漢書 (History of the [former] Han dynasty) and the *Hou Hanshu* 後漢書 (History of the latter Han dynasty) (collectively, the "Han histories") due to the loss of scroll 13, which would have contained passages from the basic annals of the early Han emperors. However, the fact that the *Essentials* devotes twelve out of its twenty scrolls of historical writings to excerpts from the Han histories seems indicative of the extent to which the Han imperium served as a model for the Zhenguan court.
17. Zhao Keyao 趙克堯 and Xu Daoxun 許道勛, *Tang Taizong zhuan* 唐太宗傳 (Biography of Emperor Taizong of the Tang dynasty) (Beijing: Renmin chubanshe, 1995), 303.
18. Zhao and Xu, *Tang Taizong zhuan*, 318–320.
19. *Zhenguan zhengyao*, 407:498–499.
20. *Jiu Tang shu*, 268:50; *Zizhi tongjian*, 308:277–279, 282.
21. Twitchett, "How to Be an Emperor: T'ang T'ai-tsung's Vision of His Role," 14.
22. *Jiu Tang shu*, 269:665; *Zhenguan zhengyao*, 407:370.
23. Li Yanshou 李延壽, *Bei shi* 北史 (History of the Northern dynasties) in *Wenyuange Siku quanshu* (Wenyuange edition of the Complete Library of

the Four Branches of Literature) 文淵閣四庫全書, vol. 267 (Taipei: Taiwan Shangwu yinshuguan, 2013), 56.195.

24. *Xin Tang shu*, 273:486 (the places of Wei's great-grandfather Zhao and his grandfather Yan are erroneously reversed); *Bei shi*, 267:195–196; Wechsler, *Mirror to the Son of Heaven: Wei Cheng at the Court of T'ang T'ai-Tsung*, 36.
25. *Bei shi*, 267:196; *Jiu Tang shu*, 269:664; Wechsler, *Mirror to the Son of Heaven: Wei Cheng at the Court of T'ang T'ai-Tsung*, 36–37.
26. *Jiu Tang shu*, 269:664.
27. *Jiu Tang shu*, 269: 665–666; *Xin Tang shu*, 274: 242–243; Wechsler, *Mirror to the Son of Heaven: Wei Cheng at the Court of T'ang T'ai-Tsung*, 59–60.
28. *Jiu Tang shu*, 269:665–667, 673–675; Wechsler, *Mirror to the Son of Heaven: Wei Cheng at the Court of T'ang T'ai-Tsung*, 4, 24.
29. *Zhenguan zhengyao*, 407:370–371; Wechsler, *Mirror to the Son of Heaven: Wei Cheng at the Court of T'ang T'ai-Tsung*, 107–115, 140, 155.
30. *Jiu Tang shu*, 269:674.
31. Wechsler, *Mirror to the Son of Heaven: Wei Cheng at the Court of T'ang T'ai-Tsung*, 1–2.
32. *Jiu Tang shu*, 269:667.
33. *Jiu Tang shu*, 269:667; Wei Zheng's involvement in the *History of the Chen Dynasty*, the *History of the Liang Dynasty*, and the *History of the Sui Dynasty*, is detailed in Cynthia L. Chennault et al., eds., *Early Medieval Chinese Texts: A Bibliographical Guide* (Berkeley, CA: Institute of East Asian Studies, 2015), 44, 167, 330–331.
34. Hung, *Qunshu zhiyao shibu yanjiu: cong Zhenguan shixue de zhiyong jingshen tanqi*, 25.
35. The *New Anecdotes from the Tang Dynasty* (*Tang xinyu* 唐新語) names Chu Suiliang 褚遂良 (596–659) instead of his father Chu Liang. However, the generally accepted view that the editorial team included Chu Liang rather than his son is reasoned as follows. Chu Liang's age and qualification at the time of the commission is closer to the other members of the editorial team. Whereas Chu Suiliang was 35 years old in the year that the *Essentials* was completed, Wei Zheng was then aged 51, and Chu Liang, Xiao Deyan, and Yu Shinan were in their seventies. Not only were the latter three contemporaries, but they were also fellow academicians since the inception of Emperor Taizong's reign. Moreover, Chu Liang is often recorded as working together with Wei Zheng and Yu Shinan during the early Zhenguan years: *Tang xinyu*, 1035:363; *Jiu Tang shu*, 268:697–698, 720; 269:677, 685; 271:539; Xie, ed., *Zhenguan zhengyao jijiao*, 37.
36. *Jiu Tang shu*, 271:539.

37. Shen Yue 沈約, *Song shu* 宋書 (History of the Song dynasty) in *Wenyuange Siku quanshu* (Wenyuange edition of the Complete Library of the Four Branches of Literature) 文淵閣四庫全書, vol. 258 (Taipei: Taiwan Shangwu yinshuguan, 2013), 428–432, 435; *Jiu Tang shu*, 271:539.
38. Yao Silian 姚思廉, *Liang shu* 梁書 (History of the Liang dynasty) in *Wenyuange Siku quanshu* (Wenyuange edition of the Complete Library of the Four Branches of Literature) 文淵閣四庫全書, vol. 260 (Taipei: Taiwan Shangwu yinshuguan, 2013), 347–348.
39. *Jiu Tang shu*, 271:539.
40. *Jiu Tang shu*, 271:539.
41. *Jiu Tang shu*, 269:697; 271.539; *Tang huiyao*, 606:41.
42. *Jiu Tang shu*, 269:677, 685.
43. *Jiu Tang shu*, 269:677, 685.
44. *Jiu Tang shu*, 269:677, 685.
45. Sheng Zhongjian 盛鐘健 et al., eds., *Sui Tang jiahua Tang guoshi bu* 隋唐嘉話唐國史補 (Fine stories from the Sui and Tang dynasties and Supplemented history of the Tang empire) (Zhejiang: Zhejiang guji chubanshe, 1986), 47–48.
46. *Jiu Tang shu*, 269:677, 680.
47. *Jiu Tang shu*, 269:678; *Zhenguan zhengyao*, 407:376
48. *Jiu Tang shu*, 269:677.
49. Jack W. Chen, "The Organization of Governance" in *The Essentials of Governance* by Wu Jing, eds. Hilde De Weerdt et al. (Cambridge: Cambridge University Press, 2020), 31.
50. *Jiu Tang shu*, 269:322, 326, 343.
51. William H. Nienhauser Jr. and Michael E. Naparstek, eds., *Biographical Dictionary of Tang Dynasty Literati* (Bloomington: Indiana University Press, 2022), 439–440.
52. *Liang shu*, 260:350.
53. Yao Silian 姚思廉, *Chen shu* 陳書 (History of the Chen dynasty) in *Wenyuange Siku quanshu* (Wenyuange edition of the Complete Library of the Four Branches of Literature) 文淵閣四庫全書, vol. 260 (Taipei: Taiwan Shangwu yinshuguan, 2013), 782.
54. *Jiu Tang shu*, 269:688.
55. *Tang xinyu*, 1035:363; Wu and Ji, eds., *Tang Taizong quanji jiaozhu*, 297; *Tang huiyao*, 606:481.
56. Wang, "Reading for rule: Emperor Taizong of Tang and *Qunshu zhiyao*," 35–36.
57. *Cefu yuangui*, 912:545, 619.
58. *Xin Tang shu*, 276:11.

59. Wang Yinglin 王應麟, *Yu Hai* 玉海 (Ocean of jades), in *Wenyuange Siku quanshu* (Wenyuange edition of the Complete Library of the Four Branches of Literature) 文淵閣四庫全書, vol. 944 (Taipei: Taiwan Shangwu yinshuguan, 2013), 449.
60. Zhang Ying 張英 and Wang Shizhen 王士禎, *Yuding yuanjian leihan* 御定淵鑑類函 (Imperially-commissioned categorized writings in the Library of Deep Insight), in *Wenyuange siku quanshu* (Wenyuange edition of the Complete Library of the Four Branches of Literature) 文淵閣四庫全書, vol. 985 (Taipei: Taiwan Shangwu yinshuguan, 2013), 786.
61. The "two hundred bolts of silk" for the *Essentials* in the *Outstanding Models from the Storehouse of Literature* differs from "a thousand bolts of plain-weave silk and five hundred lengths of coloured silk" specified in the *New Anecdotes from the Tang Dynasty* and the *Collected Writings of Emperor Taizong of the Tang Dynasty*.
62. Sometime during the second year of his reign (627) Taizong said, "I cannot hold book scrolls myself, and so have others read them and I listen to them": *Zhenguan zhengyao*, 407:486; McMullen, "The Big Cats Will Play: Tang Taizong and His Advisors," 308.
63. In a memorial to Emperor Xuanzong 玄宗 (r. 713–756) during 712/713, the commandant Yang Xiangru recommended study of the *Essentials* to understand the governing principles and learn from sagely sovereigns and faithful subordinates. In or around 780, the official Li Mi presented the *Essentials* to Emperor Dezong 德宗 (r. 779–805) for learning the essential governing principles. In a memorial accompanying the *Essentials* presented to Emperor Xianzong 憲宗 (r. 805–820) during the early ninth century, the Hanlin academician Li Jiang wrote that Taizong constantly studied and reflected on the *Essentials*, and kept it beside his seat: *Cefu yuangui*, 911.275; *Yu hai*, 944.449-450; *Lidai mingchen zouyi* 歷代名臣奏議 (Memorials of leading officials of each period), 438:518–519.
64. Wu Yun 吳云 and Ji Yu 冀宇, eds., *Tang Taizong ji* 唐太宗集 (Collected writings of Emperor Taizong of the Tang dynasty) (Xi'an: Shaanxi renmin chubanshe, 1986), 285, cited by Wang, "Reading for Rule: Emperor Taizong of Tang and *Qunshu zhiyao*," 37. I have not been able to locate this reference.
65. Assmann, *Cultural Memory and Early Civilization: Writing, Remembrance, and Political Imagination*, 71–72.
66. Assmann, *Cultural Memory and Early Civilization*, 130.
67. Aleida Assmann, "Transformations between History and Memory," *Social Research* 75, no. 1 (2008): 52.
68. Assmann, "Canon and Archive," 100, 106; Assmann, "Communicative and Cultural Memory," 113.
69. Assmann, "Canon and Archive," 97.

70. The Monograph on Classics and Literature in the *History of the Sui Dynasty* records that the palace library at the time had some 14,466 texts and 89,666 scrolls across its four bibliographical classifications. Wei Zheng 魏徵 et al., *Sui shu* 隋書 (History of the Sui dynasty) in *Wenyuange Siku quanshu* (Wenyuange edition of the Complete Library of the Four Branches of Literature) 文淵閣四庫全書, vol. 264 (Taipei: Taiwan Shangwu yinshuguan, 2013), 586.
71. The *Essentials* is listed among the historical epitomes in Endymion Wilkinson's manual of Chinese history. Wilkinson, *Chinese History: A New Manual*, 1178; Tian Xiaofei, "Literary Learning: Encyclopedias and Epitomes," in the *Oxford Handbook of Classical Chinese Literature (1000 BCE–900 CE)*, eds. Wiebke Denecke et al. (New York: Oxford University Press, 2017), 143.
72. In the preface to a catalogue of excerpted sutras, the Liang dynasty monk Sengyou 僧祐 wrote: "抄經者 蓋撮舉義要也 To epitomize a sutra is to bring out the essence of its content." Cited in Tian Xiaofei, *Beacon Fire and Shooting Star: The Literary Culture of the Liang (502–557)* (Cambridge, MA: Harvard University Asia Center, 2007), 82.
73. Tian, *Beacon Fire and Shooting Star: The Literary Culture of the Liang (502–557)*, 82.
74. Sun Wu's *Collected Essentials of Military Principles* (*Bingfa jieyao* 兵法接要) (seven scrolls) and Cao Cao's *Collected Essentials of Military Principles* (*Bingfa jieyao* 兵法接要) (three scrolls) are listed in the *History of the Sui Dynasty*'s Monograph on Classics and Literature and the *New History of the Tang Dynasty*'s Monograph on Literature: *Sui shu*, 264.633; *Xin Tang shu*, 273:95.
75. Regarded as China's earliest compendium for an imperial reader, the *Huanglan* 皇覽 (Imperial conspectus) was compiled by Wang Xiang 王象 (d. *c.* 223) et al. during 220–222 under the auspices of Cao Pi 曹丕 (r. 220–226), who was Emperor Wen 文 (r. 581–604) of the Wei dynasty (220–265). The entire work reputedly comprised forty categories and eight million characters, with one version consisting of 680 scrolls. Tian, "Literary Learning: Encyclopedias and Epitomes," 134; David R. Knechtges and Taiping Chang, eds., *Ancient and Early Medieval Chinese Literature: A Reference Guide – Part One* (Leiden: Brill, 2010), 400; David R. Knechtges and Taiping Chang, eds., *Ancient and Early Medieval Chinese Literature: A Reference Guide – Part Two* (Leiden: Brill, 2014), 1251.
76. The *Hualin bianlüe* 華林遍略 (Comprehensive digest of the Institute of the Floral Grove) was completed in 523 by Xu Mian 徐勉 (466–535) et al. for Emperor Wu of the Liang dynasty. Its size has been variously reported to be 600 scrolls, 620 scrolls, and 700 scrolls in historical writings: David R. Knechtges and Taiping Chang, eds., *Ancient and Early Medieval Chinese Literature: A Reference Guide – Part Three* (Leiden: Brill, 2014), 1707.

77. *Qunshu zhiyao*, 1:22–23 (Wei Zheng's preface); see Appendix 1.
78. *Qunshu zhiyao*, 1:22–23 (Wei Zheng's preface), at 23.
79. McMullen, "The Big Cats Will Play: Tang Taizong and His Advisors," 312.
80. Wang Yinglin's *Ocean of Jades* encyclopedia was one of the earliest texts to classify the *Qunshu zhiyao* as an encyclopedic anthology (*leishu* 類書). *Yu hai*, 944:448–449.
81. *Qunshu zhiyao*, 1:22–23 (Wei Zheng's preface); see Appendix 1.
82. The fourfold classification had been in use during the Eastern Jin dynasty (317–420): Benjamin A. Elman, "The Investigation of Things (*gewu* 格物), Natural Studies (*gezhixue* 格致學), and Evidential Studies (*kaozhengxue* 考證學) in Late Imperial China, 1600–1800," in *Concepts of Nature: A Chinese-European Cross-Cultural Perspective*, eds. Hans Ulrich Vogel and Günter Dux (Leiden: Brill, 2010), 372.
83. Wang, "Reading for rule: Emperor Taizong of Tang and *Qunshu zhiyao*," 46.
84. For example, the *Essentials* includes from *Mencius* the concept of benevolence and compassion in the ruler and the concern to maintain the loyalty of the people, but omits the Mencian ideas of human goodness being innate and the ruler being sanctioned by heaven and the people: McMullen, "The Big Cats Will Play: Tang Taizong and His Advisors," 312.
85. Guan Panpan 管盼盼, "*Qunshu zhiyao* zhuwen laiyuan chutan 群書治要注文來源初探" (Preliminary study of the sources of the *Qunshu zhiyao* annotations) *Anhui Literature* 安徽文學 2018, no.11: 9–11.
86. Guan, "*Qunshu zhiyao* zhuwen laiyuan chutan," at 24.
87. *Qunshu zhiyao*, 1:22 (Wei Zheng's preface); see Appendix 1.
88. Michael Nylan, *The Five "Confucian" Classics* (New Haven, CT: Yale University Press, 2001), 2.
89. See, for example, Wang, "Reading for Rule: Emperor Taizong of Tang and *Qunshu zhiyao*," 33–34.
90. Paul R. Goldin, *Confucianism* (London: Taylor & Francis Group, 2015), 1, 5.
91. Goldin, *Confucianism*, 5; Xinzhong Yao, "Confucianism," in *The Encyclopedia of Confucianism*, ed. Xinzhong Yao (Oxford: Routledge, 2003), 6.
92. Goldin, *Confucianism*, 5–6.
93. Nylan, *The Five "Confucian" Classics*, 5, 8, 10, 16, 33–39.
94. Nylan, *The Five "Confucian" Classics*, at 6.
95. The remaining 31 sources include nine syncretist works (*zajia* 雜家), eight legalist works (*fajia* 法家), six Daoist works (*daojia* 道家), six strategist works (*bingjia* 兵家), one logician work (*mingjia* 名家), and one Mohist work (*mojia* 墨家), as categorized by the same Monograph on Classics and Literature: *Sui shu*, 264:626–635.

96. Michael Nylan, “Ru,” in *The Encyclopedia of Confucianism*, ed. Xinzhong Yao (Oxford: Routledge, 2003), 507–509.
97. *Sui shu*, 264:627.
98. Wang, “Reading for Rule: Emperor Taizong of Tang and *Qunshu zhiyao*,” 34.
99. Wang, “Reading for Rule: Emperor Taizong of Tang and *Qunshu zhiyao*,” 34.
100. Chou Shaowen 周少文, “*Qunshu zhiyao yanjiu* 羣書治要研究” (A study of the Qunshu zhiyao), Master’s thesis, University of Taipei, 2007, 54.
101. Ban Gu 班固, *Han shu* 漢書 (History of the [former] Han dynasty) in *Wenyuange Siku quanshu* (Wenyuange edition of the Complete Library of the Four Branches of Literature) 文淵閣四庫全書, vol. 249 (Taipei: Taiwan Shangwu yinshuguan, 2013), 804–805.
102. *Sui shu*, 264:608.
103. Hung, *Qunshu zhiyao shibu yanjiu: cong Zhenguan shixue de zhiyong jingshen tanqi*, 54–56.
104. Hung, *Qunshu zhiyao shibu yanjiu: cong Zhenguan shixue de zhiyong jingshen tanqi*, at 54.
105. Hung, *Qunshu zhiyao shibu yanjiu: cong Zhenguan shixue de zhiyong jingshen tanqi*, at 55.
106. Hung, *Qunshu zhiyao shibu yanjiu: cong Zhenguan shixue de zhiyong jingshen tanqi*, at 55–56.
107. *Qunshu zhiyao*, 1:23–24 (Wei Zheng’s preface); see Appendix 1.
108. On-cho Ng and Q. Edward Wang, *Mirroring the Past: The Writing and Use of History in Imperial China* (Honolulu: University of Hawai’i Press, 2005), 117.
109. Charles Hartman and Anthony DeBlasi, “The Growth of Historical Method in Tang China,” in *The Oxford History of Historical Writing: Volume 2: 400–1400*, eds. Sarah Foot and Chase F. Robinson (Oxford: Oxford University Press, 2012), 19.
110. *Jiu Tang shu*, 269:697.
111. *Qunshu zhiyao*, vol. 1, 1 (Wei Zheng’s preface); see Appendix 1.
112. Liu Hsieh, *The Literary Mind and the Carving of Dragons*, trans. Vincent Yu-chung Shih (Hong Kong: Chinese University of Hong Kong Press, 2015), 116–119.
113. Emperor Wen prohibited the private writing of history by imperial decree in 593: *Sui shu*, 264:38.
114. *Jiu Tang shu*, 269:697.
115. Twitchett explains that the histories commissioned under Emperor Taizong did not include a new history for the Northern Wei although one was started in 622, because there were two existing histories that were considered adequate—one, the *Hou Wei shu* 後魏書 (History of the latter Wei dynasty)

by Wei Shou 魏收, and the other by Wei Tan 魏澹, either his *Wei shu* 魏書 (History of the Wei dynasty) or *Wei ji* 魏紀 (Records of the Wei), as listed in the Monographs on Classics in the *Old History of the Tang Dynasty*: *Jiu Tang shu* 269:320. Denis Twitchett, *The Writing of Official History under the T'ang* (Cambridge: Cambridge University Press, 1992), 21.

116. *Jiu Tang shu*, 269:697–698.
117. Isenbike Togan, "Court Historiography in Early Tang China: Assigning a Place to History and Historians at the Palace," in *Royal Courts in Dynastic States and Empires: A Global Perspective*, eds. Jeroen Duindam et al. (Leiden: Brill, 2011), 176.
118. Togan, "Court Historiography in Early Tang China: Assigning a Place to History and Historians at the Palace," 176.
119. Tatsuhiko Seo, "The Tang Dynasty I (618–756)," in *The Routledge Handbook of Imperial Chinese History*, eds. Victor C. Xiong and Kenneth J. Hammond (London: Routledge, 2019), 137.
120. For example, Wang Zhenping noted that "The two early Tang emperors ... learned the moral and political lessons from the previous Sui dynasty and developed consultative leadership in governing China": Wang Zhenping, *Tang China in Multi-Polar Asia: A History of Diplomacy and War* (Honolulu: University of Hawai'i Press, 2013), 202.
121. Lien-Sheng Yang, "The organization of Chinese official historiography: principles and methods of the Standard Histories from the T'ang through the Ming dynasty," in *Historians of China and Japan*, eds. W. G. Beasley and E. G. Pulleyblank (London: Oxford University Press, 1961), 44, 47.
122. *Jiu Tang shu*, 269:322.
123. De Weerdt and McMullen, "Introduction: *The Essentials of Governance from the Reign of Constancy Revealed* in Context," xlii.
124. David McMullen, "Instructing and Warning the Crown Prince and the Princes," in *The Essentials of Governance* by Wu Jing, eds. Hilde De Weerdt et al. (Cambridge: Cambridge University Press, 2020), 114.
125. *Zhenguan zhengyao*, 407:435–436; Wechsler, *Mirror to the Son of Heaven: Wei Cheng at the Court of T'ang T'ai-Tsung*, 114.
126. *Xin Tang shu*, 272:660; Wang Dingbao 王定保, *Tang zhiyan* 唐摭言 (Collected stories from the Tang dynasty) in *Wenyuange Siku quanshu* (Wenyuange edition of the Complete Library of the Four Branches of Literature) 文淵閣四庫全書, vol. 1035 (Taipei: Taiwan Shangwu yinshuguan, 2013), 802; Howard J. Wechsler, "The founding of the T'ang dynasty: Kao-tsu (reign: 618–26)," in *The Cambridge History of China Volume 3: Sui and T'ang China, 589-906, Part I*, ed. Denis Twitchett (Cambridge: Cambridge University Press, 2008), 179.

127. *Xin Tang shu*, 272:660; Song Minqiu 宋敏求, *Tang dazhaoling ji* 唐大詔令集 (Comprehensive collection of the edicts and commands of the Tang dynasty) in *Wenyuange Siku quanshu* (Wenyuange edition of the Complete Library of the Four Branches of Literature) 文淵閣四庫全書, vol. 426 (Taipei: Taiwan Shangwu yinshuguan, 2013), 721; Dong Gao 董誥 et al., *Qinding quan Tang wen* 欽定全唐文 (Imperially-authorized complete anthology of Tang dynasty prose), vol. 1634 (Shanghai: Shanghai guji chubanshe, 1995), 116.
128. *Tang huiyao*, 606:469; *Zizhi tongjian*, 308:360.
129. *Tang huiyao*, 606:822–823.
130. Wechsler, "T'ai-tsung (reign 626–49) the consolidator," 213.
131. *Jiu Tang shu*, 271:532; *Xin Tang shu*, 272:48, 236; *Cefu yuangui*, 903:22.
132. *Jiu Tang shu*, 271:532; *Xin Tang shu*, 272:48, 236.
133. *Jiu Tang shu*, 271:532; *Xin Tang shu*, 272:48, 236; *Cefu yuangui*, 903:23–24.
134. *Xin Tang shu*, 272:48, 236.
135. Andrew Seth Meyer, "The Correct Meaning of the Five Classics and the Intellectual Foundations of the Tang," Doctoral thesis, Harvard University, 1999, 31–32.
136. *Jiu Tang shu*, 269:700; 271:532; *Zhenguan zhengyao*, 407:496.
137. *Zhenguan zhengyao*, 407:496.
138. *Jiu Tang shu*, 269:700; *Zhenguan zhengyao*, 407:496.
139. Arthur F. Wright and Denis Twitchett, eds., *Perspectives on the T'ang* (London: Yale University Press, 1973), 16.
140. *Jiu Tang shu*, 269:673.
141. Song Weiche 宋維哲, "*Qunshu zhiyao* yin jing shulüe 群書治要引經述略" (Outline of the canonical works excerpted by the *Qunshu zhiyao*), *Youfeng chuming niankan* 有鳳初鳴年刊 (Annual of the Graduate School of Chinese Literature, Soochow University) 2 (2006): 151; Lam Yatyan 林溢欣, "*Qunshu zhiyao* yinshu kao 群書治要引書考" (A study of the sources excerpted by the *Qunshu zhiyao*), Master's thesis, Chinese University of Hong Kong, 2011, 16-17.
142. *Jiu Tang shu*, 268:53–57.
143. Wang, "Reading for Rule: Emperor Taizong of Tang and *Qunshu zhiyao*," 50.
144. *Zhenguan zhengyao* 407:493; *Tang huiyao*, 606:822–823.
145. Emperor Taizong and his officials showed a preference for following the ancient legendary sage rulers as their ideal of governance: Liao Yifang 廖宜方, *Tangdai de lishi jiyi* 唐代的歷史記憶 (Historical memory of the Tang dynasty) (Taipei: Guoli Taiwan daxue, 2011), 70–73.
146. Twitchett, "How to Be an Emperor: T'ang T'ai-tsung's Vision of His Role," 18–23.

147. *Zhenguan zhengyao*, 407:479.
148. Twitchett, "How to Be an Emperor: T'ang T'ai-tsung's Vision of His Role," 88–89.
149. Assmann, *Cultural Memory and Early Civilization: Writing, Remembrance, and Political Imagination*, 121–123.
150. Assmann, *Cultural Memory and Early Civilization: Writing, Remembrance, and Political Imagination*, 78–79, 103.
151. *Qunshu zhiyao*, vol. 1, 1–2 (Wei Zheng's preface); see Appendix 1.
152. Assmann, *Cultural Memory and Early Civilization: Writing, Remembrance, and Political Imagination*, 102.
153. Assmann, *Cultural Memory and Early Civilization: Writing, Remembrance, and Political Imagination*, 102.
154. The table is based on the Tenmei edition that was first published in 1787, and reprinted in 1926 as part of the *Four Branches of Literature Collection*.
155. "Confucius" is the common Latinized appellation of "Kong fuzi 孔夫子" and "Kongzi 孔子."
156. "Mencius" is the common Latinized appellation of "Mengzi 孟子."
157. The omission of the title for the *Discourse on Contemporary Affairs* is discussed in Section 0.1.

CHAPTER TWO

1. Xu Shen 許慎 and Duan Yucai 段玉裁, *Shuowen jiezi zhu* 說文解字注 (Annotated *Explanations of Simple and Compound Characters*) (Taipei: Yiwen yinshuguan, 2015), 282: "*duo cai ye, cong bei, jian sheng* 多才也 从貝臤聲"; Tang Kejing 湯可敬, *Shuowen jiezi jinshi* 說文解字今釋 (Modern translation of the *Explanations of Simple and Compound Characters*) (Changsha: Yueli shushe, 2001), 851; He Jiuying 何九盈 et al., eds., *Ci Yuan* 辭源 (Origins of words) (Beijing: The Commercial Press, 2017), 3906.
2. Xu Shen 許慎 and Xu Kai 徐鍇, *Shuowen jiezi xizhuan* 說文解字繫傳 (Appended commentary on the *Explanations of Simple and Compound Characters*) (Beijing: Zhonghua shuju, 1987), 282; Paul W. Kroll, *A Student's Dictionary of Classical and Medieval Chinese* (Leiden: Brill, 2022), 512; He et al., eds., *Ci yuan*, 3906.
3. *Shuowen jiezi zhu*, 199; Liang Jianmin 梁建民 et al., eds., *Gu Hanyu da cidian* 古漢語大詞典 (Comprehensive dictionary of ancient Chinese) (Shanghai: Shanghai cishu chubanshe, 2000), 571; *Shuowen jiezi zhu*, 484; Kroll, *A Student's Dictionary of Classical and Medieval Chinese*, 333; He et al., eds., *Ci yuan*, 3379.

4. Commentary by Zheng Xuan 鄭玄; sub-commentary by Kong Yingda 孔穎達, *Shangshu zhushu* 尚書注疏 (Annotated commentary on the *Venerable Documents*) in *Wenyuange Siku quanshu* (Wenyuange edition of the Complete Library of the Four Branches of Literature) 文淵閣四庫全書, vol. 54 (Taipei: Taiwan Shangwu yinshuguan, 2013), 202.
5. Ch'ien Mu, *Traditional Government in Imperial China: A Critical Analysis*, trans. by Chun-tu Hsueh and George O. Totten (Hong Kong: Chinese University Press, 1982), 49.
6. This anecdote is found in the *Strategies of the Warring States* (*Zhanguo ce* 戰國策), a work attributed to Liu Xiang. It is also abridged in the *Records of the Historian*, alluded to in the *Normative Discourses*, and appears in the *Essentials* as excerpts from those two texts. *Qunshu zhiyao*, 2:288 and 10:1285.
7. In Chinese, the "thousand-mile horse" is used as a metaphor for talented persons, particularly young talent: Du Ruiqing 杜瑞清 et al., eds., *New Century Chinese-English Dictionary* 新世紀漢英大詞典 (Beijing: Foreign Language Teaching and Research Press, 2016), 1321.
8. *Chan-Kuo Ts'e*, trans. James I. Crump, Jr. (Oxford: Clarendon Press, 1970), 524–525; Wang Yandong 王延棟, *Mingjia jiangjie zhanguoce* 名家講解戰國策 (Authoritative interpretation on the *Strategies of the Warring States*) (Changchun: Changchun chubanshe, 2009), 524–525.
9. Ma Qichang 馬其昶 et al., eds., *Han Changli wenji jiaozhu* 韓昌黎文集校註 (Annotated collection of the writings of Han Changli) (Shanghai: Shanghai guji chubanshe, 1998), 35. Translation based on Mei Ah Tan, "Han Yu's 'Za shuo' 雜說 (Miscellaneous Discourses): A Three-Tier System of Government," *Journal of American Oriental Society* 140, no. 4 (2020): 869–870.
10. *Qunshu zhiyao*, 7:944.
11. Assmann, *Cultural Memory and Early Civilisation: Writing, Remembrance and Political Imagination*, 114.
12. Assmann, "Transformations between History and Memory," 52.
13. Assmann, *Cultural Memory and Early Civilisation: Writing, Remembrance and Political Imagination*, 113–114, 119–120.
14. Diana Spencer, *Landscape and Roman Identity* (Cambridge, Cambridge University Press, 2010), 9; Diana Spencer, "Ρωμαίζω ... ergo sum: becoming Roman in Varro's de Lingua Latina," in *Cultural Memory and Identity in Ancient Societies*, ed. Martin Bommas (London: Continuum International Publishing Group, 2011), 45.
15. Assmann, *Cultural Memory and Early Civilisation: Writing, Remembrance and Political Imagination*, 119–120.

16. Julia Kristeva, *Desire in Language: A Semiotic Approach to Literature and Art*, trans. by Thomas Gora et al. (New York: Columbia University Press, 1980), 15, 65.
17. Jonathan Culler, *The Pursuit of Signs* (New York: Routledge, 2005), 114.
18. Wendy Swartz, *Reading Philosophy, Writing Poetry: Intertextual Modes of Making Meaning in Early Medieval China* (Cambridge, MA: Harvard University Asia Center, 2018), 3, 8.
19. Swartz, *Reading Philosophy, Writing Poetry: Intertextual Modes of Making Meaning in Early Medieval China*, 7.
20. Swartz, *Reading Philosophy, Writing Poetry: Intertextual Modes of Making Meaning in Early Medieval China*, 2.
21. Swartz, *Reading Philosophy, Writing Poetry: Intertextual Modes of Making Meaning in Early Medieval China*, 9, 17, 18.
22. Hans-Georg Moeller and Paul J. D'Ambrosio, *You and Your Profile: Identity after Authenticity* (New York: Columbia University Press, 2021), 15–16.
23. Moeller and D'Ambrosio, *You and Your Profile: Identity after Authenticity*, 119–120.
24. Simon Leys, *The Hall of Uselessness: Collected Essays* (Collingwood, Victoria: Black Inc, 2012), 248.
25. *Shiji*, 244:247, 377, 390; Commentary by Zhao Qi 趙岐; sub-commentary by Sun Shi 孫奭, *Mengzi zhushu* 孟子註疏 (Annotated commentary on the *Mencius*) (Beijing: Beijing daxue chuban she, 2000), 105.
26. *Jiu Tang shu*, 271:633; William Theodore de Bary and Irene Bloom, eds., *Sourcebook of Chinese Tradition Volume 1: From Earliest Times to 1600*, 2nd ed. (New York: Columbia University Press, 1999), 492.
27. The earliest record of the four types of occupations is found in the *Chunqiu Guliang zhuan* 春秋穀梁傳 (Guliang tradition of commentary on the Spring and Autumn annals); Commentary by Fan Ning 范寧; sub-commentary by Yang Shixun 楊士勛, *Chunqiu Guliang zhuan zhushu* 春秋穀梁傳註疏 (Annotated commentary on the Guliang tradition of commentary on the *Spring and Autumn Annals*), in *Wenyuange Siku quanshu* (Wenyuange edition of the Complete Library of the Four Branches of Literature) 文淵閣四庫全書, vol. 145 (Taipei: Shangwu yinshuguan, 2013), 742.
28. Yi Zima 毅自馬, *Xinyi Zengguang xianwen Qianzi wen* 新譯增廣賢文千字文 (New translation of the *Extended Wise Sayings* and the *Thousand Character Classic*) (Taipei: Sanmin shuju, 2010), 4.
29. "On Teaching and Learning (*Xueji* 學記)," trans. Xu Di et al., in *Chinese Philosophy on Teaching and Learning*, eds. Xu Di and Hunter McEwan (Albany: State University of New York Press, 2016), 15.

30. *Qunshu zhiyao*, 2:42. This translation of the text without annotation is adapted from *The Sacred Books of China: The Texts of Confucianism Part 1 The Shu King, The Religious Portions of the Shih King, the Hsiao King*, trans. James Legge (New York: Charles Scribner's Sons, 1899), 151.
31. See, for example, the *Essentials'* excerpt from the *Spring and Autumn Annals of Master Lü* about Zhao Jianzi 趙簡子 (d. 496) prioritizing the health of an official over the life of his prized mule. On hearing that the official would die from illness without medicine made from the liver of a white mule, Zhao sacrifices one of his two white mules so that its liver could be used for the life-saving medicine: *Qunshi zhiyao*, 8:1019.
32. *The Sacred Books of China: The Texts of Confucianism Part 1 The Shu King, The Religious Portions of the Shih King*, 150.
33. *Qunshu zhiyao*, 2:195–196.
34. *Shuowen jiezi zhu*, 10.
35. Commentary by Ban Gu 班固, *Baihu tongyi* 白虎通義 (Comprehensive discussions in the White Tiger Hall), in *Wenyuange Siku quanshu* (Wenyuange edition of the Complete Library of the Four Branches of Literature) 文淵閣四庫全書, vol. 850 (Taipei: Taiwan shangwu yinshuguan, 2013), 46.
36. Wei Zhao 韋昭, *Guoyu* 國語 (Discourses of the states), in *Wenyuange Siku quanshu* (Wenyuange edition of the Complete Library of the Four Branches of Literature) 文淵閣四庫全書, vol. 406 (Taipei: Taiwan Shangwu yinshuguan, 2013), 164.
37. For example, *Shiji,* 244:226; Sima Qian 司馬遷 and Zhang Shoujie 張守節, *Shiji zhengyi* 史記正義 (Orthodox interpretation of the *Shiji*), in *Wenyuange Siku quanshu* (Wenyuange edition of the Complete Library of the Four Branches of Literature) 文淵閣四庫全書, vol. 247 (Taipei: Taiwan Shangwu yinshuguan, 2013), 590; Huan Kuan 桓寬, *Yantie lun* 鹽鐵論 (Discourses on salt and iron), in *Wenyuange Siku quanshu* (Wenyuange edition of the Complete Library of the Four Branches of Literature) 文淵閣四庫全書, vol. 247 (Taipei: Taiwan Shangwu yinshuguan, 2013), 595–596; Liu Xiang 劉向, *Xin xu* 新序 (New order), in *Wenyuange Siku quanshu* (Wenyuange edition of the Complete Library of the Four Branches of Literature) 文淵閣四庫全書, vol. 696 (Taipei: Taiwan Shangwu yinshuguan, 2013), 192–193; Xun Yue 荀悅, *Shen jian* 申鑒 (Extended reflections), in *Wenyuange Siku quanshu* (Wenyuange edition of the Complete Library of the Four Branches of Literature) 文淵閣四庫全書, vol. 696 (Taipei: Taiwan Shangwu yinshuguan, 2013), 458.

38. *Qunshu zhiyao*, 2:292–293.
39. *Qunshu zhiyao*, 2:196; *Guoyu*, 406:164.
40. *Qunshu zhiyao*, 9:1104.
41. The historical accuracy of some aspects of this extract has been challenged. For example, Ye Youming 葉幼明 notes that Zi Xi, Zi'ao, Lord Zigao of She, and Zifan lived in the Spring and Autumn period (722–476 BCE), whereas Zhao Xizu lived in the Warring States period (475–221 BCE). However, the compilation of the passage within the *Essentials* suggests that such concerns do not affect its didactic value in learning from the documented past: Ye Youming 葉幼明, *Xinyi Xinxu duben* 新譯新序讀本 (New translation of the *New Order*) (Taipei: Sanmin shuju,1996), 23.
42. *Qunshu zhiyao*, 9:1112–1113.
43. Liu, *Xinxu*, 696:192–193.
44. *Qunshu zhiyao*, 9:1213.
45. Chu Ming-kin, "Honoring Classicist Scholarship," in *The Essentials of Governance* by Wu Jing, eds. Hilde De Weerdt et al. (Cambridge: Cambridge University Press, 2020), 227. See also, *Tang huiyao*, 606:57.
46. Oliver Moore, "On Selecting Officials," in *The Essentials of Governance* by Wu Jing, eds. Hilde De Weerdt et al. (Cambridge: Cambridge University Press, 2020), 73. See also, *Tang huiyao*, 607:9.
47. Moore, "On Selecting Officials," 78. See also, *Cefu yuangui*, 910:153.
48. *Zhenguan zhengyao*, 407:493; *Tang huiyao*, 606:822; *Zizhi tongjian*, 308:207.
49. Sheng et al., eds., *Sui Tang jiahua Tang guoshi bu*, 47–48.
50. Sheng et al., eds., *Sui Tang jiahua Tang guoshi bu*, 47–48; *Jiu Tang shu*, 269:780; *Zizhi tongjian*, 308:287; *Tang huiyao*, 606:479.
51. This translation has been adapted from Hilde De Weerdt, "Employing the Wise," in *The Essentials of Governance* by Wu Jing, eds. Hilde De Weerdt, Glen Dudbridge, and Gabe Van Beijeren (Cambridge: Cambridge University Press, 2020), 47. See also *Jiu Tang shu*, 269:626.
52. Tineke D'Haeseleer, "Debates about Punitive Expeditions," in *The Essentials of Governance* by Wu Jing, eds. Hilde De Weerdt et al. (Cambridge: Cambridge University Press, 2020), 287. See also *Wei Zheng gong jianlu*, 446:164–165.
53. Wu and Ji, eds., *Tang Taizong quanji jiaozhu*, 441–442.
54. *Zhenguan zhengyao*, 407:371; *Jiu Tang shu*, 269:675; *Xin Tang shu*, 274:251; *Wei Zheng gong jianlu*, 446:206.
55. This translation has been adapted from Hilde De Weerdt, "Employing the Wise," 40. See also, *Jiu Tang shu*, 269:675; *Xin Tang shu*, 274:251; *Wei Zheng gong jianlu*, 446:206.

56. This translation has been adapted from Hilde De Weerdt, "Employing the Wise," 48.
57. *Tang huiyao*, 606:825.
58. *Jiu Tang shu*, 269:749; *Xin Tang shu*, 272:64; *Tang da zhaoling ji*, 426:479–480; Zhang Yanyuan 張彥遠, *Lidai minghua ji* 歷代名畫記 (Records of famous paintings from each dynasty), in *Wenyuange Siku quanshu* (Wenyuange edition of the Complete Library of the Four Branches of Literature) 文淵閣四庫全書, vol. 812 (Taipei: Taiwan Shangwu yinshuguan, 2013), 342; Wu and Ji, eds., *Tang Taizong quanji jiaozhu*, 469–472.
59. Commemorative portraiture in the Chinese art originated from the Han dynasty and the standing pose was traditionally preferred for formal portraits of ancient worthies and meritorious officials for display in ceremonial halls or temples: Wen C. Fong, *Beyond Representation: Chinese Painting and Calligraphy 8th–14th Century* (New York: The Metropolitan Museum of Art, 1992), 44 and 46; Dora C. Y. Ching, "The Language of Portraiture in China," in *A Companion to Chinese Art*, eds. Martin J. Powers and Katherine R. Tsiang (Chichester: John Wiley & Son Inc, 2016), 152.
60. Patricia Ebrey, "Court Painting," in *A Companion to Chinese Art*, eds. Martin J. Powers and Katherine R. Tsiang (Chichester: John Wiley & Son Inc, 2016), 30–31.
61. Audrey Spiro, *Contemplating the Ancients: Aesthetic and Social Issues in Early Chinese Portraiture* (Berkeley: University of California Press, 1990), 11.
62. *Xin Tang shu,* 272:251.
63. This translation is adapted from Jack W. Chen, "On Greed and Baseness," in *The Essentials of Governance* by Wu Jing, eds. Hilde De Weerdt et al. (Cambridge: Cambridge University Press, 2020), 219.
64. Ralph W. Emerson, "Sermon CXXXVI," in *The Complete Sermons of Ralph Waldo Emerson*, ed. by Wesley T. Mott, vol. 4 (Columbia: University of Missouri Press, 1992), 25–26.
65. David N. Keightley, "Early Civilization in China: Reflections on How It Became Chinese," in *These Bones Will Rise Again*, ed. by Henry Rosemont, Jr. (New York: State of New York University Press, 2014), 41.
66. Amy Olberding, *Moral Exemplars in the Analects: The Good Person is That* (New York: Routledge, 2012), 20.
67. David N. Keightley, "Clean Hands and Shining Helmets: Heroic Action in Early Chinese and Greek Culture," in *These Bones Will Rise Again*, ed. by Henry Rosemont Jr. (New York: State of New York University Press, 2014), 270.

68. Keightley, “Clean Hands and Shining Helmets: Heroic Action in Early Chinese and Greek Culture,”, 272.
69. Donald Munro, *The Concept of Man in Early China* (Stanford, CA: Stanford University Press, 1969), 96.
70. Commentary by Zheng Xuan 鄭玄; sub-commentary by Kong Yingda 孔穎達, *Liji zheng yi* 禮記正義 (Orthodox exegesis of the *Records on Ritual*) (Beijing: Beijing daxue chubanshe, 2000), 1237–1238.
71. *Analects of Confucius*, trans. Burton Watson (New York: Columbia University Press, 2007), 34.
72. Munro, *The Concept of Man in Early China*, 110–112.
73. *Analects of Confucius*, 21.
74. Olberding, *Moral Exemplars in the Analects*, 13.
75. Linda Trinkaus Zagzebski, *Divine Motivation Theory* (Cambridge: Cambridge University Press, 2004), 56; Olberding, *Moral Exemplars in the Analects*, 36–37.
76. *Qunshu zhiyao*, 2:248.
77. Commentary by Wang Su 王肅, *Kongzi jiayu* 孔子家語 (School Sayings of Confucius), in *Wenyuange Siku quanshu* (Wenyuange edition of the Complete Library of the Four Branches of Literature) 文淵閣四庫全書, vol. 695 (Taipei: Taiwan shangwu yinshuguan, 2013), 31.
78. *Qunshu zhiyao*, 1:97. Most of this excerpt's annotations are not material to this discussion and have been omitted for readability. This translation of the text without annotation is adapted from *Zuo Tradition Zuozhuan*, trans. Stephen Durrant et al., vol. 2 (Seattle: University of Washington Press, 2016), 902–905.
79. Ng and Wang, *Mirroring the Past: The Writing and Use of History in Imperial China*, 42–43.
80. Wang Daokun 王道焜 and Zhao Ruyuan 趙汝源, *Zuozhuan Du Lin hezhu* 左傳杜林合注 (Commentary by Du Yu and Lin Yaosou on the *Zuo Tradition of Commentary on the Spring and Autumn Annals*), in *Wenyuange Siku quanshu* (Wenyuange edition of the Complete Library of the Four Branches of Literature) 文淵閣四庫全書, vol. 171 (Taipei: Taiwan Shangwu yinshuguan, 2013), 591.
81. *Qunshu zhiyao*, 1:135–136. This translation of the text without annotation is adapted from *Zuo Tradition Zuozhuan*, 3:1688–1689.
82. *Zuozhuan Du Lin hezhu*, 171:811–812; *Zuo Tradition Zuozhuan*, 3:1688–1693.
83. *Qunshu zhiyao*, 8:1047.

84. *Qunshu zhiyao*, 7:945, translation by *Shizi: China's First Syncretist*, 97 (with modifications).
85. *Qunshu zhiyao*, 2:286, this translation is adapted from Bruce Knickerbocker, "齊 Hereditary House 2," in *The Grand Scribe's Records Volume V.1: The Hereditary Houses of Pre-Han China Part 1* by Ssu-ma Ch'ien, ed. by William H. Nienhauser, Jr., and trans. by Weiguo Cao et al. (Bloomington: Indiana University Press, 2006), 52–64.
86. *Qunshu zhiyao*, 2:294, this translation is adapted from Ssu-ma Ch'ien, *The Grand Scribe's Records Volume VII: The Memoirs of Pre-Han China*, ed. William H. Nienhauser, Jr., trans. Tsai-fa Cheng et al. (Bloomington: Indiana University Press, 1994), 9–11.
87. This translation is adapted from Winston George Lewis, "The *Cheng-kuan cheng-yao*: A source for the study of early T'ang government," Master's thesis, University of Hong Kong, 1962, 173; Hilde De Weerdt, "Accepting Criticism," in *The Essentials of Governance* by Wu Jing, eds. Hilde De Weerdt et al. (Cambridge: Cambridge University Press, 2020), 58–59.
88. This translation is adapted from Moore, "On Selecting Officials," 75. See also *Wei Zheng gong jianlu*, 446:184.
89. This translation is adapted from Jack W. Chen, "On Profligacy and Recklessness," in *The Essentials of Governance* by Wu Jing, eds. Hilde De Weerdt et al. (Cambridge: Cambridge University Press, 2020), 213. See also, *Zizhi tongjian*, 308:349; *Cefu yuangui*, 911:251. A variation of this quote is recorded in the *Old History of the Tang Dynasty*, the *Essence of Tang Literature* (*Tang wen cui* 唐文粹), and the *Finest Flowers of the Garden of Literature*. *Jiu Tang shu*, 269:708; *Wenyuan yinghua*, 1339:583; Yao Xuan 姚鉉, *Tang wen cui* 唐文粹 (Essence of Tang literature), in *Wenyuange Siku quanshu* (Wenyuange edition of the Complete Library of the Four Branches of Literature) 文淵閣四庫全書, vol. 1343 (Taipei: Taiwan Shangwu yinshuguan, 2013), 392.
90. This translation is adapted from Moore, "On Selecting Officials," 74. See also *Tang huiyao*, 606:728; *Cefu yuangui*, 904:744.
91. This translation is adapted from Moore, "On Selecting Officials," 73. See also *Tang huiyao*, 606:670; *Cefu yuangui*, 903:258.
92. *Zhenguan zhengyao*, 407:412; *Tang huiyao*, 606:670; *Cefu yuangui*, 903:258.
93. *Zhenguan zhengyao*, 407:411; *Tang huiyao*, 606:728; *Cefu yuangui*, 904:744.
94. *Zhenguan zhengyao*, 407:370.
95. *Jiu Tang shu*, 269:418–419.
96. *Zhenguan zhengyao*, 407:379.

97. See, for example, an account dated to the sixteenth year of Zhenguan (642) with the relevant officials including the Right Vice Director of the Department of State Affairs Gao Shilian 高士廉 (575–647), the Vice Director of the Chancellery Liu Ji 劉洎 (d. 645), the Vice Director of the Secretariat Cen Wenben 岑文本 (595–645), and the Grand Master of Remonstrance Chu Suiliang: *Zhenguan zhengyao*, 407:429; *Tang huiyao*, 606:28; *Cefu yuangui*, 903:782–783; *Jiu Tang shu*, 269:781.
98. *Zhenguan zhengyao*, 407:366–367; *Jiu Tang shu*, 269:610; *Cefu yuangui*, 907:342.
99. *Qunshu zhiyao*, 2:218; *The Analects of Confucius*, 55.
100. Twitchett, "How to Be an Emperor: T'ang T'ai-tsung's Vision of His Role," 20, 24.
101. Twitchett, "How to Be an Emperor: T'ang T'ai-tsung's Vision of His Role," 20, 24.
102. Sheng et al., eds., *Sui Tang jiahua Tang guoshi bu*, 19–20; *Zizhi tongjian*, 308:328.
103. *Qunshu zhiyao*, 1:23 (Wei Zheng's preface).
104. Loubna El Amine, *Classical Confucian Political Thought: A New Interpretation* (Princeton, NJ: Princeton University Press, 2015), 130.
105. *Qunshu zhiyao*, 2:218, this translation of the text without annotation is adapted from *Confucius: Analects with Selections from Traditional Commentaries*, trans. Edward Slingerland (Indianapolis, IN: Hackett Publishing Company, Inc., 2003), 80.
106. *Confucius: Analects with Selections from Traditional Commentaries*, 80.
107. *Qunshu zhiyao*, 2:226, this translation of the text without annotation is adapted from *Confucius: Analects with Selections from Traditional Commentaries*, 177.
108. Munro, *The Concept of Man in Early China*, 97, 112, 114–115.
109. *Qunshu zhiyao*, 2:180.
110. *Qunshu zhiyao*, 1:125.
111. Munro, *The Concept of Man in Early China*, 112.
112. This translation is adapted from Lewis, "The Cheng-kuan cheng-yao: A Source for the Study of Early T'ang Government," 173.
113. *Qunshu zhiyao*, 8:1053.
114. *Qunshu zhiyao*, 5:707 and 7:961.
115. *Qunshu zhiyao*, 10:1320.
116. *Qunshu zhiyao*, 1:41 and 8:1080.
117. *Qunshu zhiyao*, 1:41.
118. *Qunshu zhiyao*, 8:1080.
119. *Qunshu zhiyao*, 2:269.
120. *Qunshu zhiyao*, 3:414, 3:417, 3:458, 3:460, 3:461, 4:558.

121. *Qunshu zhiyao*, 5:707
122. *Qunshu zhiyao*, 8:1053
123. *Qunshu zhiyao*, 7:961.
124. *Qunshu zhiyao*, 9:1152.
125. *Qunshu zhiyao*, 7:947.
126. *Qunshu zhiyao*, 10:1251.
127. *Qunshu zhiyao*, 10:1320.
128. *Qunshu zhiyao*, 1:141, 3:417, 3:479, 5:707, 6:740, 7:961, 9:1152, 10:1281.
129. *Qunshu zhiyao*, 3:404, 4:519, 5:622, 9:1152.
130. Yuri Pines, *The Everlasting Empire: The Political Culture of Ancient China and Its Imperial Legacy* (Princeton, NJ: Princeton University Press, 2012), 97.
131. *Qunshu zhiyao*, 3:414, 417.
132. *Qunshu zhiyao*, 7:961, this translation of the text without annotation is from *The Shenzi Fragments: A Philosophical Analysis and Translation*, 115.
133. *The Shenzi Fragments: A Philosophical Analysis and Translation*, 116.
134. Ng and Wang, *Mirroring the Past: The Writing and Use of History in Imperial China*, 115.

CHAPTER THREE

1. Roger T. Ames and Henry Rosemont, Jr., *The Chinese Classic of Family Reverence: A Philosophical Translation of the Xiaojing* (Honolulu: University of Hawai'i, 2009), 71.
2. Alternative methods include active or passive noncompliance, or even veiled threats of rebellion to discourage the monarch from abusing their power: Pines, *The Everlasting Empire: The Political Culture of Ancient China and Its Imperial Legacy*, 45.
3. Paul Fahr, *Remonstration als Institution: Ein Beitrag zum Herrschaftsverständnis im frühen chinesischen Kaiserreich* (Remonstration as an institution: A contribution to the concept of rulership in early imperial China) (Wiesbaden: Harrassowitz Verlag, 2021), 101. Based on Fahr's doctoral dissertation, *Remonstration als Institution* is the first book-length study of the institution of remonstration in early imperial China.
4. Ames and Rosemont, Jr., *The Chinese Classic of Family Reverence: A Philosophical Translation of the Xiaojing*, 71.
5. David Schaberg identifies these characteristics of remonstrance based on his study of the speeches in the *Zuo Tradition* and the *Discourses of the States*: David Schaberg, "Remonstrance in Eastern Zhou Historiography," *Early China* 22 (1997): 140, 142.

6. Schaberg, "Remonstrance in Eastern Zhou Historiography": 138, 140–142, 155.
7. As Paul R. Goldin observes, "Rarely did Chinese persuaders fail to refer to examples from the past that supposedly bolstered their case": Paul R. Goldin, "Non-deductive Argumentation in Early Chinese Philosophy," in *Between History and Philosophy: Anecdotes in Early China*, eds. Paul van Els and Sarah A. Queen (Albany: State University of New York Press, 2017), 46; Paul R. Goldin, "Appeals to History in early Chinese Philosophy and Rhetoric," *Journal of Chinese Philosophy* 35, no. 1 (2008): 79–96.
8. McMullen, "The Big Cats Will Play: Tang Taizong and His Advisors," 311.
9. Schaberg's study identifies forms (i) to (iv) in respect of remonstrances recorded in the *Zuo Tradition* and the *Discourses of the States*, and collectively refers to those forms as "inherited words": Schaberg, "Remonstrance in Eastern Zhou Historiography," 141, 155. Reference to something the official has heard or knows of and historical remonstrations arguably constitutes additional forms of inherited principle based on the *Essentials* remonstrances.
10. Schaberg, "Remonstrance in Eastern Zhou Historiography," 138.
11. *Qunshu zhiyao*, 1:43.
12. *Qunshu zhiyao*, 5:102–103, this translation of the text without annotation is adapted from *Zuo Tradition Zuozhuan*, 2:1024–1025.
13. For example, Gao Jiong 高熲 (*c.* 607) was condemned to death for being critical of the court and policies of Emperor Yang: Arthur F. Wright, "The Sui dynasty," in *The Cambridge History of China Volume 3: Sui and T'ang China, 589–906, Part I*, ed. Denis Twitchett (Cambridge: Cambridge University Press, 1979), 123–124.
14. *Qunshu zhiyao*, 2:225, this translation of the text without annotation is from the *Analects of Confucius*, 100.
15. Zheng Xuan's commentary on the *Classic of Family Reverence* is further discussed in Section 4.1 "China" and found in the *Collectanea from the Studio of Knowing One's Deficiencies* (*Zhi buzu zhai congshu* 知不足齋叢書): Okada Noboyuki 岡田挺之, ed., *Xiaojing Zheng zhu* 孝經鄭注 (Zheng Xuan's commentary on the *Classic of Family Reverence*), in *Zhi buzu zhai congshu* 知不足齋叢書 (Collectanea from the studio of knowing one's deficiencies), comp. Bao Tingbo 鮑廷博 (Taipei: Yiwen yinshuguan yinhang, 1966), collection 21.
16. *Qunshu zhiyao*, 2:213, this translation of the text without annotation is adapted from Ames and Rosemont, Jr., *The Chinese Classic of Family Reverence: A Philosophical Translation of the Xiaojing*, 113–114.
17. *Qunshu zhiyao*, 2:294.

18. *Qunshu zhiyao*, 2:286–287, this translation of the text without annotation is adapted from Bruce Knickerbocker, "齊 Hereditary House 2," 77–81.
19. As mentioned in Section 2.2, Guan Zhong was recommended to Lord Huan as a worthy talent by Bao Shuya.
20. *Qunshu zhiyao*, 2:286, this translation is adapted from Knickerbocker, "齊 Hereditary House 2," 60–64.
21. *Qunshu zhiyao*, 6:819–820.
22. Yi Ya 易牙, Shu Diao 豎刁, Tang the shaman 堂巫, and Prince Kaifang 公子開方.
23. Dong Zhongshu 董仲舒, *Chunqiu fanlu* 春秋繁露 (Luxuriant gems of the Spring and Autumn), in *Wenyuange Siku quanshu* (Wenyuange edition of the Complete Library of the Four Branches of Literature) 文淵閣四庫全書, vol. 181 (Taipei: Taiwan Shangwu yinshuguan, 2013), 798.
24. *Qunshu zhiyao*, 2:272–273.
25. *Shi ji*, 244:531.
26. *Qunshu zhiyao*, 10:1281.
27. *Qunshu zhiyao*, 2:305–306; 3:408; 9:1101, 1167.
28. For example, Zou Yang secures release from imprisonment through his memorial that refers to the incident of Prince Bi Gan having his heart cut out by the last ruler of the Shang dynasty: *Qunshu zhiyao*, 3:414.
29. *Qunshu zhiyao*, 1:36–38, this translation of the text without annotation is from *The Sacred Books of China: The Texts of Confucianism Part 1 The Shu King, The Religious Portions of the Shih King, the Hsiao King*, 114, 117–118.
30. *Qunshu zhiyao*, 1:52, this translation of the text without annotation is from *The Sacred Books of China: The Texts of Confucianism Part 1 The Shu King, The Religious Portions of the Shih King, the Hsiao King*, 253.
31. Tsung-Tung Chang, "A new view of King Wuding," *Monumenta Serica* 37 (1986–1987): 8; National Palace Museum, *King Wu Ding and Lady Hao: Art and Culture of the Late Shang Dynasty* (Taipei: National Palace Museum, 2012), 4, 36.
32. Ma Chiying 馬持盈, *Shi jing jinzhu jinshi* 詩經今註今釋 (*Classic of Odes* with modern annotation and translation) (Taipei: Commercial Press, 1971), 553–555.
33. Annping Chin, *The Authentic Confucius: A Life of Thought and Politics* (New York: Scribner, 2007), 44.
34. Edward L. Shaughnessy, "Western Zhou History," in *The Cambridge History of Ancient China: From the Origins of Civilization to 221 B.C.* eds. Michael Loewe and Edward L. Shaughnessy (New York: Cambridge University Press, 1999), 323.
35. For example, the recension of the *Venerable Documents* in the *Wenyuange Siku quanshu* (Wenyuange edition of the Complete Library of the Four Branches of Literature): *Shangshu zhushu*, 54:1–445.

36. Twitchett, "How to Be an Emperor: T'ang T'ai-tsung's Vision of His Role," 4.
37. Wu Jing, the author of the *Essentials of Governance from the Zhenguan Reign*, is one example.
38. Hilde De Weerdt, "Seeking Criticism," in *The Essentials of Governance* by Wu Jing, eds. Hilde De Weerdt et al. (Cambridge: Cambridge University Press, 2020), 49. See also, *Zizhi tongjian*, 308:296.
39. De Weerdt, "Seeking Criticism," 53. See also, *Lidai mingchen zouyi*, 438:707; *Wei Zheng gong jianlu*, 446:204; *Cefu yuangui*, 904:746.
40. De Weerdt, "Seeking Criticism," 51. See also, *Jiu Tang shu*, 269:653; *Zizhi tongjian*, 308:291; *Tang huiyao* 606:697; *Cefu yuangui*, 903:813.
41. De Weerdt, "Seeking Criticism," 49.
42. De Weerdt, "Accepting Criticism," 62. See also, *Jiu Tang shu*, 269:705; *Zizhi tongjian*, 308:309; *Cefu yuangui*, 903:795.
43. *Zhenguan zhengyao*, 407:383; *Jiu Tang shu*, 269:662; *Cefu yuangui*, 911:543.
44. De Weerdt, "Seeking Criticism," 53. See also, *Wei Zheng gong jianlu*, 446:204; *Cefu yuangui*, 904:746; *Lidai mingchen zouyi*, 438:707.
45. See, for example, the *Zhenguan Essentials* records such an account with Taizong speaking to attendant officials including Du Ruhui during the second year of the Zhenguan reign-period (628): *Zhenguan zhengyao*, 407:382.
46. *Zhenguan zhengyao*, 407:385; *Lidai mingchen zouyi*, 438:707; *Wei Zheng gong jianlu*, 446:204; *Cefu yuangui*, 904:746.
47. *Zhenguan zhengyao*, 407:380; *Cefu yuangui*, 903:813.
48. McMullen, "Instructing and Warning the Crown Prince and the Princes," 114. See also, *Cefu yuangui*, 904:747.
49. My calculations are based on the latest translation of the *Zhenguan Essentials* by Hilde De Weerdt et al.: Wu Jing, *The Essentials of Governance*, eds. Hilde De Weerdt et al. (Cambridge: Cambridge University Press, 2020).
50. See, for example, *Qunshu zhiyao*, 2:310–311; 3:450.
51. *Qunshu zhiyao*, 2:311.
52. *Qunshu zhiyao*, 1:94, this translation is adapted from the *Zuo Tradition Zuozhuan*, 2:726–727.
53. See, for example, *Zuo Tradition Zuozhuan*, 2:726–727.
54. De Weerdt, "Accepting Criticism," 54. See also, *Tang huiyao*, 606:663; *Jiu Tang shu*, 269:653.
55. The system of ritual propriety encompasses the roles, relationships, and institutions that facilitate conduct and communication, foster a sense of community, and provide each person with a defined standing within the family and society: Ames and Rosemont, Jr., *The Chinese Classic of Family Reverence: A Philosophical Translation of the Xiaojing*, 77.

56. *Qunshu* zhiyao, 1:118, this translation of the text without annotation is adapted from *Zuo Tradition Zuozhuan*, 3:1390–1391.
57. *Qunshu zhiyao*, 2:217, this translation of the text without annotation is from the *Analects of Confucius*, 33.
58. *Qunshu zhiyao*, 2:229. This translation of the text without annotation is from the *Analects of Confucius*, 122.
59. *Qunshu zhiyao*, 1:132.
60. Commentary by He Yan 何宴; sub-commentary by Huang Kan 皇侃, *Lunyu jijie yi shu* 論語集解義疏 (Collected commentaries on the *Analects*), in *Wenyuange Siku quanshu* (Wenyuange edition of the Complete Library of the Four Branches of Literature) 文淵閣四庫全書, vol. 195 (Taipei: Taiwan Shangwu yinshuguan, 2013), 362, 365–366, and 404.
61. Anthony DeBlasi, "On Impartiality," in *The Essentials of Governance* by Wu Jing, eds. Hilde De Weerdt et al. (Cambridge: Cambridge University Press, 2020), 160. See also, *Jiu Tang shu*, 269:419; *Wei Zheng gong jianlu*, 446:167; *Tang huiyao*, 606:47; Li Fang 李昉, *Taiping yulan* 太平御覽 (Perused by the emperor in the Taiping era, 976–984), in *Wenyuange Siku quanshu* (Wenyuange edition of the Complete Library of the Four Branches of Literature) 文淵閣四庫全書, vol. 894 (Taipei: Taiwan Shangwu yinshuguan, 2013), 522; *Cefu yuangui*, 907:599.
62. *Qunshu zhiyao*, 5:664–665.
63. *Qunshu zhiyao*, 6:740.
64. De Weerdt, "Accepting Criticism," 60–61. This remonstrance by Wei Zheng appears in a further entry at Anna M. Shields, "Obstructing Slander and Sycophancy," in *The Essentials of Governance* by Wu Jing, eds. Hilde De Weerdt et al. (Cambridge: Cambridge University Press, 2020), 203. See also, *Wei Zheng gong jianlu*, 446:165.
65. *Qunshu zhiyao*, 3:382.
66. Paul van Els and Sarah A. Queen observe that "Historicity is not the main concern of early Chinese anecdotes, as their value resided elsewhere, for example, in their ability to persuade, instruct, or entertain": Paul van Els and Sarah A. Queen, "Anecdotes in Early China," in *Between History and Philosophy: Anecdotes in Early China*, eds. Paul van Els and Sarah A. Queen (Albany: State University of New York Press, 2017), 10.
67. De Weerdt, "Accepting Criticism," 57–58.
68. *Qunshu zhiyao*, 1:87, 91; 7:882–883.
69. *Qunshu zhiyao*, 1:139–140; 2:268; 3:395, 465; 4:516, 586; 5:632, 656.
70. Assmann, "Transformations between History and Memory," 50.
71. *Qunshu zhiyao*, 2:223, this translation of the text without annotation is adapted from the *Analects of Confucius*, 91.

72. *Qunshu zhiyao*, 7:882–883. This translation is adapted from *The Book of Lieh-Tzŭ*, trans. A. C. Graham (New York: Columbia University Press, 1990), 165.

73. *Qunshu zhiyao*, 6:848; *The Spring and Autumn Annals of Master Yan*, trans. Olivia Milburn (Leiden: Brill, 2016), 274.

74. *Qunshu zhiyao*, 3:333, this translation is adapted from an entry in *Wang Fu and the Comments of a Recluse*, trans. Margaret J. Pearson (Tempe: Arizona University Press, 1989), 156. Margaret J. Pearson notes that it is a variant of a popular saying, with the earliest record in *Master Wen*, the original text of which is said to date to the fifth century BCE.

75. *Qunshu zhiyao*, 1:91; *Zuo Tradition Zuozhuan*, 1:676–677.

76. Ibid.

77. David McMullen, "On Determining the Roles of the Crown Prince and the Princes," in *The Essentials of Governance* by Wu Jing, eds. Hilde De Weerdt et al. (Cambridge: Cambridge University Press, 2020), 99–100. See also, *Jiu Tang shu*, 269:709; *Xin Tang shu*, 274:262; *Cefu yuangui*, 911:251–252; *Tang wen cui*, 1343:393; *Wenyuan yinghua*, 1339:584.

78. *Qunshu zhiyao*, 2:268, this translation of the text without annotation is adapted from Ssu-ma Ch'ien, *The Grand Scribe's Records Volume I: The Basic Annals of Pre-Han China*, ed. William H. Nienhauser, Jr., and trans. Tsai-fa Cheng et al. (Bloomington: Indiana University Press, 1994), 46.

79. Gabe Van Beijeren, "On Remaining Vigilant until the End," in *The Essentials of Governance* by Wu Jing, eds. Hilde De Weerdt et al. (Cambridge: Cambridge University Press, 2020): 337. See also, *Wei Zheng gong jianlu*, 446:185.

80. *Qunshu zhiyao*, 7:925.

81. Twitchett, "How to Be an Emperor: T'ang T'ai-tsung's Vision of His Role," 37. See also, *Zizhi tongjian*, 308:419; *Tang huiyao* 607:485.

82. Tang Taizong 唐太宗, *Di fan* 帝範 (Model for an emperor), in *Wenyuange Siku quanshu* (Wenyuange edition of the Complete Library of the Four Branches of Literature) 文淵閣四庫全書, vol. 696 (Taipei: Taiwan Shangwu yinshuguan, 2013), 587–618.

83. *Qunshu zhiyao*, 1–10.

84. The eight books in the *Essentials* that are not cited by the *Model for an Emperor* are the *History of the Zhou Dynasty*, the *Discourses of the States*, *Master Lie*, *Master Zeng*, *Master Wu*, *Master Shen*, the *Discourses on Government*, and the *Discourses on Contemporary Affairs*.

85. Other sources include Cao Jiong's 曹冏 *Liudai lun* 六代論 (Discourses of the Six Dynasties) that was intended for the guidance of the young Emperor Shao 少 of Wei (r. 239–254), and the Lu Ji's 陸機 *Wudeng lun* 五等論 (Discourse on the Five Ranks).

86. Twitchett, "How to Be an Emperor: T'ang T'ai-tsung's Vision of His Role," 50–92.
87. *Qunshu zhiyao*, 6:801–803.
88. *Qunshu zhiyao*, 6:856–861; 7:924–927.
89. *Qunshu zhiyao*, 6:859, this translation of the text without annotation is adapted from *The Chinese Martial Code*, trans. Arthur Lindsay Sadler (Rutland, VT: Tuttle Publishing, 2009), 97.
90. *Qunshu zhiyao*, 6:857; *The Chinese Martial Code*, 132–133.
91. *Qunshu zhiyao*, 8:1053; *The Seven Military Classics of Ancient China*, trans. by Ralph D. Sawyer and Mei-chün Sawyer (New York: Basic Books, 1993), 305.
92. *Qunshu zhiyao*, 6:781.
93. *Qunshu zhiyao*, 6:783.
94. *Qunshu zhiyao*, 7:925; *The Seven Military Classics of Ancient China*, 209 (with modifications).
95. *Zhenguan zhengyao*, 407:525; *Wei Zheng gong jianlu*, 446:164–165.
96. *Zhenguan zhengyao*, 407:525; D'Haeseleer, "Debates about Punitive Expeditions," 287.
97. Zeng Zhen 曾振, *Tang Taizong Li Wei gong wendui jinshi jinyi* 唐太宗李衛公問對今註今譯 (Questions and answers of Emperor Taizong of the Tang dynasty and Duke Li of Wei with modern annotation and translation) (Taipei: Taiwan Shangwu yinshuguan, 1986), 53.
98. *Qunshu zhiyao*, 6:856.
99. *Qunshu zhiyao*, 1:89.
100. *Zhenguan zhengyao*, 407:528 and 407:530; *Cefu yuangui*, 911:535 and 919:541.
101. *Zhenguan zhengyao*, 407:527 and 407:532; *Jiu Tang shu*, 269:613 and 271:786; *Tang huiyao*, 606:366 and 606:373; *Cefu yuangui*, 911:536
102. *Qunshu zhiyao*, 8:1053.
103. Ibid., 3:398 and 3:447.
104. Ibid., 7:867.
105. Ibid., 7:980.
106. Ibid., 10:1257.
107. Zeng, *Tang Taizong Li Wei gong wendui jinshi jinyi*, 193.
108. *Zhenguan zhengyao*, 407:526; D'Haeseleer, "Debates about Punitive Expeditions," 287.
109. *Di fan*, 696:615.
110. *Zhenguan zhengyao*, 407:532.; *Jiu Tang shu*, 269:613, *Tang huiyao*, 606:373–374; *Cefu yuangui*, 911:536.
111. *Qunshu zhiyao*, 6:857, this translation is adapted from *The Chinese Martial Code*, 132.

112. *Qunshu zhiyao*, 6:861, this translation of the text without annotation is from *The Chinese Martial Code*, 119.

113. *Qunshu zhiyao*, 8:1052, this translation of the text without annotation is from *The Seven Military Classics of Ancient China*, 304.

114. D'Haeseleer, "Debates about Punitive Expeditions," 290.

115. *Zhenguan zhengyao*, 407:537–538; *Wei Zheng gong jianlu*, 446:174; *Jiu Tang shu*, 269:785; *Tang huiyao*, 606:370; *Cefu yuangui*, 907:605–606 and 919:662; Du You 杜佑, *Tong dian* 通典 (Comprehensive institutions), in *Wenyuange Siku quanshu* (Wenyuange edition of the Complete Library of the Four Branches of Literature) 文淵閣四庫全書, vol. 605 (Taipei: Shangwu yinshu guan, 2013), 640.

116. *Zhenguan zhengyao*, 407:538; *Jiu Tang shu*, 269:785; *Tong dian*, 605:640; *Tang huiyao*, 606:370; *Cefu yuangui*, 907:606.

117. *Zhenguan zhengyao*, 407:538.

118. *Qunshu zhiyao*, 1:22 (Wei Zheng's preface); see Appendix 1.

119. In the Zhenguan remonstrations, only Taizong's response to Wei Zheng's remonstration dated 642 is unknown. It must be noted that although Taizong expressed approval of the advices from Wei Zheng in 632 and Ma Zhou in 637, it remains unknown whether those remonstrances were ultimately followed in the absence of further detail in the historical record.

120. Twitchett, "How to Be an Emperor: T'ang T'ai-tsung's Vision of His Role," 50.

121. *Qunshu zhiyao*, 1:18, this translation is adapted from Richard J. Lynn, "The Formation of the *Classic of Changes* (*Yijing*)," in *Sources of Chinese Tradition Volume 1: From the earliest times to 1600*, 2nd ed., eds. Wm. Theodore de Bary and Irene Bloom (New York: Columbia University Press, 1999), 323.

122. *Qunshu zhiyao*, 3:332.

123. *Qunshu zhiyao*, 10:1284.

124. Twitchett, "How to Be an Emperor: T'ang T'ai-tsung's Vision of His Role": 63.

125. *Qunshu zhiyao*, 1:37.

126. *Qunshu zhiyao*, 2:252.

127. *Qunshu zhiyao*, 6:746.

128. *Qunshu zhiyao*, 6:811, this translation is adapted from *Guanzi Political, Economic, and Philosophical Essays from Early China: A Study and Translation Volume 1,* trans. Walter A. Rickett (Boston, MA: Cheng & Tsui Company, 2001), 196.

129. *Qunshu zhiyao*, 8:1049, this translation of the text without annotation is from *The Seven Military Classics of Ancient China*, 292.

130. D'Haeseleer, "Debates about Punitive Expeditions," 294.

131. *Qunshu zhiyao*, 1:2, D'Haeseleer, "Debates about Punitive Expeditions," 294.

132. D'Haeseleer, "Debates about Punitive Expeditions," 294.
133. *Qunshu zhiyao*, 7:870.
134. *Qunshu zhiyao*, 5:667.
135. *Zhenguan zhengyao*, 407:538
136. *Qunshu zhiyao*, 1:19. *The Sacred Books of China: The I Ching*, 2nd ed., trans. James Legge (New York: Dover Publications Inc., 1963), 391–392; emphasis added.
137. *Qunshu zhiyao*, 2:189.
138. Ibid., 3:359.
139. *Qunshu zhiyao*, 8:1027, this translation of the text without annotation is from *The Annals of Lü Buwei: A Complete Translation and Study*, trans. John Knoblock and Jeffrey Riegel (Stanford, CA: Stanford University Press, 2000), 337.

CHAPTER FOUR

1. Assmann, "Canon and Archive," 100–101.
2. Assmann, "Canon and Archive," 100–102, 106.
3. Assmann, "Canon and Archive," 101–103.
4. Assmann, "Canon and Archive," 103.
5. Martin Bommas, "Pausanias' Egypt," 92.
6. Assmann, *Cultural Memory and Early Civilization: Writing, Remembrance, and Political Imagination*, 72
7. Assmann, *Cultural Memory and Early Civilization: Writing, Remembrance, and Political Imagination*, 74; Assmann, "Communicative and Cultural Memory," 111.
8. Assmann, *Cultural Memory and Early Civilization: Writing, Remembrance, and Political Imagination*, 74–75.
9. Barbie Zelizer, "Reading the Past Against the Grain: The Shape of Memory Studies," *Critical Studies in Mass Communication* 12, no. 2 (1995): 220.
10. Adrian Forty, "Introduction," in *The Art of Forgetting*, eds. Adrian Forty and Suzanne Küchler (Oxford: Berg, 2001), 2.
11. Assmann, "Canon and Archive," 97.
12. Bommas, "Pausanias' Egypt," 93.
13. Assmann, "Canon and Archive," 98.
14. Anna Lucille Boozer, "Forgetting to Remember in the Dakhleh Oasis, Egypt," in *Cultural Memory and Identity in Ancient Societies*, ed. Martin Bommas (London: Continuum International Publishing Group, 2011), 112.

15. "Pre-modern" in this volume refers to Japan before 1868, Korea before 1910, and Vietnam before 1945, respectively.
16. Denis Twitchett, "Hsüan-tsung (reign 712–56)," in *The Cambridge History of China Volume 3: Sui and T'ang China, 589–906, Part 1*, ed. Denis Twitchett (Cambridge: Cambridge University Press, 1979), 462.
17. Michael T. Dalby, "Court politics in late T'ang times," in *The Cambridge History of China Volume 3: Sui and T'ang China, 589-906, Part 1*, ed., Denis Twitchett (Cambridge: Cambridge University Press, 1979), 561.
18. *Cefu yuangui*, 911:275.
19. Wei Zheng is posthumously titled as "Wenzhen 文貞" but his title is recorded here as "Wenzheng 文正" instead to avoid the taboo of using a character in the name of the Emperor Renzong 仁宗 (r. 1022–1063) of the Song dynasty, Zhao Zhen 趙禎.
20. *Yu hai*, 944:449.
21. *Yu hai*, 944:449–450.
22. *Lidai mingchen zouyi*, 438:518–519.
23. De Weerdt and McMullen, "Introduction: *The Essentials of Governance from the Reign of Constancy Revealed* in Context," xv.
24. *Jiu Tang shu*, 268:329.
25. *Yu hai*, 944:328.
26. Dalby, "Court politics in late T'ang times," 628–629.
27. Dalby, "Court politics in late T'ang times," 628–629.
28. Chen Tiefan 陳鐵凡, "*Zuozhuan* jieben kao: cong Ying Fa suo cang Dunhuang liang juan zhi he lun *Zuozhuan* jieben yu *Qunshu zhiyao* zhi yuanyuan 左傳節本考—從英法所藏敦煌兩卷之合論左傳節本與群書治要之淵源" (A study of the abridged *Zuozhuan* based on two scrolls of Dunhuang manuscripts in British and French possession and their origins in the *Qunshu zhiyao)* in *Dalu zazhi yuwen congshu* 大陸雜誌語文叢書 (Collectanea of Mainland Chinese periodicals on oral and written language) ed. Dalu zazhi bianji weiyuanhui 大陸雜志編輯委員會 (Taipei: Dalu zazhi she, 1975), vol. 3 part 3: 279, 282–283, 285; Hao Chunwen 郝春文, *Ying cang Dunhuang shehui lishi wenxian shilu* 英藏敦煌社會歷史文獻釋錄 (Explanatory record of Dunhuang social and historical documents in British possession) (Beijing: Shehui kexue wenxian chubanshe, 2018), 359, 365–371.
29. Lionel Giles, *Descriptive Catalogue of the Chinese Manuscripts from Tunhuang in the British Museum* (London: Trustees of the British Museum, 1957), 230–231; International Dunhuang Project, accessed January 24, 2022, http://idp.bl.uk/database/oo_scroll_h.a4d?uid=2063151398;recnum=133;index=1.

30. Chen, "*Zuozhuan* jieben kao: cong Ying Fa suo cang Dunhuang liang juan zhi he lun *Zuozhuan* jieben yu *Qunshu zhiyao* zhi yuanyuan": 285–286; Wang Zhongmin 王重民, *Dunhuang guji xulu* 敦煌古籍敘錄 (Introductory records of the ancient texts at Dunhuang) (Beijing: Zhonghua shuju, 1979), 57.
31. Chen Tiefan 陳鐵凡, "Dunhuangben *Liji*, *Zuo*, *Gu* kaolüe 敦煌本禮記左穀考略" (A general study of the Dunhuang manuscripts of the *Liji*, the *Zuozhuan*, and the *Guliangzhuan*) *Kongmeng xuebao* 孔孟學報 (*Journal of the Confucius and Mencius Society*) 1971 (21): 113–159; Chen, "*Zuozhuan* jieben kao: cong Ying Fa suo cang Dunhuang liang juan zhi he lun *Zuozhuan* jieben yu *Qunshu zhiyao* zhi yuanyuan": 283–284; Li Suo 李索, *Dunhuang xiejuan Chunqiu jingzhuan jijie yiwen yanjiu* 敦煌寫卷春秋經傳集解異文研究 (Study of the variant text in the Dunhuang manuscript of the *Collected expositions on the Spring and Autumn Annals and Commentaries*) (Beijing: Zhongguo shehui kexue chubanshe, 2008), 17.
32. *Jiu Tang shu*, 269:343.
33. *Xin Tang shu*, 273:90.
34. *Song shi*, 238:787.
35. Wang Yaochen 王堯臣, *Chongwen zongmu* 崇文總目 (Catalogue of the Institute for Venerating Culture) in *Wenyuange Siku quanshu* (Wenyuange edition of the Complete Library of the Four Branches of Literature) 文淵閣四庫全書, vol. 674 (Taipei: Taiwan Shangwu yinshuguan, 2013), 4–151.
36. Di Xinming 翟新明, "*Chongwen zongmu* jiancun chaoben jiben xitong kaoshu 崇文總目見存抄本 輯本系統考述" (Systematic study of the extant manuscripts and collected editions of the *Catalogue of the Institute for Venerating Culture*), *Banben muluxue yanjiu* 版本目錄學研究 (Studies of bibliographical editions) 10 (2019): 71–78.
37. Wilkinson, *Chinese History: A New Manual*, 1858.
38. *Yu hai*, 944:459.
39. *Song shi*, 238:787.
40. Zheng Qiao 鄭樵, *Tong zhi* 通志 (Universal treatise), in *Wenyuange Siku quanshu* 文淵閣四庫全書 (Wenyuange edition of the Complete Library of the Four Branches of Literature) , vol. 374 (Taipei: Taiwan Shangwu yinshuguan, 2013), 376.
41. Zhang Ruyu 章如愚, *Qunshu kaosuo* (Critical compilation of divers books), in *Wenyuange Siku quanshu* 文淵閣四庫全書 (Wenyuange edition of the Complete Library of the Four Branches of Literature), vol. 936 (Taipei: Taiwan Shangwu yinshuguan, 2013), 138.
42. *Yu hai*, 944:459.
43. *Song shi*, 283:787.

44. Ke Weiqi 柯維騏, *Song shi xinbian* 宋史新編 (Revised history of the Song dynasty), in Xuxiu Siku quanshu 續修四庫全 (Continuation of the *Complete Library of the Four Branches of Literature*), vol. 309 (Shanghai: Shanghai guji chubanshe, 2002), 291.
45. Jiao Hong 焦竑, *Guo shi jing ji zhi* (Monograph on national history, classics, and literature), in Xuxiu Siku quanshu 續修四庫全 (Continuation of the *Complete Library of the Four Branches of Literature*), vol. 916 (Shanghai: Shanghai guji chubanshe, 2002), 491.
46. Qi Zengjun 稽曾筠 et al., *Zhejiang tong zhi* 浙江通志 (Zhejiang gazetteer) in *Wenyuange Siku quanshu* 文淵閣四庫全書 (Wenyuange edition of the Complete Library of the Four Branches of Literature), vol. 525 (Taipei: Taiwan Shangwu yinshuguan, 2013), 525:626.
47. Fu Yili 傅以禮, ed., *Siku weishou shumu tiyao* 四庫未收數目提要 (Bibliographical abstracts for the collection of books not included in the Four Branches [of Literature]) (Shanghai: Shangwu yinshu guan, 1955), 57.
48. Florence Bretelle-Establet and Karine Chemla, "Qu'était-ce qu'écrire une encyclopédie en Chine?" *Extrême-Orient Extrême-Occident* 1, no. 1 (2007): 9; Jean-Pierre Drège, "Des ouvrages classés par catégories: les encyclopédies chinoises," *Extrême-Orient Extrême-Occident* 1, no. 1 (2007): 20.
49. Hilde De Weerdt, "Aspects of Song Intellectual Life: A Preliminary Inquiry into some Southern Song Encyclopedias," *Papers on Chinese History* 3 (1994): 4.
50. The founding of the Tang dynasty marked a turning point for examining the concept of *leishu* in the history of their compilations. As the *Essentials* had its own system of thought and did not conform to the characteristics of existing *leishu*, it was generally excluded from the *leishu* classification. However, Ōbuchi Takayuki大渕貴之 argues that the *Essentials* may be considered as an exceptional *leishu* that subordinated the literary repository function to the purpose of serving as a statecraft reference: Tochio Takeshi 杤尾武, "Ruisho no kenkyū josetsu (ichi) Gishin rikuchō tōdai ruisho ryakuji 類書の研究序説一魏晉六朝唐代類書略史" (Introduction to a study on encyclopedic anthologies—brief history on the encyclopedic anthologies of the Wei, Jin, the Six Dynasties, and the Tang dynasty) *Seijō kobungaku ronshū* 成城國文學論集 10 (1978): 187; Ōbuchi Takayuki 大渕貴之, *Tōdai chokusen ruisho shotan* 唐代勅撰類書初探 (Preliminary exploration of Tang dynasty imperially commissioned encyclopedic anthologies) (Tokyo: Ken-bun shuppan, 2014), 22, 28–32.
51. *Cefu yuangui*, 912:617–619.
52. *Qinding quan Tang wen*, 1636: 310–311.

53. Pablo A. Blitstein, "The Art of Producing a Catalogue: The Meaning of 'Compilations' for the Organisation of Ancient Knowledge in Tang Times," in *Monographs in Tang Official Historiography: Perspectives from the Technical Treatises of the History of the Sui (Sui Shu)*, eds. Daniel Patrick Morgan and Damien Chaussende (Cham: Springer, 2019), 326.
54. *Tang huiyao*, 606:481; *Cefu yuangui*, 912:545, 619; *Yu hai*, 944:449; *Tang xinyu*, 1035:363; Wu and Ji, eds., *Tang Taizong quanji jiaozhu*, 297.
55. Glen Dudbridge, *Lost Books of Medieval China* (London: The British Library, 2000), 11, 18, 28.
56. The Tang empire was in effect ruled by Wu Zhao as empress during Gaozong's 高宗 (r. 649–683) reign, as empress dowager during the reign of her sons Zhongzong 中宗 (r. 684, 705–710) and Ruizong 睿宗 (r. 684–690, 710–712), and then in her own capacity, when she assumed the throne as empress regnant Wu Zetian 武則天 (r. 690–705). Not only was the court "overruled," but the number of its chief ministers were reduced. Whereas Taizong had been assisted by eight or more chief ministers and Gaozong had inherited the chief ministers that had served his father, Empress Wu worked with only three to five chief ministers and there were none to serve the Department of State Affairs (the main executive organization) while she controlled Gaozong's court. From the 660s, the empress circumvented the court by use of the private secretariat known as the "Scholars of the Northern Gate" (*Beimen xueshi* 北門學士), an informal group of skilled writers that she retained to process memorials and formulate policy: Denis Twitchett and Howard J. Wechsler, "Kao-tsung (reign 649–83) and the Empress Wu: The Inheritor and the Usurper," in *The Cambridge History of China Volume 3: Sui and T'ang China, 598–906, Part 1*, ed. Denis Twitchett (Cambridge: Cambridge University Press, 1979), 242–243, 255, 263, 268–270, 289; Richard W. L. Guisso, "The Reigns of the Empress Wu, Chung-tsung and Juitsung (684–712)," in *The Cambridge History of China Volume 3: Sui and T'ang China, 598–906, Part 1*, ed. Denis Twitchett (Cambridge: Cambridge University Press, 1979), 310–311.
57. Although the early years of Xuanzong's reign witnessed reforms that restored some *esprit de corps* to the bureaucracy through the ministerial freedom to remonstrate and greater transparency of court business, those conditions were gradually eroded from 736, as Xuanzong increasingly entrusted his government to a single chief minister who would dominate the court (e.g., Li Linfu 李林甫 (d. 752)). The central administration was further undermined by his ad hoc extra-bureaucratic appointments of specialist commissioners for economic and defense matters, reliance on his confidential secretariat, as well as the influence of his favored consort Yang Yuhuan 楊玉環 (d. 755), and

military governors in charge of the permanent professional armies: Denis Twitchett, "Hsüan-tsung (reign 712–56)," 348–350, 366–370, 378, 385–386, 409, 418, 426–429, 447, 450; C. A. Peterson, "Court and province in mid- and late T'ang," in *The Cambridge History of China Volume 3: Sui and T'ang China, 598–906, Part 1*, ed. Denis Twitchett (Cambridge: Cambridge University Press, 1979), 469–470, 474–484; Dalby, "Court politics in late T'ang times," 574–575.

58. Each province was essentially administered by a military or civil governor with wide powers over its prefectures and districts. The governors had command of local troops, the authority to levy taxes and customs, and at times, a monopoly over communications between the court, the prefectures and districts: Peterson, "Court and province in mid- and late T'ang," 487–489, 516, 518–519, 521; Mark E. Lewis, *China's Cosmopolitan Empire: The Tang Dynasty* (Cambridge, MA: The Belknap Press of Harvard University Press, 2009), 60–61.
59. The late Tang emperors relied on provincial governors and their commands to settle regional instability, subdue rebellion and separatist movements, and defend against foreign incursions: Peterson, "Court and province in mid- and late T'ang," 487–489, 493, 509; Dalby, "Court politics in late T'ang times," 583.
60. Robert M. Somers, "The end of the T'ang," in *The Cambridge History of China Volume 3: Sui and T'ang China, 598–906, Part 1*, ed. Denis Twitchett (Cambridge: Cambridge University Press, 1979), 778; Lewis, *China's Cosmopolitan Empire: The Tang Dynasty*, 71, 73.
61. Liao, *Tangdai de lishi jiyi*, 122–125.
62. De Weerdt and McMullen, "Introduction: *The Essentials of Governance from the Reign of Constancy Revealed* in Context," xlvi–lv.
63. Kondō Morishige, *Kondō seisai zenshū* 近藤正齋全集 (Collected works of Kondō Morishige), ed. Ichishima Kenkichi 市島謙吉, vol. 2 (Tokyo: Kappan Kabushiki Kaisha, 1906), 214; Kim, "*Qunshu zhiyao* huichuan kao," 127.
64. Yan Shaodang, *Riben cang Hanji zhenben zhuizong jishi: Yan Shaodang haiwai fangshu zhi* 日本藏漢籍珍本追綜紀實 嚴紹璗海外訪書志 (Record of investigation on rare Chinese texts in Japan: Monograph on foreign textual enquiries by Yan Shaodang) (Shanghai: Shanghai guji chubanshe, 2005), 177–178.
65. The Japanese reproductions of the *Essentials* were exported from Nagasaki on Chinese trading junks as follows: 13 copies in 1817; one copy in 1822, two copies in 1823, one copy in 1824, and one copy in 1825: *Tōsen shinkō narabi ni zatsuji no bu* 唐船進港并ニ雜事之部 (Various accounts of events related to the arrival of Chinese junks at port) in *Zoku Nagasaki jitsuroku taisei* 續長崎實録大成 (Sequel to the *Annals of Nagasaki*), Nagasaki bunken sōsho 長崎文献叢書 (Collectanea of Nagasaki documents), vol. 1, no. 4, ed. Kohara Hazan

小原克紹 (Nagasaki: Nagasaki bunkensha, 1974), 218, 225; Matsuura Akira 松浦章, "Imports and Exports of Books by Chinese Junks in the Edo Period," in *Copper in the Early Modern Sino-Japanese Trade*, ed. Keiko Nagase-Reimer (Leiden: Brill, 2016), 187–189.

66. Matsuura, "Imports and Exports of Books by Chinese Junks in the Edo Period," 192.
67. *Siku weishou shumu tiyao*, 57.
68. Ruan Yuan presented the rare works to the throne in three lots at different times from 1807 to 1811, and the specific timeframe when the *Essentials* was submitted remains unknown: Shanghai tushu guan 上海圖書館, *Zhongguo congshu zonglu* 中國叢書綜錄 (Comprehensive catalogue of Chinese collectanea) (Beijing: Zhonghua shuju, 1959), 151–154.
69. Weng Lianxi 翁連溪, "Yangxin dian cangshu *Wanwei biecang* 養心殿藏書宛委別藏" (Book collection of the Hall of the Cultivating Heart and the *Exclusive Collection from Wanwei*), *Zijin cheng* 紫禁城 (Imperial palace) 1991, no. 6: 43.
70. The timeframe of the discovery is dated to 1924 by Lu Renlong 盧仁龍 and to 1927 by Weng Lianxi 翁連溪: Lu Renlong 盧仁龍, "*Wanwei biecang* bianzuan shimo 宛委別藏編纂始末" (Overview of the compilation of the *Exclusive Collection from Wanwei*) *Wenxian* 文獻 (Documents) 1990, no. 1: 169; Weng, "Yangxin dian cangshu *Wanwei biecang*": 43–44.
71. Betty Peh-T'i Wei, *Ruan Yuan, 1769–1849: The Life and Work of a Major Scholar-Official in Nineteenth Century China before the Opium War* (Hong Kong: Hong Kong University Press, 2006), 238, 290.
72. Ruan Heng 阮亨, *Yingzhou bitan* 瀛舟筆談 (Notes from an immortal's boat) cited in Lu, "*Wangwei biecang* bianzuan shimo," 169.
73. *Dezong Jing Huangdi shilu* 德宗景皇帝實錄 (Veritable records of Emperor Dezong (posthumously titled 'Jing')), in *Qing shilu* 清實錄 (Veritable records of the Qing dynasty), vol. 55 (Beijing: Zhonghua shuju, 1987), 62–64.
74. *Xiaojing Zheng zhu* in *Zhi buzu zhai congshu*, collection 21. The textual reconstruction was eminently possible, as virtually all of the *Classic of Family Reverence* is compiled within the *Essentials*.
75. Qian Tong 錢侗, "Chong ke *Zhengzhu Xiaojing xu* 重刻鄭註孝經序" (Preface to the reprint of *Zheng Xuan's Commentary on the Classic of Family Reverence*), in *Zhi buzu zhai congshu* 知不足齋叢書 (Collectanea from the studio of knowing one's deficiencies), comp. Bao Tingbo 鮑廷博, collection 21 (Taipei: Yiwen yinshuguan yinhang, 1966), 1–3.
76. Sun Xingyan, *Shizi jiben* 尸子集本 (The Collected *Master Shi*), cited in *Shizi: China's First Syncretist*, 185.

77. This translation is adapted from *Shizi: China's First Syncretist*, 49.
78. Wang Weijia, "*Qunshu zhiyao* de huichuan yu Yan Kejun de jiyi chengjiu 群書治要的回傳與嚴可均的輯佚成就" (Rediscovery of the *Qunshu zhiyao* and Yan Kejun's accomplishments in textual reconstruction), Master's thesis, Fudan University, 2013, 28–30.
79. Kim, "*Qunshu zhiyao* yanjiu," 83–98.
80. *Qunshu zhiyao* 群書治要 (Essentials for bringing about order from assembled texts), in *Yueya tang congshu* 粵雅堂叢書 (Hall of Canton elegance series), ed. Wu Chongyao 伍崇曜 (China: Nanhai wushi, 1857), collection 26.
81. *Qunshu zhiyao* 群書治要 (Essentials for bringing about order from assembled texts), in *Sibu congkan* 四部叢刊 (Four branches of literature collection), ed. Zhang Yuanji 張元濟, vols. 443–458 (Shanghai: Shanghai shangwu yinshuguan, 1919).
82. *Qunshu zhiyao* 群書治要 (Essentials for bringing about order from assembled texts), in *Congshu jicheng chubian* 叢書集成初編 (Corpus of works from collectanea first series), ed. Wang Yunwu 王雲五, vols. 195–204 (Shanghai: Shangwu yinshuguan, 1937).
83. *Qunshu zhiyao* 群書治要 (Essentials for bringing about order from assembled texts), in *Wanwei biecang* 宛委別藏 (Exclusive collection from Wanwei), ed. Ruan Yuan 阮元, vols. 73–77 (Nanjing: Jiangsu guji chubanshe, 1988).
84. *Qunshu zhiyao* 群書治要 (Essentials for bringing about order from assembled texts), in *Sibu congkan* 四部叢刊 (Four branches of literature collection), ed. Wang Yunwu 王雲五, vols. 76–78 (Shanghai: Shanghai shudian, 1989).
85. *Qunshu zhiyao* 群書治要 (Essentials for bringing about order from assembled texts), in *Xuxiu Siku quanshu* 續修四庫全書 (Continuation of the *Complete Library of the Four Branches of Literature*), ed. *Xuxiu Siku quanshu* bianzuan weiyuanhui 續修四庫全書編纂委員會, vol. 1187 (Shanghai: Shanghai guji chubanshe, 2002).
86. Zhang Faxiang 張發祥, *Wenbai duizhao Qunshu zhiyao* 文白對照群書治要 (Classical-vernacular *Essentials for Bringing about Order from Assembled Texts*) (Beijing: Zhongguo caizheng jingji chubanshe, 2001).
87. *Qunshu zhiyao yizhu* 群書治要譯注 (Annotated translation of the *Essentials for Bringing about Order from Assembled Texts*), comp. Wei Zheng 魏徵 et al., trans. *Qunshu zhiyao* xuexi xiaozhu 群書治要學習小組 (Beijing: Zhongguo shudian, 2012).
88. *Qunshu zhiyao jinghua lu* 群書治要精華錄 (Essential record of the *Essentials for Bringing about Order from Assembled Texts*), comp. *Qunshu zhiyao* yizhu xiaozu 群書治要譯注小組 (Beijing: Zhongguo huaqiao chubanshe, 2013).

89. *Qunshu zhiyao jiaodingben* 群書治要校訂本 (Revised edition of the *Essentials for Bringing about Order from Assembled Texts*), comp. Wei Zheng 魏徵 et al., eds., *Qunshu zhiyao jiaodingben* bianji weiyuanhui 群書治要校訂本編輯委員會 (Beijing: Zhongguo shudian, 2015).
90. Hao Shijin 郝時晉 et al., eds., *Qunshu zhiyao xubian* 群書治要續編 (Continuation of the *Essentials for Bringing about Order from Assembled Texts*) (Beijing: Tuanjie chubanshe, 2021).
91. *Qunshu zhiyao bianjizu* 群書治要編輯組, *Qunshu zhiyao zhong xiuqizhiping de zhihui* 群書治要中修齊治平的智慧 (Wisdom of the *Qunshu zhiyao* for [self] cultivation, [family] harmony, [state] governance, and [global] peace) (Hong Kong: Sage Education Association, 2020).
92. Xiao Xiangjian 蕭祥劍, *Qunshu zhiyao xinde* 群書治要心得 (Reflections on the *Qunshu zhiyao*) (Beijing: Zhongguo huaqiao chubanshe, 2012).
93. Xiao Xiangjian, *Gunseochiyo gyeongheom* 群書治要心得 (Reflections on the *Qunshu zhiyao*), trans. Kim Seong-dong and Cho Kyung-hee (Seoul: Munhakdongne Publishing Group, 2014).
94. *Qunshu zhiyao kaoyi* bianweihui 群書治要考譯編委會, *Gu jing jin jian: Qunshu zhiyao gushi xuan* 古鏡今鑒群書治要故事選 (Ancient mirror, modern reflection: Selection of stories from the *Qunshu zhiyao*) (Beijing: Zhonghua huaqiao chubanshe, 2013).
95. Scholarship and circulation of the *Essentials* for modern relevance was advocated by the Buddhist master Chin Kung (1927–2022) since 2010: Ji Zhe, "Making a Virtue of Piety: *Dizigui* and the Discursive Practice of Jingkong's Network," in *The Varieties of Confucian Experience: Documenting a Grassroots Revival of Tradition*, ed. Sébastien Billioud (Leiden: Brill, 2018), 88–89; Association of Master Chin Kung's Friends at UNESCO, accessed 21 December 2022, www.ckunesco.com/the-governing-principles-of-ancient-china/.
96. Zelizer, "Reading the Past Against the Grain: The Shape of Memory Studies," 232.
97. Zelizer, "Reading the Past Against the Grain: The Shape of Memory Studies," 229.
98. Zelizer, "Reading the Past Against the Grain: The Shape of Memory Studies," 224.
99. David Lowenthal, *The Past is a Foreign Country – Revisited* (Cambridge: Cambridge University Press, 2015), 320–321.
100. Wang, "Reading for rule: Emperor Taizong of Tang and *Qunshu zhiyao*," 35–36.
101. There are pocketbook editions of the English edition entitled "*The Governing Principles of Ancient China*," volumes 1 to 3, and the passages of volume 1 have been printed as bookmarks: Chung Hua Cultural Education Centre(M)

Bhd 馬來西亞中華文化教育中心, *The Governing Principles of Ancient China* (Taipei: World Book Co., 2012); Chung Hua Cultural Education Centre(M) Bhd 馬來西亞中華文化教育中心, *The Governing Principles of Ancient China*, vol. 2 (Taipei: World Book Co., 2014), and Chung Hua Cultural Education Centre(M)Bhd 馬來西亞中華文化教育中心, *The Governing Principles of Ancient China*, vol. 3 (Taipei: World Book Co., 2017).

102. Jeffrey Prager, *Presenting the Past: Psychoanalysis and the Sociology of Misremembering* (Cambridge, MA: Harvard University Press, 1998), 125.
103. Barry Schwartz, "From *Abraham Lincoln and the Forge of American Memory*," in *The Collective Memory Reader*, eds. Jeffrey K. Olick et al. (New York: Oxford University Press, 2011), 246.
104. Zhou, "Qiangu qishu *Qunshu zhiyao* niepan chongsheng," 106.
105. *Zhuzi zhiyao* 諸子治要 (Essentials of governance from the various masters), comp. Wei Zheng 魏徵 and Xiao Deyan 蕭德言 (Taipei: Shijie shuju, 1962).
106. *Qunshu zhiyao zichao* 羣書治要子鈔 (Epitome of masters from the *Essentials for Bringing about Order from Assembled Texts*), comp. Wei Zheng 魏徵 et al., eds., Jiang Dejun 蔣德鈞, in *Congshu jicheng xubian* 叢書集成續編 (Continuation of the *Corpus of Works from Collectanea*), vol 16 (Taipei: Xinwenfeng chuban gongsi, 1978), 35–66.
107. Zhou, "Qiangu qishu *Qunshu zhiyao* niepan chongsheng," 106–108.
108. *Qunshu zhiyao kaoyi* 群書治要考譯 (Philological translation of the *Qunshu zhiyao*), comp. Wei Zheng 魏徵 et al., trans. Lü Xiaozu 呂孝祖and Zhao Baoyu 趙保玉 (Beijing: Tuanjie chubanshe, 2011).
109. National Centre for Preservation of Ancient Books, "Yongqing wenku sizhong chuban shuoming," 1–2.
110. National Centre for Preservation of Ancient Books, "Yongqing wenku sizhong chuban shuoming," 1–2.
111. Jürgen Habermas, *Structural Transformation of the Public Sphere: An Inquiry into a Category of Bourgeois Society*, trans. by Thomas Burger (Cambridge, MA: MIT Press, 1989), 2.
112. Habermas, *Structural Transformation of the Public Sphere: An Inquiry into a Category of Bourgeois Society*, 7.
113. Habermas, *Structural Transformation of the Public Sphere: An Inquiry into a Category of Bourgeois Society*, 35–36.
114. Habermas, *Structural Transformation of the Public Sphere: An Inquiry into a Category of Bourgeois Society*, 27–28, 36.
115. Habermas, *Structural Transformation of the Public Sphere: An Inquiry into a Category of Bourgeois Society*, 15, 21, 25.

116. Charles Holcombe, *The Genesis of East Asia 221 B.C.–AD 907* (Honolulu: University of Hawai'i Press and Association for Asian Studies Inc., 2001), 145–182; Charles Holcombe, *A History of East Asia: From the Origins of Civilization to the Twenty-First Century* (Cambridge: Cambridge University Press, 2017), 114.
117. For example, although pre-modern Vietnam was at times a Chinese province, under Chinese suzerainty, or politically independent from 939, it was always strongly influenced by Chinese culture: Charles. P. Fitzgerald, *A Concise History of East Asia* (Hong Kong: Heinemann, 1966), 259.
118. Holcombe, *The Genesis of East Asia 221 B.C.–AD 907*, 3–4, 31, 219; Holcombe, *A History of East Asia: From the Origins of Civilization to the Twenty-First Century*, 122.
119. Except for Tibet, most parts of East Asia encountered China's writing system and textual tradition first. Usage of classical Chinese was discontinued in Korea, and Vietnam in the years 1895 and 1945, respectively: Peter F. Kornicki, *The Book in Japan: A Cultural History from the Beginnings to the Nineteenth Century* (Leiden: Brill, 1998), 79; Peter Kornicki, "A Tang-Dynasty Manual of Governance and the East Asian Vernaculars," in *Sungkyun Journal of East Asian Studies* 16, no. 2 (2016): 163; Holcombe, *The Genesis of East Asia 221 B.C.–AD 907*, 5, 67; Liu Yujun 劉玉珺, "Yuenan guji mulu gailüe 越南古籍目錄概略" (Overview of the Vietnamese catalogues of old texts), in *Wenxian jikan* (Literature quarterly) 2006, no. 4: 177.
120. Holcombe, *The Genesis of East Asia 221 B.C.–AD 907*, 72–73, 165, 200.
121. A Sinitic text could be read in Chinese, Japanese, Korean, or Vietnamese, depending on the native language of the reader: Peter F. Kornicki, *Languages, Scripts, and Chinese Texts in East Asia* (Oxford: Oxford University Press, 2018), 29.
122. Holcombe, *The Genesis of East Asia 221 B.C.–AD 907*, 65–66, 75, 225.
123. Kornicki, *Languages, Scripts, and Chinese Texts in East Asia*, 26.
124. Holcombe, *A History of East Asia: From the Origins of Civilization to the Twenty-First Century*, 99.
125. Kai Vogelsang, *China und Japan: Zwei Reiche unter einem Himmel* (China and Japan: Two kingdoms under one sky) (Stuttgart: Alfred Kröner Verlag, 2020), 79.
126. Holcombe, *The Genesis of East Asia 221 B.C.–AD 907*, 38, 57, 178, 203.
127. For example, by the late ninth century, roughly half of the Chinese texts in China were available in Japan: Qian Chengjun, "A research review of Chinese books exchanged between ancient China, Japan and Korea and its influence," in *The History and Cultural Heritage of Chinese Calligraphy,*

Printing and Library Work, eds. Susan M. Allen et al. (Berlin: De Gruyter Saur, 2010), 226–229.

128. Liu Yujun 劉玉珺, *Yuenan Han Nôm guji de wenxian yanjiu* 越南漢喃古籍的文獻研究 (A documentary study of ancient Chinese and Nôm texts in Vietnam) (Beijing: Zhonghua shuju, 2007), 20.
129. Kornicki, *Languages, Scripts, and Chinese Texts in East Asia*, 130–131.
130. Holcombe, *The Genesis of East Asia 221 B.C.–AD 907*, 162–163, 168, 177, 179, 194, 198, 202, 211; Holcombe, *A History of East Asia: From the Origins of Civilization to the Twenty-First Century*, 114, 119–123.
131. Holcombe, *The Genesis of East Asia 221 B.C.–AD 907*, 47, 209.
132. Lewis, *China's Cosmopolitan Empire: The Tang Dynasty*, 120, 168.
133. Holcombe, *The Genesis of East Asia 221 B.C.–AD 907*, 52, 201–202; Lewis, *China's Cosmopolitan Empire: The Tang Dynasty*, 154, 159, 163–164, 173.
134. Holcombe, *The Genesis of East Asia 221 B.C.–AD 907*, 180–181.
135. Holcombe, *The Genesis of East Asia 221 B.C.–AD 907*, 204–205. For example, the historical records show that 217 students from Silla were studying in China in 836, and 105 students returned to Silla after completing their studies in 840; *Tang huiyao*, 606:494; *Jiu Tang shu*, 271:783; Qian, "A research review of Chinese books exchanged between ancient China, Japan and Korea and its influence," 230.
136. Early Tang China enjoyed relations with over seventy foreign countries, but there were relatively closer ties with Japan, Korea, and Vietnam as only those kingdoms fell within the realm of investiture relations proper. There was also cultural dialogue between pre-modern Japan and Korea, as exemplified by the former receiving Confucian and Buddhist traditions from Paekche during the sixth century: Holcombe, *The Genesis of East Asia 221 B.C.–AD 907*, 54, 187–189.
137. Lewis, *China's Cosmopolitan Empire: The Tang Dynasty*, 145.
138. Wu Jie 吳傑, ed., *Riben shi cidian* 日本史辭典 (Historical dictionary of Japan) (Shanghai: Fudan daxue chubanshe, 1992), 802; Shimada Kan 島田翰, *Kobun kyūsho kō* 古文舊書考 (Studies of old Chinese books) (Shanghai: Shanghai guji chubanshe, 2017), 77.
139. Yasuhiko Kimiya 木宮泰彥 (1887–1969) notes that although 19 missions are recorded, three of them were later cancelled for reasons such as inclement weather: Yasuhiko Kimiya 木宮泰彥, *Nissi kōtsūshi* 中日交通史 (History of Sino-Japanese relations), trans. by Chen Jie 陳捷 (Taipei: Shangwu yinshuguan, 1935), 99–109; Mikiso Hane and Louis G. Perez, *Premodern Japan: A Historical Survey*, 2nd ed. (Boulder, CO: Westview Press, 2015), 34.
140. The ambassadorial delegation visiting the imperial library is described in the *Nihon kōsōden yōmonshō* 日本高僧傳要文抄 (Excerpts from the biographies

of Japan's accomplished Buddhist monastics), cited in Bussho kankōkai, *Dai Nihon bukkyo zensho* 大日本佛教全文書 (Comprehensive collection of Japanese Buddhist writings), vol. 5 (Tokyo: Bussho kankōkai, 1912), 74.

141. *Jiu Tang shu*, 271:784; *Xin Tang shu*, 276:362; Naojirō Sugimoto 杉本直治郎, *Abe Nakamaro den kenkyū: shutaku hoteibon* 阿倍仲麻呂伝研究手沢補訂本 (Revised edition of a study on Abe Nakamaro) (Tokyo: Bensei Shuppan, 2006), 242–307.

142. For example, Kibi no Makibi presented numerous Chinese texts to the Heavenly Emperor Shōmu in 735, including the *Tang li* 唐禮 (Rituals of the Tang China) (130 scrolls), the *Dayan lijing* 大衍曆經 (Classic on the comprehensive calendar) (one scroll), the *Dayan li lichen* 大衍曆立成 (Successful establishment of the comprehensive calendar) (twelve scrolls), and *Yueshu yaolu* 樂書要錄 (Record of the essentials from music texts) (ten scrolls): Miyata Toshihiko 宮田俊彥, *Kibi no Makibi* 吉備眞備 (Kibi no Makibi) (Tokyo: Yoshikawa kōbunkan, 1961), 33.

143. Kozo Yamamura, ed., *The Cambridge History of Japan, Volume 3: Medieval Japan* (Cambridge: Cambridge University Press, 1990), 695.

144. Fujiwara no Sukeyo 藤原佐世, *Nihon koku genzai shomokuroku* 日本國見在書目錄 (Catalogue of extant books in Japan) (Tokyo: Hajimu shi, 1885), 26; Marian Ury, "Chinese learning and intellectual life," in *The Cambridge History of Japan, Volume 2: Heian Japan*, eds. Donald H. Shively and William H McCullough (Cambridge: Cambridge University Press, 1999), xix, 345–346.

145. Kozo, ed., *The Cambridge History of Japan, Volume 3: Medieval Japan*, 690; Sagawa Yasuko 佐川保子and Yang Ying 楊穎, "Guanyu Jiutiao ben *Wenxuan* shiyu de yanjiu 關於九條本文選識語的研究" (A language literacy study of the Kujō edition of the *Selections of Refined Literature*), *Yuwai Hanji yanjiu jikan* 域外漢籍研究集刊 (Journal of studies on Chinese texts abroad) 16 (2017): 275.

146. The other texts were the *Essentials of Governance from the Zhenguan Reign* and the *Classic of Family Reverence*: Kim, "*Qunshu zhiyao* yanjiu," 50, 55–56.

147. Kim, "*Qunshu zhiyao* yanjiu,", 55.

148. Yoshifusa Fujiwara 藤原良房 and Nobutomo Ban 伴信友, *Shoku Nihon kōki* 續日本後記 (Continuation of the *Later Records of Japan*) (Tokyo: Yoshikawa Kōbunkan, 1972), 77.

149. *Shoku Nihon kōki*, 238.

150. Shimada Kan is of the view that the *Essentials* was introduced to Japan during the reign of Emperor Ninmyō: Shimada Kan, *Kobun kyūsho kō*, 77.

151. Li Yinsheng 李寅生, *Riben tianhuang nianhao yu Zhongguo gudian wenxian guanxi zhi yanjiu* 日本天皇年號與中國古典文獻關係之研究 (A study of the

relationship between the reign-names of Japanese heavenly emperors and ancient Chinese texts) (Nanjing: Fenghuang chubanshe, 2018), 133–135; Ogura Shigeji 小倉慈司, *Jiten Nippon no nengō* 事典日本の年号 (Encyclopedia of Japanese reign-names) (Tokyo: Yoshikawa Kōbunkan, 2019), 57.

152. Fujiwara Tokihira 藤原時平 and Nobutomo Ban 伴信友, *Nihon sandai jitsuroku* 日本三代實錄 (Veritable record of three generations [of emperors] of Japan), in *Shintei zōho Kokushi taikei* 新訂增補國史大系 (Newly revised and supplemented *Complete Series of Japanese History*), eds. Katsumi Kuroita 黑板勝美 and Jirō Maruyama 丸山二郎, vol. 4 (Tokyo: Yoshikawa Kōbunkan, 1973), 342.
153. *Nihon sandai jitsuroku*, 361.
154. Hosoi Tokumin 細井德民, "Kan *Gunsho chiyō* kō rei 刊羣書治要考例" (Research on publishing the *Qunshu zhiyao*), in *Qunshu zhiyao* 群書治要 (Essentials for bringing about order from assembled texts), vol. 1 (Taipei: World Book Co., 2011), 19.
155. Hayashi Nobutaka 林信敬, "Kōsei *Gunsho chiyō* jo 校正羣書治要序 (Preface to the collated *Gunsho chiyō*)," in *Qunshu zhiyao* 群書治要 (Essentials for bringing about order from assembled texts), vol. 1 (Taipei: World Book Co., 2011), 15. Hayashi Nobutaka's preface is translated into English at Appendix 2.
156. Cited in Kim, "*Qunshu zhiyao* yanjiu," 56; Sen'ichi Hisamatsu, *Biographical Dictionary of Japanese Literature* (Tokyo: Kodansha International Ltd., 1976), 93.
157. Hanawa Hokiichi 塙保己一, *Zoku gunsho ruijū* 續群書類從 (Continuation of the *Classified Collection of Books*), scroll 886 (Tokyo: Zoku-gunsho-ruijū Kanseikai, 1982), 104.
158. Kitabatake Chikafusa, *Chronicle of Gods and Sovereigns: Translation of the Jinnō shōtōki*, trans. H. Paul Varley (New York: Columbia University Press, 1980).
159. Kitabatake, *Chronicle of Gods and Sovereigns: Translation of the Jinnō shōtōki*, 234–236.
160. Hanawa Hokiichi 塙保己一, *Gunsho ruijū* 群書類從 (Classified collection of books), scroll 449 (Tokyo: Zoku-gunsho-ruijū Kanseikai, 1986), 215.
161. Shimada, *Kobun kyūsho kō*, 77.
162. Joseph T. Sorensen, *Optical Allusions: Screens, Paintings, and Poetry in Classical Japan (ca. 800–1200)* (Leiden: Brill, 2012), 153.
163. *Saikyūki* 西宮記 (Chronicles of the Western Palace), comp. Minamoto no Takaakira 源高明, ed. Zōtei Kojitsu Sōsho Henshūbu (Tokyo: Yoshikawa kōbunkan, 1931), vol. 2, 133.
164. Ozaki Yasushi 尾崎康, "*Gunsho chiyō* to sono genson hon 群書治要とその現存本" (The *Qunshu zhiyao* and its extant editions), *Bulletin of the Shidô Bunko Institute* 斯道文庫論集 25 (1990): 135–137.

165. Other titles included the *Essentials of Governance from the Zhenguan Reign*, the *Model for an Emperor*, the *Venerable Documents*, the *Classic of Family Reverence*, and the *History of the Latter Han Dynasty*: Sagawa and Yang, "Guanyu Jiutiao ben *Wenxuan* shiyu de yanjiu," 275.
166. The library collection later became known as the Kanazawa bunko 金澤文庫: Seiichi Iwao, ed., *Biographical Dictionary of Japanese History* (Tokyo: Kodansha International Ltd., 1978), 103; Chen Chong 陳翀, "*Liang Song shiqi keben dongchuan Riben kao jian lun Jinze wenku zhi chuangjian jingwei* 兩宋時期刻本東傳日本考兼論金澤文庫之創建經緯" (A study of block-printed texts transmitted to Japan during the Song dynasty and the establishment of the Kanazawa bunko), *Journal of Xihua University (Philosophy and Social Sciences Edition)* 29, no. 3 (2010): 35–43.
167. Wu, ed., *Riben shi cidian*, 289; Kondō Morishige 近藤守重, "Yūbun koji ken go go hon Nikki toku roku ken chū 右文故事卷五 御本日記贖録卷中" (Above anecdotes scroll 5: Imperial editions of diary records (scroll 2)), in *Kondō Seisai zenshū* 近藤正齋全集 (Collected works of Kondō Morishige), ed. Ichishima Kenkichi 市島謙吉, vol. 2 (Tokyo: Kappan Kabushiki Kaisha, 1906), 393.
168. Kim, "*Qunshu zhiyao* yanjiu," 60.
169. Ozaki, "*Gunsho chiyō to sono genson hon*," 129.
170. Yoshinori Kobayashi 小林芳規, *Kanazawa bunkobon Gunsho chiyō no kun ten* 金澤文庫本群書治要の訓點 (Exegesis and punctuation of the Kanazawa bunko edition of the *Qunshu zhiyao*) (Tokyo: Oiko-shoin, 1991), 480–484; Kim, "*Qunshu zhiyao* yanjiu," 61–70.
171. Scrolls numbered 11, 15, 16, 17, 18, and 19 were recopied during 1274 to 1276, and scrolls numbered 14, 28, 29, and 30 were recopied during 1306 to 1308. The remaining scrolls of the historical section do not contain notations indicating their production dates: Fukushima Kinji 福島金治, "Kamakura chūki no kyō Kamakura no kanseki tsutō ju to sono baikai sha Kanazawa bunkobon to sono shū hen 鎌倉中期の京 鎌倉の漢籍傳授とその媒介者 金澤文庫本とその周邊" (On the Kanazawa bunko and its context: Teaching and introducing the Kanazawa Chinese texts during the mid-Kamakura period), *Kokuritsu Rekishi Minzoku Hakubutsukan kenkyuu houkoku* 國立歷史民俗博物館研究報告 (Research report of the National Museum of Japanese History) 198 (2015): 97.
172. Fukushima, "Kamakura chūki no kyō Kamakura no kanseki tsutō ju to sono baikai sha Kanazawa bunkobon to sono shū hen," 104; Yoshinori, *Kanazawa bunkobon Gunsho chiyō no kun ten*, 480.
173. Yoshinori, *Kanazawa bunkobon Gunsho chiyō no kun ten*, 485.
174. Poon, "Ricang Ping'an shidai Jiutiao jiaben *Qunshu zhiyao*," 4–5; Ozaki, "*Gunsho chiyō* to sono genson hon," 134, 137.

175. The three missing scrolls are number 4, 13, and 21: Yan Shaodang 嚴紹璗, *Ricang Hanji shanben shulu* 日藏漢籍善本書錄 (Catalogue of good editions of Chinese books in Japan) (Beijing: Zhonghua shuju, 2007), 2:1113.

176. In terms of centralized rule, the period of the Muromachi shogunate (1333–1568) for example, has been seen as a time of political weakness and social unrest: John Whitney Hall, "The Muromachi Bakufu," in *The Cambridge History of Japan, Volume 3, Medieval Japan*, ed. Kozo Yamamura (Cambridge: Cambridge University Press, 1990), 175.

177. Yan, *Ricang Hanji shanben shulu*, 2:1113.

178. Kondō Morishige 近藤守重, "Yūbun koji ken nana go sha honpu ken jō 右文故事巻七御寫本譜巻上" (Above anecdotes scroll 7: Imperial manuscript editions of registers (scroll 1)), in *Kondō Seisai zenshū* 近藤正齋全集 (Collected works of Kondō Morishige), ed. Ichishima Kenkichi 市島謙吉, vol. 2 (Tokyo: Kappan Kabushiki Kaisha, 1906), 228; Ozaki, "*Gunsho chiyō* to sono genson hon," 140.

179. Cabinet Library of the National Archives of Japan 國立公文書館内閣文庫藏, 24 January 24, 2022, www.digital.archives.go.jp/DAS/meta/listPhoto?LANG=default&BID=F1000000000000102476&ID=&TYPE=.

180. Hayashi Razan was Ieyasu's librarian and one of his closest advisors: Peter F. Kornicki, "Books in the service of politics: Tokugawa Ieyasu as custodian of the books of Japan," *Journal of the Royal Asiatic Society* 18, no. 1 (2008): 72.

181. Ozaki, "*Gunsho chiyō* to sono genson hon," 156; Zen kuni tōshōgū rengō e 全國東照宮連合會, ed., Hi isago ken kin Tokugawa Ieyasu ōyake itsuwa shū 披沙揀金徳川家康公逸話集 (Collected anecdotes of Tokugawa Ieyasu) (Tokyo: Yagishoten, 1997), 459.

182. Kornicki, "Books in the service of politics: Tokugawa Ieyasu as custodian of the books of Japan," 75.

183. Yan Shaodang 嚴紹璗, *Hanji zai Riben de liubu yanjiu* 漢籍在日本的流佈研究 (A study of the transmission of Chinese texts in Japan) (Nanjing: Jiangsu guji chubanshe, 1992), 162.

184. Ozaki, "*Gunsho chiyō* to sono genson hon," 144, 149.

185. Ozaki, "*Gunsho chiyō* to sono genson hon," 143–144.

186. Ozaki, "*Gunsho chiyō* to sono genson hon," 141–142.

187. Hosoi, "Kan *Gunsho chiyō* kō rei", 20; Ozaki, "*Gunsho chiyō* to sono genson hon": 166.

188. The differences between the Tenmei and Kansei editions are detailed in Ishihama Juntarō 石濱純太郎, *Shinagaku ronkō* 支那學論攷 (Ōsaka: Zenkoku Shobō, 1943), 71–74.

189. Ozaki, "*Gunsho chiyō* to sono genson hon," 160–161, 164–165. The Kōka edition is accessible online from the National Diet Library of Japan 國立國會圖書館, January 16, 2022, https://dl.ndl.go.jp/info:ndljp/pid/2546047?tocOpened=1.

190. The Shōwa edition, National Diet Library Digital Collections, Japan, January 20, 2022, https://dl.ndl.go.jp/info:ndljp/pid/2591404?tocOpened=1.

191. Archives Department of the Imperial Household Agency, "*Gunsho chiyō* kaisetsu 群書治要解說" (About the *Qunshu zhiyao*), in *Gunsho chiyō* 群書治要 (Essentials for bringing about order from assembled texts), volume 0 (Tokyo: Imperial Palace Library, 1941), 1–10.

192. The 13 scrolls remaining are numbers 22, 26, 31, 33, 35, 36, 37, 42, 43, 45, 47, 48, 49: e-National Treasure of National Institutes for Cultural Heritage, Japan, January 23, 2022, https://emuseum.nich.go.jp/detail?langId=en&webView=&content_base_id=100168&content_part_id=0&content_pict_id=0.

193. e-Museum of National Institutes for Cultural Heritage, Japan, January 23, 2022, https://emuseum.nich.go.jp/detail?langId=en&webView=&content_base_id=100168&content_part_id=009&content_pict_id=0.

194. Kondō, *Kondō Seisai zenshū*, 2:174, 204–215, 226–228, 262–265, 301–302, 360–361.

195. Ozaki, "*Gunsho chiyō* to sono genson hon," 170.

196. Ozaki, "*Gunsho chiyō* to sono genson hon," 121–210.

197. Shibue Chūsai 澀江抽齋 and Mori Tatsuyuki 森立之, eds., *Keiseki hōkoshi* 經籍訪古志 (Bibliography of Chinese classics in Japan) (Shanghai: Shanghai guji chubanshe, 2017), 144.

198. Shimada, *Kobun kyūsho kō*, 81.

199. Uematsu Yasushi 植松安, "*Gunsho chiyō* ni tsuki te 群書治要につきて" (About the *Qunshu zhiyao*), *Higashiajia kenkyū* 東亞研究 (East Asian studies) 2, no. 10 (1912) cited in Ozaki, "*Gunsho chiyō* to sono genson hon," 164.

200. Ishihama Juntarō 石濱純太郎, "*Gunsho chiyō* no *Rongo Tei chū* 群書治要の論語鄭注" (Zheng's Commentary on the *Analects* in the *Qunshu zhiyao*), *Higashiajia kenkyū* 東亞研究 (East Asian studies) 5, no. 6 (1915); "*Gunsho chiyō* no *Shōsho* Shun ten 群書治要の尚書舜典" (The 'Shun dian' [chapter] of the *Shang shu* in the *Qunshu zhiyao*), *Higashiajia kenkyū* 東亞研究 (East Asian studies) 5, no. 10/11 (1915), cited in Ozaki, "*Gunsho chiyō* to sono genson hon," 127, 168.

201. Takagi Bun 高木文, *Kōsho zassai* 好書雜載 (Tokyo: Inoue shoten, 1932), cited in Ozaki, "*Gunsho chiyō* to sono genson hon," 159.

202. Sasaki Isamu 佐佐木勇, "Nippon kan'on niokeru hansetsu, dō onji chū no on chū, e no han'ei nitsuite Kanazawa bunkobon *Gunsho chiyō* Kamakura

chūki no baai 日本漢音における反切 同音字注の假名音注 聲點への反映について 金澤文庫本群書治要鎌倉中期點の場合" (Linguistics aspects of the mid-Kamakura annotations to the Kamakura edition of the *Qunshu zhiyao*), *Kunigo manabu* 國語學 (Japanese linguistic studies) 53, no. 3 (2002): 93–106; Sasaki Isamu 佐佐木勇, "Kanazawa bunkobon *Gunsho chiyō* to Kuonji zō honchō bun iki to no kanjion no hikaku Kamakura jidai chūki niokeru kanseki to waka kanbun to no jion chū no sai nitsuite 金澤文庫本群書治要と久遠寺蔵本朝文粋との漢字音の比較 鎌倉時代中期における漢籍と和化漢文との字音注の差異について" (A comparative study of the Chinese phonetics in the Kamakura edition of the *Qunshu zhiyao* and the Kuonji zō edition of *Benchao wencui*), *Oto kenkyū* 音聲研究 (Phonological studies), 8, no. 2 (2004): 26–34; Sasaki Isamu 佐佐木勇, "Kuonji zō honchō bun iki Kamakura chūkiten no kan'on Kanazawa bunkobon *Gunsho chiyō* Kamakura chūkiten to no hikaku otōshite 久遠寺蔵本朝文粋鎌倉中期点の漢音聲調 金澤文庫本群書治要鎌倉中期点との比較を通して" (A comparative study of the Chinese phonetic tones in the Kamakura edition of the *Qunshu zhiyao* and the Kuonji zō edition of *Benchao wencui*), *Kuntengo to kunten shiryō* 訓点語と訓点資料 (Interpretive language and interpretive materials), 114 (2005): 43–59; Sasaki Isamu 佐佐木勇, "Kanazawa bunkobon *Gunsho chiyō* Kamakura chūkiten no kan'on nitsuite 金澤文庫本群書治要經部鎌倉中期点の漢音 聲母について" (Chinese phonetic consonants in the mid-Kamakura period annotations to the Kamakura edition of the *Qunshu zhiyao*), *Shin Ōkunigo* 新大國語 (New comprehensive Japanese linguistics), 30 (2005): 66–76.

203. Morioka Nobuyuki 森岡信幸, "Kanazawa bunko bon *Gunsho chiyō* Kamakura chūki bu no bunmatsu hyōgen omegutte 金澤文庫本群書治要鎌倉中期點經部の文末表現をめぐって" (Mid-Kamakura period expressions for sentence endings in the annotations to the Kamakura edition of the *Qunshu zhiyao*), in *Kunigo manabu ronshū Yoshinori Kobayashi hakase ki kotobuki kinen* 國語學論集 小林芳規博士喜壽記念 (Collected papers on Japanese language studies in commemoration of Dr. Yoshinori Kobayashi), ed. Yoshinori Kobayashi (Tokyo: Kyuko Shoin, 2006), 613–622.

204. Mizukami Masaharu 水上雅晴, "Riben jinze wenku guchaoben *Qunshu zhiyao* xieru de yinyi zhuji 日本金澤文庫古鈔本群書治要寫入的音義註記" (Annotations of sound and meaning in the Japanese Kamakura manuscript of the *Qunshu zhiyao*), in *Di yi jie Qunshu zhiyao guoji xueshu yantao hui lunwen ji* 第一屆群書治要國際學術研討會論文集 (Collected papers from the first international academic symposium on the *Qunshu zhiyao*), eds. Lin Chao-Cheng 林朝成 and Zhang Jui-Lin 張瑞麟 (Taipei: Wanjuanlou, 2020), 1–20.

205. Assmann, "Canon and Archive," 100.

206. National Centre for Preservation of Ancient Books, "Yongqing wenku sizhong chuban shuoming," 1.

207. Kornicki, "A Tang-Dynasty Manual of Governance and the East Asian Vernaculars," 163–164.

208. Kornicki, *Languages, Scripts, and Chinese texts in East Asia*, 131.

209. Liu, *Yuenan Han Nôm guji de wenxian yanjiu*, 20.

210. Cho Myŏngch'ae 曹命采, *Pongsa ilbonsi mun'gyŏnnok* 奉使日本時聞見錄 (Record of information from ambassadorial visits to Japan), in *Chaoxian tongxinshi wenxian xuanbian* 朝鮮通信使文獻選編 (Anthology of Joseon dynasty emissary documents), ed. Fudan daxue wenshi yanjiuyuan 復旦大學文史研究院, vol. 4 (Shanghai: Fudan daxue chubanshe, 2015), 83.

211. *Pongsa ilbonsi mun'gyŏnnok*, 83.

212. Nanmei Aoyagi 青柳綱太郎, *Jeungbo munheon bigo* 增補文獻備考 (Supplemented edition of the reference compilation of documents [on Korea]), vol. 10 (Keijō: Chōsen Kenkyūkai, 1918).

213. Chŏn In-ch'o, ed., *Han'guk sojang Chungguk hanjŏk ch'ongmok* 韓國所藏漢籍總目 (Complete list of Chinese texts in Korea) (Seoul: Hakgobang, 2005).

214. The fourth Koryŏ king, Kwangjong 光宗 (r. 949–975) studied the *Zhenguan Essentials* in 950: Zheng Lianzhi 鄭麟趾, *Koryŏsa* 高麗史 (History of the Koryŏ dynasty), vol. 1 (Tokyo: Takeki insatsusho, 1908), 31.

215. Scholars from the Korean peninsula were studying in China from the times of the Tang dynasty through to the Qing dynasty. Some participated in the civil service examination system and there were graduates working in the Chinese imperial court: Jin Jeuya 琴知雅, "Zhongguo Hanji chuanru Hanguo yanjiu 中國漢籍傳入韓國研究" (A study of the transmission of Chinese texts in Korea), *Guoji Hanxue* 國際漢學 (International Sinology) 2015, no.5: 157–158, 161; Wang Caiyun 王彩雲, "Zhongguo guji zai Hanguo 中國古籍在韓國" (Ancient Chinese texts in Korea), *Guji zhengli yanjiu xuekan* 古籍整理研究學刊 (Journal of studies on ancient book collation) no. 4 (1996): 41–44.

216. Qian, "A research review of Chinese books exchanged between ancient China, Japan and Korea and its influence," 226–229.

217. Wang, "Zhongguo guji zai Hanguo," 42.

218. Korean Old and Rare Collection Information System, accessed December 8, 2021, http://pms.nl.go.kr/korcis/search/searchResultDetail.do.

219. Liu, "Yuenan guji mulu gailüe," 183.

220. Liu Yujun 劉玉珺, *Yuenan Hanji yu Zhong Yue wenxue jiaoliu yanjiu* 越南漢籍與中越文學交流研究 (A study of Vietnam's Chinese texts and Sino-Vietnam literary exchange) (Beijing: Zhongguo shehui kexue chubanshe, 2019), 302.

221. Liu, "Yuenan guji mulu gailüe," 177–178.
222. Liu, "Yuenan guji mulu gailüe," 178–179.
223. Liu, "Yuenan guji mulu gailüe," 179.
224. He Qiannian 何仟年, "Zhonguo guji liubo Yuenan de fangshi ji dui Ruanchao wenhua de yinxiang 中國典籍流播越南的方式及對阮朝文化的影響" (How ancient Chinese texts were transmitted to Vietnam and their influence on the culture of the Nguyễn dynasty), *The Qing History Journal* 2014, no. 2: 47, 49.
225. Liu, *Yuenan Han Nôm guji de wenxian yanjiu*, 23–24.
226. *Xin Tang shu*, 274:344.
227. *Xin Tang shu*, 274:344.
228. Yan Congjian 嚴從簡, *Shuyu zhouzi lu* 殊域周咨錄 (Records of comprehensive enquiries about foreign territories) (Beijing: Zhonghua shuju, 1982), 238.
229. Liu, *Yuenan Hanji yu Zhong Yue wenxue jiaoliu yanjiu*, 298.
230. Ozaki, "*Gunsho chiyō* to sono genson hon," 165–168.
231. He, "Zhonguo guji liubo Yuenan de fangshi ji dui Ruanchao wenhua de yinxiang," 47–48.
232. *Tang xinyu*, 1035:363.
233. Jiang Xie 蔣偕, *Li xiangguo lunshi ji* 李相國論事集 (Collected discourses on [state] affairs by Chancellor Li), in *Wenyuange Siku quanshu* 文淵閣四庫全書, vol. 446 (Taipei: Taiwan Shangwu yinshuguan, 2013), 215.
234. *Jiu Tang shu*, 269:343.
235. *Tang huiyao*, 606:481.
236. *Cefu yuangui*, 911:275, 912:545, 617–619.
237. *Xin Tang shu*, 273:90; 276:11
238. *Tong zhi*, 374:376.
239. *Qunshu kaosuo*, 936:138.
240. *Yu hai*, 944: 328, 449–450, 459, 528; 948:342.
241. *Song shi*, 283:787
242. *Lidai mingchen zouyi*, 438:518–519.
243. *Song shi xinbian*, 309:291.
244. *Guo shi jing ji zhi*, 916:382, 491.
245. *Yuding yuanjian leihan*, 985:786.
246. Chen Menglei 陳夢蕾 et al., *Gujin tushu jicheng* 古今圖書集成 (Comprehensive corpus of illustrations and books from past to present), vol. 240 (Shanghai: Zhonghua shuju, 1934), 4.
247. *Zhejiang tong zhi*, 525:626.
248. *Siku weishou shumu tiyao*, 57.
249. *Qinding quan Tang wen*, 1634:195, 1636:310–311, 1639:77, 1644:487.

CONCLUSION

1. Jack W. Chen, "Anthologies," in *Literary Information in China: A History*, eds. Jack W. Chen et al. (New York: Columbia University Press, 2021), 201–202.
2. Xiaofei Tian, "Medieval Literary Anthologies," in *Literary Information in China: A History*, eds. Jack W. Chen et al. (New York: Columbia University Press, 2021), 215.
3. *Qunshu zhiyao,* 1:22–23 (Wei Zheng's preface); see Appendix 1.
4. Wang, "Reading for rule: Emperor Taizong of Tang and *Qunshu zhiyao*," 38.
5. Tian, "Medieval Literary Anthologies," 203.
6. Christopher M. B. Nugent, "Encyclopedias," in *Literary Information in China: A History*, eds. Jack W. Chen et al. (New York: Columbia University Press, 2021), 293.
7. Fitzgerald, *Son of Heaven: A Biography of Li Shih-Min, founder of the T'ang Dynasty*, 206–207.
8. The limited information concerning the *Essentials*' transmission in Korea and Vietnam precludes drawing further conclusions about its reception and usage by those polities.
9. *Di fan*, 696:617; Twitchett, "How to Be an Emperor: T'ang T'ai-tsung's Vision of His Role," 90.
10. The grand scale of sponsored scholarship in the early Tang is noted by Twitchett: Denis Twitchett, "Chen gui and Other Works Attributed to Empress Wu Zetian," *Asia Major* 16 (2003): 56.
11. *Jiu Tang shu*, 269:697–698.
12. The ritual code was entitled after the name of Taizong's reign: *Zhenguan li* 貞觀禮 (Rituals of the Zhenguan period) and presented to the throne in 633: *Xin Tang shu*, 272:193–194; Howard J. Wechsler, *Offerings of Jade and Silk* (New Haven, CT: Yale University Press, 1985), 42–44; McMullen, *State and Scholars in T'ang China*, 120–123.
13. The *Zhenguan lü* 貞觀律 (Laws of the Zhenguan period) was produced in 637: *Xin Tang shu*, 273:40; *Zizhi tongjian*, 308:291; Mark E. Lewis, *China's Cosmopolitan Empire: The Tang Dynasty*, 51.
14. *Jiu Tang shu*, 268:67, 269:695, 700–701; *Xin Tang shu*, 276:2. McMullen, *State and Scholars in T'ang China*, 72–82; Meyer, "The 'Correct Meaning of the Five Classics' and the Intellectual Foundations of the Tang," 1999.
15. The *Beitang shuchao* 北堂書鈔 (Excerpts from books in the Northern Hall) was compiled by Yu Shinan 虞世南 in *circa* 630: Wilkinson, *Chinese History: A New Manual*, 1818.

16. I include the *Zhenguan Essentials* even though it was not produced during the Zhenguan reign-period because it was written to inform Emperor Xuanzong about the strengths of the Zhenguan practice of government, and it has been used to educate later rulers and their courts on the same.
17. Harald Welzer, "Communicative Memory," in *Cultural Memory Studies: An International and Interdisciplinary Handbook*, eds. Astrid Erll and Ansgar Nünning (Berlin: Walter de Gruyter, 2008), 290.
18. Chen, *The Poetics of Sovereignty: On Emperor Taizong of the Tang Dynasty*, 90–91.
19. Cen Zhongmian 岑仲勉, *Sui Tang shi* 隋唐史 (History of the Sui and Tang dynasties) (Shijiazhuang: Hebei jiaoyu chubanshe, 2000), 107–108.
20. Lo Hsiang-lin 羅香林, *Tangdai wenhua shi* 唐代文化史 (History of the Tang dynasty culture) (Taipei: Shangwu yinshuguan, 1955), 30; Lewis, *China's Cosmopolitan Empire: The Tang Dynasty*, 34; Chen, *The Poetics of Sovereignty: On Emperor Taizong of the Tang Dynasty*, 2.
21. In classical Chinese literature, the dragon is thought to have scales on the underside of its throat that would be fatal to anyone who brushed up against them. See for example, *Han Feizi: Basic Writings*, trans. Burton Watson (New York: Columbia University Press, 2003), 79. The dragon is a metaphor for the emperor in the expression "brave the dragon's scales," which describes the risk of incurring their emperor's ire by officials offering frank advice.
22. Lewis, *China's Cosmopolitan Empire: The Tang Dynasty*, 37.
23. Assmann, "Communicative and Cultural Memory," 112–113, 117.
24. This translation is adapted from Twitchett, "How to Be an Emperor: T'ang T'ai-tsung's Vision of His Role," 57.
25. Assmann, "Communicative and Cultural Memory," 109, 112, 117.
26. Aleida Assmann, *Cultural Memory and Western Civilization: Functions, Media, Archives* (Cambridge: Cambridge University Press, 2011), 128–129.
27. *Zhenguan zhengyao*, 407:341–342; Lewis, "The Cheng-kuan Chengyao: A Source for the study of early T'ang government," 7–8; De Weerdt and McMullen, "Introduction: *The Essentials of Governance from the Reign of Constancy Revealed* in Context," xv–xvi, xix.
28. Twitchett, "Hsüan-tsung (reign 712–56)," 349.
29. Chen, *The Poetics of Sovereignty: On Emperor Taizong of the Tang Dynasty*, 26.
30. Two of the *Model for an Emperor*'s twelve chapters: Chapter 3 "Seeking Worthies" and Chapter 5 "Accepting Remonstrance." Six out of the forty chapters in the *Zhenguan Essentials*: Chapter 3 ("Employing the Wise"), Chapter 4 ("Seeking Criticism"), Chapter 5 ("Accepting Criticism"), Chapter 7 ("On Selecting Officials"), Chapter 11 ("Instructing and Warning the Crown

Prince and the Princes"), and Chapter 12 ("Reproving the Crown Prince"): Wu and Ji, eds., *Tang Taizong quanji jiaozhu*, 601–603, 606–608; *Zhenguan zhengyao*, 407: 366–402, 410–418, 434–447.

31. Many such remonstrances by Wei Zheng are recorded not least in the *Zhenguan Essentials* and the *Old History of the Tang Dynasty.* See, for example, his remonstrances to Taizong dated to the eleventh year of the Zhenguan reign-period (637): *Zhenguan zhengyao*, 407:350–353; *Jiu Tang shu*, 269:667–669.
32. Harth, "The Invention of Cultural Memory," 94.
33. De Weerdt and McMullen, "Introduction: *The Essentials of Governance from the Reign of Constancy Revealed* in Context," xlvi–lii.
34. De Weerdt and McMullen, "Introduction: *The Essentials of Governance from the Reign of Constancy Revealed* in Context," xlvii, lii–lv.
35. De Weerdt attributes the dissemination of the *Golden Mirror* and the *Model for an Emperor* to the encyclopedic work *Description géographique, historique, chronologique, politique, et physique de l'empire de la Chine et de la Tartarie chinoise* (Paris, 1735) edited by Jean-Baptiste Du Halde (1674–1743) and an English translation entitled *The General History of China, Containing a Geographical, Historical, Chronological, Political and Physical Description of the Empire of China, Chinese-Tartary, Corea and Thibet*: Hilde De Weerdt, "Modelling Tang Emperor Taizong and Chinese Governance in the Eighteenth-Century German-Speaking World," *Global Intellectual History* (2022):1, 3–4.
36. For example, Johann Gotlobb von Justi (*c.* 1717–1771), in his political treatise comparing European and non-European monarchies, devotes a chapter to Emperor Taizong, presenting him and his administration as a model for all rulers and monarchies across the earth, and Christoph Martin Wieland (1733–1813) adapted the *Golden Mirror* and the *Model for an Emperor* for his utopian novel advocating monarchical reform: De Weerdt, "Modelling Tang Emperor Taizong and Chinese Governance in the Eighteenth-Century German-Speaking World,"1–27.

APPENDIX 1

1. *Qunshu zhiyao*, 1:22–24 (Wei Zheng's preface).

APPENDIX 2

1. *Qunshu zhiyao*, 1:13–18 (Hayashi Nobutaka's Preface).

Bibliography

Ames, Roger T. "Travelling Together with *Gravitas*: The Intergenerational Transmission of Confucian Culture." In *Confucian Role Ethics: a Moral Vision for the 21st Century?*, edited by Henry Rosemont Jr. and Roger T. Ames, 157–169. Gottingen: Vandenhoeck & Ruprecht, 2016.

Ames, Roger T. and Henry Rosemont, Jr. *The Chinese Classic of Family Reverence: A Philosophical Translation of the Xiaojing*. Honolulu: University of Hawai'i, 2009.

Analects of Confucius. Translated by Burton Watson. New York: Columbia University Press, 2007.

The Annals of Lü Buwei: A Complete Translation and Study. Translated by John Knoblock and Jeffrey Riegel. Stanford, CA: Stanford University Press, 2000.

Archives Department of the Imperial Household Agency. "*Gunsho chiyō* kaisetsu 群書治要解說" (About the *Qunshu zhiyao*). In *Gunsho chiyō* 群書治要 (Essentials for bringing about order from assembled texts). Comp. by Wei Zheng 魏徵 et al., 1–10. Vol. 0. Tokyo: Imperial Palace Library, 1941.

Assmann, Aleida. "Canon and Archive." In *Cultural Memory Studies: An International and Interdisciplinary Handbook*, edited by Astrid Erll and Ansgar Nünning, 97–107. Berlin: Walter de Gruyter, 2008.

Assmann, Aleida. "Transformations between History and Memory." *Social Research* 75, no. 1 (2008): 49–72.

Assmann, Aleida. *Cultural Memory and Western Civilization: Functions, Media, Archives*. Cambridge: Cambridge University Press, 2011.

Assmann, Jan. "Kollektives Gedächtnis und kulturelle Identität." In *Kultur und Gedächtnis*, edited by Jan Assmann and Tonio Hölscher, 9–19. Frankfurt: Suhrkamp, 1988.

Assmann, Jan. "Collective Memory and Cultural Identity." Translated by John Czaplicka. *New German Critique*, vol. 65 (1995): 125–133.

Assmann, Jan. "Communicative and Cultural Memory." In *Cultural Memory Studies: An International and Interdisciplinary Handbook*, edited by Astrid Erll and Ansgar Nünning, 109–118. Berlin: Walter de Gruyter, 2008.

Assmann, Jan. *Cultural Memory and Early Civilization: Writing, Remembrance, and Political Imagination*. New York: Cambridge University Press, 2011.

Association of Master Chin Kung's Friends at UNESCO. Accessed December 21, 2022. www.ckunesco.com/the-governing-principles-of-ancient-china/.

Baihu tongyi 白虎通義 (Comprehensive discussions in the White Tiger Hall). Comp. by Ban Gu 班固. In *Wenyuange Siku quanshu* 文淵閣四庫全書 (Wenyuange edition of the Complete Library of the Four Branches of Literature), Vol. 850. Taipei: Taiwan shangwu yinshuguan, 2013.

Bei shi 北史 (History of the Northern dynasties). Comp. by Li Yanshou 李延壽. In *Wenyuange Siku quanshu* 文淵閣四庫全書 (Wenyuange edition of the Complete Library of the Four Branches of Literature), Vol. 267. Taipei: Taiwan Shangwu yinshuguan, 2013.

Blitstein, Pablo A. "The Art of Producing a Catalogue: The Meaning of 'Compilations' for the Organisation of Ancient Knowledge in Tang Times." In *Monographs in Tang Official Historiography: Perspectives from the Technical Treatises of the History of the Sui (Sui Shu)*, edited by Daniel Patrick Morgan and Damien Chaussende, 323–341. Cham: Springer, 2019.

Bommas, Martin. "Pausanias' Egypt." In *Cultural Memory and Identity in Ancient Societies*, edited by Martin Bommas, 79–108. London: Continuum Publishing Group, 2011.

The Book of Lieh-Tzŭ. Translated by A. C. Graham. New York: Columbia University Press, 1990.

Boozer, Anna Lucille. "Forgetting to Remember in the Dakhleh Oasis, Egypt." In *Cultural Memory and Identity in Ancient Societies*, edited by Martin Bommas, 109–126. London: Continuum International Publishing Group, 2011.

Bretelle-Establet, Florence and Karine Chemla. "Qu'était-ce qu'écrire une encyclopédie en Chine?" *Extrême-Orient Extrême-Occident* 1, no. 1 (2007): 7–18.

Bussho kankōkai. *Dai Nihon bukkyo zensho* 大日本佛教全文書 (Comprehensive collection of Japanese Buddhist writings). Vol. 5. Tokyo: Bussho kankōkai, 1912.

Cabinet Library of the National Archives of Japan 國立公文書館內閣文庫藏. Accessed January 24, 2022. www.digital.archives.go.jp/DAS/meta/listPhoto?LANG=default&BID=F1000000000000102476&ID=&TYPE=.

Cai Meng 蔡蒙. "*Qunshu zhiyao* suo yin *Shi zi* jiaokan yanjiu 群書治要所引尸子校勘研究" (A collative study of *Master Shi* in the *Qunshu zhiyao*). *Wenzi ziliao* 文字資料 (Textual material) 35 (2018): 84–85, 110.

Cefu yuangui 冊府元龜 (Outstanding models from the storehouse of literature). Comp. by Wang Qinruo 王欽若 and Yang Yi 楊億 et al. In *Wenyuange Siku quanshu* 文淵閣四庫全書 (Wenyuange edition of the Complete Library of the Four Branches of Literature), Vols. 902, 903, 904, 907, 910, 911, 912, 919. Taipei: Taiwan Shangwu yinshuguan, 2013.

Cen Zhongmian 岑仲勉. *Sui Tang shi* 隋唐史 (History of the Sui and Tang dynasties). Shijiazhuang: Hebei jiaoyu chubanshe, 2000.

Chan-Kuo Ts'e (Intrigues of the warring states).Translated by James I. Crump, Jr. Oxford: Clarendon Press, 1970.

Chang, Tsung-Tung. "A new view of King Wuding." *Monumenta Serica* 37 (1986–1987): 1–12.

Chen Chong 陳翀. "*Liang Song shiqi keben dongchuan Riben kao jian lun Jinze wenku zhi chuangjian jingwei* 兩宋時期刻本東傳日本考兼論金澤文庫之創建經緯" (A study of block-printed texts transmitted to Japan during the Song dynasty and the establishment of the Kanazawa bunko). *Journal of Xihua University (Philosophy and Social Sciences Edition)* 29, no. 3 (2010): 35–43.

Chen, Jack W. *The Poetics of Sovereignty: On Emperor Taizong of the Tang Dynasty.* Cambridge, MA: Harvard University Asia Center for the Harvard-Yenching Institute, 2010.

Chen, Jack W. "On Greed and Baseness." In *The Essentials of Governance* by Wu Jing, edited by Hilde De Weerdt, Glen Dudbridge, and Gabe Van Beijeren, 216–222. Cambridge: Cambridge University Press, 2020.

Chen, Jack W. "On Profligacy and Recklessness." In *The Essentials of Governance* by Wu Jing, edited by Hilde De Weerdt, Glen Dudbridge, and Gabe Van Beijeren, 208–215. Cambridge: Cambridge University Press, 2020.

Chen, Jack W. "The Organization of Governance." In *The Essentials of Governance* by Wu Jing, edited by Hilde De Weerdt, Glen Dudbridge, and Gabe Van Beijeren, 17–32. Cambridge: Cambridge University Press, 2020.

Chen, Jack W. "Anthologies." In *Literary Information in China: A History*, edited by Jack W. Chen, Anatoly Detwyler, Xiao Liu, Christopher M. B. Nugent, and Bruce Rusk, 201–204. New York: Columbia University Press, 2021.

Chen Menglei 陳夢雷 and Jiang Tingxi 蔣廷錫, *Gujin tushu jicheng* 古今圖書集成 (Comprehensive corpus of illustrations and books from past to present). Vol. 240. Shanghai: Zhonghua shuju, 1934.

Chen shu 陳書 (History of the Chen dynasty). Comp. by Yao Silian 姚思廉. In *Wenyuange Siku quanshu* 文淵閣四庫全書 (Wenyuange edition of the Complete Library of the Four Branches of Literature), Vol. 260. Taipei: Taiwan Shangwu yinshuguan, 2013.

Chen Tiefan 陳鐵凡. "Dunhuangben *Liji*, *Zuo*, *Gu* kaolüe 敦煌本禮記左穀考略" (A general study of the Dunhuang manuscripts of the *Liji*, the *Zuozhuan,* and the *Guliangzhuan*). *Kongmeng xuebao* 孔孟學報 (Journal of the Confucius and Mencius Society) 1971 (21): 113–159.

Chen Tiefan 陳鐵凡. "*Zuozhuan* jieben kao: cong Ying Fa suo cang Dunhuang liang juan zhi he lun *Zuozhuan* jieben yu *Qunshu zhiyao* zhi yuanyuan 左傳節本考 從英法所藏敦煌兩卷之合論左傳節本與群書治要之淵源" (A study of the abridged *Zuozhuan* based on two scrolls of Dunhuang manuscripts in British and French possession and their origins in the *Qunshu zhiyao*). In *Dalu zazhi yuwen congshu* 大陸雜誌語文叢書 (Collectanea of mainland Chinese periodicals on oral and written language), edited by Dalu zazhi bianji weiyuanhui 大陸雜誌編輯委員會. Vol. 3, part 3. Taipei: Dalu zazhi she, 1975.

Chennault, Cynthia L., Keith N. Knapp, Alan J. Berkowitz, and Albert E. Dien, eds. *Early Medieval Chinese Texts – A Bibliographical Guide*. Berkeley, CA: Institute of East Asian Studies, 2015.

Ch'ien Mu. *Traditional Government in Imperial China: A Critical Analysis*. Translated by Chun-tu Hsueh and George O. Totten. Hong Kong: Chinese University Press, 1982.

Chin, Annping. *The Authentic Confucius: A Life of Thought and Politics*. New York: Scribner, 2007.

The Chinese Martial Code. Translated by Arthur Lindsay Sadler. Rutland, VT: Tuttle Publishing, 2009.

Ching, Dora C. Y. "The Language of Portraiture in China." In *A Companion to Chinese Art*, edited by Martin J. Powers and Katherine R. Tsiang, 136–157. Chichester: John Wiley & Son Inc, 2016.

Chŏn In-ch'o, ed. *Han'guk sojang Chungguk hanjŏk ch'ongmok* 韓國所藏漢籍總目 (Complete list of Chinese texts in Korea). Seoul: Hakgobang, 2005.

Chongwen zongmu 崇文總目 (General catalogue of the Institute for Venerating Culture). Comp. by Wang Yaochen 王堯臣. In *Wenyuange Siku quanshu* 文淵閣四庫全書 (Wenyuange edition of the Complete Library of the Four Branches of Literature), Vol. 674. Taipei: Taiwan Shangwu yinshuguan, 2013.

Chou Shaowen 周少文. "Qunshu zhiyao yanjiu 羣書治要研究" (A study of the *Qunshu zhiyao*). Master's thesis, University of Taipei, 2007.

Chu Ming-kin. "Honoring Classicist Scholarship." In *The Essentials of Governance* by Wu Jing, eds. Hilde De Weerdt, Glen Dudbridge, and Gabe Van Beijeren, 225–239. Cambridge: Cambridge University Press, 2020.

Chung Hua Cultural Education Centre(M)Bhd 馬來西亞中華文化教育中心. *The Governing Principles of Ancient China – Volumes One, Two, and Three*. Taipei: World Book Co, 2012–2017.

Chunqiu fanlu 春秋繁露 (Luxuriant gems of the Spring and Autumn). By Dong Zhongshu 董仲舒. In *Wenyuange Siku quanshu*文淵閣四庫全書 (Wenyuange edition of the Complete Library of the Four Branches of Literature), Vol. 181. Taipei: Taiwan Shangwu yinshuguan, 2013.

Chunqiu Guliang zhuan zhushu 春秋穀梁傳註疏 (Annotated commentary on the *Guliang Tradition of Commentary on the Spring and Autumn Annals*). Commentary by Fan Ning 范寧. Sub-commentary by Yang Shixun 楊士勛. In *Wenyuange Siku quanshu* 文淵閣四庫全書 (Wenyuange edition of the Complete Library of the Four Branches of Literature), Vol. 145. Taipei: Shangwu yinshuguan, 2013.

Confucius: Analects with Selections from Traditional Commentaries. Translated by Edward Slingerland. Indianapolis, IN: Hackett Publishing Company, Inc, 2003.

Culler, Jonathan. *The Pursuit of Signs*. New York: Routledge, 2005.

D'Haeseleer, Tineke. "Debates about Punitive Expeditions." In *The Essentials of Governance* by Wu Jing, edited by Hilde De Weerdt, Glen Dudbridge, and Gabe Van Beijeren, 285–299. Cambridge: Cambridge University Press, 2020.

Dalby, Michael T. "Court politics in late T'ang times." In *The Cambridge History of China Volume 3: Sui and T'ang China, 589–906, Part 1*, edited by Denis Twitchett, 561–681. Cambridge: Cambridge University Press, 1979.

de Bary, William Theodore. "Epilogue: Why Confucius Now?" In *Confucianism for a Modern World*, edited by Daniel A. Bell and Hahm Chaibong, 361–372. Cambridge: Cambridge University Press, 2003.

de Bary, William Theodore and Irene Bloom, eds. *Sourcebook of Chinese Tradition Volume 1: From Earliest Times to 1600*. 2nd ed. New York: Columbia University Press, 1999.

De Weerdt, Hilde. "Aspects of Song Intellectual Life: A Preliminary Inquiry into some Southern Song Encyclopedias." *Papers on Chinese History* 3 (1994): 1–27.

De Weerdt, Hilde. "Accepting Criticism." In *The Essentials of Governance* by Wu Jing, edited by Hilde De Weerdt, Glen Dudbridge, and Gabe Van Beijeren, 54–64. Cambridge: Cambridge University Press, 2020.

De Weerdt, Hilde. "Employing the Wise." In *The Essentials of Governance* by Wu Jing, edited by Hilde De Weerdt, Glen Dudbridge, and Gabe Van Beijeren, 35–48. Cambridge: Cambridge University Press, 2020.

De Weerdt, Hilde. "Seeking Criticism." In *The Essentials of Governance* by Wu Jing, edited by Hilde De Weerdt, Glen Dudbridge, and Gabe Van Beijeren, 49–53. Cambridge: Cambridge University Press, 2020.

De Weerdt, Hilde. "Modelling Tang Emperor Taizong and Chinese Governance in the Eighteenth-Century German-Speaking World." *Global Intellectual History* (2022): 1–27, DOI: 10.1080/23801883.2022.2104741

De Weerdt, Hilde and David McMullen. "Introduction: *The Essentials of Governance from the Reign of Constancy Revealed* in Context." In *The Essentials of Governance* by Wu Jing, edited by Hilde De Weerdt, Glen Dudbridge, and Gabe Van Beijeren, xv–lxii. Cambridge: Cambridge University Press, 2020.

DeBlasi, Anthony. "On Impartiality." In *The Essentials of Governance* by Wu Jing, edited by Hilde De Weerdt, Glen Dudbridge, and Gabe Van Beijeren, 156–161. Cambridge: Cambridge University Press, 2020.

Denecke, Wiebke. *The Dynamics of Masters Literature: Early Chinese Thought from Confucius to Han Feizi*. Cambridge, MA: Harvard University Asia Center, 2010.

Dezong Jing Huangdi shilu 德宗景皇帝實錄 (Veritable records of Emperor Dezong (posthumously titled "Jing")). In *Qing shilu* 清實錄 (Veritable records of the Qing dynasty). Vol. 55. Beijing: Zhonghua shuju, 1987.

Di fan 帝範 (Model for an emperor). By Tang Taizong 唐太宗. In *Wenyuange Siku quanshu* 文淵閣四庫全書 (Wenyuange edition of the Complete Library of the Four Branches of Literature), Vol. 696. Taipei: Taiwan Shangwu yinshuguan, 2013.

Di Xinming 翟新明. "Chongwen zongmu jiancun chaoben jiben xitong kaoshu 崇文總目見存抄本、輯本系統考述" (Systematic study of the extant manuscripts and collected editions of the *General Catalogue of the Institute for Venerating Culture*). *Banben muluxue yanjiu* 版本目錄學研究 (Studies of bibliographical editions) 10 (2019): 71–78.

Drège, Jean-Pierre. "Des ouvrages classés par catégories: les encyclopédies Chinoises." *Extrême-Orient Extrême-Occident* 1, no. 1 (2007): 19–38.

Du Ruiqing 杜瑞清, Zhao Gangli 趙崗利, Zhao Gang 趙剛, Jiang Yajun 姜亞軍, and Liu Hui 劉輝, eds. *New Century Chinese-English Dictionary* 新世紀漢英大詞典. Beijing: Foreign Language Teaching and Research Press, 2016.

Dudbridge, Glen. *Lost Books of Medieval China*. London: The British Library, 2000.

e-Museum of National Institutes for Cultural Heritage, Japan. Accessed January 23, 2022. https://emuseum.nich.go.jp/detail?langId=enaicaiw=&content_base_id=100168&content_part_id=009&content_pict_id=0.

e-National Treasure of National Institutes for Cultural Heritage, Japan. Accessed January 23, 2022. https://emuseum.nich.go.jp/detail?langId=enaicaiw=&content_base_id=100168&content_part_id=0&content_pict_id=0.

Ebrey, Patricia. "Court Painting." In *A Companion to Chinese Art*, edited by Martin J. Powers and Katherine R. Tsiang, 27–46. Chichester: John Wiley & Son Inc, 2016.

El Amine, Loubna. *Classical Confucian Political Thought: A New Interpretation.* Princeton, NJ: Princeton University Press, 2015.

Elman, Benjamin A. "The Investigation of Things (*gewu* 格物), Natural Studies (*gezhixue* 格致學), and Evidential Studies (*kaozhengxue* 考證學) in Late Imperial China, 1600–1800." In *Concepts of Nature: A Chinese-European Cross-Cultural Perspective*, edited by Hans Ulrich Vogel and Günter Dux, 368–399. Leiden: Brill, 2010.

Emerson, Ralph Waldo. "Sermon CXXXVI." In *The Complete Sermons of Ralph Waldo Emerson*, edited by Wesley T. Mott, 25–26. Vol. 4. Columbia: University of Missouri Press, 1992.

The Essentials of Governance. By Wu Jing. Edited by Hilde De Weerdt, Glen Dudbridge, and Gabe van Beijeren. Cambridge: Cambridge University Press, 2020.

Fahr, Paul. *Remonstration als Institution: Ein Beitrag zum Herrschaftsverständnis im frühen chinesischen Kaiserreich (Remonstration as an institution: A contribution to the concept of rulership in early imperial China)*. Wiesbaden: Harrassowitz Verlag, 2021.

Fitzgerald, Charles P. *Son of Heaven: A Biography of Li Shih-Min, founder of the T'ang Dynasty*. Cambridge: Cambridge University Press, 1933.

Fitzgerald, Charles P. *A Concise History of East Asia*. Hong Kong: Heinemann, 1966.

Fong, Wen C. *Beyond Representation: Chinese Painting and Calligraphy 8th–14th Century*. New York: The Metropolitan Museum of Art, 1992.

Forty, Adrian. "Introduction." In *The Art of Forgetting*, edited by Adrian Forty and Suzanne Küchler, 1–18. Oxford: Berg, 2001.

Fukushima Kinji 福島金治. "Kamakura chūki no kyō Kamakura no kanseki tsutō ju to sono baikai sha Kanazawa bunkobon to sono shū hen 鎌倉中期の京 鎌倉の漢籍傳授とその媒介者 金澤文庫本とその周邊" (On the Kanazawa bunko and its context: Teaching and introducing the Kanazawa Chinese texts during the mid-Kamakura period). Kokuritsu Rekishi Minzoku Hakubutsukan kenkyuu houkoku 國立歷史民俗博物館研究報告 (Research report of the National Museum of Japanese History) 198 (2015): 91–110.

Giles, Lionel. *Descriptive Catalogue of the Chinese Manuscripts from Tunhuang in the British Museum*. London: Trustees of the British Museum, 1957.

Goldin, Paul R. "Appeals to History in early Chinese Philosophy and Rhetoric." *Journal of Chinese Philosophy* 35, no. 1 (2008): 79–96.

Goldin, Paul R. *Confucianism*. London: Taylor & Francis Group, 2015.

Goldin, Paul R. "Non-deductive Argumentation in Early Chinese Philosophy." In *Between History and Philosophy: Anecdotes in Early China*, edited by Paul van Els and Sarah A. Queen, 41–62. Albany: State University of New York Press, 2017.

Gong Yueguo 鞏曰國 and Zhang Yanli 張豔麗. "*Qunshu zhiyao* suo jian *Guanzi* yiwen kao 群書治要所見管子異文考" (A study of the variant text in the *Qunshu zhiyao*'s excerpts from *Master Guan*). *Guanzi xuekan* 管子學刊 (Journal of Master Guan) 3 (2015): 12–16, 34.

Goodman, Howard L. *Ts'ao P'i Transcendent: The Political Culture of Dynasty-founding in China at the end of the Han*. Seattle, WA: Scripta Serica, 1998.

Guan Panpan 管盼盼. "*Qunshu zhiyao* zhuwen laiyuan chutan 群書治要注文來源初探" (Preliminary study of the sources of the *Qunshu zhiyao* annotations). *Anhui Literature* 安徽文學 2018, no.11: 9–11.

Guanzi Political, Economic, and Philosophical Essays from Early China: A Study and Translation, Volume 1. Translated by Walter A. Rickett. Boston, MA: Cheng & Tsui Company, 2001.

Guisso, Richard W. L. "The Reigns of the Empress Wu, Chung-tsung and Juitsung (684–712)." In *The Cambridge History of China Volume 3: Sui and T'ang China, 598–906, Part 1*, edited by Denis Twitchett, 290–332. Cambridge: Cambridge University Press, 1979.

Guisso, Richard W. L. *Wu Tse-T'ien and the Politics of Legitimation in T'ang China*. Bellingham: Western Washington Press, 1978.

Gunsho ruijū 群書類從 (Classified collection of books). Comp. by Hanawa Hokiichi 塙保己一. Scroll 449. Tokyo: Zoku-gunsho-ruijū Kanseikai, 1986.

Guo shi jing ji zhi 國史經籍志 (Monograph on national history, classics, and literature). By Jiao Hong 焦竑. In *Xuxiu Siku quanshu* 續修四庫全書 (Continuation of the *Complete Library of the Four Branches of Literature*). Vol. 916. Shanghai: Shanghai guji chubanshe, 2002.

Guoyu 國語 (Discourses of the states). Commentary by Wei Zhao 韋昭. In *Wenyuange Siku quanshu* 文淵閣四庫全書 (Wenyuange edition of the Complete Library of the Four Branches of Literature), Vol. 406. Taipei: Taiwan Shangwu yinshuguan, 2013.

Habermas, Jürgen. *Structural Transformation of the Public Sphere: An Inquiry into a Category of Bourgeois Society*. Translated by Thomas Burger. Cambridge, MA: MIT Press, 1989.

Hall, John Whitney. "The Muromachi Bakufu." In *The Cambridge History of Japan: Volume 3, Medieval Japan*, edited by Kozo Yamamura, 175–230. Cambridge: Cambridge University Press, 1990.

Han Feizi: Basic Writings. Translated by Burton Watson. New York: Columbia University Press, 2003.

Hane, Mikiso and Louis G. Perez. *Premodern Japan: A Historical Survey*. 2nd ed. Boulder, CO: Westview Press, 2015.

Hanshu 漢書 (History of the [former] Han dynasty). Comp. by Ban Gu 班固. In *Wenyuange Siku quanshu* 文淵閣四庫全書 (Wenyuange edition of the Complete Library of the Four Branches of Literature), Vol. 249. Taipei: Taiwan Shangwu yinshuguan, 2013.

Hao Chunwen 郝春文. *Ying cang Dunhuang shehui lishi wenxian shilu* 英藏敦煌社會歷史文獻釋錄 (Explanatory record of Dunhuang social and historical documents in British possession). Beijing: Shehui kexue wenxian chubanshe, 2018.

Hao Shijin 郝時晉, Liang Guangyu 梁光玉, and Xiao Xiangjian 蕭祥劍, eds. *Qunshu zhiyao xubian* 群書治要續編 (Continuation of the *Essentials for Bringing about Order from Assembled Texts*). Beijing: Tuanjie chubanshe, 2021.

Harth, Dietrich. "The Invention of Cultural Memory." In *Cultural Memory Studies: An International and Interdisciplinary Handbook*, edited by Astrid Erll and Ansgar Nünning, 85–96. Berlin: Walter de Gruyter, 2008.

Hartman, Charles and Anthony DeBlasi. "The Growth of Historical Method in Tang China." In *The Oxford History of Historical Writing: Volume 2: 400–1400*, edited by Sarah Foot and Chase F. Robinson, 17–36. Oxford: Oxford University Press, 2012.

Hayashi Nobutaka 林信敬. "Kōsei *Gunsho chiyō* jo 校正羣書治要序 (Preface to the collated *Gunsho chiyō*)." In *Qunshu zhiyao* 群書治要 (Essentials for bringing about order from assembled texts). Comp. by Wei Zheng 魏徵, Chu Suiliang 褚遂良, and Yu Shinan 虞世南. Vol. 1, 13–18. Taipei: World Book Co., 2011.

He Jiuying 何九盈, Wang Ning 王寧, and Dong Kun 董琨, eds. *Ci Yuan* 辭源 (Origins of words). Beijing: The Commercial Press, 2017.

He Qiannian 何仟年. "Zhonguo guji liubo Yuenan de fangshi ji dui Ruanchao wenhua de yinxiang 中國典籍流播越南的方式及對阮朝文化的影響" (How ancient Chinese texts were transmitted to Vietnam and their influence on the culture of the Nguyễn dynasty). *The Qing History Journal* 2014, no. 2: 45–54.

Holcombe, Charles. *The Genesis of East Asia 221 B.C.–AD 907*. Honolulu: University of Hawai'i Press and Association for Asian Studies Inc, 2001.

Holcombe, Charles. *A History of East Asia: From the Origins of Civilization to the Twenty-First Century.* Cambridge: Cambridge University Press, 2017.

Hosoi Tokumin 細井德民. "Kan *Gunsho chiyō* kō rei 刊羣書治要考例" (Research on publishing the *Gunsho chiyō*). In *Qunshu zhiyao* 群書治要 (Essentials for bringing about order from assembled texts). Comp. by Wei Zheng 魏徵, Chu Suiliang 褚遂良, and Yu Shinan 虞世南. Vol. 1, 19–21. Taipei: World Book Co., 2011.

Hou Jianming 侯健明. "Jinzeben *Qunshu zhiyao* dui *Shiji Hanshu* jiaozheng shisan ze 金澤本群書治要對史記漢書校正十三則" (Thirteen collative corrections to the *Records of the Historian* and the *History of the Former Han Dynasty* from the Kamakura edition of the *Qunshu zhiyao*). *Guji zhengli yanjiu jikan* 古籍整理研究季刊 (Journal of ancient book collation studies) 4 (2020): 50–54.

Huang Lipin 黃麗頻. "Lun *Qunshu zhiyao* dui *Lao zi* de qujing yu shijian 論群書治要對老子的取徑與實踐" (An essay on the teachings and practice of the *Old Master* in the *Qunshu zhiyao*). *Dong Hwa Journal of Chinese Studies* 31 (2020): 1–31.

Huang Sheng-Sung 黃聖松, ed. *Di er jie Qunshu zhiyao guoji xueshu yantao hui lunwen ji* 第二屆群書治要國際學術研討會論文集 (Collected papers of the second international academic symposium on the *Qunshu zhiyao*). Taipei: Wanjuanlou, 2021.

Hung Kuan-Chih 洪觀智. *Qunshu zhiyao shibu yanjiu: cong Zhenguan shixue de zhiyong jingshen tanqi* 羣書治要史部研究 從貞觀史學的致用精神談起 (The pragmatism of historiography in the Zhenguan period: A study of the *Qunshu zhiyao*'s historical excerpts). Taipei: Huamulan wenhua chubanshe, 2016.

International Dunhuang Project. Accessed January 24, 2022. http://idp.bl.uk/database/oo_scroll_h.a4d?uid=2063151398;recnum=133;index=1.

Ishihama Juntarō 石濱純太郎. *Shinagaku ronkō* 支那學論攷. Ōsaka: Zenkoku Shobō, 1943.

Itō Mieko 伊藤美重子. "Ruisho ni tsuite 類書について" (About the *leishu*). *Bulletin of the Sinological Society of Ochanomizu University* 24 (2005): 1–16.

Jeungbo munheon bigo 增補文獻備考 (Supplemented edition of the reference compilation of documents [on Korea]). Comp. by Nanmei Aoyagi 青柳綱太郎. Vol. 10. Keijō: Chōsen Kenkyūkai, 1918.

Ji Zhe. "Making a Virtue of Piety: *Dizigui* and the Discursive Practice of Jingkong's Network." In *The Varieties of Confucian Experience: Documenting a Grassroots Revival of Tradition*, edited by Sébastien Billioud, 61–89. Leiden: Brill, 2018.

Jin Jeuya 琴知雅. "Zhongguo Hanji chuanru Hanguo yanjiu 中國漢籍傳入韓國研究" (A study of the transmission of Chinese texts in Korea). *Guoji Hanxue* 國際漢學 (International Sinology) 2015, no.5: 156–165.

Jiu Tang shu 舊唐書 (Old history of the Tang dynasty). Comp. by Liu Xu 劉昫 et al. In *Wenyuange Siku quanshu* 文淵閣四庫全書 (Wenyuange edition of the Complete Library of the Four Branches of Literature), Vols. 268–269, 271. Taipei: Taiwan Shangwu yinshuguan, 2013.

Keightley, David N. "Clean Hands and Shining Helmets: Heroic Action in Early Chinese and Greek Culture." In *These Bones Will Rise Again*, edited by Henry Rosemont, Jr., 253–281. New York: State of New York University Press, 2014.

Keightley, David N. "Early Civilization in China: Reflections on How It Became Chinese." *In These Bones Will Rise Again*, edited by Henry Rosemont, Jr., 37–73. New York: State of New York University Press, 2014.

Kern, Martin. "Cultural Memory and the Epic in Early Chinese Literature: The Case of Qu Yuan 屈原 and the *Lisao* 離騷." *Journal of Chinese Literature and Culture* 9, no. 1 (2022): 131–169.

Kim Kwang-Il 金光一. "*Gunseochiyo* ui ilbon jeonrae 群書治要의 일본 전래" (The transmission of the *Qunshu zhiyao* in Japan). *Junggugeomunhak* 중국어문학 (Chinese literature) 2008, no. 52: 47–70.

Kim Kwang-Il 金光一. "Qunshu zhiyao yanjiu 群書治要研究" (A study of the *Qunshu zhiyao*). Doctoral thesis, Fudan University, 2010.

Kim Kwang-Il 金光一. "*Jeong-gwanjichi* uiilonseo *Gunseochiyo* 貞觀之治의이론서群書治要" (*Qunshu zhiyao*: the theory book of the "good government of the Zhenguan era"). *Dongyoung munhwa* 東亞文化 (East Asian culture) 2011, no. 49: 123–127.

Kim Kwang-Il 金光一. "*Qunshu zhiyao* huichuan kao 群書治要回傳考" (A study of the *Qunshu zhiyao*'s re-introduction). *Lilunjie* 理論界 (Theory horizon) 9 (2011): 125–127.

Kitabatake Chikafusa. *Chronicle of Gods and Sovereigns: Translation of the Jinnō shōtōki*. Translated by H. Paul Varley. New York: Columbia University Press, 1980.

Knechtges, David R. and Taiping Chang, eds. *Ancient and Early Medieval Chinese Literature: A Reference Guide – Parts One, Two, and Three.* Leiden: Brill, 2010–2014.

Knickerbocker, Bruce. "齊 Hereditary House 2." In *The Grand Scribe's Records Volume V.1: The Hereditary Houses of Pre-Han China Part 1* by Ssu-ma Ch'ien, edited by William H. Nienhauser, Jr. and translated by Weiguo Cao, Zhi Chen, Scott Cook, Hongyu Huang, Bruce Knickerbocker, William H. Nienhauser, Jr., Wang Jing, Zhang Zhenjun, and Zhao Hua, 31–130. Bloomington: Indiana University Press, 2006.

Kondō Morishige 近藤守重. *Kondō Seisai zenshū* 近藤正齋全集 (Collected works of Kondō Morishige), edited by Ichishima Kenkichi 市島謙吉. Tokyo: Kappan Kabushiki Kaisha, 1906.

Kondō Morishige 近藤守重. "Yūbun koji ken go go hon Nikki toku roku ken chū 右文故事卷五 御本日記黷録卷中" (Above anecdotes scroll 5: Imperial editions of diary records (scroll 2)). In *Kondō Seisai zenshū* 近藤正齋全集 (Collected works of Kondō Morishige), edited by Ichishima Kenkichi 市島謙吉. Vol. 2. Tokyo: Kappan Kabushiki Kaisha, 1906.

Kondō Morishige 近藤守重. "Yūbun koji ken nana go sha honpu ken jō 右文故事卷七御寫本譜卷上" (Above anecdotes scroll 7: Imperial manuscript editions of registers (scroll 1)). In *Kondō Seisai zenshū* 近藤正齋全集 (Collected works of Kondō Morishige), ed. Ichishima Kenkichi 市島謙吉. Vol. 2. Tokyo: Kappan Kabushiki Kaisha, 1906.

Kongzi jiayu 孔子家語 (School Sayings of Confucius). Commentary by Wang Su 王肅. In *Wenyuange Siku quanshu* 文淵閣四庫全書 (Wenyuange edition of the Complete Library of the Four Branches of Literature), Vol. 695. Taipei: Taiwan shangwu yinshuguan, 2013.

Korean Old and Rare Collection Information System. Accessed December 8, 2021. http://pms.nl.go.kr/korcis/search/searchResultDetail.do.

Kornicki, Peter F. *The Book in Japan: A Cultural History from the Beginnings to the Nineteenth Century*. Leiden: Brill, 1998.

Kornicki, Peter F. "Books in the service of politics: Tokugawa Ieyasu as custodian of the books of Japan." *Journal of the Royal Asiatic Society* 18, no. 1 (2008): 71–82.

Kornicki, Peter. "A Tang-Dynasty Manual of Governance and the East Asian Vernaculars." *Sungkyun Journal of East Asian Studies* 16, no. 2 (2016): 163–177.

Kornicki, Peter F. *Languages, Scripts, and Chinese texts in East Asia*. Oxford: Oxford University Press, 2018.

Koryŏsa 高麗史 (History of the Koryŏ dynasty). Comp. by Zheng Lianzhi 鄭麟趾. Vol. 1. Tokyo: Takeki insatsusho, 1908.

Kozo Yamamura, ed. *The Cambridge History of Japan Volume 3: Medieval Japan*. Cambridge: Cambridge University Press, 1990.

Kristeva, Julia. *Desire in Language: A Semiotic Approach to Literature and Art*. Translated by Thomas Gora, Alice Jardine, and Leon S. Roudiez. New York: Columbia University Press, 1980.

Kroll, Paul W. *A Student's Dictionary of Classical and Medieval Chinese*, 3rd ed. Leiden: Brill, 2022.

Lam Yatyan 林溢欣. "Cong *Qunshu zhiyao* kan Tang chu *Sunzi* banben xitong 從群書治要看唐初孫子版本系統" (A study of the early Tang editions of the *Art of War* based on the *Qunshu zhiyao*). *Guji zhengli yanjiu jikan* 古籍整理研究季刊 (Journal of ancient book collation studies) 3 (2011): 62–68.

Lam Yatyan 林溢欣. "Cong Riben cang juanzi ben *Qunshu zhiyao* kan *Sanguo zhi* jiaokan ji qi banben wenti 從日本藏卷子本群書治要看三國志校勘及其版本問題" (A matter of textual collation and editions of the *Records of the Three Kingdoms* based on the Kamakura edition of the *Qunshu zhiyao*). *Journal of Chinese Studies* 53 (2011): 193–215.

Lam Yatyan 林溢欣. "*Qunshu zhiyao* yinshu kao群書治要引書考" (A study of the sources excerpted by the *Qunshu zhiyao*). Master's thesis, Chinese University of Hong Kong, 2011.

Lam Yatyan 林溢欣. "*Qunshu zhiyao* yin *Wu Yue chunqiu* tanwei 群書治要引吳越春秋探微" (Exploring the *Qunshu zhiyao*'s excerpts from the *Spring and Autumn Annals of [the states of] Wu and Yue*). *Guji zhengli yanjiu jikan* 古籍整理研究季刊 (Journal of ancient book collation studies) 1 (2019): 19–23.

Lerer, Seth. "Medieval English Literature and the Idea of the Anthology." *Publications of the Modern Language Association of America* 118, no. 5 (2003): 1251–1267.

Lewis, Mark E. *China's Cosmopolitan Empire: The Tang Dynasty*. Cambridge, MA: The Belknap Press of Harvard University Press, 2009.

Lewis, Winston George. "The Cheng-kuan cheng-yao: A source for the study of early T'ang government." Master's thesis, University of Hong Kong, 1962.

Leys, Simon. *The Hall of Uselessness: Collected Essays*. Collingwood: Black Inc., 2012.

Li Suo 李索. *Dunhuang xiejuan Chunqiu jingzhuan jijie yiwen yanjiu* 敦煌寫卷春秋經傳集解異文研究 (Study of the variant text in the Dunhuang manuscript of the *Collected expositions on the Spring and Autumn Annals and Commentaries*). Beijing: Zhongguo shehui kexue chubanshe, 2008.

Li xiangguo lunshi ji 李相國論事集 (Collected discourses on [state] affairs by Chancellor Li). Comp. by Jiang Xie 蔣偕. In *Wenyuange Siku quanshu* 文淵閣四庫全書 (Wenyuange edition of the Complete Library of the Four Branches of Literature), vol. 446. Taipei: Taiwan Shangwu yinshuguan, 2013.

Li Yinsheng 李寅生. *Riben tianhuang nianhao yu Zhongguo gudian wenxian guanxi zhi yanjiu* 日本天皇年號與中國古典文獻關係之研究 (A study of the relationship between the reign-names of Japanese heavenly emperors and ancient Chinese texts). Nanjing: Fenghuang chubanshe, 2018.

Liang Jianmin 梁建民, Wang Jianyin 王劍引, Yu Wanli 虞萬里, and Zhou Weiliang 周偉良, eds. *Gu Hanyu da cidian* 古漢語大詞典 (Comprehensive dictionary of ancient Chinese). Shanghai: Shanghai cishu chubanshe, 2000.

Liang shu 梁書 (History of the Liang dynasty). Comp. by Yao Silian 姚思廉. In *Wenyuange Siku quanshu* 文淵閣四庫全書 (Wenyuange edition of the Complete Library of the Four Branches of Literature), Vol. 260. Taipei: Taiwan Shangwu yinshuguan, 2013.

Liao Yifang 廖宜方. *Tangdai de lishi jiyi* 唐代的歷史記憶 (Historical memory of the Tang dynasty). Taipei: Guoli Taiwan daxue, 2011.

Lidai mingchen zouyi 歷代名臣奏議 (Memorials from leading officials of each period). Comp. by Yang Shiqi 楊士奇et al. In *Wenyuange Siku quanshu* 文淵閣四庫全書 (Wenyuange edition of the Complete Library of the Four Branches of Literature), Vol. 438. Taipei: Taiwan Shangwu yinshuguan, 2013.

Lidai minghua ji 歷代名畫記 (Records of famous paintings from each dynasty). By Zhang Yanyuan 張彥遠. In *Wenyuange Siku quanshu* 文淵閣四庫全書 (Wenyuange edition of the Complete Library of the Four Branches of Literature), Vol. 812. Taipei: Taiwan Shangwu yinshuguan, 2013.

Liji zheng yi 禮記正義 (Orthodox exegesis of the *Records on Ritual)*. Commentary by Zheng Xuan 鄭玄; sub-commentary by Kong Yingda 孔穎達. Beijing: Beijing daxue chubanshe, 2000.

Lin Chao-Cheng 林朝成 and Zhang Jui-Lin 張瑞麟, eds. *Di yi jie Qunshu zhiyao guoji xueshu yantao hui lunwen ji* 第一屆群書治要國際學術研討會論文集 (Collected papers of the first international academic symposium on the *Qunshu zhiyao*). Taipei: Wanjuanlou, 2020.

Liu Guangpu 劉廣普 and Kang Weipo 康維波. "*Qunshu zhiyao* de nongye sixiang yanjiu 群書治要的農業思想研究" (A study of the *Qunshu zhiyao*'s discourse on agriculture). *Theoretic Observation* 理論觀察 12 (2014): 87–90.

Liu Haitian 劉海天 and Li Ping 李萍. "*Qunshu zhiyao* bianzuan yuanze tanshu: guanyu 'Zhenguan zhi zhi' zhengzhi lunli sixiang zhi tedian 群書治要編纂原則探述 關於貞觀之治政治倫理思想之特點" (An analysis of the compilation principles of the *Qunshu zhiyao*: the characteristics of the politico-ethical philosophy of the 'good government of the Zhenguan era'). *Modern Philosophy* 現代哲學 2 (2019): 149–154.

Liu Hsieh. *The Literary Mind and the Carving of Dragons*. Translated by Vincent Yu-chung Shih. Hong Kong: Chinese University of Hong Kong Press, 2015.

Liu Peide 劉佩德. "*Qunshu zhiyao Shuofu* suoshou *Yuzi* hejiao 群書治要說郛所收鬻子合校" (Collating *Master Yu* as received in the *Qunshu zhiyao* and the *Shuofu*). *Guanzi xuekan* 管子學刊 (Journal of Master Guan) 14 (2014): 88–90.

Liu Yujun 劉玉珺. "Yuenan guji mulu gailüe 越南古籍目錄概略" (Overview of the Vietnamese catalogues of old texts). *Wenxian jikan* (Literature quarterly) 2006, no. 4: 177–189.

Liu Yujun 劉玉珺. *Yuenan Han Nôm guji de wenxian yanjiu* 越南漢喃古籍的文獻研究 (A documentary study of ancient Chinese and Nôm texts in Vietnam). Beijing: Zhonghua shuju, 2007.

Liu Yujun 劉玉珺. *Yuenan Hanji yu Zhong Yue wenxue jiaoliu yanjiu* 越南漢籍與中越文學交流研究 (A study of Vietnam's Chinese texts and Sino-Vietnam literary exchange). Beijing: Zhongguo shehui kexue chubanshe, 2019.

Liu Yuli 劉余莉 and Zhang Chao 張超. "Cong *Qunshu zhiyao* zhidao sixiang lun Rujia shengxian zhengzhi tixi 從群書治要治道思想論儒家聖賢政治體系" (An essay on the Confucian system of governance by sages based on the political discourse of the *Qunshu zhiyao*). *Confucius Studies* 孔子研究 4 (2021): 33–41, 156–158.

Lo Hsiang-lin 羅香林. *Tangdai wenhua shi* 唐代文化史 (History of the Tang dynasty culture). Taipei: Shangwu yinshuguan, 1955.

Lowenthal, David. *The Past is a Foreign Country – Revisited*. Cambridge: Cambridge University Press, 2015.

Lu Renlong 盧仁龍. "Wanwei biecang bianzuan shimo 宛委別藏編纂始末" (Overview of the compilation of the *Exclusive Collection from Wanwei*). *Wenxian* 文獻 (Documents) 1990, no. 1: 168–178.

Lunyu jijie yi shu 論語集解義疏 (Collected commentaries on the *Analects*). Commentary by He Yan 何宴. Sub-commentary by Huang Kan 皇侃. In *Wenyuange Siku quanshu*文淵閣四庫全書 (Wenyuange edition of the Complete Library of the Four Branches of Literature), Vol. 195. Taipei: Taiwan Shangwu yinshuguan, 2013.

Lynn, Richard J. "The Formation of the *Classic of Changes* (*Yijing*)." In *Sources of Chinese Tradition Volume 1: From the earliest times to 1600*, 2nd ed. Edited by Wm Theodore de Bary and Irene Bloom, 318–325. New York: Columbia University Press, 1999.

Ma Chiying 馬持盈. *Shi jing jinzhu jinshi* 詩經今註今釋 (*Classic of Odes* with modern annotation and translation). Taipei: Commercial Press, 1971.

Ma Qichang 馬其昶 and Ma Maoyuan 馬茂元, eds. *Han Changli wenji jiaozhu* 韓昌黎文集校註 (Annotated collection of the writings of Han Changli). Shanghai: Shanghai guji chubanshe, 1998.

Matsuura Akira 松浦章. "Imports and Exports of Books by Chinese Junks in the Edo Period" in *Copper in the Early Modern Sino-Japanese Trade*, edited by Keiko Nagase-Reimer, 175–196. Leiden: Brill, 2016.

McMullen, David. *State and Scholars in T'ang China*. Cambridge: Cambridge University Press, 1988.

McMullen, David. "The Big Cats Will Play: Tang Taizong and His Advisors." *Journal of Chinese Studies* 57 (2013): 299–340.

McMullen, David. "Bureaucrats and Cosmology: The Ritual Code of T'ang China." In *Critical Readings on Tang China*, edited by Paul W. Kroll, vol. 1, 295–345. Leiden: Brill, 2018.

McMullen, David. "Instructing and Warning the Crown Prince and the Princes." In *The Essentials of Governance* by Wu Jing, edited by Hilde De Weerdt, Glen Dudbridge, and Gabe Van Beijeren, 113–119. Cambridge: Cambridge University Press, 2020.

McMullen, David. "On Determining the Roles of the Crown Prince and the Princes." In *The Essentials of Governance* by Wu Jing, edited by Hilde De Weerdt, Glen Dudbridge, and Gabe Van Beijeren, 99–104. Cambridge: Cambridge University Press, 2020.

Mengzi zhushu 孟子註疏 (Annotated commentary on the *Mencius*). Commentary by Zhao Qi 趙岐 and sub-commentary by Sun Shi 孫奭. Beijing: Beijing daxue chuban she, 2000.

Meyer, Andrew Seth. "The Correct Meaning of the Five Classics and the Intellectual Foundations of the Tang." Doctoral thesis, Harvard University, 1999.

Miyata Toshihiko 宮田俊彥. *Kibi no Makibi* 吉備眞備 (Kibi no Makibi). Tokyo: Yoshikawa kōbunkan, 1961.

Mizukami Masaharu 水上雅晴. "Riben jinze wenku guchaoben *Qunshu zhiyao* xieru de yinyi zhuji 日本金澤文庫古鈔本群書治要寫入的音義註記" (Annotations of sound and meaning in the Japanese Kamakura manuscript of the *Qunshu zhiyao*). In *Di yi jie Qunshu zhiyao guoji xueshu yantao hui lunwen ji* 第一屆群書治要國際學術研討會論文集 (Collected papers from the first international academic symposium on the *Qunshu zhiyao*), edited by Lin Chao-Cheng 林朝成 and Zhang Jui-Lin 張瑞麟, 1–20. Taipei: Wanjuanlou, 2020.

Moeller, Hans-Georg and Paul J. D'Ambrosio. *You and Your Profile: Identity after Authenticity*. New York: Columbia University Press, 2021.

Moore, Oliver. "On Selecting Officials." In *The Essentials of Governance* by Wu Jing, edited by Hilde De Weerdt, Glen Dudbridge, and Gabe Van Beijeren, 72–83. Cambridge: Cambridge University Press, 2020.

Morioka Nobuyuki 森岡信幸. "Kanazawa bunko bon *Gunsho chiyō* Kamakura chūki bu no bunmatsu hyōgen omegutte 金澤文庫本群書治要鎌倉中期點經部の文末表現をめぐって" (Mid-Kamakura period expressions for sentence endings in the annotations to the Kamakura edition of the *Qunshu zhiyao*). In *Kunigo manabu ronshū Yoshinori Kobayashi hakase ki kotobuki kinen* 國語學論集 小林芳規博士喜壽記念 (Collected papers on Japanese language studies in commemoration of Dr. Yoshinori Kobayashi), edited by Yoshinori Kobayashi, 613–622. Tokyo: Kyuko Shoin, 2006.

Munro, Donald. *The Concept of Man in Early China*. Stanford, CA: Stanford University Press, 1969.

Naojirō Sugimoto 杉本直治郎. *Abe Nakamaro den kenkyū: shutaku hoteibon* 阿倍仲麻呂伝研究手沢補訂本 (Revised edition of a study on Abe Nakamaro). Tokyo: Bensei Shuppan, 2006.

National Centre for Preservation of Ancient Books. "Yongqing wenku sizhong chuban shuoming 永青文庫四種出版說明" (Note on the publication of the four types from the Eisei Bunko Collection). In *Qunshu zhiyao* 群書治要 (Essentials for bringing about order from assembled texts). Comp. by Wei Zheng 魏徵 et al. Vol. 1, 1–2. Beijing: National Library of China Press, 2019.

National Cheng Kung University of Taiwan. "Di yi jie *Qunshu zhiyao* guoji xueshu yantao hui huiyi lunwenji 第一屆群書治要國際學術研討會會議文集"

(Collected papers of the first international academic symposium on the *Qunshu zhiyao*). Accessed June 14, 2019. www.chinese.ncku.edu.tw/p/406-1142-194026,r1185.php?Lang=zh-tw.

National Cheng Kung University of Taiwan."Di er jie *Qunshu zhiyao* guoji xueshu yantao hui第二屆群書治要國際學術研討會" (Second international academic symposium on the *Qunshu zhiyao*). Accessed September 26, 2022. https://chinese.ncku.edu.tw/p/404-1142-210922.php?Lang=zh-tw.

National Cheng Kung University of Taiwan. *"Di san jie Qunshu zhiyao xueshu yantaohui* 第三屆群書治要學術研討會*"* (The third academic symposium on the *Qunshu zhiyao*). Accessed September 26, 2022. https://chinese.ncku.edu.tw/p/404-1142-228167.php?Lang=zh-tw.

National Diet Library Digital Collections—the Shōwa edition. Accessed January 20, 2022. https://dl.ndl.go.jp/info:ndljp/pid/2591404?tocOpened=1.

National Diet Library of Japan 國立國會圖書館. Accessed January 16, 2022. https://dl.ndl.go.jp/info:ndljp/pid/2546047?tocOpened=1.

National Palace Museum. *King Wu Ding and Lady Hao: Art and Culture of the Late Shang Dynasty.* Taipei: National Palace Museum, 2012.

Ng, On Cho and Q. Edward Wang. *Mirroring the Past: The Writing and Use of History in Imperial China*. Honolulu: University of Hawai'i Press, 2005.

Ngo, Kelly. "Cultural Memory of Early Tang China in the *Qunshu zhiyao* 群書治要 (Essentials for bringing about order from assembled texts)." *Journal of the European Association for Chinese Studies* 4 (2023): 199–222. https://doi.org/10.25365/jeacs.2023.4.ngo

Nienhauser Jr., William H. and Michael E. Naparstek, eds. *Biographical Dictionary of Tang Dynasty Literati*. Bloomington: Indiana University Press, 2022.

Nihon koku genzai shomokuroku 日本國見在書目錄 (Catalogue of extant books in Japan). By Fujiwara no Sukeyo 藤原佐世. Tokyo: Hajimu shi, 1885.

Nihon sandai jitsuroku 日本三代實錄 (Veritable record of three generations [of emperors] of Japan). By Fujiwara Tokihira 藤原時平 and Nobutomo Ban 伴信友. In *Shintei zōho Kokushi taikei* 新訂增補國史大系 (*Newly revised and supplemented Complete Series of Japanese History*), edited by Katsumi Kuroita 黑板勝美 and Jirō Maruyama 丸山二郎. Vol. 4. Tokyo: Yoshikawa Kōbunkan, 1973.

Nugent, Christopher M. B. "Encyclopedias." In *Literary Information in China: A History*, edited by Jack W. Chen, Anatoly Detwyler, Xiao Liu, Christopher M. B. Nugent, and Bruce Rusk, 291–294. New York: Columbia University Press, 2021.

Nylan, Michael. *The Five "Confucian" Classics.* New Haven, CT: Yale University Press, 2001.

Nylan, Michael. "Ru" in *The Encyclopedia of Confucianism*, edited by Xinzhong Yao, 507–509. Oxford: Routledge, 2003.

Ōbuchi Takayuki 大渕貴之. *Tōdai chokusen ruisho shotan* 唐代勅撰類書初探 (Preliminary exploration of Tang dynasty imperially commissioned encyclopedic anthologies). Tokyo: Ken-bun shuppan, 2014.

Ogura Shigeji 小倉慈司. *Jiten Nippon no nengō* 事典日本の年号 (Encyclopedia of Japanese reign-names). Tokyo: Yoshikawa Kōbunkan, 2019.

Olberding, Amy. *Moral Exemplars in the Analects: The Good Person is That*. New York: Routledge, 2012.

"On Teaching and Learning (*Xueji* 學記)." Translated by Xu Di, Yang Liuxin, Hunter McEwan, and Roger T. Ames. In *Chinese Philosophy on Teaching and Learning*, edited by Xu Di and Hunter McEwan, 9–18. Albany: State University of New York Press, 2016.

Ozaki Yasushi 尾崎康. "*Gunsho chiyō* to sono genson hon 群書治要とその現存本" (The *Qunshu zhiyao* and its extant editions). *Bulletin of the Shidô Bunko Institute* 斯道文庫論集 25 (1990): 121–210.

Peterson, C. A. "Court and province in mid- and late T'ang." In *The Cambridge History of China Volume 3: Sui and T'ang China, 598–906, Part 1*, edited by Denis Twitchett, 464–560. Cambridge: Cambridge University Press, 1979.

The Pheasant Cap Master (He guan zi): A Rhetorical Reading. Translated by Carine Defoort. New York: State University of New York Press, 1997.

Pines, Yuri. *The Everlasting Empire: The Political Culture of Ancient China and Its Imperial Legacy*. Princeton, NJ: Princeton University Press, 2012.

Pongsa ilbonsi mun'gyŏnnok 奉使日本時聞見錄 (Record of information from ambassadorial visits to Japan). By Cho Myŏngch'ae 曹命采. In *Chaoxian tongxinshi wenxian xuanbian* 朝鮮通信使文獻選編 (Anthology of Joseon dynasty emissary documents), edited by Fudan daxue wenshi yanjiuyuan 復旦大學文史研究院. Vol. 4. Shanghai: Fudan daxue chubanshe, 2015.

Poon Ming Kay 潘銘基. "*Qunshu zhiyao* suo zai *Wenzi* yiwen yanjiu 群書治要所載文子異文研究" (A study of the variant text in the *Qunshu zhiyao*'s excerpts from *Master Wen*). *Xingda zhongwen xuebao* 興大中文學報 (Journal of the Chinese Department of the National Chung Hsing University) 44 (2018): 1–27.

Poon Ming Kay 潘銘基. "Ri cang Ping'an shidai Jiutiaojia ben *Qunshu zhiyao* yanjiu 日藏平安時代九条家本群書治要研究" (A study of the *Qunshu zhiyao* from Japan's Heian period). *Journal of Chinese Studies* 67 (2018): 2–42.

Poon Ming Kay 潘銘基. "Lun *Qunshu zhiyao* jingbu suojian Tang chu jingxue fengshang 論群書治要經部所見唐初經學風尚" (An essay on early Tang classical scholarship as seen in the canonical section of the *Qunshu zhiyao*). *Shumu jikan* 書目季刊 (Bibliography quarterly) 53, no. 3 (2019): 1–27.

Prager, Jeffrey. *Presenting the Past: Psychoanalysis and the Sociology of Misremembering*. Cambridge, MA: Harvard University Press, 1998.

Qian Chengjun. "A research review of Chinese books exchanged between ancient China, Japan and Korea and its influence." In *The History and Cultural Heritage of Chinese Calligraphy, Printing and Library Work*, edited by Susan M. Allen, Lin Zuzao, Cheng Xiaolan, and Jan Bos, 226–241. Berlin: De Gruyter Saur, 2010.

Qian Tong 錢侗. "Chong ke *Zhengzhu Xiaojing xu* 重刻鄭註孝經序" (Preface to the reprint of *Zheng Xuan's Commentary on the Classic of Family Reverence*). In *Zhi buzu zhai congshu* 知不足齋叢書 (Collectanea from the studio of knowing one's deficiencies). Compiled by Bao Tingbo 鮑廷博. Collection 21. Taipei: Yiwen yinshuguan yinhang, 1966.

Qinding quan Tang wen 欽定全唐文 (Imperially authorized complete anthology of Tang dynasty prose). Comp. by Dong Gao 董誥 et al. Vols. 1634, 1636, 1639, 1644. Shanghai: Shanghai guji chubanshe, 1995.

Qunshu kaosuo 群書考索 (Critical compilation of divers books). By Zhang Ruyu 章如愚. In *Wenyuange siku quanshu* 文淵閣四庫全書 (Wenyuange edition of the Complete Library of the Four Branches of Literature), Vol. 936. Taipei: Taiwan Shangwu yinshuguan, 2013.

Qunshu zhiyao 群書治要 (Essentials for bringing about order from assembled texts). Comp. by Wei Zheng 魏徵 et al. In *Yueya tang congshu* 粵雅堂叢書 (Hall of Canton elegance series), edited by Wu Chongyao 伍崇曜. China: Nanhai wushi, 1857. Collection 26.

Qunshu zhiyao 群書治要 (Essentials for bringing about order from assembled texts). Comp. by Wei Zheng 魏徵 et al. In *Sibu congkan* 四部叢刊 (Four branches of literature collection), edited by Zhang Yuanji 張元濟. Vols. 443–458. Shanghai: Shanghai shangwu yinshuguan, 1919.

Qunshu zhiyao 群書治要 (Essentials for bringing about order from assembled texts). Comp. by Wei Zheng 魏徵 et al. In *Congshu jicheng chubian* 叢書集成初編 (Corpus of works from collectanea first series), edited by Wang Yunwu 王雲五. Vols. 195–204. Shanghai: Shangwu yinshuguan, 1937.

Qunshu zhiyao 群書治要 (Essentials for bringing about order from assembled texts). Comp. by Wei Zheng 魏徵 et al. In *Wanwei biecang* 宛委別藏 (Exclusive collection from Wanwei), edited by Ruan Yuan 阮元. Vols. 73–77. Nanjing: Jiangsu guji chubanshe, 1988.

Qunshu zhiyao 群書治要 (Essentials for bringing about order from assembled texts). Comp. by Wei Zheng 魏徵 et al. In *Sibu congkan* 四部叢刊 (Four branches of literature collection), edited by Wang Yunwu 王雲五. Vols. 76–78. Shanghai: Shanghai shudian, 1989.

Qunshu zhiyao 群書治要 (Essentials for bringing about order from assembled texts). Comp. by Wei Zheng 魏徵 et al. In *Xuxiu Siku quanshu* 續修四庫全書 (Continuation of the *Complete Library of the Four Branches of Literature*), edited by *Xuxiu Siku quanshu* bianzuan weiyuanhui 續修四庫全書編纂委員會. Vol. 1187. Shanghai: Shanghai guji chubanshe, 2002.

Qunshu zhiyao 群書治要 (Essentials for bringing about order from assembled texts). Comp. by Wei Zheng 魏徵, Chu Suiliang 褚遂良, and Yu Shinan 虞世南. Taipei: World Book Co., 2013.

Qunshu zhiyao bianjizu 群書治要編輯組, ed. *Qunshu zhiyao zhong xiuqizhiping de zhihui* 群書治要中修齊治平的智慧 (Wisdom of the *Qunshu zhiyao* for [self] cultivation, [family] harmony, [state] governance, and [global] peace). Hong Kong: Sage Education Association, 2020.

Qunshu zhiyao jiaodingben 群書治要校訂本 (Revised edition of the *Essentials for Bringing about Order from Assembled Texts)*. Comp. by Wei Zheng 魏徵 et al. Edited by *Qunshu zhiyao* jiaodingben bianji weiyuanhui 群書治要校訂本編輯委員會. Beijing: Zhongguo shudian, 2015.

Qunshu zhiyao jinghua lu 群書治要精華錄 (Essential record of the *Essentials for Bringing about Order from Assembled Texts*). Comp. by *Qunshu zhiyao* yizhu xiaozu 群書治要譯注小組. Beijing: Zhongguo huaqiao chubanshe, 2013.

Qunshu zhiyao kaoyi 群書治要考譯 (Philological translation of the *Qunshu zhiyao)*. Comp. by Wei Zheng 魏徵 et al. Translated by Lü Xiaozu 呂孝祖 and Zhao Baoyu 趙保玉. Beijing: Tuanjie chubanshe, 2011.

Qunshu zhiyao kaoyi bianweihui 群書治要考譯編委會. *Gu jing jin jian: Qunshu zhiyao gushi xuan* 古鏡今鑒群書治要故事選 (Ancient mirror, modern reflection: Selection of stories from the *Qunshu zhiyao)*. Beijing: Zhonghua huaqiao chubanshe, 2013.

Qunshu zhiyao yizhu 群書治要譯注 (Annotated translation of the *Essentials for Bringing about Order from Assembled Texts)*. Comp. by Wei Zheng 魏徵 et al. Annotated and translated by *Qunshu zhiyao* xuexi xiaozhu 群書治要學習小組. Bejing: Zhongguo shudian, 2012.

Qunshu zhiyao zichao 羣書治要子鈔 (Epitome of masters from the *Essentials for Bringing about Order from Assembled Texts).* Comp. by Wei Zheng 魏徵 et al. Edited by Jiang Dejun 蔣德鈞. In *Congshu jicheng xubian* 叢書集成續編 (Continuation of the *Corpus of Works from Collectanea*), Vol. 16, 35–66. Taipei: Xinwenfeng chuban gongsi, 1978.

Ren Yu 任煜. "Ri cang Liancang chaoben *Qunshu zhiyao Shi* tanlun 日藏鐮倉抄本群書治要詩探論" (An essay on the *Qunshu zhiyao*'s excerpts from the *Odes* in the Japanese Kamakura manuscript). *Dangan* 檔案 (Archives) 1 (2020): 33–40.

The Sacred Books of China: The I Ching, 2nd ed. Translated by James Legge. New York: Dover Publications Inc., 1963.

The Sacred Books of China: The Texts of Confucianism Part 1 The Shu King, The Religious Portions of the Shih King, the Hsiao King. Translated by James Legge. New York: Charles Scribner's Sons, 1899.

Sagawa Yasuko 佐川保子 and Yang Ying 楊穎. "Guanyu Jiutiao ben *Wenxuan* shiyu de yanjiu 關於九條本文選識語的研究" (A language literacy study of the Kujō edition of the *Selections of Refined Literature*). *Yuwai Hanji yanjiu jikan* 域外漢籍研究集刊 (Journal of studies on Chinese texts abroad) 16 (2017): 259–277.

Saikyūki 西宮記 (Chronicles of the Western Palace). Compiled by Minamoto no Takaakira 源高明, edited by Zōtei Kojitsu Sōsho Henshūbu. Vols. 1–2. Tokyo: Yoshikawa kōbunkan, 1931.

Sasaki Isamu 佐佐木勇. "Nippon kan'on niokeru hansetsu, dō onji chū no on chū, e no han'ei nitsuite Kanazawa bunkobon *Gunsho chiyō* Kamakura chūki no baai 日本漢音における反切 同音字注の假名音注 聲點への反映について 金澤文庫本〈群書治要〉鎌倉中期點の場合" (Linguistics aspects of the mid-Kamakura annotations to the Kamakura edition of the *Qunshu zhiyao*). *Kunigo manabu* 國語學 (Japanese linguistic studies) 53, no. 3 (2002): 93–106.

Sasaki Isamu 佐佐木勇. "Kanazawa bunkobon *Gunsho chiyō* to Kuonji zō honchō bun iki to no kanjion no hikaku Kamakura jidai chūki niokeru kanseki to waka kanbun to no jion chū no sai nitsuite 金澤文庫本群書治要と久遠寺蔵本朝文粋との漢字音の比較 鎌倉時代中期における漢籍と和化漢文との字音注の差異について" (A comparative study of the Chinese phonetics in the Kamakura edition of the *Qunshu zhiyao* and the Kuonji zō edition of *Benchao wencui*). *Oto kenkyū* 音聲研究 (Phonological studies), 8, no. 2 (2004): 26–34.

Sasaki Isamu 佐佐木勇. "Kanazawa bunkobon *Gunsho chiyō* Kamakura chūkiten no kan'on nitsuite 金澤文庫本群書治要經部鎌倉中期点の漢音 聲母について" (Chinese phonetic consonants in the mid-Kamakura period annotations to the Kamakura edition of the *Qunshu zhiyao*). *Shin Ōkunigo* 新大國語 (New comprehensive Japanese linguistics), 30 (2005): 66–76.

Sasaki Isamu 佐佐木勇. "Kuonji zō honchō bun iki Kamakura chūkiten no kan'on Kanazawa bunkobon *Gunsho chiyō* Kamakura chūkiten to no hikaku otōshite 久遠寺蔵本朝文粋鎌倉中期点の漢音聲調 金澤文庫本群書治要鎌倉中期点との比較を通して" (A comparative study of the Chinese phonetic tones in the Kamakura edition of the *Qunshu zhiyao* and the Kuonji zō edition of *Benchao wencui*). *Kuntengo to kunten shiryō* 訓点語と訓点資料 (Interpretive language and interpretive materials), 114 (2005): 43–59.

Schaberg, David. "Remonstrance in Eastern Zhou Historiography." *Early China* 22 (1997): 133–179.

Schwartz, Barry. "From *Abraham Lincoln and the Forge of American Memory*." *In The Collective Memory Reader*, edited by Jeffrey K. Olick, Vered Vinitzky-Seroussi, and Daniel Levy, 242–247. New York: Oxford University Press, 2011.

Seiichi Iwao, ed. *Biographical Dictionary of Japanese History.* Tokyo: Kodansha International Ltd, 1978.

Sen'ichi Hisamatsu. *Biographical Dictionary of Japanese Literature*. Tokyo: Kodansha International Ltd, 1976.

The Seven Military Classics of Ancient China. Translated by Ralph D. Sawyer and Mei-chün Sawyer. New York: Basic Books, 1993.

Shanghai tushu guan 上海圖書館. *Zhongguo congshu zonglu* 中國叢書綜錄 (Comprehensive catalogue of Chinese collectanea). Beijing: Zhonghua shuju, 1959.

Shangshu zhushu 尚書注疏 (Annotated commentary on the *Venerable Documents*). Commentary by Zheng Xuan 鄭玄; sub-commentary by Kong Yingda 孔穎達. In *Wenyuange Siku quanshu* 文淵閣四庫全書. Vol. 54. Taipei: Taiwan Shangwu yinshuguan, 2013.

Shaughnessy, Edward L. "Western Zhou History." In *The Cambridge History of Ancient China: From the Origins of Civilization to 221 B.C.*, edited by Michael Loewe and Edward L. Shaughnessy, 292–351. New York: Cambridge University Press, 1999.

Shields, Anna M. "Obstructing Slander and Sycophancy." In *The Essentials of Governance* by Wu Jing, edited by Hilde De Weerdt, Glen Dudbridge, and Gabe Van Beijeren, 199–204. Cambridge: Cambridge University Press, 2020.

Shen jian 申鑒 (Extended reflections). By Xun Yue 荀悅. In *Wenyuange Siku quanshu* 文淵閣四庫全書. Vol. 696. Taipei: Taiwan Shangwu yinshuguan, 2013.

Sheng Zhongjian 盛鐘健, Huang Shaojun 黃紹筠, and Zhang Songyue 張嵩岳, eds. *Sui Tang jiahua Tang guoshi bu* 隋唐嘉話 唐國史補 (Fine stories from the Sui and Tang dynasties and Supplemented history of the Tang empire). Zhejiang: Zhejiang guji chubanshe, 1986.

The Shenzi Fragments: A Philosophical Analysis and Translation. Translated by Eirik Lang Harris. New York: Columbia University Press, 2016.

Shibue Chūsai 澁江抽齋 and Mori Tatsuyuki 森立之, eds. *Keiseki hōkoshi* 經籍訪古志 (Bibliography of Chinese classics in Japan). Shanghai: Shanghai guji chubanshe, 2017.

Shiji 史記 (Records of the historian). By Sima Qian 司馬遷. In *Wenyuange Siku quanshu* 文淵閣四庫全書 (Wenyuange edition of the Complete Library of the Four Branches of Literature), Vol. 244. Taipei: Taiwan Shangwu yinshuguan, 2013.

Shiji zhengyi 史記正義 (Orthodox interpretation of the *Shiji*). By Sima Qian 司馬遷. Commentary by Zhang Shoujie 張守節. In *Wenyuange Siku quanshu*

文淵閣四庫全書 (Wenyuange edition of the Complete Library of the Four Branches of Literature), Vol. 247. Taipei: Taiwan Shangwu yinshuguan, 2013.

Shimada Kan 島田翰. *Kobun kyūsho kō* 古文舊書考 (Studies of old Chinese books). Shanghai: Shanghai guji chubanshe, 2017.

Shizi: China's First Syncretist. Translated by Paul Fischer. New York: Columbia University Press, 2012.

Shoku Nihon kōki 續日本後記 (Continuation of the *Later Records of Japan*). Comp. by Yoshifusa Fujiwara 藤原良房 and Nobutomo Ban 伴信友. Tokyo: Yoshikawa Kōbunkan, 1972.

Shuowen jiezi xizhuan 說文解字繫傳 (Appended commentary on the *Explanations of Simple and Compound Characters*). By Xu Shen 許慎. Commentary by Xu Kai 徐鍇. Beijing: Zhonghua shuju, 1987.

Shuowen jiezi zhu 說文解字注 (Annotated *Explanations of Simple and Compound Characters*). By Xu Shen 許慎. Commentary by Duan Yucai 段玉裁. Taipei: Yiwen yinshuguan, 2015.

Shuyu zhouzi lu 殊域周咨錄 (Records of comprehensive enquiries about foreign territories). By Yan Congjian 嚴從簡. Beijing: Zhonghua shuju, 1982.

Siku weishou shumu tiyao 四庫未收數目提要 (Bibliographical abstracts on the collection of books not included in the *Four Branches [of Literature]*). Edited by Fu Yili 傅以禮. Shanghai: Shangwu yinshu guan, 1955.

Somers, Robert M. "The end of the T'ang." In *The Cambridge History of China Volume 3: Sui and T'ang China, 598–906, Part 1*, edited by Denis Twitchett, 682–789. Cambridge: Cambridge University Press, 1979.

Song shi 宋史 (History of the Song dynasty). Comp. by Tuoketuo 托克托 et al. In *Wenyuange Siku quanshu* 文淵閣四庫全書 (Wenyuange edition of the Complete Library of the Four Branches of Literature), Vol. 287. Taipei: Taiwan Shangwu yinshuguan, 2013.

Song shi xinbian 宋史新編 (Revised history of the Song dynasty). Comp. by Ke Weiqi 柯維騏. In *Xuxiu Siku quanshu* 續修四庫全書 (Continuation of the *Complete Library of the Four Branches of Literature*). Vol. 309. Shanghai: Shanghai guji chubanshe, 2002.

Song shu 宋書 (History of the Song dynasty). Comp. by Shen Yue 沈約. In *Wenyuange Siku quanshu* 文淵閣四庫全書 (Wenyuange edition of the Complete Library of the Four Branches of Literature), Vol. 258. Taipei: Taiwan Shangwu yinshuguan, 2013.

Song Weiche 宋維哲. "*Qunshu zhiyao* yin jing shulüe 群書治要引經述略" (Outline of the canonical works excerpted by the *Qunshu zhiyao). Youfeng chuming niankan* 有鳳初鳴年刊 (Annual of the Graduate School of Chinese Literature, Soochow University) 2 (2006): 147–160.

Song Yushun 宋玉順. "*Qunshu zhiyao* fanying de Qi wenhua zhiguo linian ji qi yingxiang 群書治要反映的齊文化治國理念及其影響" (Qi political culture and its influence in the *Qunshu zhiyao*). *Guanzi xuekan* 管子學刊 (Journal of Master Guan) 2 (2018): 76–81.

Sorensen, Joseph T. *Optical Allusions: Screens, Paintings, and Poetry in Classical Japan (ca. 800–1200).* Leiden: Brill, 2012.

Spencer, Diana. *Landscape and Roman Identity*. Cambridge: Cambridge University Press, 2010.

Spencer, Diana. "Ρωμαίζω … ergo sum: becoming Roman in Varro's de Lingua Latina." In *Cultural Memory and Identity in Ancient Societies*, edited by Martin Bommas, 43–60. London: Continuum International Publishing Group, 2011.

Spiro, Audrey. *Contemplating the Ancients: Aesthetic and Social Issues in Early Chinese Portraiture.* Berkeley: University of California Press, 1990.

The Spring and Autumn Annals of Master Yan. Translated by Olivia Milburn. Leiden: Brill, 2016.

Ssu-ma Ch'ien. *The Grand Scribe's Records Volume I: The Basic Annals of Pre-Han China*. Edited by William H. Nienhauser, Jr. and translated by Tsai-fa Cheng, Zongli Lu, William H. Nienhauser, Jr., and Robert Reynolds. Bloomington: Indiana University Press, 1994.

Ssu-ma Ch'ien. *The Grand Scribe's Records Volume VII: The Memoirs of Pre-Han China*. Edited by William H. Nienhauser, Jr. and translated by Tsai-fa Cheng, Zongli Lu, William H. Nienhauser, Jr., and Robert Reynolds. Bloomington: Indiana University Press, 1994.

Struve, Lynn A. "Introduction to the Symposium: Memory and Chinese Text." *Chinese Literature: Essays, Articles, Reviews (CLEAR)* 27 (2005): 1–4.

Sui shu 隋書 (History of the Sui dynasty). Comp. by Wei Zheng 魏徵 et al. In *Wenyuange Siku quanshu* 文淵閣四庫全書 (Wenyuange edition of the Complete Library of the Four Branches of Literature), Vol. 264. Taipei: Taiwan Shangwu yinshuguan, 2013.

Swartz, Wendy. *Reading Philosophy, Writing Poetry: Intertextual Modes of Making Meaning in Early Medieval China*. Cambridge, MA: Harvard University Asia Center, 2018.

Ta Kung Pao 大公報. "*Qunshu zhiyao* luntan yi gu jian jin 群書治要論壇以古鑒今 (Seminars on the *Essentials for Bringing about Order from Assembled Texts*—Using the past to reflect on the present)." Accessed February 17, 2022. http://paper.takungpao.com/html/2013-04/27/content_37_6.htm.

Taiping yulan 太平御覽 (Perused by the emperor in the Taiping era, 976–984). Compiled by Li Fang 李昉. In *Wenyuange Siku quanshu* 文淵閣四庫全

書 (Wenyuange edition of the Complete Library of the Four Branches of Literature), Vol. 894. Taipei: Taiwan Shangwu yinshuguan, 2013.

Tan, Mei Ah. "Han Yu's 'Za shuo' 雜說 (Miscellaneous Discourses): A Three-Tier System of Government." *Journal of American Oriental Society* 140, no. 4 (2020): 859–874.

Tang da zhaoling ji 唐大詔令集 (Comprehensive collection of the edicts and commands of the Tang dynasty). Comp. by Song Minqiu 宋敏求. In *Wenyuange Siku quanshu* 文淵閣四庫全書 (Wenyuange edition of the Complete Library of the Four Branches of Literature), Vol. 426. Taipei: Taiwan Shangwu yinshuguan, 2013.

Tang huiyao 唐會要 (Essential records of the Tang dynasty). Comp. by Wang Pu 王溥. In *Wenyuange Siku quanshu* 文淵閣四庫全書 (Wenyuange edition of the Complete Library of the Four Branches of Literature), Vols. 606–607. Taipei: Taiwan Shangwu yinshuguan, 2013.

Tang Kejing 湯可敬. *Shuowen jiezi jinshi* 說文解字今釋 (Modern translation of the *Explanations of Simple and Compound Characters*). Changsha: Yueli shushe, 2001.

Tang wen cui 唐文粹 (Essence of Tang literature). By Yao Xuan 姚鉉. In *Wenyuange Siku quanshu* 文淵閣四庫全書 (Wenyuange edition of the Complete Library of the Four Branches of Literature), Vol. 1343. Taipei: Taiwan Shangwu yinshuguan, 2013.

Tang xinyu 唐新語 (New anecdotes from the Tang dynasty). Comp. by Liu Su 劉肅. In *Wenyuange Siku quanshu* 文淵閣四庫全書 (Wenyuange edition of the Complete Library of the Four Branches of Literature), Vol. 1035. Taipei: Taiwan Shangwu yinshuguan, 2013.

Tang zhiyan 唐摭言 (Collected stories from the Tang dynasty). Comp. by Wang Dingbao 王定保. In *Wenyuange Siku quanshu* 文淵閣四庫全書 (Wenyuange edition of the Complete Library of the Four Branches of Literature), Vol. 1035. Taipei: Taiwan Shangwu yinshuguan, 2013.

Tatsuhiko Seo. "The Tang Dynasty I (618–756)." In *Routledge Handbook of Imperial Chinese History*, edited by Victor C. Xiong and Kenneth J. Hammond, 126–143. London: Routledge, 2019.

Tian Xiaofei. *Beacon Fire and Shooting Star: The Literary Culture of the Liang (502–557)*. Cambridge, MA: Harvard University Asia Center, 2007.

Tian Xiaofei. "Literary Learning: Encyclopedias and Epitomes." In *The Oxford Handbook of Classical Chinese Literature (1000 BCE–900 CE)*, edited by Wiebke Denecke, Wai-yee Li, and Xiaofei Tian, 132–146. New York: Oxford University Press, 2017.

Tian Xiaofei. "Medieval Literary Anthologies." In *Literary Information in China: A History*, edited by Jack W. Chen, Anatoly Detwyler, Xiao Liu,

Christopher M. B. Nugent, and Bruce Rusk, 215–223. New York: Columbia University Press, 2021.

Tochio Takeshi 栃尾武. "Ruisho no kenkyū josetsu (ichi) Gishin rikuchō tōdai ruisho ryakuji 類書の研究序説一 魏晉六朝唐代類書略史" (Introduction to a study on encyclopedic anthologies – brief history on the encyclopedic anthologies of the Wei, Jin, the Six Dynasties and the Tang dynasty). *Seijō kobungaku ronshū* 成城國文學論集 10 (1978): 157–211.

Togan, Isenbike. "Court Historiography in Early Tang China: Assigning a Place to History and Historians at the Palace." In *Royal Courts in Dynastic States and Empires: A Global Perspective*, edited by Jeroen Duindam, Tülay Artan, and Metin Kunt, 171–198. Leiden: Brill, 2011.

Tong dian 通典 (Comprehensive institutions). By Du You 杜佑. In *Wenyuange Siku quanshu* 文淵閣四庫全書 (Wenyuange edition of the Complete Library of the Four Branches of Literature), Vol. 605. Taipei: Shangwu yinshu guan, 2013.

Tong zhi 通志 (Universal treatise). By Zheng Qiao 鄭樵. In *Wenyuange Siku quanshu* 文淵閣四庫全書. Vol. 374. Taipei: Taiwan Shangwu yinshuguan, 2013.

"Tōsen shinkō narabi ni zatsuji no bu 唐船進港并ニ雜事之部 (Various accounts of events related to the arrival of Chinese junks at port)." In *Zoku Nagasaki jitsuroku taisei* 續長崎實録大成 (Sequel to the *Annals of Nagasaki*), Nagasaki bunken sōsho 長崎文献叢書 (Collectanea of Nagasaki documents). Vol. 1, no. 4, edited by Kohara Hazan 小原克紹. Nagasaki: Nagasaki bunkensha, 1974.

Twitchett, Denis. "Hsüan-tsung (reign 712–56)." In *The Cambridge History of China Volume 3: Sui and T'ang China, 589–906, Part 1*, edited by Denis Twitchett, 333–463. Cambridge: Cambridge University Press, 1979.

Twitchett, Denis. *The Writing of Official History under the T'ang*. Cambridge: Cambridge University Press, 1992.

Twitchett, Denis. "How to Be an Emperor: T'ang T'ai-tsung's Vision of His Role." *Asia Major* 9, no. 1/2 (1996): 1–102.

Twitchett, Denis. "Chen gui and Other Works Attributed to Empress Wu Zetian." *Asia Major* 16 (2003): 33–109.

Twitchett, Denis and Howard J. Wechsler. "Kao-tsung (reign 649–83) and the Empress Wu: The Inheritor and the Usurper." In *The Cambridge History of China Volume 3: Sui and T'ang China, 598–906, Part 1*, edited by Denis Twitchett, 242–289. Cambridge: Cambridge University Press, 1979.

Ury, Marian. "Chinese Learning and Intellectual Life." In *The Cambridge History of Japan, Volume 2: Heian Japan*, edited by Donald H. Shively and William H McCullough, 341–389. Cambridge: Cambridge University Press, 1999.

Van Beijeren, Gabe. “On Remaining Vigilant until the End.” In *The Essentials of Governance* by Wu Jing, edited by Hilde De Weerdt, Glen Dudbridge, and Gabe Van Beijeren, 325–338. Cambridge: Cambridge University Press, 2020.

van Els, Paul and Sarah A. Queen. “Anecdotes in Early China.” In *Between History and Philosophy: Anecdotes in Early China*, edited by Paul van Els and Sarah A. Queen, 1–37. Albany: State University of New York Press, 2017.

Vogelsang, Kai. *China und Japan: Zwei Reiche unter einem Himmel (China and Japan: two kingdoms under one sky)*. Stuttgart: Alfred Kröner Verlag, 2020.

Wang Caiyun 王彩雲. “Zhongguo guji zai Hanguo 中國古籍在韓國” (Ancient Chinese texts in Korea). *Guji zhengli yanjiu xuekan* 古籍整理研究學刊 (Journal of studies on ancient book collation) no. 4 (1996): 41–44.

Wang, Fan. “Reading for Rule: Emperor Taizong of Tang and *Qunshu zhiyao*.” In *The Edinburgh History of Reading: Early Readers*, edited by Mary Hammond, 31–53. Edinburgh: Edinburgh University Press, 2020.

Wang Fu and the Comments of a Recluse. Translated by Margaret J. Pearson. Tempe: Arizona University Press, 1989.

Wang Weijia. “*Qunshu zhiyao* de huichuan yu Yan Kejun de jiyi chengjiu 群書治要的回傳與嚴可均的輯佚成就” (Rediscovery of the *Qunshu zhiyao* and Yan Kejun’s accomplishments in textual reconstruction). Master’s thesis, Fudan University, 2013.

Wang Wenhui 王文暉. “Cong guxieben *Qunshu zhiyao* kan tongxingben *Kong zi jiayu* cunzai de wenti 從古寫本群書治要看通行本孔子家語存在的問題” (A study of the received *School Sayings of Confucius* based on an early manuscript edition of the *Qunshu zhiyao*). *Zhongguo dianji yu wenhua* 中國典籍與文化 (Chinese texts and culture) 4 (2018): 113–119.

Wang Yandong 王延棟. *Mingjia jiangjie zhanguoce* 名家講解戰國策 (Authoritative interpretation on the *Strategies of the Warring States*). Changchun: Changchun chubanshe, 2009.

Wang Zhenping. *Tang China in Multi-Polar Asia: A History of Diplomacy and War*. Honolulu: University of Hawai’i Press, 2013.

Wang Zhongmin 王重民. *Dunhuang guji xulu* 敦煌古籍敘錄 (Introductory records of the ancient texts at Dunhuang). Beijing: Zhonghua shuju, 1979.

Wechsler, Howard J. *Mirror to the Son of Heaven: Wei Cheng at the Court of T’ang T’ai-tsung*. London: Yale University Press, 1974.

Wechsler, Howard J. *Offerings of Jade and Silk.* New Haven, CT: Yale University Press, 1985.

Wechsler, Howard J. “T’ai-tsung (reign 626–49) the consolidator.” In *The Cambridge History of China Volume 3: Sui and T’ang China, 589–906, Part I*, edited by Denis Twitchett, 188–241. Vol. 3. Cambridge: Cambridge University Press, 2008.

Wechsler, Howard J. "The founding of the T'ang dynasty: Kao-tsu (reign: 618–26)." In *The Cambridge History of China Volume 3: Sui and T'ang China, 589–906, Part I*, edited by Denis Twitchett, 150–187. Cambridge: Cambridge University Press, 2008.

Wei, Betty Peh-T'i. *Ruan Yuan, 1769–1849: The Life and Work of a Major Scholar-Official in Nineteenth Century China before the Opium War*. Hong Kong: Hong Kong University Press, 2006.

Wei Zheng gong jianlu 魏鄭公諫錄 (Record of the remonstrations of Lord Wei Zheng). Comp. by Wang Fangqing 王方慶. In *Wenyuange Siku quanshu* 文淵閣四庫全書 (Wenyuange edition of the Complete Library of the Four Branches of Literature), Vol. 446. Taipei: Taiwan Shangwu yinshuguan, 2013.

Welzer, Harald. "Communicative Memory." In *Cultural Memory Studies: An International and Interdisciplinary Handbook*, edited by Astrid Erll and Ansgar Nünning, 285–298. Berlin: Walter de Gruyter, 2008.

Weng Lianxi 翁連溪. "Yangxin dian cangshu *Wanwei biecang* 養心殿藏書 宛委別藏" (Book collection of the Hall of the Cultivating Heart and the *Exclusive collection from Wanwei*). *Zijin cheng* 紫禁城 (Imperial palace) 1991, no. 6: 43–44.

Wenyuan yinghua 文苑英華 (Finest flowers in the garden of literature). Comp. by Li Fang 李昉 et al. In *Wenyuange Siku quanshu* 文淵閣四庫全書 (Wenyuange edition of the Complete Library of the Four Branches of Literature), Vol. 1336. Taipei: Taiwan Shangwu yinshuguan, 2013.

Wilkinson, Endymion Porter. *Chinese History: A New Manual*, 6th ed. Cambridge, MA: Endymion Wilkinson c/o Harvard University Asia Center, 2022.

Wright, Arthur F. "T'ang T'ai-Tsung and Buddhism." In *Perspectives on the T'ang*, edited by Arthur F. Wright and Denis Twitchett, 239–263. New Haven, CT: Yale University Press, 1973.

Wright, Arthur, F. "T'ang T'ai-Tsung: The Man and the Persona." In *Essays on T'ang Society*, edited by John Curtis Perry and Bardwell L. Smith, 17–32. Leiden: Brill, 1976.

Wright, Arthur, F. "The Sui dynasty." In *The Cambridge History of China Volume 3: Sui and T'ang China, 589–906, Part I*, edited by Denis Twitchett, 48–149. Cambridge: Cambridge University Press, 1979.

Wright, Arthur F. and Denis Twitchett, eds. *Perspectives on the T'ang*. London: Yale University Press, 1973.

Wu Jie 吴傑, ed. *Riben shi cidian* 日本史辭典 (Historical dictionary of Japan). Shanghai: Fudan daxue chubanshe, 1992.

Wu Yun 吳云 and Ji Yu 冀宇, eds. *Tang Taizong ji* 唐太宗集 (Collected writings of Emperor Taizong of the Tang dynasty). Xi'an: Shaanxi renmin chubanshe, 1986.

Wu Yun 吴云 and Ji Yu 冀宇, eds. *Tang Taizong quanji jiaozhu* 唐太宗全集校注 (Collation and annotation of the complete works of Emperor Taizong of the Tang dynasty). Tianjin: Tianjin guji chubanshe, 2004.

Xiao Xiangjian 蕭祥劍. *Qunshu zhiyao xinde* 群書治要心得 (Reflections on the *Qunshu zhiyao*). Beijing: Zhongguo huaqiao chubanshe, 2012.

Xiao Xiangjian. *Gunseochiyo gyeongheom* (Reflections on the *Qunshu zhiyao*). Translated by Kim Seong-dong and Cho Kyung-hee. Seoul: Munhakdongne Publishing Group, 2014.

Xiaojing Zheng zhu 孝經鄭注 (Zheng Xuan's commentary on the *Classic of Family Reverence*). Edited by Okada Noboyuki 岡田挺之. In *Zhi buzu zhai congshu* 知不足齋叢書 (Collectanea from the studio of knowing one's deficiencies). Comp. by Bao Tingbo 鮑廷博, collection 21. Taipei: Yiwen yinshuguan yinhang, 1966.

Xie Baocheng 謝保成, ed. *Zhenguan zhengyao jijiao* 貞觀政要集校 (Collected annotations of the *Essentials of Governance from the Zhenguan Reign*). Beijing: Zhonghua shuju, 2003.

Xin Tang shu 新唐書 (New history of the Tang dynasty). Comp. by Ouyang Xiu 歐陽修 and Song Qi 宋祁. In *Wenyuange Siku quanshu* 文淵閣四庫全書 (Wenyuange edition of the Complete Library of the Four Branches of Literature), Vols. 272–274, 276. Taipei: Taiwan Shangwu yinshuguan, 2013.

Xin xu 新序 (New order). By Liu Xiang 劉向. In *Wenyuange Siku quanshu* 文淵閣四庫全書 (Wenyuange edition of the Complete Library of the Four Branches of Literature), Vol. 696. Taipei: Taiwan Shangwu yinshuguan, 2013.

Xinjiao Songben Guangyun 新校宋本廣韻 (New collated Song edition of the *Guangyun* [rime dictionary]). By Chen Pengnian 陳彭年 et al. Edited by Li Tianfu 李添富, Zhang Linxia 張玲霞, Li Juanjuan 李鵑娟, Yang Zhengxiang 楊徵祥, Liu Yafen 劉雅分, Huang Shuru 黃淑汝, Li Wanru 李宛儒, and Chen Zhiyuan 陳志源. Taipei: Hongye wenhua, 2001.

Yan Shaodang 嚴紹璗. *Hanji zai Riben de liubu yanjiu* 漢籍在日本的流佈研究 (A study of the transmission of Chinese texts in Japan). Nanjing: Jiangsu guji chubanshe, 1992.

Yan Shaodang 嚴紹璗. *Riben cang Hanji zhenben zhuizong jishi: Yan Shaodang haiwai fangshu zhi*日本藏漢籍珍本追綜紀實 嚴紹璗海外訪書志 (Record of investigation on rare Chinese texts in Japan: Monograph on foreign textual enquiries by Yan Shaodang). Shanghai: Shanghai guji chubanshe, 2005.

Yan Shaodang 嚴紹璗. *Ricang Hanji shanben shulu* 日藏漢籍善本書錄 (Catalogue of good editions of Chinese books in Japan). Beijing: Zhonghua shuju, 2007.

Yantie lun 鹽鐵論 (Discourses on salt and iron). By Huan Kuan 桓寬. In *Wenyuange Siku quanshu* 文淵閣四庫全書 (Wenyuange edition of the Complete Library of the Four Branches of Literature), Vol. 247. Taipei: Taiwan Shangwu yinshuguan, 2013.

Yang Lien-Sheng. "The organization of Chinese official historiography: principles and methods of the Standard Histories from the T'ang through the Ming dynasty." In *Historians of China and Japan*, edited by W. G. Beasley and E. G. Pulleyblank, 44–59. London: Oxford University Press, 1961.

Yao Xinzhong. "Confucianism" in *The Encyclopedia of Confucianism*, edited by Xinzhong Yao, 1–11. Oxford: Routledge, 2003.

Yasuhiko Kimiya 木宮泰彥. *Nissi kōtsūshi* 中日交通史 (History of Sino-Japanese relations). Translated by Chen Jie 陳捷. Taipei: Shangwu yinshuguan, 1935.

Ye Youming 葉幼明. *Xinyi Xinxu duben* 新譯新序讀本 (New translation of the *New Order*). Taipei: Sanmin shuju,1996.

Yi Zima 毅自馬. *Xinyi Zengguang xianwen Qianzi wen* 新譯增廣賢文千字文 (New translation of the *Extended Wise Sayings* and the *Thousand Character Classic*). Taipei: Sanmin shuju, 2010.

Yoshinori Kobayashi 小林芳規. *Kanazawa bunkobon Gunsho chiyō no kun ten* 金澤文庫本群書治要の訓點 (Exegesis and punctuation of the Kanazawa bunko edition of the *Qunshu zhiyao*). Tokyo: Oiko-shoin, 1991.

Yu hai 玉海 (Ocean of jades). Comp. by Wang Yinglin 王應麟. In *Wenyuange Siku quanshu* 文淵閣四庫全書 (Wenyuange edition of the Complete Library of the Four Branches of Literature), Vol. 944. Taipei: Taiwan Shangwu yinshuguan, 2013.

Yuding yuanjian leihan 御定淵鑑類函 (Imperially-commissioned categorized writings in the Library of Deep Insight). Comp. by Zhang Ying 張英 and Wang Shizhen 王士禎. In *Wenyuange Siku quanshu* 文淵閣四庫全書 (Wenyuange edition of the Complete Library of the Four Branches of Literature), Vol. 985. Taipei: Taiwan Shangwu yinshuguan, 2013.

Zagzebski, Linda Trinkaus. *Divine Motivation Theory.* Cambridge: Cambridge University Press, 2004.

Zelizer, Barbie. "Reading the Past Against the Grain: The Shape of Memory Studies." *Critical Studies in Mass Communication* 12, no. 2 (1995): 214–239.

Zen kuni tōshōgū rengō e 全國東照宮連合會, ed. *Hi isago ken kin Tokugawa Ieyasu ōyake itsuwa shū* 披沙揀金德川家康公逸話集 (Collected anecdotes of Tokugawa Ieyasu). Tokyo: Yagishoten, 1997.

Zeng Zhen 曾振. *Tang Taizong Li Wei gong wendui jinshi jinyi* 唐太宗李衛公問對今註今譯 (Questions and answers of Emperor Taizong of the Tang dynasty and Duke Li of Wei with modern annotation and translation). Taipei: Taiwan Shangwu yinshuguan, 1986.

Zhang Faxiang 張發祥. *Wenbai duizhao Qunshu zhiyao* 文白對照群書治要 (Classical-vernacular *Essentials for Bringing about Order from Assembled Texts*). Beijing: Zhongguo caizheng jingji chubanshe, 2001.

Zhao Keyao 趙克堯 and Xu Daoxun 許道勛. *Tang Taizong zhuan* 唐太宗傳 (Biography of Emperor Taizong of the Tang dynasty). Beijing: Renmin chubanshe, 1995.

Zhejiang tong zhi 浙江通志 (Zhejiang gazetteer). Comp. by Qi Zengjun 稽曾筠, Li Wei 李衛, Shen Yiji 沈翼機, and Fu Wanglu 傅王露. In *Wenyuange Siku quanshu* 文淵閣四庫全書 (Wenyuange edition of the Complete Library of the Four Branches of Literature), Vol. 525. Taipei: Taiwan Shangwu yinshuguan, 2013.

Zheng Kaiyue 鄭凱月. "*Qunshu zhiyao* xuanlu *Kongzi jiayu* yanjiu 群書治要選錄孔子家語研究" (A study of the *School Sayings of Confucius* as excerpted in the *Qunshu zhiyao*). Master's thesis, University of Wales Trinity Saint David, 2020.

Zhenguan zhengyao 貞觀政要 (Essentials of governance from the Zhenguan reign). By Wu Jing 吳兢. In *Wenyuange Siku quanshu* 文淵閣四庫全書 (Wenyuange edition of the Complete Library of the Four Branches of Literature), Vol. 407. Taipei: Taiwan Shangwu yinshuguan, 2013.

Zhou Li 周勵. "Qiangu qishu *Qunshu zhiyao* niepan chongsheng 千古奇書群書治要涅槃重生 (An ancient and extraordinary text – the revival of the *Qunshu zhiyao*)." *China Western Development* 西部大開發, 2012, no. 7: 106–108.

Zhuzi zhiyao 諸子治要 (Essentials for bringing about order from the various masters). Comp. by Wei Zheng 魏徵 and Xiao Deyan 蕭德言. Taipei: Shijie shuju, 1962.

Zizhi tongjian 資治通鑑 (Comprehensive mirror in aid of governance). By Sima Guang 司馬光. In *Wenyuange Siku quanshu* 文淵閣四庫全書 (Wenyuange edition of the Complete Library of the Four Branches of Literature), Vol. 308. Taipei: Taiwan Shangwu yinshuguan, 2013.

Zoku gunsho ruijū 續群書類從 (Continuation of the *Classified Collection of Books*). Comp. by Hanawa Hokiichi 塙保己一. Scroll 886. Tokyo: Zoku-gunsho-ruijū Kanseikai, 1982.

Zuo Tradition Zuozhuan. Translated by Stephen Durrant, Wai-yee Li, and David Schaberg. Seattle: University of Washington Press, 2016.

Zuozhuan Du Lin hezhu 左傳杜林合注 (Commentary by Du Yu and Lin Yaosou on the *Zuo Tradition of Commentary on the Spring and Autumn Annals*). Edited by Wang Daokun 王道焜 and Zhao Ruyuan 趙汝源. In *Wenyuange Siku quanshu*文淵閣四庫全書 (Wenyuange edition of the Complete Library of the Four Branches of Literature), Vol. 171. Taipei: Taiwan Shangwu yinshuguan, 2013.